Personnel Selection

Adding Value Through People

FOURTH EDITION

Mark Cook

John Wiley & Sons, Ltd

Other Wiley Editorial Offices

John Wiley & Sons Inc., 111 River Street, Hoboken, NJ 07030, USA

Jossey-Bass, 989 Market Street, San Francisco, CA 94103-1741, USA

Wiley-VCH Verlag GmbH, Boschstr. 12, D-69469 Weinheim, Germany

John Wiley & Sons Australia Ltd, 33 Park Road, Milton, Queensland 4064, Australia

John Wiley & Sons (Asia) Pte Ltd, 2 Clementi Loop #02-01, Jin Xing Distripark, Singapore 129809

John Wiley & Sons Canada Ltd, 22 Worcester Road, Etobicoke, Ontario, Canada M9W 1L1

Wiley also publishes its books in a variety of electronic formats. Some content that appears in print may not be available in electronic books.

Library of Congress Cataloging-in-Publication Data

Cook, Mark, 1942–
    Personnel Selection : adding value through people / Mark Cook. – 4th ed.
       p. cm.
    Includes bibliographical references and index.
    ISBN 0-470-85082-5 (Cloth : alk. paper) – ISBN 0-470-85083-3 (Paper : alk. paper)
    1. Employee selection. I. Title.

    HF5549.5.S38C66 2004
    658.3'112–dc21

                             2003008913

British Library Cataloguing in Publication Data

A catalogue record for this book is available from the British Library

ISBN 10: 0-470-85083-3 (P/B)
ISBN 13: 978-0-470-85083-1 (P/B)
ISBN 10: 0-470-85082-5 (H/B)
ISBN 13: 978-0-470-85082-4 (H/B)

Typeset in 10/12pt Palatino by Laserwords Private Limited, Chennai, India
Printed and bound in Great Britain by Antony Rowe Ltd, Chippenham, Wiltshire
This book is printed on acid-free paper responsibly manufactured from sustainable forestry in which at least two trees are planted for each one used for paper production.

Personnel Selection

FOURTH EDITION

Contents

Preface to the first edition

When I first proposed writing this book, I thought it self-evident that personnel selection and productivity are closely linked. Surely an organisation that employs poor staff will produce less, or achieve less, than one that finds, keeps and promotes the right people. So it was surprising when several people, including one anonymous reviewer of the original book proposal, challenged my assumption and argued that there was no demonstrated link between selection and productivity.

Critics are right, up to a point – there has never been an experimental demonstration of the link. The experiment could be performed, but might prove very expensive. First, create three identical companies. Second, allow company A to select its staff by using the best techniques available, require company B to fill its vacancies at random (so long as the staff possess the minimum necessary qualifications), and require company C to employ the people company A identified as least suitable. Third, wait a year and then see which company is doing best, or – if the results are very clear-cut – which companies are still in business. No such experiment has been performed, although fair employment laws in the USA have caused some organisations to adopt at times personnel policies that are not far removed from the strategy for company B.

Perhaps critics meant only to say that the outline overlooked other more important factors affecting productivity, such as training, management, labour relations, lighting and ventilation, or factors which the organisation cannot control, such as the state of the economy, technical development, foreign competition, and political interference. Of course all of these affect productivity, but this does not prove that – other things being equal – an organisation that selects, keeps and promotes good employees will not produce more, or produce better, than one that does not.

Within-organisation factors that affect productivity are dealt with by other writings on industrial/organisational psychology. Factors outside the organisation, such as the state of world trade, fall outside the scope of psychology.

Centre for Occupational Research Ltd
10 Woodlands Terrace, Swansea SA1 6BR, UK

Preface to the fourth edition

Every chapter of the fourth edition has been revised to incorporate new research or new ideas, so that the amount of change in each chapter serves as an index of the amount of interesting new research in different areas. The chapters on assessment centres, personality tests, ability tests, interviewing and biographical methods include a lot of new material. Personality tests in particular have been very extensively researched, with numerous important meta-analyses appearing. The areas of references, ratings and work samples have been altered least. Every chapter has been rewritten, even where there is not so much new research to report.

The most obvious change is the replacement of the conventional Conclusions section at the end of each chapter by lists of Key Points, Key References and Useful Websites.

An encouraging trend which is continuing is the increasing volume of research originating in the UK and Europe, covering many aspects of selection. However, much more European research is needed, especially in the areas of equal opportunities and differential validity.

I would like to thank the many people who have helped me to prepare this fourth edition. First, I would like to thank the many researchers in the selection area who have generously sent me accounts of research in press or in progress. Second, I would like to thank the students on the Applied Psychology Masters course at the University of Cardiff, whose questions and comments over the last 15 years have shown me where the earlier editions needed change. Third, I would like to thank Karen Howard for her help with the figures. Finally, I would like to thank John Wiley for their support and help with the three previous editions of *Personnel Selection*.

Centre for Occupational Research Ltd
10 Woodlands Terrace, Swansea SA1 6BR, UK

CHAPTER 1

Old and new selection methods

We've always done it this way

Why selection matters

Clark Hull is better known, to psychologists at least, as an animal learning theorist, but very early in his career he wrote a book on aptitude testing (Hull, 1928) in which he described ratios of output of best to worst performers in a variety of occupations. In an ideal world, two people doing the same job under the same conditions will produce exactly the same amount, but in the real world, some employees produce more than others. Hull was the first psychologist to ask how much workers differ in productivity, and he discovered the principle that should be written in letters of fire on every manager's office wall: *the best is twice as good as the worst*.

Human resource (HR) managers sometimes find that they have difficulty convincing colleagues that HR departments also make a major contribution to the organisation's success. Because HR departments are not making things or selling things, some colleagues think they are not adding any value to the organisation. This represents a very narrow approach to the way in which organisations work, which completely overlooks the fact that an organisation's most important asset is its staff.

Psychologists have devised techniques for showing how finding and keeping the right staff adds value to the organisation. The *rational estimate* technique (described in detail in Chapter 13) estimates how much workers who are doing the same job vary with regard to the value of their contribution. This gives the HR manager an estimate of the difference in value between an average performer and a good performer in any given job. For computer programmers, Schmidt, Gast-Rosenberg and Hunter's (1980) rational estimates indicated that a good programmer is worth over $10,000 a year more than an average programmer. Schmidt *et al.* also propose a rule of thumb, that the difference in value between a good worker and an average worker will be between 40% and 70% of the salary for the job. If the salary is £30,000, then the difference in value to the organisation between a good manager and an average manager will fall between £12,000 and £21,000. These estimates clearly indicate that the HR manager can add a great deal of value to the organisation by finding good managers in the first place, which is what this book is about, as well as by making managers good through training and development, and by keeping them good through avoiding poor morale, high levels of stress, etc.

Differences in value of the order of £12–42,000 per employee mount up across an organisation. Schmidt and Hunter (1981) generated a couple of examples for the public sector in the USA:

- A small employer, such as the Philadelphia police force (5,000 employees), could save $18 million a year by using psychological tests to select the best (Schmidt & Hunter, 1981).
- A large employer, such as the US Federal Government (4 million employees), could save $16 billion a year. Or, to reverse the perspective, the US Federal Government is losing $16 billion a year by not using tests.

Some critics see a flaw in Schmidt and Hunter's calculations. Every company in the country cannot employ *the best* computer programmers or budget analysts; someone has to employ *the rest*. Good selection cannot increase national productivity, only the productivity of employers who use good selection methods to grab more than their fair share of talent. At present, employers are free to do precisely that. The rest of this book explains *how*.

Recruitment

Figure 1.1 summarises the successive stages of recruiting and selecting an academic for a British university. The *advertisement* attracts applicants, who complete and return an *application form*. Some applicants' *references* are taken up, and the rest are excluded from further consideration. Candidates with satisfactory references are short-listed and invited for *interview*, after which the post is filled. The employer tries to attract as many applicants as possible and then pass them through a series of filters, until the number of surviving candidates equals the number of vacancies.

Recruitment sources

There are many ways in which employers can try to attract applicants, such as advertisements, agencies (public or private), word of mouth, the Internet, 'walk-ins' (people who come in and ask if there are any vacancies), job fairs, etc. Employers should analyse recruiting sources carefully to determine which of these find effective employees who stay with them. Employers also need to check whether their recruitment methods are finding a representative applicant pool in terms of gender, ethnicity and disability.

Realistic job previews

Many organisations paint a rosy picture of what is really a boring and unpleasant job because they fear no one would apply for it otherwise. In the USA, *realistic job previews* (Bretz & Judge, 1998) are widely used to tell applicants what being, for example, a call-centre worker is really like – fast-paced, closely supervised, routine to the point of being boring and solitary.

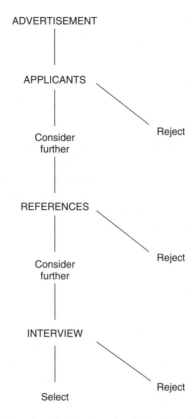

Figure 1.1   Successive stages in selecting academic staff at a British university

The more carefully worded the advertisement and the job description, the fewer unsuitable applicants will apply.

Informal recruitment

Applicants are sometimes recruited by word of mouth, usually through existing employees. Besides being cheaper, the 'grapevine' finds employees who stay longer (*low turnover*) according to several researchers (e.g. Saks, 1994), possibly because they have a clearer idea about what the job really involves. Fair employment agencies (e.g. the (British) Commission for Racial Equality) generally dislike informal recruitment; they argue that recruiting an all-white workforce's friends is unfair because it tends to perpetuate an all-white workforce.

Selection by the classic trio

Having recruited a good, and representative, field of applicants, the employer then tries to select the most suitable person(s). Many organisations still select by using the traditional trio of *application form, letter of reference* and *interview*.

Application form

The role of the application form is to act as the first filter, choosing a relatively small number of applications to process further. This procedure is known as *sifting*. Research suggests that sifting is not always done very effectively. Machwirth, Schuler and Moser (1996) used *policy-capturing* analyses to reconstruct the way in which personnel managers sift applications. This approach works back from the decisions that the manager makes about a set of applications, to infer the basis on which the manager makes those decisions. Machwirth *et al.* have found that what the managers *do*, according to the policy-capturing analysis, often differs from what they *say*, when asked to describe how they sift. Managers say that they sift on the basis of proven ability and previously achieved position, but in practice they are likely to reject applicants because the application looks untidy or badly written.

Fairness and sifting

Davison and Burke (2000) reviewed 49 studies of gender bias in simulated employment decisions, and found bias against female applicants by female as well as male sifters. The less job information that is given, the greater the discrimination against females. In the UK, the Commission for Racial Equality recommends that application sifting should be done by two people. In the USA, the Equal Employment Opportunities Commission (EEOC) *Guide to Pre-Employment Inquiries* lists a wide range of application-form questions that are suspect because they may not be *job related*. These include questions about marital status, children, childcare, hair or eye colour, gender, military service or discharge, age, availability over holidays or weekends (which may discourage some religious minorities), height and weight, arrest records, etc.

A continuing concern is whether applicants tell the truth on application forms, although there is not much good quality research on this issue. Keenan (1997) asked UK graduates which answers on their application forms they had 'made up...to please the recruiter'. Hardly any admitted to giving false information about their degree, but most (73%) admitted that they were not honest about their reasons for choosing the company to which they were applying. More worryingly, 40% felt no obligation to be honest about their hobbies and interests.

Improving application forms: weighted application blanks

Application forms can be converted into *weighted application blanks* by analysing past and present employees for predictors of success (*see* Chapter 5). One study found that American female bank clerks who did not stay in the job long tended to be under 25 years of age, single, living at home, to have had several jobs, etc. (Robinson, 1972), so banks could reduce turnover by screening out applicants with these characteristics. (Robinson's biodata would probably not be legal today, however, because it specifies *female* bank clerks.)

Improving application sifting: training and experience (T&E) ratings

In the USA, application sifting is assisted by *training and experience (T&E) ratings* (*see* Chapter 9), which seek to quantify applicants' training and experience instead of relying on arbitrary judgements made by the sifter (McDaniel, Schmidt & Hunter, 1988).

Improving application forms: behavioural competences

Applicants are asked to describe things that they have done which relate to key competences for the job. For example, the competence *ability to influence others* is assessed by the request to 'describe an occasion when you had to persuade others to accept an unpopular course of action'.

Improving application forms: minimum qualifications

Levine *et al.* (1997) generated lists of minimum qualifications by asking a panel of experts to state what experience or qualifications a 'barely acceptable' employee ought to have. The results for pharmacy technicians indicated that the organisation had previously specified more experience than was needed, and that there were more ways of gaining that experience than was realised.

Background investigation (positive vetting)

The application form contains the information that the applicant chooses to provide about him- or herself. Some employers make their own checks on the applicant, covering criminal history, driving record, financial and credit history, education and employment history, and possibly even reputation and lifestyle. This is common practice in the USA, where specialist agencies exist to carry out the process. In the UK, background investigations are recommended for childcare workers, and are used for government employees with access to confidential information, a process that is known as *positive vetting*. The Criminal Records Bureau has been set up to supply information on the criminal records of people applying for work which gives access to children.

References

References work on the principle that the best way of finding out about someone is to ask someone who knows him or her well, such as a former employer or schoolteacher. The principle is sound – former employers may have valuable information. However, the practice is less perfect, and research reviewed in Chapter 4 shows that references often do not contribute much to finding effective employees.

Interview

The final hurdle is almost always the interview. A British survey of major companies, published in the *Times 1000*, found only one company that never interviewed (Robertson & Makin, 1986).

Box 1.1   Normal distribution

The Astronomer Royal of Belgium in the nineteenth century, Adolphe Quetelet, plotted a graph of the height of 100,000 French soldiers (Figure 1.2). The soldiers' heights formed a bell-shaped distribution, called the *normal distribution*.

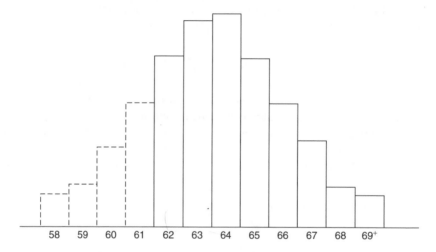

Figure 1.2   Distribution of height, in inches, for nineteenth-century French soldiers. *Note:* The distribution has been estimated for men less than 5 ft 2in tall who were not accepted as soldiers because they were too short

Other naturally occurring measurements when plotted as a graph also produce a normal distribution. Examples include chest diameter, vital capacity (how much air the person can draw into his or her lungs – still a selection requirement for the fire brigade), the time it takes to react to a sound, and the activity of the autonomic nervous system.

Role of the Internet

Advertising, making applications, sifting applications and even assessment can now be carried out electronically, which can make the whole process far quicker. People now talk of making 'same-day offers', whereas traditional approaches took weeks or even months to fill vacancies.

- More and more jobs are advertised on the Internet, through the employer's own website or through numerous recruitment sites.

- People seeking jobs can post their details on websites for potential employers to evaluate. This gives the job seeker an opportunity that did not exist before. Previously, people could make speculative applications to possible employers, but could not advertise themselves on a global scale.
- Many employers now use electronic application systems, eliminating the need for the conventional paper application form. This makes it easier both to use electronic sifting systems, and to construct more sophisticated filtering systems. Half a dozen questions can screen out clearly unsuitable applicants, saving both employer and applicant time, before going on to collect more detailed information from the rest.
- Some employers are replacing their conventional paper application forms by short questionnaires that are completed over the Internet. Formerly HR staff inferred, for example, leadership potential from what applicants said they did at school or university. The new systems assess it more directly by a set of standard questions. This saves time that would otherwise be spent reading application forms, and could ensure more standardised assessment of core competences. In effect the conventional application form or CV has been replaced by a short personality questionnaire, which has been moved forward from its usual position at the short-list stage. No research has been published on how such systems work.
- Software has been developed that scans applications and CVs to check whether they match the job's requirements. This is much quicker than conventional sifting of paper applications by HR staff. The Restrac system can search 300,000 CVs in 10 seconds. Automated sifting systems can also eliminate bias based on ethnicity, disability or gender. Sifting software can scan paper applications, or its input can be electronic. Apparently President Clinton used one to select his aides from thousands of applicants.
- Aptitude tests or assessments of personality can be completed over the Internet by the applicant. This saves both time and travel costs.

However, Internet recruitment and selection is associated with a number of potential problems.

- Not everyone has access to the Internet. Surveys (Bartram, 2000) suggest that there are gender, ethnicity and age differences, which will have possible legal implications, as well as differences in income and education, which will tend to exclude the less fortunate.
- Electronic media do not bypass the problems that arise with paper. It is just as easy to lie through a keyboard as it is on paper or in person, and just as easy to give the answer you think that the employer wants to hear.
- Sifting electronically may be very fast, but it is not necessarily any more accurate. Accuracy depends on the decision rules that are used in sifting, which in turn depend on the quality of the research that the employer has done. Reports (Bartram, 2000) suggest some scanning systems do nothing more sophisticated than search for key words, and that once applicants get wise to this, they will take care to include as many as possible.

Researching accuracy of selection

Is there any reason why employees should not continue to be selected by application form, reference and interview? Most occupational psychologists will answer yes. Psychological research shows that references and interviews are inaccurate selection methods. Accuracy can be divided into two issues, namely reliability and validity. A good selection method is:

- *reliable* – meaning that it gives a consistent account of the person being assessed
- *valid* – meaning that it selects good applicants and rejects bad ones.

Reliability

Physical measurements (e.g. the dimensions of a piece of a furniture) are usually so reliable that their consistency is taken for granted. However, selection assessments are often not so consistent. At their worst they may be so inconsistent that they convey little or no information. Conway, Jako and Goodman (1995) have reviewed interview research, and found the conventional (unstructured) interview very unreliable. Two interviewers who see the same candidate will produce ratings that correlate on average by only 0.37, which means that their opinions are very different. If two interviewers reach different opinions, at least one of them must be wrong – but which one?

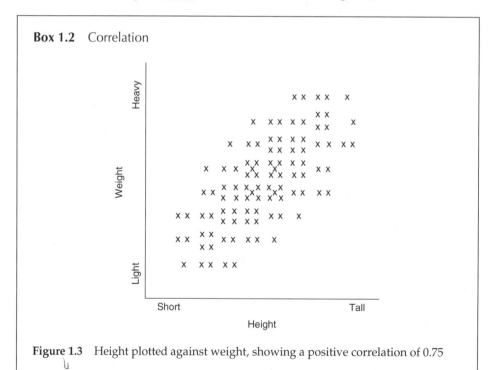

Box 1.2   Correlation

Figure 1.3   Height plotted against weight, showing a positive correlation of 0.75

Height and weight are *correlated*; tall people usually weigh more than short people, and heavy people are usually taller than light people. Height and weight are not perfectly correlated – there are plenty of short fat and tall thin exceptions to the rule (*see* Figure 1.3).

The correlation coefficient summarises how closely two measures like height and weight go together. A perfect one-to-one correlation gives a value of +1.00. If two measures are completely unrelated, the correlation is zero (0.00). Height and weight correlate by about 0.75. Sometimes two measures are inversely, or negatively, correlated. For example, the older people are, the less fleet of foot they (generally) are.

Validity

A valid selection method accepts good applicants and rejects poor ones. The basic building block of selection research is the *validation study*. A typical validation study collects two sets of data, namely the *predictor* and the *criterion*. Interviewer ratings form the predictor, while some index of work performance forms the criterion (Figure 1.4). Note that the interviewer's opinion of the candidates has to be quantified, as does the criterion measure of work performance. The researcher then computes a *correlation* (*see* Box 1.2) between the predictor and criterion data, which is the *validity coefficient*. Validation research is discussed in greater detail in Chapter 10.

A good selection method is also *cost-effective*; it saves the employer more in increased output than it costs to use (psychologists call cost-effectiveness *utility*; *see* Chapter 13).

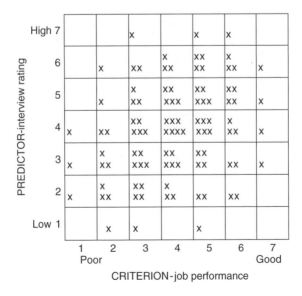

Figure 1.4 Schematic representation of a validity study, showing predictor and criterion data

The criterion problem: defining good work performance

Selection research compares a *predictor*, meaning an selection test, with a *criterion*, meaning an index of the worker's work performance. The *criterion* side of selection research presents greater problems than the *predictor* side because it requires researchers to define good work performance. The criterion problem can be very simple when work generates something that can be counted, such as widgets manufactured per day, or sales per week. The criterion problem can be made very simple if the organisation has an appraisal system whose ratings can be used. The supervisor rating criterion is widely used, because it is almost always available (in the USA), because it is unitary, and because it is hard to argue with.

On the other hand, the criterion problem can soon get very complex if one wants to dig a little deeper into what constitutes effective performance. Questions about the real nature of work or the true purpose of organisations soon arise. Is success better measured objectively by counting units produced, or is it better measured subjectively by informed opinion? Is success at work unidimensional or multi-dimensional? Who decides whether work is successful? Different supervisors may not agree. Management and workers may not agree. The organisation and its customers may not agree.

Objective criteria are many and various. Some are more objective than others. For example, *training grades* often involve some subjective judgement in rating written work. *Personnel* criteria, such as advancement/promotion, length of service, turnover, punctuality, absence, disciplinary action, accidents and sickness, are easy to collect. However, they may be very unreliable, and they often have skewed distributions. Analyses of selection research (Lent, Aurbach & Levin, 1971) have shown that a subjective criterion – the global supervisor rating – was clearly the favourite, used in 60% of studies. Criteria of work performance are discussed in greater detail in Chapter 11.

Looking for alternatives

The first research to be published on the interview, as long ago as 1915, showed that six personnel managers did not agree about a common set of applicants. Many more research studies since then have confirmed that interviews have less than perfect reliability and fairly poor validity. Research on the letter of reference similarly showed it to be unreliable and to have limited validity. These research findings prompted both personnel managers and psychologists to look for a better alternative. The various offerings over the years divide into the following:

- psychological tests
- group exercises
- work sample tests

– or any combination of these, and traditional methods. Intensive assessments of a group of applicants by multiple methods are often known as *assessment centres* (*see* Chapter 8).

Psychological tests

Alfred Binet wrote the first *intelligence test* in France in 1904. The Binet assesses children individually, whereas personnel selectors usually want to test adults in groups. A committee of American psychologists wrote the world's first adult group ability test, to classify US army recruits when America entered the First World War in 1917.

The *personality questionnaire* also owes its origin to the Great War. By 1917, armies had discovered that many men could not stand the stress of continuous battle. The US army devised a screening test, known as the Woodworth Personal Data Sheet, which was surprisingly sophisticated for its day. Questions were excluded if more than 25% of the healthy controls gave the keyed answer, or if the neurotic group did not give the keyed answer at least twice as often as the controls. Many items from Woodworth's test still feature in modern questionnaires. For example:

- Do you usually sleep well?
- Do you worry too much about little things?
- Does some particular useless thought keep coming into your mind to bother you?

Behavioural tests have been used for at least 3,000 years. The Book of Judges (Chapter 7, verses 4–7) tells how Gideon raised an army to 'smite' the Midianites, and found that he had too many volunteers. He used a simple test of fieldcraft to exclude the inexperienced from his army. He told the volunteers to go and take a drink from the nearby river, and he then selected only those who remained on their guard even while slaking their thirst.

Group exercises and assessment centres

Until 1942 the British army selected officers by Commanding Officer's recommendation and a panel interview. By 1942 this system was proving ineffective because the panels did not like or could not understand candidates with a grammar-school education or 'communist' opinions. The War Office Selection Board (WOSB) that replaced the panels used *group exercises*, both leaderless group discussions and more practical tasks, such as building a bridge across a wide gap with short lengths of timber. The WOSB was the model for the British Civil Service Selection Board (CSSB). In the USA, a similar intensive assessment programme was used by the Office of Strategic Services (OSS), forerunner of the CIA, to select spies. These early programmes inspired the *assessment centre* for evaluating managers, first used by AT&T in 1956. Assessment centres are discussed in greater detail in Chapter 8.

Work sample tests

In 1913 the Boston streetcar system asked Hugo Munsterberg to find a way of reducing the number of accidents. Munsterberg found that some drivers were poor at judging speed and closing distance (whether the streetcar would reach a pedestrian before the pedestrian had managed to get out of its way), so he devised a work sample test to assess judgement of closing distances and relative speeds. Work samples were used very extensively in military selection and classification programmes in World War Two. Work samples are discussed in Chapter 9.

Weird and wonderful methods

It is very difficult to select good staff, and quite impossible to make the right choice every time, so most personnel managers are conscious of frequent failures and always on the look-out for better methods. Some are led astray by extravagant claims for semi-magical methods.

Graphology

> ... a hail-fellow-well-met who liked to eat and drink; who might attract women of the class he preyed on by an overwhelming animal charm. I would say in fact he was a latent homosexual...and passed as a man's man...capable of conceiving any atrocity and carrying it out in an organised way.

This is a graphologist's assessment of Jack the Ripper based on what might be one of his letters (*see* Figure 1.5). No one knows who really wrote the letter or committed the murders, so no one knows if the graphologist is right.

Graphology is widely used in personnel selection in France, by 85% of all companies according to Klimoski and Rafaeli (1983). Far fewer companies in the UK and the USA use it. Robertson and Makin (1986) reported that 7 to 8 per cent of major UK employers sometimes used graphology. If handwriting accurately reflected personality or work performance, it would offer a very cost-effective selection method, because candidates could be assessed from their application forms. Nor is it obviously absurd to suppose that handwriting reflects personality. However, Klimoski and Rafaeli conclude that research evidence indicates that 'graphology is not a viable assessment method', as two graphologists analysing the same handwriting sample independently show very poor agreement about the writer's personality. Graphologists' ratings of realtors (estate agents) are completely unrelated to supervisors' ratings and to actual sales figures.

Graphologists often ask people to write pen pictures of themselves, so the assessment is not based solely on handwriting. (The content of the letter in Figure 1.5 reveals quite a lot about the writer's mentality – the author enclosed half a human kidney and claims to have eaten the other half.) Neter and Ben-Shakhar (1989) reviewed 17 studies, comparing graphologists and

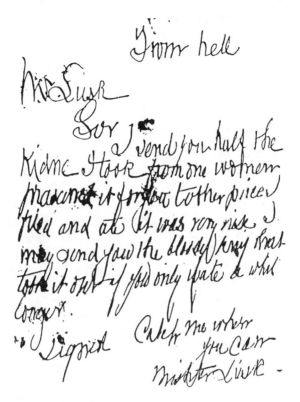

Figure 1.5 A letter attributed to Jack the Ripper

non-graphologists, rating neutral and *content-laden* scripts (such as pen pictures). With content-laden scripts, the non-graphologists, who know nothing about analysing handwriting, achieve better results than graphologists, which suggests that they interpret *what* people write, not *how* they write it, and interpret it better than the graphologists. With neutral scripts, neither group achieves better than zero validity, suggesting either that there is no useful information in handwriting, or that no one at present knows how to extract it.

Handwriting can be a *sign* or a *sample*. A personnel manager who complains that he or she cannot read an applicant's writing judges it as a *sample*; legible handwriting may be needed for the job. The graphologist who infers repressed homosexuality from handwriting interprets the latter as a *sign* of something far removed from putting pen to paper.

Polygraph

The polygraph, also known as the lie detector, was once widely used in the USA to check staff who have the opportunity to steal. The principle of the polygraph is sound – anxiety causes changes in respiration, pulse and skin conductance – but its practice has drawbacks. The polygraph creates a high rate of *false positives* – people who appear to have something to hide but in fact do not, and who may be nervous about the polygraph, but not because they are lying. The polygraph is likely to miss criminals and psychopaths, because these individuals do not see lies as lies or because they do not respond physically to threat, and might well miss a spy who has been trained to mask physical reactions. US law now prohibits use of the polygraph for most types of employee.

Selection and fair employment law

In addition to reliability and validity, selectors must bear in mind fair employment and equal opportunities laws. The law has shaped selection practices in the USA for 40 years, since the Civil Rights Act (CRA) of 1964 prohibited discrimination in employment on grounds of race, colour, religion, national origin or gender. Later laws in the USA also covered age and disability. Similar laws exist in the UK, namely the Race Relations Act (1976), the Sex Discrimination Act (1975) and the Disability Discrimination Act (1995). Figure 1.6 shows how fair employment laws work in the USA. Other developed countries, including the UK, have followed the same general model and adopted many of the key concepts. If selection excludes too many non-whites or women, it is said to create *adverse impact*. The employer can remove the adverse impact by *quota hiring* to 'get the numbers right'. Alternatively, the employer can argue that the adverse impact is justified because the selection test is *job related* or – in psychologists' terms – valid. The employer who succeeds in proving that the

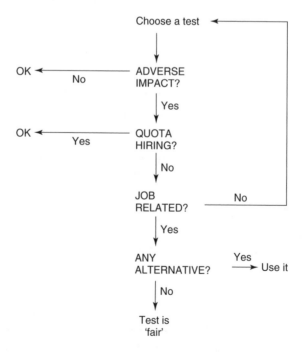

Figure 1.6   Stages in deciding whether a test is legally 'fair'

test is *job related* faces one last hurdle – proving that there is no *alternative test* that is equally valid but which does not create adverse impact.

Note that adverse impact is not what the lay person thinks of as 'discrimination'. Adverse impact does not mean turning away minorities in order to keep the job open for white males, or otherwise deliberately treating minorities differently. Adverse impact means that the selection method results in more majority persons getting through than minority persons. Adverse impact means that an employer can be proved guilty of discrimination by setting standards that make no reference to race or gender, and that may seem well-established, 'common-sense' practice. The important *Griggs* case in the USA ruled that high-school diplomas and ability tests created adverse impact, because fewer African–American applicants had diplomas or reached the pass mark set on the ability test. Height, weight and strength tests for police, fire brigade and armed forces create adverse impact because they exclude more women. In the UK, some employers sift out applicants who have been unemployed for more than six months, on the grounds that they will have lost the habit of working. The Commission for Racial Equality (CRE) argues that this creates adverse impact because unemployment is higher among ethnic minorities. Adverse impact assesses the *effect* of the selection method, not the *intentions* of the people who devised it.

Adverse impact is a very serious matter for employers. It creates a presumption of discrimination, which the employer must disprove, possibly in court. This will cost a great deal of time and money, and may create damaging publicity. Selection methods that do not create adverse impact are therefore highly desirable, but unfortunately they are not always easy to find.

Current selection practice

In the USA

Figure 1.7 summarises a recent survey of 251 US employers (Rynes, Orlitsky & Bretz, 1997), which found that reference checks are the most frequently used method, followed by structured interviews, drug tests, and then unstructured interviews. Biodata, assessment centres and psychological tests (of either personality or ability) are rarely used. New graduates are likely to be assessed by educational achievement or through a trial work period – methods that are not generally used for experienced applicants.

One survey (Harris, Dworkin & Park, 1990) delves a little deeper and asks *why* personnel managers choose or do not choose different selection methods. The most important factor was accuracy, and the least important factors were cost and – surprisingly, perhaps – risk of unfairness. Factors of middling importance were fakability, offensiveness to applicant, and how many other companies use the method. Interviews, although very widely used, were recognised as not being very accurate, as well as being easy to fake. Harris *et al.* suggest that personnel managers are aware of the interview's shortcomings, but continue to use it because it serves other purposes besides

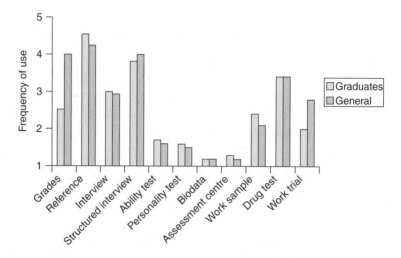

Figure 1.7 Survey of 251 American employers, showing methods used to select graduate entrants and experienced staff. Data taken from Rynes *et al.* (1997). 1 = never, 3 = sometimes, 5 = always

assessment. By contrast, Terpstra and Rozell (1997) asked personnel managers why they did *not* use particular methods. Some they did not consider useful, such as structured interviews and mental ability tests. Some they had not heard of, such as biodata. They did not use mental ability tests because of legal worries.

In the UK

The most recent British survey (Hodgkinson, Daley & Payne, 1995) finds that the classic trio is still almost universal, but that it is being joined by other methods (*see* Figure 1.8).

Graduate recruitment

Keenan (1995) reports a survey of UK graduate recruitment. At the screening stage, employers use the application form, interview and reference. For the final decision, all employers use the interview again, and nearly half of them use assessment centres. Clark (1992) surveyed British executive recruitment agencies which are used by many employers to fill managerial positions. They all used interviews, most (81%) used references, nearly half (45%) used psychological tests, and they rarely used biodata or graphology.

University staff

Foster, Wilkie and Moss (1996) confirm that staff in UK universities are still selected by application form, reference and interview, and that psychological tests and assessment centres are virtually never used. Nearly half of their sample say that they use biodata, but in fact they have probably confused it

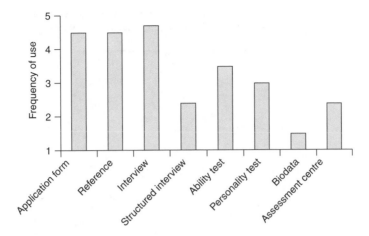

Figure 1.8 Selection methods used by 176 UK employers. Data taken from Hodgkinson *et al.* (1995). 1 = never, 3 = sometimes, 5 = always

with the conventional application form. However, most universities do use one addition to the classic trio that might have some value – they ask the applicant to make a presentation to existing academic staff.

Small business

Most surveys look at large employers, who have specialised personnel departments who know something about selection. However, one-third of the UK workforce work for small employers with fewer than 10 staff, where such expertise is likely to be lacking. Bartram *et al.* (1995) found that small employers rely on interview, at which they try to assess the applicant's honesty, integrity and interest in the job, rather than his or her ability. One in five use work samples or tests of literacy and numeracy, and a surprising one in six use tests of ability or aptitude. Bartram characterises small employers' approach to selection as 'casual'.

In Europe

The Price-Waterhouse–Cranfield survey (Dany & Torchy, 1994) covers 12 Western European countries and nine methods. Table 1.1 reveals a number of interesting national differences.

- The French favour graphology, but no other country does.
- Application forms are widely used everywhere except in The Netherlands.
- References are widely used everywhere, but are less popular in Spain, Portugal and The Netherlands.
- Psychometric testing is most popular in Spain and Portugal, and least popular in West Germany and Turkey.
- Aptitude testing is most popular in Spain and The Netherlands, and least popular in West Germany and Turkey.

Table 1.1   The Price-Waterhouse–Cranfield survey of selection methods in 12 Western European countries: percentage of employers using method.

	AF	IV	Psy	Gph	Ref	Apt	AC	Grp
UK	97	71	46	1	92	45	18	13
Ireland	91	87	28	1	91	41	7	8
France	95	92	22	57	73	28	9	10
Portugal	83	97	58	2	55	17	2	18
Spain	87	85	60	8	54	72	18	22
Germany	96	86	6	6	66	8	13	4
Netherlands	94	69	31	2	47	53	27	2
Denmark	48	99	38	2	79	17	4	8
Finland	82	99	74	2	63	42	16	8
Norway	59	78	11	0	92	19	5	1
Sweden	na	69	24	0	96	14	5	3
Turkey	95	64	8	0	69	33	4	23

Source: Reproduced from Dany & Torchy (1994) by permission of Thomson Publishing Services.
Methods: AF = application form; IV = interview panel; Psy = psychometric testing; Gph = graphology; Ref = reference; Apt = aptitude test; AC = assessment centre; Grp = group selection methods.

- Assessment centres are not used much, but are most popular in Spain and The Netherlands.
- Group selection methods are not used much, but are most popular in Spain and Portugal.

Further afield

Very much less is known about selection in other parts of the world. Recent surveys of New Zealand (Taylor, Mills & O'Driscoll, 1993) and Australia (Di Milia, Smith & Brown, 1994) found a very similar picture to that in the UK. Interview, references and application are virtually universal, with personality tests, ability tests and assessment centres only being used by a minority. Arthur *et al.* (1995) described selection in Nigeria and Ghana, where interviews were nearly universal (90%) and references were widely used (46%); paper-and-pencil tests were less frequently used, as were work samples (19%) and work simulations (11%).

The most recent survey covers no less than 20 countries, although some samples are rather small (Ryan *et al.*, 1999). Mental ability tests are used most in Belgium, The Netherlands and Spain, and least in Italy and the USA. Personality tests are used most in Spain, and least in Germany and the USA. Projective tests are used most in Portugal, Spain and South Africa, and least in Germany, Greece, the UK, Ireland, Italy and Singapore. Drug tests are used most in Portugal, Sweden and the USA, and least in Italy, Singapore and Spain.

Acceptability of selection methods to candidates

In times of high unemployment, employers may feel that they can afford to take less notice of candidates' reactions; in times of labour shortage, unpopular methods could drive applicants away. Candidates' views of selection methods may shape their opinion of the organisation and their decision as to whether to accept a job offer. A recent survey in Belgium (Stinglhamber, Vandenberghe & Brancart, 1999) even reports that a candidate who does not like an organisation's assessment methods may stop buying its products.

Surveys also indicate that some assessment methods are more popular with applicants than others (Steiner & Gilliland, 1996; Ryan & Ployhart, 2000). Candidates like interviews, work samples and assessment centres, but they do not like biodata, peer assessment or personality tests. Smither *et al.* (1993) reported that candidates regard more job-related approaches, such as simulations, interviews and more concrete ability tests (e.g. vocabulary, maths), as fairer. They regard personality tests, biodata and abstract ability tests (letter sets, etc.) as less fair because they are less job related. Steiner and Gilliland (1996) found that preferences in the USA and France are broadly similar, with two exceptions. Personality tests and graphology are more acceptable in France, although they are still not very popular. Research indicates that people like selection methods which are job related, but they do not like being assessed on aspects which they cannot change, such as personality.

Key points

In Chapter 1 you have learnt the following.

- Employees vary greatly in value, so selection matters.
- Traditional methods of selection (application form, letter of reference and interview) are not very accurate, so employers who rely on them are probably not selecting very effectively.
- Selection research compares a selection test, known as a *predictor*, with work performance, known as the *outcome* or *criterion*. This is called a *validity study*, and it yields a *validity coefficient*.
- Selection methods should be *reliable* – that is, give a consistent account of the candidate.
- Selection methods should be *valid* – that is, accept good candidates and reject poor candidates.
- Deciding which application to proceed with and which to reject is called *sifting*. It is often done inefficiently or unfairly.
- Conventional paper application methods can be improved.
- The Internet may greatly change the application process.
- Selection methods must conform with fair employment legislation.
- The problem with fair employment is not deliberate or *direct discrimination*, but *adverse impact*, whereby the method results in fewer women or minority

persons being successful. Adverse impact will create problems for the employer, so it should be avoided if possible.
- Non-traditional methods include psychological tests, assessment centres and work sample tests.
- Magical methods such as graphology rarely work.
- Selection in developed countries follows broadly similar patterns, with some local variations.
- Some selection methods are more acceptable to candidates than others.

Key references

Bartram (2000) discusses the role of the Internet in recruitment and selection.

Dany and Torchy (1994) describe the Price-Waterhouse–Cranfield survey which studies selection methods in 12 European countries.

Davison and Burke (2000) review research on gender bias in application sifting.

Murphy and Davidshofer (2000) is an up-to-date textbook of psychological testing.

Neter and Ben-Shakhar (1989) analyse research on the value of graphology as a selection method.

Ryan and Ployhart (2000) review research on the acceptability of selection methods to candidates.

Ryan *et al.* (1999) describe selection methods in 20 countries, including the USA and the UK.

Rynes *et al.* (1997) describe a survey of selection methods in the USA.

Schmidt and Hunter (1981) present some striking data on the possible savings that can be achieved by effective selection.

Useful websites

www.bps.org.uk/about/psychometric.cfm. The British Psychological Society's Psychological Testing Centre.
www.checkpast.com. A (US) background checking agency.
www.factsffinder.com. Another (US) background checking agency.
www.hrzone.com. Offers advice on a range of human resource issues in the USA.
www.hr-guide.com. Offers advice and information on a range of human resource issues in the USA.
www.incomesdata.co.uk. Income Data Services, a UK company that reports interesting research on human resource issues, including a survey of selection tests.
www.restrac.com. The leading American résumé scanning service.
www.siop.org. (US) Society for Industrial and Organisational Psychology, includes details of conferences, and *The Industrial/Organisational Psychologist*.

CHAPTER 2

Job description and job analysis

*If you don't know where you're going, you'll end up
somewhere else*

Introduction

Selectors should always start by deciding what they are looking for. In the
UK, this is often done very inefficiently (but not necessarily very quickly – I
once sat through a three-hour discussion of what or who we wanted in a new
head of department, which succeeded only in concluding that we didn't really
want a psychoanalyst, but would otherwise like the 'best' candidate. I didn't
feel that my time had been usefully spent).

Job description and person specification

Traditional British practice recommends selectors to write a job description
and a person specification. Job descriptions start with the job's official title
('Head of Contracts Compliance Unit') and then say how the job fits into
the organisation ('organising and leading a team of seven implementing [a
London borough] Council's contracts compliance policy'), before listing the
job's main duties.

1. Devise and implement management control systems and procedures.
2. Introduce new technology to the Unit.
3. Develop strategies for fighting discrimination, poverty, apartheid and
   privatisation.

Job descriptions commonly fall into one of two traps. First, they list every
duty – important or unimportant, frequent or infrequent, routinely easy or very
difficult – without indicating which is which. Second, they lapse into a vague,
sub-literate 'managementspeak' (of 'liaising', 'resourcing', 'monitoring', etc.)
instead of explaining precisely what the successful applicant will find him-
or herself doing. Many job descriptions aim to list anything the person might
ever be asked to do, so that the employee cannot subsequently say 'that's not
part of my job'.

Person specifications also suffer from vagueness and 'managementspeak'.
Having dealt with the specifics ('must have personnel management qualifications, must speak Mandarin Chinese'); many UK person specifications waste

time stating that the applicant must be keen, well motivated and energetic – as if any employer is likely to want idle, unmotivated employees. American job descriptions usually focus much more sharply on *KSAs – knowledge, skills and aptitudes*. Ideally, the person specification indicates which selection tests to use.

Competences

Over the last 25 years, the personnel world has adopted with great enthusiasm the *competence* approach. Jacobs (1989) offers a typical definition of competence: 'an observable skill or ability to complete a managerial task successfully'. To some extent the competence approach starts from the conventional job description/person specification approach. To some extent, in the UK, it is inspired by the National Vocational Qualifications (NVQ) scheme, which describes jobs in competence terms. For example, the National Health Service lists 35 separate main competences for healthcare assistants, such as 'assist clients to access and use toilet facilities'. The NVQ system is primarily geared to training and to awarding qualifications, not to selection. In the UK, people talk of *competences*, meaning achieving an acceptable standard for which an NVQ might be awarded, and the model covers all jobs. In the USA, people talk of *competencies*, meaning achieving a very high standard, and are more likely to be talking about managers and professionals. Dulewicz (1994) supplies a list of 40 competencies for managers in general, including *development of subordinates, extra-organisational awareness* and *business sense*.

From the selector's point of view, competences are often a very mixed bag:

- specific skills or knowledge that workers will acquire as part of their training but would not possess beforehand (e.g. knowing how to serve meals and drinks on an aircraft)
- more generalised skills or knowledge that organisations might wish to select for (e.g. communicating well in writing)
- aptitudes that would make it easier for a person to acquire more specific competences (e.g. flexibility, or ability to learn quickly)
- personality characteristics (e.g. resilience, tolerance). Of Dulewicz's list of 40 managerial competences, no less than 10 competences look like personality traits.

Lists of competences are often very long, giving rise to the suspicion that statistical analysis would show that many of them are highly correlated. Dulewicz's 40 managerial competences group into 11 'supra-competences'. Fletcher (1997) considers that competence 'must stand a good chance of winning any competition for the most over-worked concept in HR management in the late 1980s/early 1990s'.

Job analysis methods

Job descriptions and person specifications can be drawn up by a committee in half a day. *Job analysis* is much more ambitious, much more detailed and has many more uses. Some methods require complex statistical analysis.

Collecting information for job analysis

The job analyst can choose from at least nine methods of collecting information about work, arranged below in a rough order from the most mechanistic and behaviourist to the most subjective or phenomenological.

1. Film or video recording.
2. Written records of sales, accidents, etc.
3. Observation is useful for simple jobs, but may not make sense of higher-level jobs.
4. Structured questionnaires completed by workers and/or supervisors.
5. Diaries are used for jobs with very little structure, such as that of a university lecturer (college professor).
6. Open-ended questionnaires are more suitable for higher-level jobs with diverse tasks.
7. Interviews take account of aspects of work that observation cannot, such as plans, intentions, meaning and satisfaction. The person who sees his or her work as 'laying bricks' differs from the person who sees it as 'building a cathedral'.
8. Group interviews with workers are more economical and iron out idiosyncrasies.
9. Participation. Some psychologists think that the only way to understand a job is to do it, or to spend as much time as possible alongside someone else who is doing it. Some psychologists researching USAAF flight crew selection in World War Two went to the lengths of learning to fly themselves.

The trend is increasingly towards structured methods, in which information is compared with a large database describing hundreds of jobs.

Ways of analysing information

Having collected information about the work being done, the researcher faces the task of making sense of it. This can be done subjectively, by a committee, or by two types of formal statistical analysis.

Subjective analysis

After spending a month, a week or an afternoon watching people doing the job, or talking to them, the analyst writes down his or her impressions. This is often good enough as the basis for writing a job description, but it does not really merit the title 'analysis'.

Rational analysis

Official analyses of jobs group them by rational methods – that is, by committee and consultation. This helps to ensure that the analysis makes sense to the organisation and will be accepted by them.

Statistical analysis I: factor analysis

Job analysis typically generates very large datasets. For example, Krzystofiak Newman and Anderson (1979) had a matrix of 1700 × 750 ratings, which is far too large to make any sense of 'by eye', so statistical analysis is essential. Factor analysis correlates scores for different jobs, to find factors of job performance (see Box 2.1).

Box 2.1   Factor analysis

Table 2.1 shows (fictitious) correlations between performance on six typical school subjects, in a large sample. The correlations between English, French and German are all fairly high – people who are good at one tend to be good at the others. Similarly, the correlations between Maths, Physics and Chemistry are fairly high. However, the correlations between subjects in different sets (e.g. English Literature × Physics) are much lower. This all suggests that people who are good at one language tend to be good at another, while people who are good at one science tend to be good at another. There are *eight* school subjects, but only *two* underlying abilities. Clear groupings in small sets of correlations can be seen by inspection. Larger sets of less clear correlations can only be interpreted by *factor analysis*, which calculates how many *factors* are needed to account for the observed correlations.

Table 2.1   (Fictitious) correlations between school subject marks.

	M	P	C	E	F
M (Maths)					
P (Physics)	0.67				
C (Chemistry)	0.76	0.55			
E (English)	0.33	0.23	0.25		
F (French)	0.23	0.31	0.30	0.77	
G (German)	0.11	0.21	0.22	0.80	0.67

Statistical analysis II: cluster analysis

Cluster analysis groups jobs according to similarity of ratings (see Box 2.2). Cluster analysis groups *people*, whereas factor analysis groups *tasks*. Each is useful to the selector in different ways.

Box 2.2   Cluster analysis

A typical job analysis has data from 1,700 workers and 60 scores for each, generating a 1,700 × 60 (= 102,000) matrix. One could try to search through this by hand to pick out people with similar profiles, but this would be very tedious and very inaccurate. Cluster analysis calculates the similarity of every possible pair of profiles, and then groups profiles by similarity.

An example

Krzystofiak, Newman and Anderson (1979) wrote a 754-item Job Analysis Questionnaire for use in a power utility (power station) that employed nearly 1,900 individuals in 814 different jobs. Employees rated how often they performed nearly 600 tasks. Krzystofiak *et al.* first factor-analysed their data and extracted 60 factors, representing 60 themes in the work of the 1,900 employees. The profile for the company's Administrator of Equal Employment Opportunity showed that his work had the following six themes (in order of importance):

1. personnel administration
2. legal, commissions, agencies and hearings
3. staff management
4. training
5. managerial supervision and decision making
6. non-line management.

Similar profiles were drawn up for every employee. Knowing that a particular job has six main themes gives the selector a much clearer idea of how to recruit and select for it. If personnel could find a good test of each of the 60 factors, they would have a perfect all-purpose test battery for every one of the 800-jobs in the plant.

Krzystofiak *et al.* then cluster-analysed their data (see Box 2.2) to sort employees into groups whose jobs were similar. One cluster consisted of the following:

- rate analyst III
- statistical assistant
- research assistant
- affirmative action staff assistant
- co-ordinator, distribution service
- environmental co-ordinator
- statistician
- power production statistician.

These eight jobs had quite a lot in common, but they all came from different departments, so their similarity might easily have been overlooked. Knowing which posts have much in common helps when planning training, staff succession, cover for illness, etc.

Selected job analysis techniques: an overview

Over the last 30 years, job analysis techniques have multiplied almost as prolifically as personality inventories. In this chapter there is only space to describe six or seven of the most widely used techniques. In general terms, job analysis systems can be divided into *job-oriented*, *content-oriented* and *attribute-oriented* techniques.

- *Job-oriented techniques.* concentrate on the work being done ('installing cable pressurisation systems', 'locating the source of an automobile engine knock').
- *Content-oriented techniques.* are more concerned with what the worker does to accomplish the job ('attention to detail', 'use of written materials'). The Position Analysis Questionnaire (PAQ) exemplifies this approach.
- *Attribute-oriented techniques.* describe jobs in terms of the traits or aptitudes that are needed to perform them (good eyesight, verbal fluency, manual dexterity). The PAQ lists attributes as well as job content.

*Dictionary of Occupational Titles/O*NET*

The (US) *Dictionary of Occupational Titles (DOT)* provides detailed descriptions of thousands of jobs. For example:

> Collects, interprets and applies scientific data to human and animal behavior and mental processes, formulates hypotheses and experimental designs, analyses results using statistics, writes papers describing research, provides therapy and counselling for groups or individuals. Investigates processes of learning and growth, and human interrelationships. Applies psychological techniques to personnel administration and management. May teach college courses.

DOT's account of a psychologist's work is actually a composite of several types of psychologist – academic, clinical and occupational. Few psychologists do everything listed in DOT's description. DOT also includes ratings of the complexity of each job, which have been widely used in research on intellectual ability. DOT is now being superseded by a database called O*NET (Peterson *et al.*, 2001), which will include details of the following:

- experience requirements
- worker requirements
- worker characteristics
- occupational requirements, including generalised work activities (e.g. inspecting equipment, structures or materials, electronic and electrical repair)

- occupation-specific requirements
- occupation characteristics.

Critical incident technique (CIT)

CIT is the oldest job analysis technique, devised by Flanagan (1954) to analyse failure in military pilot training during World War Two. He found the reasons that were given for failure either too vague to be helpful (e.g. 'poor judgement') or completely circular ('lack of inherent flying ability'). Flanagan identified the critical requirements of flying by collecting accounts of *critical incidents* which caused recruits to be rejected. These included what led up to the incident, what the recruit did, what the consequences were, and whether the recruit was responsible for them. Typical incidents included trying to land on the wrong runway or coming in to land too high. CIT is open-ended and flexible, but can be time consuming. In modern CIT, hundreds or even thousands of accounts are collected and then sorted by similarity to identify the main themes in effective and ineffective performance. CIT is the basis of *behaviourally anchored rating scales (BARS)* (*see* Chapter 4), and of some structured interviewing systems (*see* Chapter 3).

Repertory grid technique (RGT)

Loosely based on *personal construct theory*, RGT is popular in the UK. The informant is asked to think of a good worker, an average worker and a poor worker, and then to state which two differ from the third, and how (*see* Figure 2.1). In the grid in Figure 2.1, the informant states in the first row that a good ambulance worker can be distinguished from average and poor workers by 'commitment', and in the second row that a good ambulance supervisor can be distinguished from average and poor workers by 'fairness'. The informant is usually asked to apply each distinction to every person in the grid, making it possible to calculate the overlap of the *constructs* 'commitment' and 'fairness'. When using RGT for job analysis, one probes the constructs by asking the informant for specific behavioural examples of commitment (e.g. willing to stay on after the end of the shift if there is an emergency call).

Fleishman job analysis survey, including physical abilities analysis

Fleishman and Mumford (1991) list 52 abilities (e.g. oral comprehension), each of which is rated on a seven-point rating, with explanations of how each differs from related but separate abilities (e.g. written comprehension and oral expression). Fleishman's abilities include nine purely physical abilities (listed in Table 9.1, page 201). Detailed physical job analysis is particularly important when women and the disabled are applying for jobs that are traditionally done by men, or which require physical abilities.

Elements > Sorts	Good ambulance person	Average ambulance person	Poor ambulance person	Good ambulance service supervisor	Average ambulance service supervisor	Poor ambulance service supervisor	Good ambulance service manager	••• Constructs
1	[X]	[ ]	[ ]	X			X	••• Commitment
2				[X]	[ ]	[ ]	X	••• Fairness
3	[X]			[X]	X		[X]	••• Calmness
4			[ ]			[ ]		•••
etc.								

Figure 2.1 Repertory grid technique (RGT) used in job analysis. The elements are various 'role figures' (e.g. good ambulance supervisor). The three elements that are used to start each set are denoted by []

Personality-related Position Requirement Form (PPRF)

Traditional job analysis systems tended to emphasise those abilities that are needed for the job. However, with the growing popularity of personality testing in selection, new systems are emerging that also assess personality requirements. Raymark, Schmit and Guion's (1997) Personality-Related Position Requirement Form (PPRF) contains items in the following format.

Effective performance in this position requires the person to:
– take control in group situations
                    not required/helpful/essential

Preliminary results indicate that leadership is needed in management but not in cashiers, while a friendly disposition is needed in sales assistants but not in caretakers. By contrast, conscientiousness seems to be needed in every job. The PPRF enables selectors to use personality measures in a more focused way, and to be able to justify assessing aspects of personality if challenged about this.

Job components inventory (JCI)

The JCI was developed in the UK (Banks *et al.*, 1983) for jobs requiring limited skill, and has five principal sections, namely tools and equipment, perceptual and physical requirements, maths, communication, decision making and responsibility.

Future-oriented job analysis (FOJA)

Landis, Fogli and Goldberg (1998) have devised a job analysis system to describe jobs that do not yet exist, to meet the criticism that job analysis is essentially backward looking. FOJA is used for three new entry-level jobs in the insurance industry.

Position analysis questionnaire (PAQ)

The PAQ is probably the most widely used job analysis technique. Despite its title, it is not in fact a questionnaire, but a structured interview schedule (McCormick, Jeanneret and Mecham, 1972). The PAQ is completed by a trained job analyst who collects information from workers and supervisors. However, the analyst does not simply record what the informant says, but forms his or her own judgement about the job. The information that the PAQ collects covers nearly 200 elements, divided into six main areas (*see* Table 2.2).

Elements are rated for *importance to the job, time spent doing each, amount of training required*, etc. The completed PAQ is analysed by comparing it with a very large American database. The analysis proceeds by a series of linked stages as follows.

1. *Profile of 32 job elements.* The original factor analysis of PAQ items identified 32 dimensions which underlie all forms of work (e.g. watching things from a distance, being aware of bodily movement and balance, making decisions, dealing with the public).
2. *Profile of 76 attributes.* These are the aptitudes, interests or temperament that the person needs to perform the job elements (McCormick *et al.*,

Table 2.2 Six main divisions of the Position Analysis Questionnaire (PAQ), and their illustrative job elements.

PAQ division	Illustrative job elements
1. Information input	Use of written materials
	Near visual differentiation (i.e. good visual acuity at short range)
2. Mental processes	Level of reasoning in problem solving, coding/decoding
3. Work output	Use of keyboard devices, assembling/disassembling
4. Relationships with other people	Instructing, contacts with public or customers
5. Job context	High temperature, interpersonal conflict
6. Other	Specified work space, amount of job structure

1972). Aptitude attributes include *movement detection* (being able to detect the physical movement of objects and to judge their direction) and *selective attention* (being able to perform a task in the presence of distracting stimuli). Temperament attributes include empathy and influencing people. The attribute profile provides the selector with a detailed person specification.

3. *Recommended psychological tests.* The attribute profile leads naturally on to suggestions for tests to assess the attributes. If the job needs manual dexterity, the PAQ output suggests using the pegboard test of gross dexterity of the General Aptitude Test Battery (GATB) (*see* Chapter 6). Recommendations for tests for interests and temperament are also made, mostly for the Myers Briggs Type Indicator.

4. *Job component validity (JCV) data.* Based on the job's component elements, estimates are generated of the likely validity of the nine abilities assessed by the GATB (Table 6.9, page 117), as well as estimates of likely average scores (Jeanneret, 1992).

5. *Comparable jobs and remuneration.* The job element profile is compared with the PAQ's extensive database, in order to identify other jobs with similar requirements, and to estimate the appropriate salary in US$. Arvey and Begalla (1975) obtained PAQ ratings for 48 home-makers (housewives) and found that the most similar job in PAQ's database was police officer, followed by home economist, airport maintenance chief, kitchen helper and firefighter – all trouble-shooting, emergency-handling jobs. Arvey and Begalla also calculated the average salary paid for the 10 jobs most similar to that of housewife ($740 a month, at 1968 prices).

Reliability and validity of job analysis techniques

Reliability

McCormick *et al.* (1972) reported acceptable inter-rater reliabilities for the PAQ, and Banks *et al.* (1983) found that Job Components Inventory ratings by workers and supervisors correlate reasonably for most scales and most jobs. Re-test reliabilities are not calculated very often for job analysis measures, because they are so long and complicated to complete. Wilson *et al.* (1990) reported that repeating sections of the inventory can demonstrate good reliability.

Validity

Research on validity of job analysis faces a dilemma that is familiar to psychologists. If results agree with 'common sense', they are dismissed as redundant ('telling us what we already know'). If results do not agree with common sense, they are simply dismissed as wrong. Evidence for the validity of job analysis derives from demonstrating that its results make sense, and from showing that job analysis leads to more accurate selection (see below).

Analysis of the work of senior (UK) civil servants found nine factors and 13 clusters of jobs. Dulewicz and Keenay (1979) sent details of the clusters to the civil servants who contributed the data, and asked if they agreed with the classification and whether they had been correctly classified. Only 7% considered the classification to be unsatisfactory, and only 11% disagreed with their personal classification.

Job analysis should differentiate jobs that differ, but give the same picture of the same job, in different plants or organisations. Banks *et al.* (1983) found that Job Component Inventory (JCI) ratings distinguished four clerical jobs from four engineering jobs, proving that the JCI can find a difference where a difference ought to exist. Banks *et al.* also showed that JCI ratings were the same for mail-room clerks in different companies, proving that the JCI does not find a difference where there should not be one.

Some doubts have been cast on the PAQ's validity by research which shows that PAQ ratings by experts, supervisors, people doing the job and students inter-correlated almost perfectly (Smith & Hakel, 1979). If workers or students can analyse jobs, why pay for experts? The students were given only the name of the job, so how could they describe it accurately? Perhaps the PAQ is only generating stereotyped impressions of jobs, and not really analysing them. However, Cornelius, DeNisi and Blencoe (1984) were able to show that the more the students knew about the job, the better their PAQ ratings agreed with those of the experts, which confirms the PAQ's validity. Furthermore, very high levels of student–expert agreement are partly an artefact, based on the PAQ's *does not apply* ratings – everyone knows that college professors (university lecturers) do not use powered hand tools as part of their job. When *does not apply* ratings are excluded from the analysis, agreement between students and experts is further reduced. These results imply that the PAQ genuinely analyses jobs, and is not just a complicated way of measuring stereotypes. Morgeson and Campion (1997) point out that most job analysis techniques rely on subjective judgement, so are open to the many (they list 16) types of bias that have been documented for such judgements. For example, judgements may be subject to conformity pressures, if management or the trades (labour) union has definite views about the nature of the job. This will create very reliable ratings, where everyone agrees with everyone else, but these ratings are not necessarily valid.

Uses of job analysis

Job analysis has a variety of uses, in selection in particular and in personnel work in general – so many uses in fact that one wonders how personnel departments ever managed without it. Some uses are directly connected with selection.

1. *Write accurate, comprehensive job descriptions* which help to recruit the right applicants.
2. *Aid the interviewer.* If the interviewer knows exactly what the job involves, he or she can concentrate on assessing knowledge, skills and abilities.

Otherwise the interview can only assess the candidate *as a person*, which may give poor results and allow biases to creep in.

3. *Distinguish between what should be selected for and what can be trained for.* Some competences can be readily acquired by most people by training, so do not need to be selected for, whereas others may be difficult or almost impossible to train for, so must be selected for. Jones *et al.* (2001) showed that experts achieve a high degree of consensus on the trainability of the competences that are needed for school-teaching.

4. *Choose selection tests.* A good job analysis identifies the knowledge, skills and abilities that are needed, allowing the selector to choose the right tests.

5. *Classification.* This involves assigning new employees to the tasks that they are best suited for, assuming they have not been appointed to a specific job.

6. *Defend selection tests.* In the case of *Arnold v Ballard*, a good job analysis allowed an employer to require high-school education, although general educational requirements are rarely accepted as fair in the USA (*see* Chapters 9 and 12). Job analysis is legally required by the Equal Employment Opportunities Commission in the USA if the employer needs to use selection methods that create adverse impact.

7. *Transfer selection tests.* Jobs can be grouped into families for which the same selection procedure can be used. If jobs are similar, then (1) selection tests for job A can be used for job B without separate validation, and (2) selection procedures in organisation C can be used in organisation D, again without separate validation. However, fair employment legislation in the USA may not allow selection procedures to be transferred without proof that there are no significant differences between jobs. Job analysis can provide the necessary proof.

Some uses of job analysis allow more elaborate selection methods to be devised.

8. *Devise structured interview systems.* Structured interviews (*see* Chapter 3) have proved much more accurate than conventional interviews, but require a detailed job analysis.

9. *Write selection tests. I. Content validation.* Job analysis allows selectors to write a selection test whose content so closely matches the content of the job that it is *content valid* (*see* Chapter 10), which means that it can be used, legally in the USA, without further demonstration of its validity.

10. *Write selection tests. II. Synthetic validation.* Krzystofiak, Newman and Anderson (1979) found 60 factors in power-station jobs. If the employer could find an adequate test of each factor, they could *synthesise* a different set of tests for every job, according to the factors involved in each job (*see* Chapter 10). The PAQ's job component validity (see above) approaches this in a different way by using the job's PAQ profile to calculate which GATB tests to use and what weight to give each score for a particular job.

Besides helping to improve selection, job analyses are useful in other areas of human resource management.

11. *Vocational guidance.* Job analysis identifies jobs which are similar with regard to the work done and the attributes needed, so someone interested in job X, where there are currently no vacancies, can be recommended to try jobs Y and Z instead.
12. *Rationalise training.* Job analysis identifies jobs that have a lot in common, which enables employers to rationalise training provision.
13. *Succession planning.* Job analysis can be used to plan promotions, and to find avenues to promote under-represented minorities.
14. *Plan performance appraisal systems.* Job analysis identifies the dimensions to be rated in performance appraisal.
15. *Criterion development.* Selection research needs a criterion or measure of work performance. Detailed analysis of the job may make it easier to distinguish between good and bad employees.
16. Carrying out a job analysis, or studying the results of one, focuses the organisation's mind on what they are doing and why, which is often very useful.

Using job analysis to select workers

Analysis by PAQ of the job of plastics injection-moulding setter in a UK plant identified seven attributes that were needed in workers (*see* Table 2.3), and then recommended a suitable test for each attribute (Raven's Standard Progressive Matrices for intelligence, an optician's eye chart for visual acuity, etc.) (Sparrow *et al.*, 1982). Sparrow's work illustrates the use of job analysis first to generate a person specification, and then to choose appropriate selection tests. This may seem obvious, but it is surprising how many employers even now do not do this, which places them in a very dangerous position if someone complains about their selection methods. If the employer cannot state why they are using Raven's Standard Progressive

Table 2.3 Job analysis by the Position Analysis Questionnaire, showing choice of tests for the job of plastic injection-moulding setter.

Attribute	Test
Long-term memory	Wechsler Memory Scale
Intelligence	Standard Progressive Matrices
Short-term memory	Wechsler Memory Scale
Near visual acuity	Eye chart at 30 cm
Perceptual speed	Thurstone Perceptual Speed Test
Convergent thinking	Standard Progressive Matrices
Mechanical ability	Birkbeck Mechanical Comprehension Test

Source: Reproduced from Sparrow *et al.* (1982) by permission of the British Psychological Society.

Matrices, they will find it extremely difficult to justify themselves if it turns out that this method creates an adverse impact on some sections of the population.

More ambitiously, job analysis systems can be linked to aptitude batteries. Gutenberg *et al*. (1983) correlated the validity of the General Aptitude Test Battery (GATB) for 111 jobs with PAQ ratings for decision making and information processing, and found correlations with general mental ability, but not with dexterity. Mecham (cited in McCormick, DeNisi & Shaw, 1979) analysed 163 jobs for which both GATB and PAQ data were available, and then asked two questions.

1. Does the PAQ profile for a job correlate with the GATB profile for the same job? If PAQ indicates that the job needs spatial ability, do people who are doing the job tend to have high spatial ability scores on the GATB?
2. Does the PAQ profile for a job correlate with GATB profile validity for the same job? If the PAQ indicates that the job needs spatial ability, do people with high spatial ability scores on the GATB perform the job better?

The answer to both questions was yes. The correlation between the PAQ profile and the GATB profile across jobs was 0.71. The correlation between the PAQ profile and GATB validity across jobs was lower, but still positive (0.43). This research implies that each job needs a particular set of attributes, which can be identified by the PAQ and then assessed by the GATB. However, some American psychologists would question this, and have argued (*see* Chapter 6) that general mental ability predicts work performance for all jobs, and that differences in the profile of abilities add little or no predictive power.

Improving selection validity

From the selector's viewpoint, job analysis has validity if it results in more accurate selection decisions. Three meta-analyses have shown that personality testing (Tett, Jackson and Rothstein, 1991), structured interviewing (Wiesner and Cronshaw, 1988) and situational judgement tests (McDaniel *et al*., 2001) achieve higher validity when based on job analysis.

'Hammer in search of a nail'

Sometimes job analysis identifies skills or attributes for which no test is readily available. For example, job descriptions frequently list awareness of others as a necessary competence, but it is difficult to assess this successfully (*see* Chapter 6). Many selectors tend to reverse their perspective in an unhelpful way and do not ask 'What does the job need and how can we assess it?' but 'What assessments have we got and how can we fit them to the job in question?'.

The future of job analysis

Is job analysis essential?

The work of Schmidt, Hunter and Pearlman (reviewed in greater detail in Chapter 6) suggests that analysis of jobs might not need to be very detailed for selection purposes. Pearlman, Schmidt and Hunter (1980) concluded that deciding a job is 'clerical' was all the job analysis needed to choose tests that predicted productivity. (One should bear in mind that during the 1970s and 1980s the Schmidt–Hunter–Pearlman group developed the view that *all* jobs in the USA could be selected for by a combination of general mental ability and dexterity, which clearly does not leave much scope for detailed job analysis in guiding choice of test.) Smith (1994) suggests that mental ability may be a 'universal' of selection – something that is needed, or useful, in every job. Smith suggests two other universals, namely energy and 'work importance'. Hunt (1996) analysed performance data for 18,000 hourly-paid entry-level employees, and suggested eight dimensions of generic work behaviour, such as attendance, thoroughness, schedule flexibility (willingness to change working hours if needed), and absence of unruliness, drug misuse or theft.

Even if Pearlman's conclusions are correct, it would probably be difficult to act on them at present. Deciding that a job is 'clerical', and using a clerical test for selection, may satisfy common sense and may be good enough for Pearlman *et al.*, but it will probably not satisfy the Equal Employment Opportunities Commission if there are complaints about the composition of the workforce. The full detail and complexity of the PAQ may be needed to prove that a clerical job really is clerical. Similarly, an American employer who has proved that the GATB selects wool-pullers in plant A, and wants to use the GATB to select wool-pullers in plant B, may have to analyse both wool-pulling jobs in order to prove that they really are the same.

Is job analysis becoming obsolete?

Latham and Wexley (1981) described a long rating schedule for janitors in which item 132 read:

Places a deodorant block in urinal   almost never – almost always

The rest of the janitor's day was documented in similarly exhaustive detail. Management and the HR professions have begun to question this type of approach. Rapid change implies less need for task-specific skills and more need for general abilities to adapt, solve problems, define one's own direction and work in teams. Job analysis is backward looking and encourages cloning, whereas organisations need to be forward looking. Job analysis assumes that the job exists apart from the employee who holds it, whereas organisations are being 'de-jobbed', meaning that employees work on a fluid set of activities which change rapidly so no job descriptions exist. Current management trends also suggest a shift towards broad personal characteristics rather than long lists of specific skills or competences. *Total quality management* (TQM) emphasises customer service skills, self-direction, self-development and team development skills. The quest for *high-performance organisations* – a buzzword in the USA in the 1990s – lists the qualities that employees need, namely teamwork, customer service and leadership. This represents a shift of emphasis from very specific (and hence very numerous) skills or competences to a few very broad abilities or traits – a shift of emphasis from the job to the person. In the USA this may create problems, since the emphasis for many years has been on the importance of job relatedness in selection. Wood and Payne (1998) suggest that the key dimensions which selectors will be assessing in future will be integrity, learning ability, creativity and resilience (because more and more employees are claiming compensation for the effect of work stress).

Key points

In Chapter 2 you have learnt the following.

- It is absolutely vital to decide what you are looking for before starting any selection programme. If you fail to do this, you will be unlikely to make good selection decisions, and you will be unable to justify your selection methods if they are questioned or become the subject of legal dispute.
- Conventional job descriptions and person specifications are better than nothing.
- Competence frameworks are also useful, although they are often conceptually rather confused.
- Quantitative or statistical analysis is usually essential to make sense of large sets of data about work.
- Job analysis can identify the main themes in a specific job, or in whole sets of jobs, or in work in general.
- Job analysis methods include some that are fairly open-ended, such as the critical incident technique, and some that are more structured, such as the Position Analysis Questionnaire.
- Job analysis can improve selection systems.
- Job analysis has many other uses as well as guiding selection.
- Job analysis needs to look forward as well as backward.

Key references

Krzystofiak *et al*. (1979) describe the use of factor analysis and cluster analysis in a large set of job analysis data.

Landis *et al*. (1998) describe a future-oriented job analysis system.

McCormick *et al*. (1972) describe the original research on the PAQ.

Morgeson and Campion (1997) analyse possible sources of bias and error in job analysis ratings.

Pearlman *et al*. (1980) argue that detailed job analysis is not always essential for selection.

Raymark *et al*. (1997) describe a job analysis system that is specifically geared to personality requirements and assessment.

Smith (1994) suggests that there are several 'universals' or attributes that are needed in all jobs.

Sparrow *et al*. (1982) describe a UK example of use of the PAQ to guide selection.

Useful websites

www.doleta.gov/programs/onet/. O*NET site.
www.ijoa.org. Institute of Job and Occupational Analysis.
www.oalj.dol.gov/libdot.htm. *Dictionary of Occupational Titles*.
www.paq.com. PAQ Services Inc.

CHAPTER 3

The interview

I know one when I see one

Introduction

Interviews have been used to assess people for a long time – promotion, to lieutenant in the Royal Navy in 1800 was decided by an interview with three captains. Interviews are used very widely today, and the Price-Waterhouse–Cranfield survey (Dany & Torchy, 1994) confirms that 80 to 100% of European employers interview prospective staff, the only exception being Turkey, where 64% of employers interview staff. Interviews are similarly popular in North America (Rynes *et al.*, 1997).

Interviews vary widely. They can be as short as three minutes, or as long as two hours. There may be one interviewer, or several. If there are several interviewers, they may interview together, as a panel or board, or separately. The public sector in the UK favours panel interviews, in which the candidate faces 5, 10 or even 20 interviewers. In campus recruitment, candidates often go through a series of interviews.

In the past, interviews were often rather casual affairs. The interviewer had no job description or person specification. If asked what he or she was looking for, the interviewer might say 'someone who will fit in here' or 'the right sort of person'. The interviewer had no prepared questions, took no notes, and made no ratings or quantitative assessment of the candidates. This type of interview probably still takes place quite often, but most large employers have been forced to ask themselves whether their selection methods are valid and fair. The traditional casual unstructured interview was very often neither, so the need to select efficient staff and to avoid unfair employment claims has caused many employers to conduct their interviewing more systematically. In particular, *structured interviewing* has become very popular.

Different interviews seek to assess different attributes of candidates. In a review of 47 studies, mostly in the USA, Huffcutt *et al.* (2001) found that personality dimensions were most frequently assessed (35%), followed by applied social skills (28%) and mental ability (16%). Interviews were less often used to assess knowledge and skills (10%), interests and preferences (4%), organisational fit (3%) or physical attributes (4%). As Huffcutt *et al.* note, it is slightly odd that interviews are so widely used to assess personality and mental ability, given that tests of both are widely available, and are possibly more accurate and certainly more economical to use. On the other hand, the interview may be particularly well suited to assessing social skills, since it is itself a social encounter.

Reliability and validity

The interview is a test or assessment, so we can ask how reliable and valid it is, and compute correlations between interviewer ratings and work performance data to find out the answer to this question.

Reliability

Conway *et al.* (1995) analysed 160 researches and concluded that interviewers agreed to the extent of 0.77 if they saw the same interview, but only to the extent of 0.53 if they saw different interviews with the same candidate. The difference arises because candidates do not perform consistently at different interviews. Conway *et al.* argued that 0.53 is the better estimate of interview reliability in practice, because inconsistency of candidate behaviour is an inherent limitation of the interview. They also found that interviews are more reliable if they are based on a job analysis, and if the interviewers are trained.

Box 3.1   Interviewer reliability

Reliability is usually measured by the correlation between two sets of measures. If two interviewers each rate 50 applicants, the correlation between their ratings estimates the *inter-rater reliability*, also known as the *inter-observer* or *inter-judge reliability*.

Validity

We tend to talk about the 'validity of the interview' when perhaps we should really be referring to the validity of the interview *for assessing sales potential* or *for assessing intellectual ability*. The interview is used to assess a wide variety of skills, abilities, personality, attitudes, etc., and the very popularity of the interview may derive from its versatility. It has this feature in common with several other selection methods, such as assessment centres and biodata. A mental ability test, on the other hand, can only assess mental ability. In practice, selection interviews are usually used to make a simple decision – to hire or not – and are often validated against a global assessment of how well the person does the job. The interviewer may be asked to make 10 ratings of diverse characteristics, but it is frequently the case that all 10 ratings will be highly correlated. In this context, perhaps it is appropriate to talk about the 'validity of the interview'.

Research on interview validity has been reviewed frequently, from Wagner (1949) and Ulrich and Trumbo (1965) to Posthuma, Morgeson and Campion (2002). Most of the earlier reviews concluded that interviews were not a very good way of choosing productive workers and rejecting unproductive ones, a fact which took a very long time to begin to penetrate the consciousness of line managers or HR departments.

Earlier reviews were *narrative reviews*, meaning that authors did not use any formal quantitative means of summarising the research that was reviewed. The human mind, however expert or impartial, is not very good at summarising large bodies of complex numerical information. Narrative reviews often fail to enlighten because they first list 10 studies which find that interviews predict job performance, then list 10 studies that do not, and finish by listing 20 studies that are inconclusive. Readers typically react to narrative reviews by exclaiming 'Do interviews work or not? The psychologists don't seem to be able to make up their minds!'. At their worst, narrative reviews are like projective tests – reviewers read into the research whatever conclusions they want to find.

Meta-analytic reviews pool the results of many different researches, to produce a single estimate of the correlation between the predictor and the criterion. A meta – analysis of selection data typically reports median correlation, weighted by sample size (because research on interview validity based on 10,000 individuals clearly carries more weight than research based on 50 individuals). Dunnette (1972) reported the first meta-analysis of interview validity; 30 validity coefficients in the American petroleum industry had a very low average (0.13). Hunter and Hunter (1984) obtained a similarly low average validity (0.11).

Box 3.2   Median

The median is a form of average, in which scores are arranged in order from lowest to highest. The value halfway between the highest and the lowest scores is the median. Thus the median of 4, 6, 7, 8 and 18 is 7. The median is less affected by extreme values than is the conventional arithmetic mean.

What does a correlation of 0.11 mean? The usual way of interpreting a correlation is to calculate how much *variance* it accounts for, by squaring it. A rating of a candidate by an unstructured one-to-one interview explains only 1 percent ($0.10^2 = 0.01$) of the variance in later success in the job. The other 99 percent of employee effectiveness remains unaccounted for. The largest correlations that can be obtained in practice in selection research (0.50–0.60) account for only a quarter to a third of the variance in performance, a point that is frequently made by critics of psychological testing. But is it realistic to expect more than this? Performance at work is influenced by a host of other factors, such as management, organisational climate and co-workers, economic climate and the working environment, as well as by the assessable characteristics of the individual worker. In psychological research, correlations of 0.80 or 0.90, which the 'variance accounted for' argument implies that tests ought to have, rarely occur, unless the researcher is doing something trivial like correlating a measure with a thinly disguised version of itself.

Table 3.1 Summary of three meta-analyses of interview validity, by Wiesner and Cronshaw (1988) (W & C), Huffcutt and Arthur (1994) (H & A) and McDaniel *et al*. (1994) (McD). Huffcutt and Arthur distinguish four levels of structure: the value for structured interviews is the highest level and the value for unstructured interviews is the lowest level.

	W & C	H & A	McD
1 Unstructured	0.17	0.11	0.18
1a One to one	0.11		
1b Board	0.21		
2 Structured	0.34	0.34	0.24
2a One to one	0.35		
2b Board	0.33		
3 All interviews	0.26	0.22	0.20

Three subsequent and much larger meta-analyses present a more complex and sometimes more favourable picture. Wiesner and Cronshaw (1988) analysed 160 validities from research in Germany, France and Israel as well as the USA. Huffcutt and Arthur (1994) set out to replicate Hunter and Hunter's earlier study of the interview as a selection test for entry-level jobs, based on 114 studies. The review by McDaniel *et al*. (1994) covers 245 correlations from a total sample of 86,000 individuals. Row 3 of Table 3.1 gives average validities of between 0.20 and 0.26. As Wiesner and Cronshaw remarked, the interview may not be quite such a poor predictor as many occupational psychologists had assumed. However, row 3 is probably an overestimate of the validity of the typical interview, because it includes research using structured interview systems. Row 1 shows that the interview as generally practised in the UK – the unstructured interview – achieves an overall validity of only 0.11 to 0.18. Wiesner and Cronshaw's review distinguishes between one-to-one and board or panel interviews, and finds that one-to-one unstructured interviews have a very low validity (0.11).

Validity for different characteristics

Attempts to identify which characteristics interviews can assess accurately are limited by the point already noted, that the outcome measure is usually a global rating of work performance. Huffcutt *et al*.'s (2001) meta-analysis shows that interview ratings of some attributes (e.g. creativity) correlate better with supervisor ratings of overall job performance than do interview ratings of other attributes (e.g. persuasiveness). However, this is not the same as showing that interviews are better at assessing creativity than persuasiveness, because creativity and persuasiveness in the workplace are not being assessed, only overall performance. McDaniel *et al*.'s meta-analysis reported that *psychological interviews* which try to assess personality were less successful than *situational interviews* that ask hypothetical questions of the form 'what would you do if . . .?', or *job-related interviews* which assess training, experience and interests.

Interviews are often used to assess what is variously referred to as 'organisational fit', 'chemistry' or 'the right type'. Sometimes this may be just a code word for the interviewer's prejudices or reluctance to explain him- or herself, but it could refer to legitimate organisation-specific requirements which the interview could be used to assess. Rynes and Gerhart (1990) report that interviewers from the same organisation agree about candidates' fit, showing that the concept is not idiosyncratic. However, fit cannot be related to objective data such as grade-point average, but is related to appearance, which suggests an irrational element. An important part of fit is *values congruence* – whether the candidate has the same ideas about what matters in work as the organisation. Cable and Judge (1997) reported that interviewers could assess whether the candidate's values matched those of the organisation. However, they were not very accurate, which suggests that it might be better to assess candidates' values more directly by paper-and-pencil tests. Latham and Skarlicki (1995) found that the interview predicts *organisational citizenship* fairly well.

Box 3.3   Organisational citizenship

This means volunteering to do things that are not in the job description, helping others, following rules willingly, and publicly supporting the organisation – all highly desirable behaviours in employees.

Reasons for poor validity

Why is the conventional unstructured interview apparently such a poor predictor of work performance?

Interviewers differ

Most validity studies pool data from a number of interviewers, thereby mixing good, bad and indifferent interviewers. Perhaps interview validity would be better estimated from how well *good* interviewers do.

Interviewer motivation

Anyone who has spent a day interviewing knows how one's attention can start to wander by the late afternoon. Brtek and Motowidlo (2002) showed that college students watching videotaped interviews can make more accurate ratings if they try. Being told that they will have to explain their ratings to the researchers makes them pay more attention to the interview, which results in more accurate ratings.

Interviewee's impression management

The interviewee wants to get the job, and does whatever he or she thinks will help to achieve this in the way of self-promotion, self-enhancement, etc. People are expected to present themselves well at interview, and one often hears interviewers complaining that a candidate 'didn't make an effort'. Higgins, Judge and Ferris (2000) reported a meta-analysis which showed that people who seek to ingratiate themselves and self-promote in the interview do succeed in getting better ratings. This may be a source of error, but not necessarily. It may be that ingratiators and self-promoters are at some level better performers in the workplace. Silvester *et al.* (2002) showed that the type of explanation that people offer for past failures affects the impression they create. Admitting that the failure was the candidate's fault ('I didn't revise hard enough') was better received than blaming other people.

Interview coaching

Students at universities in the UK are often offered 'how to be interviewed' courses. Maurer *et al.* (1998) studied the effects of such courses in US fire and police services, and found that people who had been on such a course did better in subsequent interviews. Further analysis (Maurer *et al.*, 2001) showed that coaching seems to work by teaching people to be more organised, to think about their answers, and even to make notes, before answering. However, Maurer's research describes a highly structured interview which asks only factual questions. Taking a long time to answer and making notes before doing so might not secure a good rating in more interactive interviews.

Interviewee lying

One step on from presenting oneself well is outright lying. Ekman's research suggests that interviewers may be unable to detect this (Ekman and O'Sullivan, 1991). Of five sets of experts who ought to be good at detecting lies, namely the Secret Service, CIA, FBI, National Security Agency and Drug Enforcement Agency, only one did better than would be expected by chance.

Rating artefacts

Pooling data from many interviewers risks the results being obscured by known errors in subjective ratings, such as *leniency*. Some interviewers mark everyone generously, while others mark everyone harshly. If the criterion ratings are generous, the harsh interviewer will appear to make consistently bigger mistakes than the generous rater. The harsh interviewer may really be less accurate, or may just be using the rating scale differently. More sophisticated statistical analysis can correct for this problem. Dreher, Ash and Hancock (1988) argued that many studies use crude analyses, so may underestimate interview validity. However, two studies (Pulakos *et al.*, 1996; Moser & Reuter, 2001) found that more sophisticated analysis of interviewer ratings makes no difference to interview validity.

Criterion reliability

Validity coefficients are low because the interview is trying to predict the unpredictable. The interviewer's judgement is compared with a *criterion* of good work performance. Supervisor ratings, the most commonly used criterion, have limited reliability (0.60 at best) – one supervisor agrees only moderately well with another supervisor. Validity coefficients can be corrected for criterion unreliability. Such correction raised Hunter and Hunter's estimate for interview validity from 0.11 to 0.14.

Range restriction

Validity coefficients may be low because *range* is *restricted*. Suppose that only the top 50% of interview performers are hired. The other 50% cannot contribute data to the validity coefficient because they did not get the job, and there are therefore no data on their work performance. Figure 3.1 shows the effect on the validity coefficient – a (potentially) large correlation is greatly reduced. Validity should ideally be calculated from a sample of applicants, but usually has to be estimated from a sample of successful applicants. Range is almost always restricted in selection research because few organisations can afford to employ people who are judged to be unsuitable, simply to allow

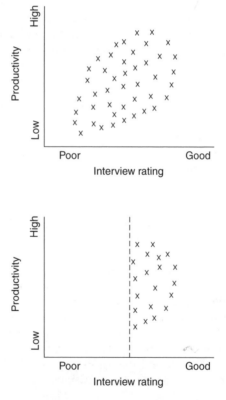

Figure 3.1 Restriction of range. In the lower distribution, everyone with a lower interview rating has been excluded from the analysis. A very low correlation results. The upper distribution shows the results that would have been obtained if everyone was employed regardless of interview rating

Table 3.2 Summary of three meta-analyses of interview validity, by Wiesner and Cronshaw (1988) (W & C), Huffcutt and Arthur (1994) (H & A) and McDaniel *et al.* (1994) (McD), *with validity corrected for restricted range and criterion reliability.*

	W & C	H & A	McD
Unstructured	0.31	0.20	0.33
Structured	0.62	0.57	0.44
All interviews	0.47	0.37	0.37

psychologists to calculate better estimates of validity. Nearly all research settles for correlating interview ratings with success within the minority of selected applicants.

Validity coefficients can be corrected for restricted range, which further increases Hunter and Hunter's (1984) estimate of interview validity from 0.14 to 0.22. Salgado and Moscoso (2002) confirmed that range restriction is a real problem in interview research. Averaging across 38 researches, they found that the standard deviation (SD) of interview ratings of successful applicants was 61% of the SD for all applicants. Table 3.2 gives validities for the three meta-analyses of interview validity, after correction for restricted range and criterion unreliability. (The corrections were made as part of *validity generalisation analysis*, which is described fully in Chapter 6.) The corrections increase the validity coefficients considerably so that validity for all interviews ranges from 0.37 to 0.47, while the validity for unstructured interviews ranges from 0.20 to 0.33.

Reliability and validity: the upper limit of the interview?

The reliability of a selection method sets an upper limit on its possible validity. If the measure does not correlate with itself perfectly, it cannot correlate with an outcome perfectly either. Unstructured interviews are very unreliable, so cannot be expected to achieve high validity. Conway *et al.* (1995) estimated the maximum possible validity of the unstructured interview to be no higher than 0.34. Structured interviews (see above) on the other hand will be able to achieve much higher validity, as they are much more reliable.

Incremental validity

The interview may not be very accurate in itself, but can it improve the prediction made by other methods, perhaps by covering aspects of work performance that other selection methods fail to cover? Schmidt and Hunter (1998) argue that unstructured interviews will provide little or no incremental validity over mental ability tests, because unstructured interviews are highly correlated with mental ability in the first place. Figure 3.2 illustrates Schmidt and Hunter's argument. The figure shows two predictors, namely interview and mental ability tests, and an outcome, namely work performance. Where

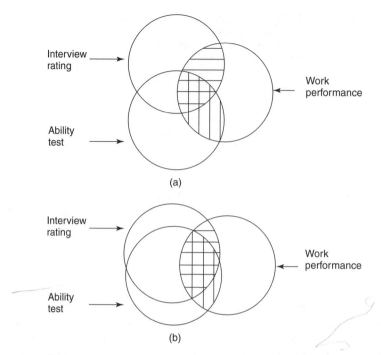

Figure 3.2 Schematic representation of the relationship between two predictors (mental ability test and interview) and work performance, (a) where the predictors are not highly correlated and (b) where they are highly correlated

the predictor circles overlap the outcome circle, the tests are achieving validity. In Figure 3.2a, the two predictors do not correlate much, so their circles do not overlap much, whereas in Figure 3.2b the two predictors are highly correlated, so their circles overlap a lot. Note the effect on the overlap between predictor and outcome circles. In Figure 3.2a the predictors explain more of the outcome, whereas in Figure 3.2b, they explain less of it, because they both cover the same ground. Schmidt and Hunter argue that this is what happens with unstructured interview and mental ability tests – they do correlate highly, so they do not add much to each other. Cortina *et al.* (2000) provided empirical confirmation of this, as they found that an unstructured interview adds little to tests of conscientiousness and mental ability. McDaniel *et al.* (1994) asked what happens if the interviewer knows the test scores while giving the interview. This is sometimes done in the hope of using the interview to confirm or clarify the test data. However, McDaniel's meta-analysis showed that knowledge of the test data resulted in much lower interview validity. Perhaps knowing the test data means that the interviewer does not try hard enough.

Improving the interview

The traditional interview has very limited validity, which implies that HR departments should be thinking in terms of either replacing it with more accurate methods, or improving it. Assuming that the interview is here to stay, what can be done to improve it?

Select interviewers

Interviewing is shared between all senior staff in many organisations. It seems intuitively plausible that some people will be better interviewers than others, and research appears to confirm this. Vernon and Parry (1949) found one naval recruiting assistant who made much better decisions than the Royal Navy's test battery, which usually far out-performed interviewers. Ghiselli (1966a) also found one interviewer (himself) whose accuracy in selecting stockbrokers over 17 years yielded a personal validity coefficient of 0.51. More recently, Dipboye et al. (2001) confirmed that different interviewers' decisions vary widely in accuracy. However, Pulakos et al. (1996) questioned whether interviewers really vary. They analysed data from 62 interviewers and found that individual validity coefficients varied widely, from a minimum of −0.10 to a maximum of 0.65. At first sight, these results seem to confirm very strongly the view that interviewers differ. However, Pulakos et al. noted that the average number of interviews analysed for each interviewer was 25, and they pointed out that correlations calculated on small samples (e.g. 25) are very unreliable. They suggested that the variation in interviewer performance might arise from sampling error rather than from true differences in interviewer accuracy. This implies that if the 62 interviewers conducted another 25 interviews, the 'good' interviewers might do very much less well, while the 'poor' interviewers might on average 'improve'. It also implies that an organisation that wants to select good interviewers will need a large sample of interviews on which to base its decisions. Telling some managers that they cannot give interviews because they are not very good at them might create problems in many organisations.

Use more than one interviewer

Wiesner and Cronshaw (1988) compared one-to-one with panel or board interviews. Rows 1a and 1b of Table 3.1 show clearly that two or more interviewers obtain far better results than just one, in conventional unstructured interviews. Perhaps two or more interviewers have more time to make notes, listen to what the candidate is saying, plan their next question, etc. Perhaps two or more interviewers are also less likely to be swayed by idiosyncratic biases. Conway et al. (1995) found that panel interviews are more reliable than one-to-one interviews. Many employers insist on panel interviews, and equal opportunities agencies also recommend their use.

Use the same interviewers throughout

Sharing interviewing means that different candidates, even for the same job, are interviewed by different interviewers. Huffcutt and Woehr (1999) compared 23 studies in which the same interviewers interviewed all candidates with 100 studies in which different interviewers interviewed different candidates, and found that using the same interviewers throughout significantly improves interview validity.

Train interviewers

Conway *et al.* (1995) analysed 160 studies and found that training makes interviewing more reliable. Huffcutt and Woehr (1999) compared 52 studies where interviewers were trained with 71 studies where they were not, and found that training significantly improves interview validity. Stevens (1998) found that training changes interviewer behaviour. Improvements include asking more open questions and more 'performance-differentiating' questions, and being less likely to stray from the point. The use of untrained interviewers will make it much more difficult to defend selection methods if the latter are challenged.

Take notes

Some interviewers refrain from taking notes on the argument that this distracts the candidate. On the other hand, an increasing number of organisations require interviewers to make notes which the organisation then keeps in case there is subsequent dispute. Huffcutt and Woehr (1999) compared 55 studies where interviewers did not take notes with 68 studies where they did, and found that taking notes significantly improved interview validity. Two recent studies suggest a more complex picture. Middendorf and Macan (2002) found that taking notes resulted in better recall of what happened in the interview, but not in greater accuracy. In fact, the more words that were written, the poorer the accuracy of the interview. Burnett *et al.* (1998) found that the type of notes made a difference. Notes about what the interviewee *said* were linked to more accurate assessment, whereas notes about what the interviewee *did* (e.g. made eye contact) were linked to less accurate assessment. However, the participants in both studies were watching videotaped interviews, not giving the interviews themselves. In real interviews, the interviewer also has to ask the questions, sometimes think up the questions, and control the interview, all of which leaves less time for note taking.

Make ratings

Taylor and Small (2002) compared interviews that used descriptively anchored rating scales with ones that did not, and found that the former achieved higher average validity (Figure 4.2 on page 69 gives an example of a descriptively anchored rating scale). Note, however, that all of the interviews included in the analysis were structured interviews. It seems likely that unstructured interviews will benefit from using sophisticated ratings, too, but we cannot conclude this from Taylor and Small's analysis.

Structured interviews

The biggest improvement to the interview is *structured interviewing*, which has developed rapidly since 1980. Structured interviewing does *not* mean following the 'seven-point plan', or agreeing who asks what before the interview starts. That is no more than good interviewing practice. Structured interview systems structure every part of the interview (Campion, Palmer & Campion, 1997).

- Interviewers' questions are structured often to the point of being completely scripted.
- Interviewers' judgements are structured by rating scales, checklists, etc.
- Some structured interview systems – but not all of them – forbid the interviewer to ask any follow-up, probing or clarifying questions.
- The traditional last phase of the interview – in which the interviewee is asked if he or she has any questions – is sometimes dropped on the grounds that interviewees could bias the interviewers by asking a silly question.

Structured interviewing systems start with a detailed job analysis, which ensures that the questions and judgements are job related. Structured interviews largely deprive interviewers of their traditional autonomy. Such interviews not only offer better validity; they are also legally safer, being closely job related, and not allowing the interviewer to wander off into irrelevant and possibly dangerous areas. Some structured interview systems also ensure that every interview is the same, which avoids one source of possible complaint. Structured interviews are beginning to be used in the UK, in local government, the financial sector, and for sales, manufacturing and the hotel industry (Barclay, 2001). There are several structured interview systems in current use, which were devised in the USA, Canada and Germany:

- situational interview (Latham *et al.*, 1980)
- patterned behaviour description interview (Janz, 1982)
- comprehensive structured interview (Campion, Pursell and Brown, 1988)
- structured behavioural interview (Motowidlo *et al.*, 1992)
- multimodal interview (Schuler & Moser, 1995)
- empirical interview (Schmidt & Rader, 1999).

Situational interviews (Latham *et al.*, 1980) are developed from *critical incidents* (*see* Chapter 2) of particularly effective or ineffective behaviour:

> The employee was devoted to his family. He had only been married for 18 months. He used whatever excuse he could to stay at home. One day the fellow's baby got a cold. His wife had a hangnail or something on her toe. He didn't come to work. He didn't even phone in.

The incidents are rewritten as questions:

> Your spouse and two teenage children are sick in bed with a cold. There are no friends or relatives available to look in on them. Your shift starts in three hours. What would you do in this situation?

The company supervisors who describe the incidents also agree 'benchmark' answers for good, average and poor workers.

- I'd stay at home – my spouse and family come first (poor).
- I'd phone my supervisor and explain my situation (average).
- Since they only have colds, I'd come to work (good).

At the interview, the questions are read out, the candidate replies, and he or she is rated against the benchmarks. The questions are phrased to avoid suggesting socially desirable answers to candidates. The situational interview looks forward, asking candidates what they would do on some future occasion.

Patterned behaviour description interviews (Janz, 1982) also start by analysing the job with critical incidents, but differ from the situational interview in two ways. First, the patterned behaviour interviewer plays a more active role than the situational interviewer, being 'trained to redirect [applicants] when their responses strayed from or evaded the question'. Secondly, the patterned behaviour interview looks *back*, focusing on actual behaviour that occurred in the past. A typical question reads as follows:

> Balancing the cash bag (day's accounts) is always the bottom line for a cashier position, but bags can't always balance. Tell me about the time your experience helped you discover why your bag didn't balance.

Taylor and Small (2002) reported a meta-analysis that compared forward-oriented or hypothetical questions (30 studies) with past-oriented or experience-based questions (19 studies), and found that the two did not differ significantly in validity. However, they did suggest that the two types of questions may assess fundamentally different things. Situational questions, they argue, assess what people know (i.e. ability), whereas behaviour description questions describe what people have done, so also reflect typical performance (i.e. personality). Questions about past work behaviour are not always possible for people with no employment experience, such as school leavers or new graduates.

Comprehensive structured interviews (Campion, Pursell & Brown, 1988) have four sections, namely job knowledge, job simulation, worker requirements and a situational section. Worker requirements are assessed by questions like: 'Some jobs require climbing ladders to the height of a five-storey building and going out on a catwalk to work. Give us your feelings about performing a task such as this.' The fourth section uses the same situational interview technique as that of Latham *et al.* (1980). As in the situational interview, no attempt is made to probe or follow up – the emphasis is on consistency of administration.

The structured behavioural interview technique was devised for a consortium of American telecommunications companies (Motowidlo *et al.*, 1992). Like other structured interview techniques, it is based on critical incidents. This approach gives interviewers a more active role, asking supplementary probing questions.

The multimodal interview, which was devised in Germany (Schuler & Moser, 1995), has eight sections, including an informal rapport-building conversation at the beginning, standardised questions on choice of career and organisation, multi-stage questions on experience, a realistic job preview, and situation questions. The multi-stage questions cover such areas as experience of working in groups, and probe into problems that arose and what the candidate did to solve them.

The empirical interview also starts with a job analysis. Good performers are interviewed to identify 10 to 15 themes in effective performance (e.g. teamwork). The panel then develops around 120 possible interview questions, and tests them in interviews with 30 outstanding performers and 30 unsatisfactory performers. They select the questions that best distinguish between good and poor employees. Unlike other structured interview systems, the empirical interview does not favour any particular type of question, past behaviour, future behaviour, etc. All types of questions are included, and are used if they succeed in the empirical keying phase – even apparently vague questions such as 'Are you competitive?'. Candidates are interviewed by telephone, the interview is tape-recorded, and it is later scored by someone else. It is strange how seldom interviews are recorded, given how difficult it is to remember everything that the candidate says, or to take accurate and detailed notes. The empirical interview has been used extensively for a wide range of jobs, including sales, teaching, production work and management.

Validity of structured interviews

Reviews of interview validity confirm that structured interviews achieve far better results than conventional interviews. Two analyses (Wiesner & Cronshaw, 1988; Huffcutt & Arthur, 1994) found validity for structured interviews to be twice that for unstructured interviews (*see* Tables 3.1 and 3.2). The third analysis (McDaniel *et al.*, 1994) found a smaller difference, possibly because these researchers defined structure differently. Wiesner and Cronshaw's analysis found that structured interviews work equally well whether there is one interviewer or several. However, structured interviews based on formal job analysis do achieve better results (0.87), corrected for restricted range and criterion unreliability.

Schmidt and Rader (1999) reported an analysis of 209 researches on the empirical interview. Table 3.3 shows that the empirical interview has good validity for the conventional supervisor rating criterion. Their review also shows that the empirical interview can predict other aspects of work performance, namely output, sales, and staying with the organisation. Only absence is less well predicted. As Schmidt and Rader note, no other previous research had shown the interview to be capable of predicting sales, output or absence.

Table 3.3 Summary of research on the empirical interview (corrected validity is validity corrected for restricted range and reliability).

	Number of researches	Uncorrected validity	Corrected validity
Supervisor rating	33	0.19	0.40
Production records	5	0.29	0.40
Sales	41	0.15	0.40
(Low) absenteeism	7	0.10	0.19
Tenure	21	0.28	0.39

Note: Data taken from Schmidt & Rader (1999).

Latham and Sue-Chan (1999) reported an analysis of 19 studies of the situational interview that achieved a validity of 0.33, which increased to 0.46 when corrected for restricted range and unreliability of work performance measures.

Accumulating research on structured interviewing now makes it possible to compare different types. Huffcutt *et al.* (2002) compared 31 studies of the situational interview with 20 studies of the behaviour description interview and overall found relatively little difference, the corrected validities being 0.44 and 0.50, respectively. However, Figure 3.3 suggests that the situational interview may not be suitable for high-complexity jobs.

Incremental validity

Schmidt and Hunter (1998) concluded that structured interviews will provide 0.12 incremental validity over mental ability tests, because both have good predictive validity, and because they are not highly correlated. Cortina *et al.*

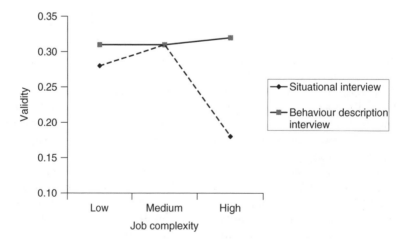

Figure 3.3 Validity of situational and behaviour description interviews for jobs of high, medium and low complexity. Data taken from Huffcutt *et al.* (in press)

(2000) confirmed that a structured interview has considerable incremental validity over tests of mental ability and conscientiousness.

Interview or spoken questionnaire?

Very structured interviews, such as Latham's situational interview, blur the distinction between interview and paper-and-pencil test. If the interviewer reads from a script and does not interact with the candidate, what is his or her function? Why not print the questions in a question book, and ask candidates to answer them in writing? This would be much quicker and cheaper. Schmidt and Rader (1999) give one answer to this question – the interview format does not give people time to prepare a carefully thought out answer, which might not be entirely frank.

Resistance

The structured interview deprives interviewers of most of their traditional autonomy. They have to follow a script, they have to use rating scales, and they are not allowed to chat with candidates or tell them about the organisation. In some forms of structured interviewing they are reduced to being a substitute for a written test. This may mean that interviewers will start to deviate from their prescribed role unless they are closely monitored. In many organisations the managers who give the interviews are more powerful than the human resource management department, who bring in structured interviewing and try to maintain its quality. These points suggest that structured interviewing systems may not always achieve such good results in practice.

Construct validity of the interview

Recent research has compared interview ratings with other assessments, usually psychological tests. This gives some indication as to what the interview is *actually* assessing (which is not necessarily what it is *intended* to assess).

Mental ability

Two meta-analyses (Huffcutt, Roth & McDaniel, 1996; Salgado & Moscoso, 2002) both found the correlation between interview rating and tested mental ability to be around 0.40, confirming that the interview makes a moderately good disguised mental ability test. The less structured the interview, the more it tends to measure mental ability. The lower the level of the job, the more the interview tends to measure mental ability. The more the interview tends to measure mental ability, the more it also predicts job performance (i.e. the more valid it is). It is quite surprising that the conventional interview turns out to be assessing mental ability to such an extent. Huffcutt *et al.* (2001) found that only 16% of interviews are intended to assess mental ability. Nor does it seem likely that most candidates, interviewers, human resource managers or lay people regard interviews as mental ability tests.

Job knowledge

Structured interviews correlate quite well with paper-and-pencil job knowledge tests. Critics might say that this is not surprising because many structured interviews are little more than oral job knowledge tests.

Personality

Salgado and Moscoso (2002) also reported data for personality. Table 3.4 shows that ratings in unstructured interviews correlate with the five main factors in personality. In other words, interview ratings are based partly on the applicant's extraversion, anxiety, etc., whether or not the interview is intended to assess these attributes. Structured interview ratings are less affected by personality.

Social skill

Unstructured interviews assess social skill, which as noted earlier is hardly surprising as the unstructured interview is a social encounter. However, structured interviews correlate surprisingly well with the applicant's social skill, which may suggest that structured interviews do not entirely succeed in excluding irrelevant considerations from the interviewers' decisions.

How the interviewer reaches a decision

Ideally, the interviewer will listen carefully to everything the candidate says, and reach a wise decision based on all of the information available. Research has documented a number of ways in which interviewers depart from this ideal.

Table 3.4   Meta-analysis of construct validity of unstructured and structured interviews.

	Unstructured interview		Structured interview	
	r	ρ	r	ρ
Mental ability	0.20	0.41	0.14	0.28
Job knowledge	–	–	0.27	0.53
Grade-point average	0.06	0.13	0.08	0.17
Social skill	0.22	0.46	0.34	0.65
Neuroticism	0.17	0.38	0.04	0.08
Extraversion	0.16	0.34	0.10	0.21
Openness	0.14	0.30	0.04	0.09
Agreeableness	0.12	0.26	0.06	0.12
Conscientiousness	0.13	0.28	0.08	0.17

Source: Reproduced from Salgado & Moscoso (2002) by permission of The Experimental Psychology Society.
Note: r = raw correlation; ρ = correlation corrected for restricted range and reliability of both measures.

1. *Interviewers make up their minds before the interview.* Interviewers usually have some information about candidates before the interview starts, from CV, application form, etc. A meta-analysis of 19 earlier studies (Olian, Schwab & Haberfeld, 1988) reported that qualifications accounted for 35% of the variance in selection decisions.
2. *Interviewers make up their minds quickly.* A frequently cited study by Springbett (1958) showed that interviewers make up their minds after only 4 minutes of a 15-minute interview, although his methodology was not very subtle. Other studies have since shown that interviewers often reach decisions early in the interview.
3. *The interviewer forms a first impression.* Male interviewers react against perfume or aftershave, regardless of the sex of the applicant, whereas female interviewers favour it, also regardless of the sex of the applicant (Baron, 1983). Female applicants for management positions create the best impression by being conventionally but not severely dressed (Forsythe, Drake & Cox, 1985).
4. *The interviewer looks for reasons to reject.* Springbett (1958) found that just one bad rating was sufficient to reject 90% of candidates. Looking for reasons to reject is a rational strategy if the organisation has plenty of good applicants.
5. *The interviewer relies on an implicit personality theory.* Andrews (1922) described an interviewer who hired a salesman who proved to be a disaster, and for ever after would not employ anyone who had ever sold adding machines. Why not? Because the disastrous salesman had previously sold adding machines. The interviewer reasoned as follows:
   - People who sell adding machines are poor salesmen.
   - This candidate formerly sold adding machines.
   - Therefore he will be a poor salesman.

The interviewer's reasoning was obviously faulty, as someone must be good at selling adding machines.

Complex judgement in the interview

Defenders of the interview argue that a good interviewer can see patterns in the information, which mechanistic methods such as checklists and weighted application blanks miss. However, research casts considerable doubt on the interviewer's claim to be doing something so complex that no other method can replace him or her. Research suggests that:

1. human experts never perform better than a system
2. human experts do not use information in as complex a manner as they claim
3. models of experts can do better than the expert in person.

Expert vs. system

Experts like to think that they combine information intuitively. Indeed, some experts make a positive virtue of not being able to explain how they reach their judgements, and say that it is all done by 'nose', 'ear', 'eye', 'gut' or 'hunch'. Fifty years ago, Meehl (1954) reviewed 20 studies comparing mechanistic systems with human experts, and concluded that system always predicted as well as expert, and often better. Expert never did better than system. Research since 1954 has not disproved Meehl's conclusion. Hitt and Barr (1989) used a *paper-person* and *video-person* method, in which both relevant and irrelevant information was systematically varied. They found that interviewers used the irrelevant information (race and gender) more than the relevant information (experience and education).

Box 3.4   Multiple correlation and regression

A correlation describes the relationship between two variables (e.g. predictor and criterion). Often the selector has several predictors – a set of test scores, a number of interview ratings, etc. A *multiple correlation*, denoted by R, takes account of inter-correlations between predictors. A multiple regression summarises the information in a set of ratings, or a set of tests. The multiple regression also identifies redundancy in a set of ratings or tests. Suppose that four interview ratings all predict productivity quite well: 0.40, 0.45, 0.42, 0.45. If each rating provides independent information, the combination of the four would give a very much better prediction than any one of the four. If the four ratings are highly inter-correlated – as is much more likely – the prediction from all four combined will not be much better than the prediction from any individual rating. Selection research shows that adding new tests to a selection battery soon brings diminishing returns; adding new tests after the third or fourth rarely increases R by a significant or worthwhile amount. Regression can be used to calculate *weightings* for using several scores in combination. For example, score A is weighted +0.25, score B is weighted +0.05 and score C is weighted +0.07. B and C get lower weights because they cover some of the same ground as A.

Does the expert use information in a complex manner?

Research on how experts make decisions mostly uses the *ANOVA (analysis of variance) paradigm*. The researcher constructs sets of cases in which information is systematically varied, asks experts to assess each case, and then deduces how the experts reached their decisions. If the expert accepts one set of cases and rejects another, and the only feature distinguishing the two sets is exam results, it follows that the expert's decisions are based on exam grades, and exam grades alone. Experts claim that they do not think as simplistically as this. They say that they use *configurations* (e.g. exam grades are important in young candidates, but not for people over 30 – an *interaction* of age and grades).

ANOVA studies have found that experts rarely use configurations, even simple ones like 'exam grades count for younger but not for older candidates'. Most of their decisions fit a *linear additive* model: superior exam grades (plus point), good vocabulary (plus point), young (plus point) and keen (plus point) equals four plus points. For example, one study (Graves & Karren, 1992) found that professional interviewers rating paper candidates made little use of interactions in six cues, apart from giving extra low ratings for the combination of poor oral communication and poor interpersonal skills. Another study found evidence of personnel managers using cues in a complex manner but not wisely. Hitt and Barr (1989) reported that 'managers. . . make different attributions when comparing a black 45-year-old woman with 10 years of experience and a master's degree with a white 35-year-old man with 10 years of experience and a master's degree'. Managers used race and sex in a complex manner to make their decisions, but basing decisions on either could create major problems for their employer. Personnel managers join an illustrious company – doctors, nurses, psychologists, radiologists, prison governors, social workers – all of whom claim to make very sophisticated judgements, and all of whom show little evidence of actually doing so.

A model of the expert is better than the expert

ANOVA studies can construct a model of the expert's thought processes, and this model can then be used to make a fresh batch of decisions. The results are unexpected – the model performs better than the expert it was derived from. The model never has 'off-days'; it always performs as well as the expert's best performance. An organisation could preserve the wisdom of its best personnel manager by constructing a model of his or her decisions, and continue to use his or her expertise after he or she had left. However, Dougherty *et al.* (1986) reported that although models of poor interviewers were better than the interviewers themselves, the same was not true for a good interviewer.

Bias in the interview

Bias in the interview can take two forms. First, the interviewer may discriminate, more or less openly. For example, he or she may mark down female candidates because they are female, or may think that women are less suitable for the job, or may ask women questions that men are not asked, or may think suitable candidates have characteristics that men are more likely to possess than women (e.g. an interest in football). These are all examples of what people think of as bias. Second, the interview may create an adverse impact, in the absence of any intended or unintended bias by the interviewer. For example, fewer women than men are successful. The interview provides an ideal opportunity for the exercise of whatever bias(es) the interviewer has, because he or she cannot help knowing every applicant's gender, ethnicity, age, social background, physical attractiveness, etc., and because the interviewer often is not required to explain his or her thought processes or justify his or her decisions (whereas selectors can use psychological tests or biographical methods, without seeing the applicants or knowing their gender, ethnicity, etc.).

Are interviewers biased against women?

Earlier research on application sifting (Arvey, 1979a) found consistent bias against women. The most recent review (Huffcutt *et al.*, 2001) found that unstructured interviews do create some adverse impact on women, whereas structured interviews do not. The research reviewed is nearly all North American, so one cannot safely assume that similar results will be found in other countries, given how widely attitudes to gender vary.

Are interviewers biased by race?

The meta-analysis by Huffcutt *et al.* (2001) shows that unstructured interviews do create some adverse impact on non-white Americans, especially interviews that assess intellectual ability and experience. One reason why structured interviews are popular is the belief that they do not have an adverse impact on ethnic minorities in the USA, which Huffcutt *et al.* appeared to confirm. However, Bobko and Roth (1999) concluded that structured interviews do create some adverse impact on African Americans, to the extent of about a quarter of a standard deviation. Roth *et al.* (2002) pointed out that adverse impact computations for interviews are often made in organisations where the interview is used after applicants have already been screened (e.g. by tests). Pre-screening by tests will tend to restrict the range of ability of those interviewed, and may possibly lead to an underestimate of the adverse impact of the structured interview. Roth *et al.* corrected for this restriction of range and found that structured interviews created a fairly large adverse impact, ranging from 0.36 to 0.56 standard deviations. Prewett-Livingston *et al.* (1996) found that interviews show *own race bias*, where whites favour whites, blacks favour blacks, Hispanic Americans favour other Hispanic Americans, etc. No research on this important issue has yet been reported for the UK or Europe.

Box 3.5   d statistic

The *d statistic* is used to estimate the size of a difference (e.g. between males and females), and hence the extent of adverse impact. The d statistic calculates how many standard deviations separate the means. For gender differences in physical performance, large values of d are sometimes found (e.g. 1.5, which means that the male mean is 1.5 SDs higher than the female mean). For gender differences in measures of intellectual performance, values of d are close to zero, which means that there is no difference in male and female means.

Are interviewers biased against older applicants?

Finkelstein, Burke and Raju (1995) summarised a number of studies, and concluded that younger raters rate older people less favourably if they are not provided with job-relevant information.

Are interviewers biased by accent?

George Bernard Shaw once remarked that no Englishman can open his mouth without making other Englishmen despise him. A Canadian study (Kalin & Rayko, 1978) found that candidates with foreign accents received less favourable ratings.

Are interviewers biased by appearance?

Most people can agree whether someone is conventionally 'good-looking' or not. A number of studies have shown that this has quite a strong effect on interview ratings. Marlowe, Schneider and Nelson (1996) found that managers prefer highly attractive candidates, and concluded that 'less attractive candidates, especially women, would have little chance of securing the job'.

Are interviewers biased by weight?

Pingitore *et al.* (1994) found that interviewers were biased against overweight applicants, especially if body shape and size were central to the interviewer's own self-concept. The study used actors, whose apparent body weight in the 'overweight' condition was increased by 20% by make-up and padding. The effect is very strong, accounting for 35% of the variance in decisions overall, and nearly 50% for apparently overweight females. Roehling (1999) reviewed extensive evidence of consistent negative stereotypes of overweight people as lacking in self-discipline, being lazy, having emotional problems or being less able to get on with others, and found overweight people discriminated against at 'virtually every stage of the employment cycle, including selection'.

Are interviewers biased by liking?

The more the interviewer likes the candidate, the more likely he or she is to make an offer (Anderson & Shackleton, 1990). Liking may of course be based on job-related competence, but may equally well arise from irrational biases.

Law and fairness

Terpstra, Mohamed and Kethley (1999) noted that unstructured interviews are the most frequent source of dispute in the USA. They estimated how many complaints one would expect for any selection method, given its frequency of use in the USA. Unstructured interviews are complained about twice as often as would be expected, whereas structured interviews are only complained about half as often as would be expected. Terpstra *et al.* found another reason to commend structured interviews to employers. When structured interviews are the subject of complaint, the employer always wins the case. This does not happen with unstructured interviews, where 40% of employers lose their case. Williamson *et al.* (1997) analysed 130 American court cases in order to identify features of the interview that help employers to defend themselves against claims of unfairness. They found two main themes. The first is *structure* – the use of standard sets of questions, limiting interviewer discretion and ensuring that all interviews are the same. The second is *objectivity and job relatedness* – the use of objective, specific, behavioural criteria as opposed to vague, global, subjective criteria, and also an interviewer who is trained and familiar with the job's requirements. However, the use of multiple interviewers or panel interviews made no difference to whether employers won their cases. Clearly structured interviewing is much better in terms of achieving fairness and avoiding losing fair employment claims.

In the UK, the Equal Opportunities Commission's *Code of Practice* states that 'questions posed during interviews [should] relate *only* to the requirements of the job. Where it is necessary to discuss personal circumstances and their effect upon ability to do the job, this should be done in a neutral manner, equally applicable to all applicants.'

Key points

In Chapter 3 you have learnt the following.

- Meta-analysis pools many researches to draw a single conclusion, and is a vital tool for understanding selection research.
- Conventional unstructured interviews have poor reliability and poor validity.
- Interviewees try to present themselves in a good light, and may sometimes even fail to tell the truth about themselves. This will prove to be a feature that interviews share with many other selection systems which will be discussed in succeeding chapters.
- Selection research tends to underestimate validity through built-in limitations in the research paradigm.
- Interviews can be improved by training interviewers, using rating, taking notes and using panels.
- Structured interviews are based on job analysis, and control the interview format and questions, while providing detailed rating systems. Research indicates that they are highly reliable and achieve good validity. Structured interviews may be more like orally administered tests.
- Research suggests that the question format in structured interviews is not critical.
- Interviewers do not always reach decisions very efficiently or rationally.
- Interviewers may be biased by many factors, including gender, ethnicity, age, appearance, weight, accent or liking.
- Interviewers' thought processes may be less complex than those interviewers suppose.
- Unstructured interviews have been the subject of many fair employment claims, many of which have been successful. Structured interviews have been the subject of fewer claims, far fewer of which have proved successful.

Key references

Bobko and Roth (1999) find that structured interviews do create some adverse impact in the USA.

Campion *et al.* (1997) describe 15 aspects of interview structure.

Conway *et al.* (1995) present a review of the reliability of interview ratings.

Huffcutt and Arthur (1994) review research on the validity of interviews for entry-level positions.

Latham *et al.* (1980) describe a structured interview technique known as the situation interview.

McDaniel *et al.* (1994) present a meta-analytic review of interview validity, covering outcome predicted and type of interview.

Pingitore *et al.* (1994) describe research showing how interviewers are biased by weight.

Posthuma *et al.* (2002) review the most recent themes in selection interview research.

Salgado and Moscoso (2002) analyse research on the interview's construct validity – what the interview actually assesses, which is not necessarily the same as what it is intended to assess.

Schmidt and Rader (1999) describe a structured interview technique known as the empirical interview.

Taylor and Small (2002) compare forward-looking questions with backward-looking questions.

Wiesner and Cronshaw (1988) review research on interview validity, distinguishing between structured and unstructured interviews, and single interviewers and panels or boards.

Williamson *et al.* (1997) analyse US fair employment cases involving interviews.

Useful websites

www.hr-guide.com. Includes 98 interview questions.
www.bdt.net. Devoted to Janz's behaviour description interviewing.
www.spb.ca.gov/int1.htm. How to write structured interviews, by California State Personnel Board.

CHAPTER 4

References and ratings

The eye of the beholder

Introduction

Interviews allow the applicant to speak for him- or herself, on the principle that the best way of finding out about someone is to ask them. References and ratings work on a different principle – that the best way of finding out about someone is to ask someone who knows him or her well (former employers, schoolteachers, colleagues or fellow trainees). They have seen the candidate all day every day, perhaps for years, and can report how he or she usually behaves, and what he or she is like on 'off days'.

References

The Price-Waterhouse–Cranfield survey (*see* Table 1.1, page 18) found references widely used throughout Western Europe. Similarly, most American employers take up references on new employees (Rynes *et al.*, 1997). References may be structured (questions, checklists, ratings) or unstructured ('Tell me what you think of John Smith in your own words'). Unstructured references are still widely used on both sides of the Atlantic. Moser and Rhyssen (2001) note that references can be used for two different purposes – either to check facts, or to get an opinion on the quality of the candidate's work.

Reliability

American research suggests that references are unreliable. Referees agree among themselves very poorly about applicants for (US) civil service jobs, with 80% of correlations lower than 0.40. References given by supervisors bore no relation to references given by acquaintances, while references given by supervisors and co-workers (who both see the applicant at work) agreed only very moderately (Mosel & Goheen, 1959). Inter-referee agreement can be compared with a larger body of research on reliability of performance appraisal and 360-degree feedback (where people are rated by supervisors, peers and subordinates). Agreement between raters is always fairly low (0.60 at best, and often much less). Murphy and Cleveland (1995) make the point that different people see different sides of the target person, so would not all be expected to say the same thing about him or her. And if they did all say the same thing, what would be the point of asking more than one person?

Some very early British research approached the problem from a different angle, and found references more useful. In the 1940s, the Civil Service Selection Board (CSSB) collected references from school, college, armed services and former employers (Wilson, 1948). CSSB staff achieved moderately good inter-rater reliability (0.73) in assessments of candidates based on references alone. The CSSB used five or six references, not two or three, which may increase reliability. Note that Wilson is addressing a different issue to Mosel and Goheen, namely whether the panel agree about what the five or six referees collectively are saying about the candidate, not whether they all agree with each other.

Validity

Mosel and Goheen reported several investigations of the Employment Recommendation Questionnaire (ERQ), a structured reference request form that was developed by the US Civil Service. The ERQ covers the following:

- occupational ability – skill, carefulness, industry, efficiency
- character and reputation
- whether the applicant is specially qualified in any particular branch of trade in which he or she seeks employment
- whether you would employ him or her in a position of the kind he or she seeks
- whether the applicant has ever been discharged from any employment to your knowledge, and if so, why.

Mosel and Goheen (1958) analysed ERQ data for various groups in the federal civil service and armed forces. For some occupations the ERQ had zero validity, while for other occupations it achieved very limited validity, represented by correlations of 0.20 to 0.30. Summarising all of the available US data, Reilly and Chao (1982) concluded that reference checks give poor predictions of supervisor ratings ($r = 0.18$) and turnover ($r = 0.08$). Shortly afterwards, Hunter and Hunter's (1984) review calculated the average validity of reference checks for supervisor ratings of 0.26. Hunter and Hunter quote higher average validity for the reference than Reilly and Chao, because they correct for unreliability of work performance measures.

European research

References for candidates for UK naval officer training by head teachers correlate moderately well (0.36, corrected for restricted range) with training grade in naval college (Jones and Harrison, 1982). Jones & Harrison argue that head teachers are more likely (than, say, former employers) to write careful and critical references, because they know they will be writing naval college references for future pupils, and because their own credibility is at stake. Moser and Rhyssen (2001) report a low but positive validity (0.20) for telephone references for German sales staff and supervisors. They note that their study was subject to the usual limitations of validity research – restricted range, leniency, and reliability of work performance measure – which all reduce the validity coefficient.

Reasons for poor validity

Referees may lack the time or motivation to write careful references, or they may follow a hidden agenda to retain good staff and 'release' poor staff, by writing deliberately untrue references.

Leniency

Numerous researches report that most references are positive (this has been nicknamed the 'Pollyanna effect' after the little girl who wanted to be nice to everyone). Early research by Mosel and Goheen (1958) found that ERQ ratings were highly skewed, with 'outstanding' or 'good' opinions greatly outnumbering 'satisfactory' or 'poor' opinions. Candidates were hardly ever rated as 'poor'. More recently, Grote, Robiner and Haut (2001) presented two parallel surveys of US psychologists. The first set of psychologists said that they would disclose negative information in the references they wrote, but the second set complained that they were rarely given any negative information in the references they received. It is not hard to see why this happens. Referees are usually nominated by the candidate, who will obviously choose someone who is likely to give them a good reference. These days many employers fear that an unfavourable reference may result in a libel suit. However, if referees are reluctant to say anything negative, references must remain a poor source of information. Murphy and Cleveland (1995) noted that performance appraisal has a similar problem – pervasive leniency – and suggested some reasons for this. Managers can observe employees' shortcomings but have no incentive to communicate them to others, and many reasons not to (fear of creating ill feeling, not wanting to admit that they have poor employees because this reflects on their management, etc.). Murphy's argument implies that references could be an excellent source of information, if only referees could be persuaded to part with it.

Idiosyncrasy

Baxter et al. (1981) searched medical school files to find 20 cases where the same two referees had written references for the same two applicants (see Figure 4.1). If references are useful, what referee A says about applicant X ought to resemble what referee B says about applicant X. Analysis of the qualities listed in the letters revealed a different and much less encouraging pattern. What referee A said about applicant X did not resemble what referee B said about applicant X, but did resemble what referee A said about applicant Y. Each referee had his or her own idiosyncratic way of describing people, which came through no matter who he or she was describing. The free-form reference appears to tell you more about its author than it does about its

	Candidate X		Candidate Y
Referee A		A g r e	
	Idiosyncratic	e m	way of describing people
Referee B		e n t	

Figure 4.1 Schematic representation of the study by Baxter *et al.* (1981) of letters of reference

subject. Aamodt, Nagy and Thompson (1998) confirm this, showing that a referee who describes one candidate in terms of conscientiousness will tend to describe another in terms of conscientiousness as well. Differences in reference writing may reflect personality (of the author, not the candidate). Judge and Higgins (1998) showed that happier people write more favourable references.

Free-form references

Colarelli, Hechanova-Alampay and Canali (2002) examined 532 letters describing 169 applicants for psychologist posts at a US university, and made global ratings of the favourability of each letter. These proved to have near zero (0.19) inter-referee reliability, and zero validity when correlated with number of publications. It is much more difficult to assess the validity of the free-form reference, as it is complex and unquantified. There is obviously much more to reference letters than global favourability. Range *et al.* (1991) have discussed some of the complexities of hinting at weaknesses in an ostensibly favourable reference. The problem with private languages of this type is that they are easily misunderstood. Loher *et al.* (1997) attempted a content analysis of reference letters, but found no relationships between the types of words used, or the types of evidence given, and the overall impact of the reference. It is difficult to see how free-form references can be validated by the conventional validation paradigm. This does not necessarily mean that they are not useful. Perhaps we need to develop subtler ways of assessing validity.

Improving the reference

Various attempts have been made to improve the reference, with mixed results.

Forced-choice format

Carroll and Nash (1972) used a forced-choice reference rating form. Items in each pair are equated for social desirability, but only one statement predicts job success:

- has many worthwhile ideas/completes all assignments
- always works fast/requires little supervision.

Scores predicted performance ratings 4 months after hire quite well in university clerical workers.

Key-word counting

Peres and Garcia (1962) factor-analysed data from 625 reference letters for engineering applicants, and found five factors that distinguished good from poor candidates (*see* Table 4.1). Many years later, Aamodt, Bryan and Whitcomb (1993) applied Peres and Garcia's lists to the selection of trainee teachers, and found that counting *mental agility* key words predicts mental ability, while counting *urbanity* key words predicts teaching performance ratings. The key-word method may partially solve the leniency problem, by allowing a referee who wants to be really positive to say someone is intelligent not just once, but four times. Key-word counting can only be done with free-form references, and has difficulties with the documented idiosyncrasy of reference writers. As Aamodt *et al.* (1998) showed, some referees tend to describe people in terms of conscientiousness more than others, so the organisation would need a baseline for each referee. However, scanning software would make key-word counting techniques much more feasible.

Relative percentile method

McCarthy and Goffin (2001) have described the *relative percentile method (RPM)*, and report that it gives substantially better validity than conventional ratings in a Canadian military sample. The RPM is a 100-point scale, in which the referee says what percentage of young people aged 16 to 25 years score lower than the target on, for example, responsibility. McCarthy and Goffin estimate that the method's validity is 0.42. The technique may work by allowing people to be lenient (the mean percentile given was 80!), but also to differentiate at the top end of the scale, giving someone whom they consider to be really responsible 95 rather than 85.

What is the purpose of the reference?

We have been assuming that employers use references to evaluate potential employees, although research suggests that this is unlikely to be very successful. However, perhaps the reference really serves another purpose. The

Table 4.1 Examples of words relating to five factors in letters of reference.

Co-operation	Mental agility	Urbanity	Vigour	Dependability
good-natured	imaginative	talkative	hustling	precise
accommodating	ingenious	chatty	active	persistent
congenial	insightful	forward	energetic	methodical
likeable	knowledgeable	bold	self-driving	tenacious
co-operative	intelligent	sparkling	vigorous	determined

Source: From Peres & Garcia (1962).

reference gives the employer control over the employee, even after he or she has left. The employer can refuse a reference or give a bad one, and so block the employee's chance of getting another job. To be certain of obtaining a good reference, the employee must avoid doing anything that might offend the employer. According to this argument, the reference system is used by employers to control existing staff, not to assess new staff. However, recent changes in the law will probably make this much more difficult.

Law and fairness

In the USA, employers find that the law has placed them in a very difficult position with regard to references. Little and Sipes (2000) note that more and more Americans are suing employers over unfavourable references, which has resulted in more and more employers providing only *minimal* references. These give dates of employment, job title and possibly salary, but do not express any opinion about performance at work. This renders the reference next to valueless as a selection assessment. The effective collapse of the reference system will deprive employers of potentially useful information about prospective employees. It will also deprive good employees of an opportunity to let other employers know about their virtues. People who lose their jobs because of sexual abuse of children or violent behaviour at work can get another job, and do the same thing again, because the next employer is not warned about them. American courts have now introduced the concept of *negligent referral* – that is, failing to disclose information to another employer about serious misconduct at work. This means that employers risk being sued by the employee if they write a bad reference, and they risk being sued by the next employer if they do not! In order to try to preserve the reference system, many states in the USA have passed immunity laws that restore 'privilege' to reference letters, meaning that employees cannot sue if the information is given in good faith, even if it proves to be not entirely correct. These laws require the employer to show the reference to the employee and to allow him or her to correct it, or to include his or her version of events.

In the UK, the 1994 case of *Spring v Guardian Assurance* (Parry, 1999) made it possible to sue if a reference was inaccurate, whereas previously one also had to prove *malice* – that is, that the referee *knew* the reference was inaccurate. A number of libel cases involving references have been tried since. The last few years have also seen Data Protection Acts that give people right of access to personal data held on them by organisations. At the time of writing, no one knows for certain whether this will include reference letters. It has been suggested that the employer who *writes* the reference is not obliged to show it to the candidate, but that prospective employers who *receive* it are. This implies that everyone will be able to gain access to their references, which in turn implies that American-style minimal references may be increasingly used in the UK.

The reference is certainly one of the most under-researched areas in person-nel selection. There have been barely enough studies to justify a meta-analysis of validity. Little research has been attempted on the widely used free-form reference, and promising leads, such as the forced-choice format, are not followed up. Sample sizes are often barely adequate. Yet research is urgently needed, because most employers still use references. This includes psychologists, both in the UK and in the USA, who continue to rely on references to select students and each other.

Ratings

American personnel practice uses ratings a lot – far more than UK personnel work. In personnel selection, ratings can be used as the *predictor*, but are more often used as the *criterion*. Ratings that are used as the *predictor* in selection are usually made by external referees (see above), or by the candidate's peers. *Criterion* ratings were traditionally made by a supervisor or manager, but increasingly ratings by co-workers and subordinates are being used as well (so-called '360-degree feedback').

Rating systems usually contain upwards of six scales, often many more. However, it is normally a mistake to multiply rating scales, because factor analysis (see Box 2.1) almost always shows that a large number of ratings reduce to a much smaller number of factors. Ratings are used for regular performance appraisals in American industry, so they are big business. Performance appraisals often determine promotion, salary or even survival, so rating systems come under keen scrutiny.

The *graphic rating scale* is the conventional rating scale format:

efficient |---|---|---|---|---|---|---| inefficient

Different formats vary the number of scale points, or supply *anchors* for each point ('very', 'fairly', 'slightly,' etc.).

The *behaviourally anchored rating scale (BARS)* format tries to make each point of the scale more meaningful to the rater, thus making ratings less arbitrary. BARS writing proceeds by the following four stages.

1. *Choose the dimensions.* Israeli tank commanders listed five dimensions for tank crews, namely *efficiency* (with which weaponry is operated), *effort, proficiency in maintenance, proficiency in manoeuvre* and *teamwork* (Shapira & Shirom, 1980).
2. *List examples of good, average and poor work.* The same supervisors, working individually, write descriptions of *critical incidents* (*see* Chapter 2) of good, average and poor performance. Up to 900 incidents may be described. The incidents are sifted in order to exclude duplicates, incidents that are too vague, and ones that raters could not observe.
3. *Sort the items.* Supervisors work through the revised list of incidents, and assign each incident to one of the dimensions listed in stage 1. Incidents that are not assigned to the same dimension by 75% of supervisors are discarded.

Box 4.1 Standard deviation

The standard deviation does two things. It describes how one person compares with others, and it summarises the variability of the whole distribution. Standard deviation is usually abbreviated to SD.

A distribution is completely summarised by its mean and SD, so long as it is *normal* – that is bell-shaped and symmetrical. (Distributions of some natural scores, such as height, are normal; distributions of constructed scores, such as IQs, are made normal.)

The SD can be used, like the percentile, to describe someone's height, without reference to any particular system of measurement. A man who is 6′2″ tall is 2 SDs above the mean. Anyone who understands statistics will know how tall that is, whether the local units of height are metres, feet and inches, or cubits.

---

4. *Scale the incidents.* Supervisors scale incidents that survive stage 3, on a seven-point scale. If the *standard deviation* (*see* Box 4.1) of supervisors' ratings exceeds 1.5, the incident is discarded, because supervisors do not agree well enough on its weighting.

Figure 4.2 illustrates a typical BARS. Behaviourally anchored rating scales are claimed to reduce leniency and to increase inter-rater agreement. Shapira and Shirom (1980) found correlations between different BARSs to be fairly low, suggesting that raters were not just rating the same thing five times under different headings. Other authors are sceptical about the advantages of BARSs over simpler rating formats (Borman, 1979). BARSs are highly specific, so a new set has to be developed for each job. Variations on the theme include the behavioural observation scale (BOS) and the behavioural expectation scale (BES).

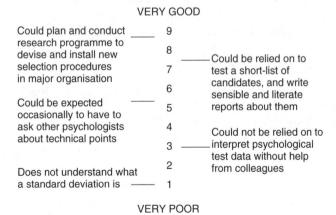

Figure 4.2 An (invented) example of a behaviourally anchored rating scale (BARS) for rating occupational psychologists

Peer assessments

Research dating back to the 1920s has found that people are surprisingly good at predicting who among their peers will succeed, and that they are surprisingly honest, too. Even when they know that their opinions will help to determine who gets selected or promoted, people say (fairly) willingly what they think of each other, and are (relatively) uninfluenced by who they like and who they dislike. Sometimes rating scales are used, and sometimes forced-choice formats. In *peer nomination*, each subject nominates the best or worst performers in the group, usually in order of effectiveness or ineffectiveness. In *peer ranking*, each subject rank orders the whole group from best to worst. Subjects do not usually judge themselves. Peer assessments do not work well unless the group numbers at least 10.

Military research

The US and Israeli armed services have researched peer assessments extensively. Early research found that peer ratings of US Marine officers were a better predictor both of success in officer candidate school and of combat performance than several objective tests. Israeli research (Tziner & Dolan, 1982) reported very high correlations between peer evaluations and admission to officer school, in large male and female samples. Peer assessments had higher predictive validity than almost any other test, including mental ability tests, interview rating, and rating by commanding officer. A review (Lewin & Zwany, 1976) of US army and navy research found correlations centring in the 0.20s and 0.30s. Peer assessment has been most popular in the armed services, where people are less likely (or less able) to complain. Peer ratings are unpopular if they are used *administratively* (i.e. to make decisions about promotion, etc.). McEvoy and Buller (1987) reported that peer ratings were more acceptable if they were used to develop staff than if they were used to select them. Zazanis, Zaccaro and Kilcullen (2001) reported that peer ratings predicted success in Special Forces training in the US army quite well, whereas ratings by army staff assessors did not predict success at all.

Civilian research

The earliest review (Kane & Lawler, 1978) analysed 19 studies and concluded that peer *nominations* achieved an average validity of 0.43. Military studies achieved higher validities than civilian studies. However, Kane and Lawler calculated these medians from the *best validity* achieved in each study, not from *all validities* reported, so the medians were probably an overestimate. Peer nominations predicted objective criteria (graduation, promotion, survival) better than supervisor ratings. Nominations for specific criteria ('will make a good officer') were more accurate than nominations for vague criteria ('extravert', 'emotional'). Kane and Lawler concluded that nominations were best used for predicting leadership. They also concluded that peer *ratings* were less valid than nominations, probably because everyone is rated, not just the highly visible extremes. Validity was equally good for civilian and military studies.

Reilly and Chao (1982) reviewed peer evaluations for MBA graduates, managers, life insurance agents, sales staff, pharmaceutical scientists, and secretaries, and calculated average validities for the following three criteria:

1. training   0.31
2. promotion   0.51
3. performance ratings   0.37.

Hunter and Hunter (1984) calculated a new *meta-analysis* for peer ratings, against the following three criteria:

1. supervisor ratings   0.49
2. training grades   0.36
3. promotion   0.49.

In Hunter and Hunter's review of *alternative tests* (alternative to ability tests), peer ratings were clearly superior to biodata, reference checks, college grades or interview. Hunter and Hunter placed peer ratings third in order of suitability for promotion decisions, but did not list it as a predictor for initial selection. The review by Schmitt *et al.* (1984) of 31 validity coefficients for supervisor/peer assessments, mostly of managers, found a mean validity of 0.43, the highest of any of eight classes of predictor. Why are peer assessments such good predictors? There are several theories about this.

1. *Friendship.* Popular people get good peer evaluations and promotion. This is not necessarily mere bias, if making oneself liked is part of the job.
2. *Consensus.* Traditional references rely on two or three opinions, whereas peer assessments use half a dozen or more. Multiple assessors cancel out each others' errors.
3. *Best vs. usual performance.* When supervisors or staff assessors are present, people do their best. If they try less hard when supervisors are not there, their peers can observe this.
4. *No place to hide.* In military research, the group is together 24 hours a day, faced with all kinds of challenges – physical, mental and emotional – so they get to know each other very well and cannot keep anything hidden. Amir *et al.* (1970) argued that peer assessments work because soldiers know what is needed in an officer, and because they know that their own survival may one day depend on being led by the right person.

Usefulness

Peer assessment is very cheap. The selectors get between 10 and 100 expert opinions about each subject, entirely free. Peer assessments generally have good validity, and sometimes it is very good. Peer assessment has two main disadvantages. First, it is unpopular, and secondly, it presupposes that applicants spend long enough together to get to know each other really well. The disadvantages effectively limit peer assessment to predicting promotability in uniformed, disciplined services. Kane and Lawler (1978) questioned whether peer assessments often add any *new* information. Hollander found that peer nominations correlated very well with pre-flight training grade, so they did not contribute any unique variance (no other study has considered this issue). In practice, peer assessments are not used very widely, if at all, to make routine selection or promotion decisions. Probably no one really believes that peer assessment will work if it is used, and is *known to be used*, within an organisation year in, year out.

Key points

In Chapter 4 you have learnt the following.

- References can be either free form or structured by ratings.
- References are rarely a useful source of information, as they generally lack reliability or validity.
- American research shows that references rarely contain any negative information.
- The traditional free-form reference is difficult to study quantitatively.
- The nature or purpose of the reference seems rather unclear.
- The law in the USA and the UK seems to have placed employers in an impossible position, so that the future of the reference is in doubt.
- References have the potential to communicate valuable information if the right format can be identified. Some variations on the reference request may have promise.
- Ratings by peers can be useful in limited circumstances, such as uniformed, disciplined workforces.

Key references

Baxter *et al.* (1981) document the problems of idiosyncrasy in reference writers.

Grote *et al.* (2001) describe American research on the consistent favourability of references.

Jones and Harrison (1982) describe UK research on reference validity for Royal Navy officer selection which finds better evidence of validity.

Kane and Lawler (1978) review early civilian and military research on peer rating.

Little and Sipes (2000) describe the dilemma in which the law seems to have placed American employers over references.

McCarthy and Goffin (2001) describe research on the relative percentile method which appears to get better results with references.

Mosel and Goheen (1958) describe early US public sector research on the validity of structured references.

Murphy and Cleveland (1995) review research on performance appraisal which has much in common with reference research.

Parry (1999) reviews recent legal development affecting references in the UK.

Zazanis *et al*. (2001) describe recent research on peer ratings.

CHAPTER 5

Weighted application blanks and biodata

How old were you when you learned to swim?

Introduction

Over 80 years ago, Goldsmith (1922) devised an ingenious new solution to an old problem – selecting people who could endure selling life insurance. She took 50 good, 50 poor and 50 middling salesmen from a larger sample of 502 salesmen, and analysed their application forms. She identified factors that collectively distinguished good from average and average from bad, namely age, marital status, education, (current) occupation, previous experience (of selling insurance), belonging to clubs, whether the candidate was applying for full- or part-time selling, and whether the candidate himself had life insurance. Binary items (married/single) were scored $+1/-1$. Scoring continuous variables such as age or education was more complicated: the best age was 30–40 years, with both younger and older age bands scoring less well. Non-linear scoring systems have remained a feature of many biographical measures ever since. Low scorers in Goldsmith's sample almost all failed as insurance salesmen. The small minority of high scorers formed half of a slightly larger minority who succeeded at selling life insurance (*see* Figure 5.1).

Goldsmith had turned the conventional application form into a *weighted application blank (WAB)*. The principle is familiar to anyone with motor insurance. The insurance company analyses its records to find what type of person has more accidents (people who drive sports cars, people who live in London, people who run bars, etc). Insurers do not rely on common sense, which might well suggest that younger drivers with faster reflexes will be safer. Instead they rely on their records, which show that young drivers on average are a bad risk. If insurers can calculate premiums from occupation, age and address, perhaps personnel managers can use application forms as a convenient but very powerful way of selecting employees.

There are two main forms of biographical predictor, namely the weighted application blank and the biographical inventory or biodata. Both start by analysing past applicants to identify facts or items that are linked to the outcome one is trying to predict. Both can be purely (even mindlessly) empirical. Items can be included if they predict the outcome, regardless of whether they 'make sense' or not. Both approaches need very large numbers to be feasible,

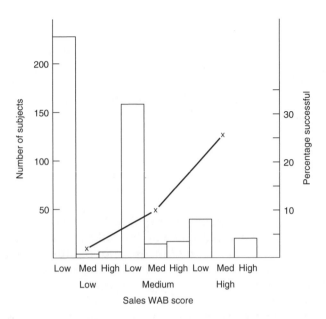

Figure 5.1   Results from the first published weighted application blank (WAB) (data taken from Goldsmith, 1922)

and both must be cross-validated before being used (i.e. items must be shown to work in both of two separate samples). Consequently, both are expensive to set up (but cheap to use thereafter). Both approaches are backward-looking – they will find 'more of the same' (e.g. more managers like present successful managers). This may be a problem in rapidly changing industries.

Uses of weighted application blanks

Taxi drivers

Viteles (1932) devised a seven-item WAB for taxi drivers, which rejected 60% of the poorest drivers while rejecting only 22% of the best, after they had been screened by mental ability tests.

Department-store staff

WABs were often used to select department-store staff. Mosel (1952) found that the ideal saleswoman was between 35 and 54 years old, had 13 to 16 years of formal education, had over 5 years of selling experience, weighed over 160 pounds, had worked on her *next to last* job for *under* 5 years, lived in a boarding house, had worked on her *last* job for *over* 5 years, was between 4'11" and 5'2" high, had between one and three dependants, was widowed, and had lost no time from work during the last 2 years. It is difficult to explain why the ideal saleswoman stayed a long time in her *last* job, but had left her *next to last* job more quickly.

Clerical turnover

WABs have often been used to predict clerical turnover. Buel (1964) compared female clerks who left within 9 months with those who stayed longer, and found 16 differentiating items. Soon after, the company moved from city centre to suburb, which meant that three of the 16 items ceased to be relevant. The WAB still achieved a reasonable validity.

Pea-canners

WABs have been used for very humble jobs. Dunnette and Maetzold (1955) devised a WAB to reduce turnover in cannery workers:

> the typically stable Green Giant production worker lives [locally], has a telephone, is married and has no children, is not a veteran [ex-serviceman], is either young (under 25) or old (over 55), weighs more than 150 pounds but less than 175, has obtained more than ten years of education, has worked for Green Giant . . .

This profile retained its predictive validity over three successive years, and into three other Green Giant canneries, but did not work for non-seasonal cannery workers. Permanent cannery workers who stay the course have family and domestic responsibilities, whereas the profile for seasonal workers identifies young college students, or semi-retired people, both of whom want a short-term job.

Chartered accountants

Harvey-Cook and Taffler (2000) used biographical methods to predict success in accountancy training in the UK, which was showing very high drop-out rates. They came up with a surprisingly traditional set of predictors, namely school and university grades, being head-boy or head-girl at school, and going to a public (i.e. private) school.

Some WAB items are familiar to personnel managers. They include (absence of) frequent job changes, being born locally, being referred by an existing employee, owning a home, being married, belonging to clubs and organisations, and playing sports or physical games. Some make sense when you know they work, but need a very devious mind to predict ("doesn't want a relative contacted in case of emergency", as a predictor of employee theft), and some are bizarre (no middle initial given, again a predictor of employee theft). Physique is often mentioned. Usually extremes of height or weight tend to be bad signs.

Biodata

The classic WAB is invisible and unfakable. It is invisible because the applicant expects to complete an application blank. It is unfakable to the extent that many items could be verified independently, if the employer could afford the time and expense. The classic WAB has tended to be supplanted since the 1960s by *biodata* or *biographical inventory*. Table 5.1 lists some typical biodata questions. Biodata uses a questionnaire format with multiple-choice answers and loses the invisibility of the WAB because it is clear to the candidate that he or she is being assessed.

Biodata items can be divided into *hard* items, which are verifiable but also often intrusive, like item 6 in Table 5.1, and *soft* items, which cause less offence but are easier to fake, like item 5. Mael (1991) has noted that some items are *controllable*, while others are not – one chooses one's exercise pattern but not one's parents' ages. Biodata in the US public sector and military tend to avoid non-controllable items, because the latter make biodata harder to defend against criticism. Kleiman and Faley (1990) found that items asking about present behaviour prove as successful as items asking about past behaviour,

Table 5.1   Some typical biodata items.

1. How old was your father when you were born?
   (a) about 20   (b) about 25   (c) about 30   (d) about 35   (e) I don't know

2. How many hours in a typical week do you engage in physical exercise?
   (a) none   (b) up to 1 hour   (c) 2 to 3 hours   (d) 4 to 5 hours   (e) over 5 hours

3. In your last year at school, how many hours in a typical week did you study outside class hours?
   (a) none   (b) up to 2 hours   (c) 2 to 4 hours   (d) 5 to 8 hours   (e) over 8 hours

4. How old were you when you first kissed someone romantically?
   (a) 12 or   (b) 13 or 14   (c) 15 or 16   (d) over 16   (e) never kissed
       under   anyone
                                                                                   romantically

5. How interested in current affairs are you?
   (a) not at all   (b) slightly   (c) fairly   (d) very   (e) extremely

6. Which best describes your present height/weight ratio?
   (a) definitely   (b) somewhat   (c) slightly   (d) just right   (e) underweight
       overweight   overweight   overweight

7. How often did you play truant from school?
   (a) never   (b) once or twice (c) 3 to 10   (d) once a   (e) once a week
                                         times   month   or more

8. What do you think of children who play truant from school?
   (a) very   (b) strongly   (c) disapprove   (d) unconcerned (e) can
       strongly   disapprove   sympathise
       disapprove

9. How would your superiors at work describe you?
   (a) very lazy   (b) fairly lazy   (c) average   (d) quite hard   (e) very hard
                                                            working   working

10. How many times did you have to take your driving test?
    (a) once   (b) twice   (c) three times   (d) four or   (e) never taken
                                                            more times   it

and suggested that they will prove more acceptable. Some biodata items contain questions about attitudes, such as item 8 in Table 5.1. Other biodata items ask what other people think of you, such as item 9, which is verifiable, at least in theory.

Biodata and personality inventory

Many biographical items look very like personality inventory items. What is the conceptual difference between personality inventory questions, like those listed in Chapter 7, and biodata questions like those listed in Table 5.1?

1. The personality inventory infers from items to trait, and then from trait to work performance. Most biodata, by contrast, infer directly from item to work performance, without any intervening variable such as 'dominance' or 'conscientiousness' (although the trend in some quarters is to use biographical factors or even personality traits as intervening variables in biodata).
2. Personality inventories have fixed keys, whereas biodata items are re-keyed for each selection task.
3. Overall, biodata questions are more likely to be factual than personality questions, although biodata measures include many non-factual questions.
4. Personality inventory questions are carefully phrased to elicit a rapid, unthinking reply, whereas biodata items often sound quite clumsy in their desire to specify precisely the information that they want. For example:

With regard to personal appearance, as compared with the appearance of my friends, I think that:
• Most of my friends have a better appearance
• I am equal to most of them in appearance
• I am better than most of them in appearance
• I don't feel strongly one way or the other.

In a personality inventory this would read more like:
• I am fairly happy about the way I look   True/False.

Sometimes the distinction between personality inventory and biodata inventory is so fine that one wonders whether the choice of title reflects no more than the authors' perception of what is acceptable in their organisation.

Biodata keyed to personality dimensions

Mael and Hirsch (1993) described a biodata measure keyed to the US military's personality inventory, ABLE, and found that the biodata achieves *incremental validity* over ABLE and mental ability tests in predicting leadership ratings. Similar research in the UK was reported by Wilkinson (1997), using Eysenck's extraversion and neuroticism. Keying a biodata measure to known personality dimensions gives it psychological meaning, and may ensure more generalised validity, but also raises the question of why the personality measure is not used in the first place.

Constructing biographical measures

Sources of biodata items

Biodata items have been derived from a number of sources. Russell *et al.* (1990) used *retrospective life experience essays*, in which Naval Academy students describe a group effort, an accomplishment at school, a disappointment and a stressful event. Many studies have used Glennon, Albright and Owens' (1963) *Catalog of Life History Items*, which lists 484 biographical items.

Empirical keying

Traditional biographical methods were purely empirical. If poor clerical workers were underweight, or had no middle initial, or lived in Balham, those facts entered the scoring key. Purely empirical measures offend psychologists, who like to feel that they have a theory. They are not happy knowing that canary breeders make dishonest employees – they want to know *why*. Ideally they would like to have *predicted* from their theory of work behaviour that canary breeders will make dishonest employees. Critics of pure empiricism also argue that a measure with a foundation of theory is more likely to hold up over time and across different employers, and may be easier to defend.

Factorial keying

The first attempt to give biodata a more theoretical basis relied on *factor analysis* to identify themes in biographical information. If the 'no middle initial' item proved to be linked to half a dozen other items, all to do with, for example, sense of belonging, one has some idea why it relates to work performance, one can explain to critics why it is included, and one can perhaps search for better items to reflect the underlying theme. Factor analysis requires linear scoring methods. Mumford and Owens (1987) reviewed 21 factorial studies and listed the seven most commonly found factors, namely adjustment, academic achievement, intellectual/cultural pursuits, introversion/extraversion, social leadership, maturity and career development.

Rational keying

Some approaches select items to reflect particular themes. Miner (1971) stated specific hypotheses about eliteness motivation – for example, that status-conscious Americans will serve (as officers of course) in the Navy or Air Force, but not in the Army. Recent studies (e.g. Fine & Cronshaw, 1994) use a *behavioural consistency* approach. If job analysis indicates that the job needs good organisational skills, items are written that reflect this, either on the job ('How often do you complete projects on time?') or off the job if the organisation is recruiting new employees ('To what extent do you prepare when going off on holiday?'). Recently, researchers have increasingly used *rational scales* based on intervening constructs. A job analysis indicates that the job requires stress tolerance, so the researchers try to devise biographical indicators of likely stress tolerance (Stokes & Cooper, 2001). Factorial and empirical approaches can be used as well to check that the stress items do all reflect one single theme, and that they do predict work performance. This approach has two advantages. First, it has a logic to it, so it is easier to defend, and second, it is more versatile – a biodata measure for stress tolerance can be used for any job that creates stress.

Reiter-Palmon and Connelly (2000) compared rational and empirical construction methods and found that they worked equally well, although the empirical keys tended to contain more unexplainable items (e.g. good grades predicted by admitting to often taking feelings out on parents). Hough and Paullin (1994) compared measures constructed by empirical, factorial and rational methods, and found that the rational approach gives slightly better results than the factorial approach. Graham *et al.* (2002) found that certain item types seem to predict work performance better. These include items that are verifiable through records, such as lateness for work, or that reflect others' opinions, such as item 9 in Table 5.1. Items that record the candidate's own opinion of him- or herself and which are not verifiable, like item 5 in Table 5.1, were less successful.

Option keying vs. linear rating

Biographical measures were traditionally scored by *option keying*, using tables drawn up by Strong in 1926 and revised by England in 1961. Table 5.2 illustrates the method for one of 88 WAB items from Mitchell and Klimoski's (1982) study of trainee realtors (estate agents), where the criterion of success was achieving licensed status. Columns 1 and 2 show that successful realtors are more likely to own their own home, and less likely to rent a flat or live with relatives. Column 4 assigns a scoring weight from Strong's tables; larger percentage differences get higher weights. This technique allows for non-linear relationships.

Linear rating methods have become more popular. These assume that the various answers constitute a scale. This rating format allows analysis by

Table 5.2   A sample WAB item.

	Licensed	Unlicensed	Difference	Weight
Do you:				
Own your own home?	81	60	21	5
Rent your home?	3	5	−2	−1
Rent an apartment?	9	25	−16	−4
Live with relatives?	5	10	−5	−2

Source: Reproduced from Mitchell & Klimoski (1982) by permission of the American Psychological Association © 1982.

correlation and factor analysis. Mael and Hirsch (1993) suggest that some apparently non-linear relationships arise by chance, and they suggest that 'the hand of reason' should sometimes modify scoring keys. They cite the example of the question 'How many years did you play chess in high school?'. If the answer 'three years' was less closely linked to work performance than the adjacent answers of 'two years' or 'four years,' strict application of option keying would assign less weight to three years than to either two or four years. By contrast, 'the hand of reason' suggests that the relationship is more likely to be linear, and sets the scoring accordingly. Devlin, Abrahams and Edwards (1992) compared various biodata scoring methods and found that they made little difference to biodata validity.

Cross-validation and shrinkage

The essential last step in writing a biodata is cross-validation. The original sample is used to construct the biographical measure. Validity can only be calculated from a second *cross-validation* or *hold-out* sample. A WAB or biodata inventory that has not been cross-validated should not be used for selection. Biographical measures are particularly likely to *shrink* on cross-validation, because they can easily capitalise on chance differences between the original samples.

Biographical classification

Owens uses biodata to *classify* people. Scores on his Biographical Question-naire are factor-analysed, and the factor scores are then cluster-analysed, to group people with common patterns of prior experience. Brush and Owens (1979) classified oil company employees into 18 biographical subgroups, and then compared different bio-groups. For example, bio-group 5 (higher *personal values* and very high *trade skills, interest* and *experience*) had lower termination rates than bio-group 6 (low on *family relationships* and very low on *achievement motivation, self-confidence* and *personal values*). Owens (1976) found that salesmen came from only three (of nine) biodata groups (one-time *college athletes, college politicians* and *hard workers*), and that biodata group membership predicted survival in selling very successfully.

Validity

There is an extensive body of research in America and the UK on biodata validity, much of it unpublished. Two recent reviews offer apparently very similar overall estimates of biodata validity.

- Bliesener (1996) reported a meta-analysis of 165 biodata validities, and found a mean validity of 0.30.
- Bobko and Roth (1999) also reported a meta-analysis, based in part on two earlier meta-analyses (but not Bliesener's) and in part on two large

American studies (Gandy *et al.*, 1989; Rothstein *et al.*, 1990). They reported a value of 0.28.

Neither analysis corrects for either restricted range or unreliability, so they represent conservative estimates of biodata validity. Biodata are evidently a fairly effective predictor. However, on closer inspection Bliesener's value is not in fact the same as that of Bobko *et al.* Bliesener's overall uncorrected correlation is actually considerably higher than 0.30, at 0.39. He does something very unusual in selection research – he makes corrections that *reduce* the size of the validity coefficient. He identifies five methodological shortcomings of biodata research which he thinks inflate validity. For example, concurrent designs achieve higher validity than predictive ones, although the latter are generally thought to be superior. Pure biodata achieve lower validity than biodata that include many attitude or personality items. Standard scoring keys (i.e. those already written in some other research) achieve lower validity than ones that have been written specially, which may capitalise on chance more. Correcting each individual validity coefficient for the presence of such factors reduced the overall validity from 0.39 to 0.30.

Different outcomes

Biodata have been used more extensively than other selection measures to predict a variety of work-related outcomes (as well as some non-work-related outcomes, such as credit rating). Table 5.3 summarises some of this research. (These analyses are not entirely independent, because the same original researches may be included in more than one review.) Table 5.3 indicates the following.

- Biodata can successfully predict a wide variety of work behaviour.

Table 5.3   Summary of validity of biodata for seven work related outcomes.

Review	R & C		H & H		Schm		B & H		Bl		
	k	r	k	r	k	r	k	r	k	r	r_{net}
Proficiency rating	15	0.36	12	0.37	29	0.32	26	0.32	16	0.32	0.23
Production	6	0.46			19	0.21	10	0.31			
Objective performance [a]									19	0.53	0.30
Training success			11	0.30	18	0.25			49	0.36	0.22
Promotion			17	0.26							
Absence/turnover					28	0.21	15	0.25			
Tenure	13	0.32	23	0.26			18	0.32	39	0.22	0.15
Creativity									19	0.43	0.32

Notes: R & C = Reilly & Chao (1982); H & H = Hunter & Hunter (1984); Schm = Schmitt *et al.* (1984); B & H = Barge & Hough (1986); Bl = Bliesener (1996).
k = number of studies; r = uncorrected correlation; r_{net} = correlation corrected for methodological shortcomings.
[a] Bliesener's objective performance category includes both production figures and sales, and absence.

- Validity is higher for Bliesener's objective performance category which covers sales, production and absence.
- Validity is generally lower for predicting tenure.

Different types of work

Biodata have also been used for a wide range of types of work. All three meta-analyses (Reilly & Chao, 1982; Mumford & Owens, 1987; Bliesener, 1996) found that biodata achieve good validity for most occupations, with the possible exception of the military, where Bliesener found a validity of only 0.19. Bliesener found biodata validity to be highest for clerical work. The data shown in Table 5.4 are validities pooled across different criteria, including training, tenure and salary, as well as supervisor rating and conventional output measures.

Several reviews and meta-analyses have been reported for specific occupations.

- Funke *et al.* (1987) reported a meta-analysis of 13 studies using biographical measures to predict research achievement in science and technology, and found an overall corrected validity of 0.47.
- Two reviews of sales staff agreed on a validity of 0.27/0.28 for sales figures, but disagreed on validity for rated sales ability. Vinchur *et al.* (1998) found it to be considerably higher at 0.52, whereas Farrell and Hakstian (2001) found it to be lower at 0.33.
- Hunter and Burke (1994) reported an uncorrected validity of 0.27 in 21 studies predicting success in pilot training. They found an unexpected moderator variable in date. Researches reported before 1961, including many large-scale World War Two studies, achieved good validity, whereas those reported after 1961 had poorer results.

Bliesener's analysis found a very large gender difference – biodata work far better for women (0.51) than for men (0.27). This may be mediated by differences between occupations, as biodata work better for occupations

Table 5.4 Summary of validity of biodata for six areas of work.

Study	M & O		R & C		Bl		
	k	r	k	r	k	r	r_{net}
Managers	21	0.35	7	0.38	11	0.42	0.27
Sales	17	0.35	5	0.50	24	0.23	0.27
Factory/craftsperson	14	0.46					
Clerical	13	0.46	6	0.52	22	0.46	0.39
Military	13	0.34	9	0.30	33	0.25	0.19
Science/engineering			15	0.41	16	0.41	0.33

Notes: M & O = Mumford & Owens (1987); R & C = Reilly & Chao, 1982; Bl = Bliesener (1996).
k = number of studies; r = uncorrected correlation; r_{net} = correlation corrected for methodological shortcomings.

where many women work, such as clerical jobs, and less well for occupations where fewer women work, such as the armed forces.

Incremental validity

Biodata are often used in conjunction with other methods, which raises the question of incremental validity. Does the combination of, for example, biodata and mental ability test improve much on the validity that can be achieved by either method used alone? Schmidt and Hunter (1998) have argued that the 0.50 correlation between biodata and mental ability reported by Rothstein *et al.* (1990) means that biodata will not achieve much incremental validity. However, some studies have reported incremental validity. Mael and Ashworth (1995) found that biodata improve on mental ability tests in predicting attrition in army recruits. Mount, Witt and Barrick (2000) found that biodata have incremental validity on mental ability and the big five personality factors for clerical work. McManus and Kelly (1999) found that the big five and biodata each achieve incremental validity on each other in predicting contextual performance – a variant of the concept of organisational citizenship.

Validity generalisation and transportability

Early research concluded that WABs and biodata did not seem to 'travel well', and tended to be specific to the organisations in which they were developed. However, Laurent (1970) succeeded in writing a biodata inventory that predicted managerial effectiveness in New Jersey, and which travelled to Norway, Denmark and The Netherlands, survived translation, and still retained good predictive validity. (Translating biodata inventories can be difficult. Education systems differ from one country to another, so 'How many GCSEs did you pass?' means nothing outside the UK.)

The best data on transportability come from the *Aptitude Index Battery* (*AIB*), a biodata inventory used by the North American insurance industry since the 1930s, and dating in part back to 1919. The AIB is a composite measure, covering personality and interest items as well as biographical items. It is currently called *Career Profile* and is part of the *Exsel* system. Figure 5.2 shows that success was closely related to AIB score, and it also shows how few succeed in insurance, even from the highest score bands. Figure 5.3 shows schematically the distribution of AIB scores against the composite survival and sales criterion, and suggests that the AIB is essentially a screening test that eliminates potential failures but does not necessarily identify successes. Brown (1981) analysed AIB data for over 12,000 insurance sales staff from 12 large US life insurance companies. Validity generalisation analysis showed that the AIB's mean true validity coefficient was 0.26. The AIB was valid for all 12 insurance companies, but proved to be more valid for larger, better-run companies that recruited through press adverts and agencies than for smaller companies that recruited by personal contacts. The AIB has been rewritten and re-scored a dozen times, but has retained some continuity.

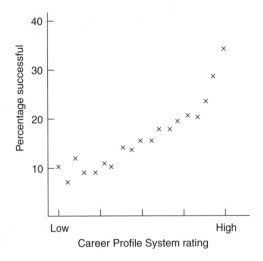

Figure 5.2 Predictive validity of the Career Profile System (CPS) (successor to the Aptitude Index Battery), showing that the higher the CPS score, the greater the proportion of applicants who 'survive'

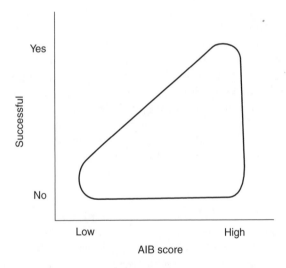

Figure 5.3 Schematic representation of the relationship between AIB score and success in selling insurance

Consortium measures

Biographical measures need large samples, which appears to rule them out for all except very large employers such as the insurance industry. One answer for organisations that do not employ vast numbers is the *consortium* biodata – one produced by several employers. Consortium measures also deal with the problem of specificity to particular jobs, criteria of performance, or organisations. Rothstein *et al.* (1990) suggested that biodata do not appear to 'travel well' because they are usually keyed inside one single organisation, which will tend to limit their generality. Their *Supervisory Profile Record (SPR)* is derived from 39 organisations, and proved to have highly generalisable validity, being unaffected by organisation, sex, race, supervisory experience, social class or education. Schmidt and Rothstein (1994) analysed SPR data for 79 separate organisations and found an overall corrected validity of 0.36 and relatively little variation in validity from one organisation, or type of supervisor, to another. The US Federal Government uses a biodata college for graduate entrants, known as the *Individual Achievement Record*, and finds that its validity generalises well across different occupations and government agencies (Gandy *et al.* 1989). Carlson *et al.* (1999) have described the *Manager Profile Record*, which was developed within one organisation but has been used successfully in 24 others to predict salary increase and promotion. Carlson *et al.* placed more emphasis on items that had a sound rational or behavioural justification than on empirical keying.

The need for secrecy?

Early studies published their WABs in full, confident that pea-canners and shop assistants did not read the *Journal of Applied Psychology* and therefore could not discover the right answers to give. However, if the scoring system becomes known, biodata can lose predictive power. Hughes, Dunn and Baxter (1956) wrote a new form of AIB which worked well while it was still experimental, but lost its validity as soon as it was used for actual hiring (*see* Figure 5.4). Field managers scored the forms and were supposed to use them to reject unsuitable applicants. Instead, they guided favoured applicants into giving the right answers. When scoring was moved back to head office, the AIB regained its validity. It is doubtful whether any selection method can be kept entirely secret these days because all of them come under intense legal scrutiny.

Construct validity

There seem to be few studies that have compared biodata with other methods, such as personality or ability tests. Rothstein *et al.* (1990) reported a large correlation with mental ability in a single large study, but we lack any meta-analyses. We therefore have no clear picture of what biodata are assessing, or how they compare with other assessment measures.

Fakability

The traditional WAB can only be faked if the subject lies. Early research gave conflicting accounts of how often people do this. Of 17 verifiable items used to select police officers (Cascio, 1975), only two showed a substantial discrepancy, namely age when first married and number of full-time jobs held up to the present. On the other hand, Goldstein (1971) checked information given by applicants for a nursing aid post against what previous employers

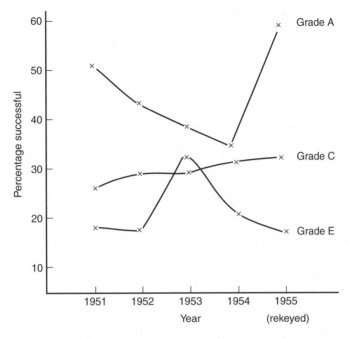

Figure 5.4   Results obtained with the Aptitude Index Battery (AIB) between 1951 and 1954. Data taken from Hughes *et al.* (1956)

said, and found that many applicants inflated both their salary and the length of time they had been employed. More seriously, a quarter gave reasons for leaving their last job that the employer did not agree with, and no less than 17% listed as their last employer someone who denied ever having employed them. Owens (1976) was right to say that more research is needed on the accuracy of WAB and biodata information. Unfortunately, very little has been reported.

Biodata inventories may be more prone to faking because they are more visible, and because many biodata items are not objective or verifiable. Research on biodata faking has a series of parallels with research on faking personality inventories (discussed in Chapter 7).

- People who are directed to 'fake good' can usually improve their biodata scores (Lautenschlager, 1994).
- People who are directed to fake good distort their answers far more than job applicants (Becker & Colquitt, 1992), so directed faking studies may be misleading.
- The extent of faking by real job applicants is uncertain. Becker and Colquitt (1992) reported that only three of 25 items were answered differently by job applicants. These items were less historical, objective and verifiable. On the other hand, Stokes, Hogan and Snell (1993) compared applicants with people who already had the job, and found that their answers were much

more 'socially desirable' in areas such as preferred working climate, work style, or personal and social adjustment.

Research also suggests several possible ways of dealing with faking in biodata, again tending to repeat approaches that have been tried with personality tests.

- More objective and verifiable items create fewer differences between applicants and people who already have the job (Stokes *et al.*, 1993).
- More complex option-keying scoring methods are less fakable than simple linear scoring systems (Kluger, Reilly and Russell, 1991). However, Stokes *et al.* (1993) found that complex scoring does not seem to prevent applicants giving different responses to those given by people who already have the job.
- Warning people that the biodata included a lie-detection scale (which it did not) reduced faking (Schrader & Osburn, 1977). This solution involves misleading people, so is neither feasible nor desirable in practice.
- A trick question about experience with a non-existent piece of electrical equipment, the 'Sonntag connector', caught out one-third of applicants (Pannone, 1984). This third obtained better overall scores on the biodata, but their biodata score correlated less well with a written job knowledge test, suggesting that they were not better applicants. This approach is unethical, and might not work for long in practice.
- Shermis *et al.* (1996) described a faking good scale, modelled on faking good scales in personality measures, consisting of 12 items along the lines of 'I have never violated the law while driving a car'.

Biographical measures, fairness and the law

If WAB/biodata items are linked to race, sex, disability or age, these protected minorities may obtain lower scores on biodata measures, so giving rise to claims of *adverse impact*. Most research has focused on ethnicity in the USA. The early review by Reilly and Chao (1982) concluded that biodata did not, by and large, create an adverse impact for ethnic minorities applying for work as bus drivers, clerical staff, army recruits or supervisors. Subsequently, a meta-analysis by Schmitt, Clause and Pulakos (1996) concluded that only fairly small Afro/white differences were found in biodata scores, represented by a d value of 0.20. The most recent analysis by Bobko and Roth (1999) is less optimistic, and concludes that the Afro/white difference is 0.33. Biodata do create adverse impact, although not as much as mental ability tests. Although this is the case, Sharf (1994) notes that biodata *have not been challenged directly under the Civil Rights Act*. Perhaps everyone thought that there was no adverse impact problem. One study reports that using biodata can reduce adverse impact. The combination of Supervisory Profile Record and mental ability test, while predicting only slightly better than the mental ability tests alone, creates less adverse impact (Rothstein *et al.* 1990).

Item analyses

The differences discussed above are in total score, but it is also possible to analyse adverse impact at the item level. An early researcher found one predictor of employee theft that he did not have much hesitation about not using, namely being non-white. Other ways in which biographical measures might discriminate against protected groups are more subtle. Having a city-centre address as opposed to a suburban one in Detroit distinguished thieves from non-thieves, but also tended to distinguish white from non-white groups. A similar problem could arise with disability. For example, items about participation in sport could discriminate against disabled people.

Sharf (1994) considers that it is unclear whether biodata could be challenged legally item by item, so a few items creating adverse impact may not matter. In fact it is extremely unlikely that no gender, age, ethnicity or disability differences would be found in any of 50 to 100 biographical questions. However, if many items show, for example, ethnicity differences, it tends to follow that total scores will also differ. Two recent studies (Whitney & Schmitt, 1997; Schmitt & Pulakos, 1998) found significant black/white differences in a high proportion of biodata items (25% and 31%, respectively). Whitney and Schmitt noted that if we can explain the differences in terms of, say, different cultural values, we shall have a better understanding of which items to exclude in future biodata. Unfortunately, they were unable to find any systematic explanation for the differences in their sample.

Privacy

As Table 5.1 shows, some biodata items can be very intrusive. In the *Soroka v Dayton-Hudson* case, a department store was sued by a job applicant who claimed that he had been asked intrusive questions about politics and religion, contrary to the Constitution of the State of California (Merenda, 1995). The case was settled out of court, so no definitive ruling emerged. Use of biodata in the USA is complicated by the fact that the 52 states all have their own different laws about privacy, so questions about, for example, credit rating are legal in some states but illegal in others (Sharf, 1994).

Some psychologists have proposed the 'Washington Post' test for biodata face validity. Imagine headlines in the *Washington Post*. One headline reads 'Psychologists reject people for paratroop training school because they don't like colour blue', which sounds arbitrary and unfair. Another headline reads 'Psychologists reject people for paratroop training school because they are afraid of heights', which sounds much more reasonable.

Key points

In Chapter 5 you have learnt the following.

- Biographical methods are mostly used in North America, and to some extent in the UK.

- There are two biographical approaches, namely weighted application blanks, which are scored from the application form, and biodata, which are separate questionnaires and so more visible to the candidate.
- Biographical measures can predict work performance and other related aspects of workplace behaviour, such as tenure, training success, promotion, absence and creativity.
- Biodata can be purely empirical, or they can be guided by either a theory of, for example, eliteness motivation, or a relevant construct such as stress tolerance.
- Biodata face the same problem of quality of information being compromised by impression management or outright faking.
- Biodata rarely seem to attract litigation, but can look unfair or arbitrary to candidates.
- Biodata do create some adverse impact on American minorities.

Key references

Bliesener (1996) presents the most recent meta-analytical review of biodata validity.

Brown (1981) describes research on the insurance industry's biodata system.

Dunnette and Maetzold (1955) describe an early weighted application blank for cannery workers.

Harvey-Cook and Taffler (2000) describe a recent UK biographical selection process for chartered accountants.

Hughes et al. (1956) describe how a biodata measure lost validity when its scoring was compromised.

Mael (1991) presents a classification of different types of biodata items.

Mael and Hirsch (1993) compare purely empirical with more rational scoring methods for biodata.

Owens and Schoenfeldt (1979) describe an elaborate system of biodata classification.

Rothstein et al. (1990) describe the development of a generic biodata known as the Supervisory Profile Record.

Shermis et al. (1996) describe a biodata faking good scale.

Useful websites

www.limra.com. American life insurance industry site that includes details of current selection systems.

CHAPTER 6

Tests of mental ability

'a...man of paralysing stupidity ...'

Introduction

In Orwell's *1984*, the main character, Winston Smith, has a neighbour called Parsons, who is dismissively characterised as 'A fattish but active man of paralysing stupidity ... At the ministry he was employed in some subordinate post for which intelligence was not required' (Orwell, 1949/1984, pp. 174–5). Orwell clearly thinks that some jobs need intelligent people (while some exist that do not). Tests of mental ability are widely used in personnel selection. They also have a multi-faceted history of controversy and unpopularity going back to the 1960s.

- In 1969, Arthur Jensen published an article entitled 'How Much Can We Boost IQ and Scholastic Achievement', which stated the evidence on heritability of mental ability more forcefully than people in the USA were either used to or cared for. The original studies were then re-read more carefully, and their defects were noted.
- Critics claimed that Burt's separated identical twin study contained fabricated data. This claim has been disputed, but the Burt affair left many people thinking that all research on heritability was suspect, or even that mental ability tests in general had been discredited.
- Jensen raised the issue of ethnicity differences in mental ability, notorious for its ability to 'generate more heat than light'.
- Jensen argued that remedial education, on which the American government was spending very large sums, was achieving little or nothing.
- The Civil Rights Act of 1964 led within a few years to most American employers abandoning mental ability testing because of adverse impact problems that have still not been solved today.

In the 1990s, controversy about mental ability tests was revived by Herrnstein and Murray's (1994) *The Bell Curve*, which covers much the same ground as Jensen did a quarter of a century earlier (heritability, ethnic differences, remedial education), and which has been at least as widely publicised. *The Bell Curve* adds one new controversial element, namely the possible existence of an 'under-class' of people whose employment prospects are limited by low mental ability.

Overview of mental ability tests

General mental ability, aptitude and achievement

An *achievement test* assesses how much someone knows about a particular body of knowledge (e.g. use of Microsoft Excel). An *aptitude test* assesses how easy it would be for someone to acquire knowledge they do not at present possess (e.g. of computer programming). A *test of general mental ability* seeks to assess how good someone is at understanding and using information of all types.

Achievement tests

In the USA, Short Occupational Knowledge Tests (SOKTs) are available for a range of occupations (motor mechanic, electrician, plumber, etc.). Achievement tests are also known as *job knowledge* or *trade* tests. Such tests are rarely used in selection in the UK, where employers usually rely on professional qualifications, National Vocational Qualifications (NVQs) or completed apprenticeships.

Aptitude tests

Aptitudes that are widely assessed include clerical aptitude (General Clerical Test), mechanical aptitude (Bennett Mechanical Comprehension Test), programming aptitude (Computer Programmer Aptitude Battery) and dexterity (Crawford Small Parts Dexterity Test). Aptitudes often correlate fairly well with general mental ability. Sometimes a number of aptitude tests are combined to form a *multiple aptitude battery*.

Tests of general mental ability

General mental ability is also referred to as cognitive ability (or abilities), intelligence, or (confusingly, in the USA) 'aptitudes'. When people keep changing the name for something, this is often a sign of unease. General mental ability tests are the most controversial level of ability testing, for a variety of reasons, some of which are outlined at the beginning of the chapter. Mental ability tests use many different types of item. Items vary in content, which may be verbal, numerical or abstract. Items also vary in difficulty and in universality. For example, few people in the UK, however bright or dim, know the distance from Denver to Dallas, but adding 5 to 6 should be possible for anyone whose culture uses numbers. Table 6.1 illustrates the test writer's dilemma – seeking to write a test of ability to use information in general, but having to assess this ability through specific questions. Some tests deal with this problem by including many and varied problems, while others try to find problems that depend as little as possible on learned information.

The items in Table 6.1 look very diverse, and 'common sense' would expect the ability to answer one to have little to do with the ability to answer another. For example, 'common sense' suggests that knowing what a word means

Table 6.1   Nine varied items from a mental ability test: note that these are not 'real' items from a 'real' test, but are typical of mental ability test items.

1.   What does the word 'impeach' mean?

preserve   accuse   give a sermon   propose

2. What number comes next? 2   4   9   16   25...

29   36   45   100

3. How far is it from Dallas to Denver in miles?

50   300   600   2,000

4. How much is 5 plus 6?

11   12   56   1

5. Big is to little as tall is to...

short   height   long   thin

6. What is the rate of income tax for incomes over £40,000 a year?

25%   40%   75%   90%

7. If John Smith buys a car for £6,000 and a boat for £5,000, how much will he spend altogether?

£10,000   £11,000   £65,000   £5,000

8. Divide the largest number by the next to smallest number, and then multiply the result by the next to largest number: 20   15   11   14   5   2

110   60   10   300

depends on education and home background, whereas complex reasoning and mental arithmetic items, such as item 8, are likely to require quite different abilities. The items in Table 6.1 are fictitious, but results obtained with similar problems in real tests show fairly high positive correlations. This reflects what Spearman discovered nearly 100 years ago, from which he developed the theory of general intelligence – that people who are good at one intellectual task tend to be good at others.

Bias in testing

Problems arise when one identifiable section of the population tested does worse than another, which gives rise to the claim that items were selected so as to favour one group. For example, item 6 in Table 6.1 may be 'biased' against people who earn too little to be concerned about the rate of tax that their income attracts.

More specialised tests

There are many variations on the basic theme of the mental ability test. Some specialised ability tests vary the *content* of what is being tested.

Creativity or divergent thinking

In 1956, Americans awoke to find a Russian satellite circling the earth, and started asking why the Russians had achieved this before them. One answer that was widely offered was creativity. It was claimed that the American education system, and the tests which it used, favoured convergent thinkers – that is, people who could remember textbook answers to questions, but could not think creatively. Many tests of creativity were developed, but most of them failed the *discriminant validity* test. They correlated with standard tests of mental ability as well as they correlated with other tests of creativity, thus failing to demonstrate that they were measuring anything new.

Social intelligence tests

These have an even longer history; the George Washington test first appeared in 1926. Being able to understand others and get along with them, it is claimed, is both a vital skill in work, and one which very intelligent people often lack. Social intelligence tests use photos, drawings or written descriptions of interpersonal problems. These tests also tend to fail the discriminant validity test, proving to be so highly correlated with other tests of general intelligence that there is no reason to suppose they measure anything different.

Emotional intelligence tests

Goleman (1995) made the claim that success at work was '80% dependent on emotional intelligence and only 20% on IQ'. On closer inspection, this turns out to derive from an analysis of job descriptions, not of test validity. The concept of emotional intelligence is very similar to that of social intelligence. Being able to understand others and get along with them is important in work, and is not measured by conventional intelligence tests. However, tests of emotional intelligence differ in format. Most of them use self-rating and have no time limit, making them more like personality tests. What we need is research demonstrating that emotional intelligence can be separated from conventional intelligence, and that it predicts work performance. Research showing how emotional intelligence relates to personality traits such as empathy and sociability is also required, otherwise we cannot be sure that we are not measuring a familiar concept under a new name. Davies, Stankov and Roberts (1998) reported that emotional intelligence measures tend to be unreliable and to be highly correlated with well-established personality factors. It may well be that social/emotional intelligence cannot be assessed successfully by paper-and-pencil means, but will require behavioural tests, which are much more difficult to devise and time-consuming to use. Dulewicz and Higgs (2000) have suggested that emotional intelligence may be assessable by ratings from peers or subordinates, which would not serve well for selection.

Situational judgement or 'common sense'

McDaniel *et al.* (2001) argued that social intelligence tests are examples of tests of situational judgement, or common sense. The category also includes various measures of supervisor judgement. Their review shows that situational judgement tests correlate quite well with both work performance (0.34) and tests of general mental ability (0.39). McDaniel and Nguyen (2001) reported correlations between situational judgement and three personality factors, namely agreeableness, conscientiousness and (low) neuroticism, which suggests that situational judgement is a broader concept. Situational judgement tests create less adverse impact on ethnic minorities in the USA, but do generate gender differences, favouring women (Weekley & Jones, 1999). Clevenger *et al.* (2001) reported that situational judgement tests have incremental validity over measures of job knowledge and conscientiousness.

Other variations in ability testing change the way in which the measure is *administered*.

Structured learning exercises (SLEs)

The Computer Rules Test requires candidates first to learn and then to apply a computer operating system devised specially for the test. All of the information that is needed to do the test correctly is provided as part of the test, thereby (it is hoped) avoiding problems of culture bias in item content. SLEs assess how quickly people can learn new information and principles. It is claimed that the SLE format reduces adverse impact, but no research data have been published that confirm this.

Computerised testing

Computerised forms of existing paper-and-pencil tests usually give similar results, although van der Vijver and Harsveld (1994) reported that people using the computer work faster but less accurately, especially on simpler tests (e.g. clerical checking). Computerised testing does not have to present a fixed sequence of questions, but can be tailored to the individual's performance. If the candidate does well the questions get harder, but if the candidate does poorly the questions get easier, until the candidate reaches his or her own limit. Computerised testing seems to be especially popular in military testing programmes. Carey (1994) found that computerised tests add little extra validity to conventional tests, but do reduce adverse impact on minority applicants.

Internet testing

A computerised test can be completed over the Internet, and many electronic recruiting systems (discussed on page 6) include online assessment of ability or personality. Testing people over the Internet poses a number of problems. Is the person who is doing the test really John Smith or someone else? How can you stop people applying several times under different names and so giving themselves unfair practice on the test? How can you protect your copyright, and prevent unauthorised use of the test by unqualified users? Bartram (2000) considers that all of these problems can be solved. However, he suggests that supervised testing centres may be needed, which would involve loss of much of the convenience of the Internet. It is easy to write your own test, but difficult and expensive to write one that is (a) reliable, (b) valid, (c) has useful normative data and (d) does not create adverse impact. There are large numbers of dubious-looking tests on the Internet that probably fail to do all or even any of these four things. It is easy to generate dubious tests in paper form, but the Internet allows them to be distributed widely, and possibly to cause more damage by giving people information that is not true or which they cannot handle.

Video-based testing

Several video-based selection tests have been described in North America (Dalessio, 1994) and Germany (Schuler, Diemand & Moser, 1993). Including sound and moving pictures allows the tester to create a richer test, especially suitable perhaps for work involving a lot of contact with the public, or for trying to assess social/emotional intelligence.

Biological testing

This approach derives from experimental psychology or psychophysiology, and uses multiple-choice reaction time, or speed of response of the brain or nervous system. Such approaches have great promise for avoiding cultural difference problems, but are not yet sufficiently well developed to be used in selection.

DNA testing

Research has already identified genes associated with high and low mental ability (Plomin, 2002). In the future it may be possible to assess mental ability from a sliver of skin or a drop of saliva. DNA testing would bypass entirely many problems of measurement, such as item bias, test anxiety or motivation. However, DNA testing would also assess inborn potential, unaffected by culture, upbringing, education and training, or social disadvantage.

Interpreting test scores

Ability tests produce *raw scores*, which mean very little in themselves. The raw score is interpreted by comparing it with *normative data* (e.g. scores for 1,000 apprentices), which tells the tester whether the score is above the mean or below it, and how far above or below it. Several systems are used to interpret raw scores.

1. *Mental age and intelligence quotient (IQ)* were used by the earliest tests – a person with a mental age of five does as well on the test as the average 5-year-old. IQ was originally calculated by dividing mental age by actual (chronological) age, and multiplying by 100.
2. *Percentiles* interpret the raw score in terms of what percentage of the norm group scores lower than the candidate. Percentiles are easy for the lay person to understand, and can be used irrespective of the shape of the distribution of raw scores.

Box 6.1   Percentiles

For a sample of 466 UK health service managers, a raw score of 7 on the Graduate and Managerial Assessment – Numerical translates to a percentile of 30, meaning that someone who scores 7 obtains a better score than 30% of health service managers.

---

3. *Standard scores* are based on standard deviations and the normal distribution. In Figure 6.1, candidate A's raw score is 1.6 SDs above average, while candidate B's raw score is 0.4 SDs below average. The simplest standard score system is the z score, in which A's z score is +1.6 and B's z score is −0.4. All other standard score systems are variations on the z-score theme, designed to be easier to use by eliminating decimals and signs. Standard scores can be misleading if the distribution of scores is not normal.

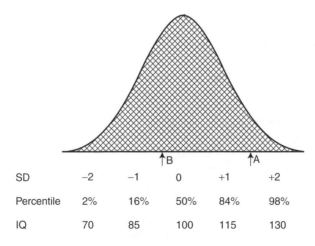

SD	−2	−1	0	+1	+2
Percentile	2%	16%	50%	84%	98%
IQ	70	85	100	115	130

Figure 6.1   Distribution of mental ability scores, showing mean, standard deviations, percentiles and IQs

---

Box 6.2   z scores

The raw score is converted into a z score using the formula $z = $ (raw score − sample mean)/sample SD. On the AH4 test, candidate A's raw score is 98, while the normative sample's mean and SD are 75.23 and 14.58, respectively. Calculating z gives a value of +1.6, which shows that candidate A scores 1.6 SDs above the norm group mean. Candidate B's raw score is 66, which gives a z score of −0.40, which means that B scores 0.4 SDs below the norm group mean.

Box 6.3   Deviation IQ

The deviation IQ is a form of standard score in which the mean is set at 100 and the SD is set at 15. Thus candidate A's IQ is $100 + (15 \times 1.6)$, which is 124, while candidate B's IQ is $100 + (15 \times -0.4)$, which is 94.

Norms

The normative sample should be large, relevant and preferably recent. Comparing a candidate with 2,000 people who have applied for the same job as the candidate within the last 3 years is clearly better than comparing him or her with 50 people who were doing a roughly similar job in Czechoslovakia in the 1930s.

Reliability

Psychological tests are never perfectly reliable. If the same person does the test twice at an interval of 3 months, he or she will not give exactly the same answers and will not obtain exactly the same score. If a group of people do an ability test twice, the two sets of scores should correlate by 0.90 or better, showing that the test measures a stable attribute. This is called *re-test reliability*.

Error of measurement

A simple formula based on re-test reliability and standard deviation of test scores gives the test's *error of measurement*, which estimates how much test scores might vary on re-test. An IQ test with a re-test reliability of 0.90 has an error of measurement of five IQ points. This means that one in three re-tests will vary by five *or more* points, so clearly it would be a mistake for Smith who scores an IQ of 119 to regard him- or herself as superior to Jones who scores 118. If they take the test again in 3 months' time, Smith might score 116 and Jones might score 121. One of the many reasons why psychologists avoid using IQs is that they tend to create a false sense of precision. One reason why untrained people should not use psychological tests is that they probably do not understand error of measurement.

Internal consistency reliability

Many test manuals also give the *split half reliability* or *alpha coefficient*, which relates to the measure's internal consistency. Poor internal consistency reliability means that the test is too short, or that the items do not relate to a single common theme. Suppose that a 'test' asks 10 questions, each of which assesses a different attribute. Scoring each item and then summing the scores to give a total score will generate a completely meaningless number. Calculating an alpha coefficient for such a 'test' will give a near zero alpha value. The same will happen if a test consists largely, or even entirely, of questions that do not assess anything at all. One reason why employers should avoid 'home-made' tests is the risk of finding that they do not measure anything.

Box 6.4   Standard error of measurement (s.e.m.)

s.e.m. is calculated by the simple formula $SD \times \sqrt{(1 - r)}$, where SD is the standard deviation of test scores, and r is the test's reliability. For AH4, this gives a value of 5.33.

The validity of mental ability tests

In 1918, Link published a validation study for American munitions workers using a battery of nine ability tests. The most successful test, the Woodworth Wells Cancellation test, correlated very well (0.63) with a month's production figures for 52 shell inspectors. Link can probably claim the credit for the first published validity coefficient for psychological tests. Since 1918, thousands of similar studies have been reported. Early validation research has been summarised by Dorcus and Jones (1950) and Super and Crites (1962). Early attempts to summarise validation research used the *narrative review*, whose deficiencies were noted in Chapter 3 (unsystematic, subjective and possibly even biased). Ghiselli (1966b) reported the first meta-analysis of validation research on ability tests. He collected hundreds of validity coefficients, classified them by test type, job type and measure of work performance, and then calculated median validity. Figure 6.2 presents his distributions of validity coefficients for four test × job pairs. Ghiselli found reviewing the literature depressing:

> A confirmed pessimist at best, even I was surprised at the variation in findings concerning a particular test applied to workers on a particular job. We certainly never expected the repetition of an investigation to give the same results as the original. But we never anticipated them to be worlds apart.

Ghiselli's distributions of validity coefficients had generally low averages, around 0.30. Modern meta-analyses suggest that Ghiselli's estimate of 0.30 was accurate. Bobko and Roth (1999) summarised earlier research (*see* Table 6.2) and reported an average uncorrected correlation between mental ability and work performance of 0.30. A correlation of 0.30, as critics were quick to note,

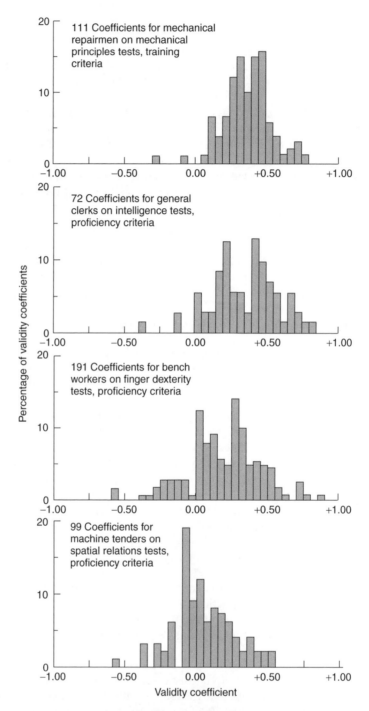

Figure 6.2   Four distributions of validity coefficients for four combinations of test and criterion. Reproduced with permission from Ghiselli, 1966b

Table 6.2 Summary of correlation between mental ability and work performance: note that correlations are not corrected for reliability or restricted range.

Source	Total n	r	Notes
Hunter & Hunter (1984)	32,124	0.29	Meta-analysis
McHenry *et al.* (1990)	4,039	0.39	Project A study
Schmitt *et al.* (1984)	3,597	0.22	Meta-analysis (performance rating)
Schmitt *et al.* (1984)	1,793	0.43	Meta-analysis (work sample)
Overall		0.30	

Note: Data taken from Bobko & Roth (1999).

accounts for only 9% of the variance in work performance. Ghiselli's review made people start asking whether it was worth using tests that appeared to contribute so little information, especially when they were becoming very unpopular, and beginning to meet difficulties with fair employment laws. Industrial psychologists started trying to find out why test validity varied so much, and why it varied around such a low average. During the 1960s and early 1970s they suggested three linked answers, namely moderator variables, situational specificity and the 0.30 barrier. Eventually, however, these proved to be incorrect.

Moderator variables

The test × work performance correlation is *moderated* by some third factor. *Perceptual speed* may correlate well with clerical proficiency where work is routine and fast, but poorly or not at all where work is more varied and less rushed; pace and variety *moderate* the predictive validity of *perceptual speed* (the example is fictional). Possible moderator variables are numerous, and include the nature of the job, the way the organisation operates, the type of people applying for vacancies, geographical location, etc.

Situational specificity

This is a more pessimistic hypothesis, developed as the search for moderators failed to find them. So many factors affect test validity, in such a complex manner, that it is impossible to construct a model that predicts validity in any particular setting. The right tests for a particular job in a particular organisation can only be found by conducting a *local validation study*.

The 0.30 barrier

This is the most pessimistic explanation of all. Mischel (1968) argued that psychological tests never correlate better than 0.30 with any outcome, because they are founded on a fundamentally incorrect model of broad internal dispositions that do not really exist. If there is not any such thing as mental ability or personality, it is not surprising that tests of either fail to predict work performance.

Validity generalisation

However, the answer did not lie in moderator variables or situational specificity, and the 0.30 barrier proved illusory for tests of mental ability. Most critics had overlooked Ghiselli's reminder that:

> Averages of validity coefficients. . .are distorted by the fact that reliability of tests and criteria varies from one investigation to another. Furthermore. . .the workers used differ in range of talent, so that in cases of extensive restriction there is marked attenuation of the validity coefficient. Errors of these sorts. . .are likely to reduce the magnitude of the average validity coefficient. Therefore the trends in validity coefficients to be reported here may well be underestimates.

The critics could be forgiven for this oversight, given that Ghiselli did not develop his own argument fully. Meta-analysis makes some sense of validation studies, but still leaves a fairly confused and depressing picture, because it fails to take into account four limitations of the typical validity study:

1. sampling error
2. restricted range
3. criterion reliability
4. test reliability.

Sampling error

The biggest limitation in validation research is *sampling error*. Correlations calculated from small samples vary greatly, and most validity research has used fairly small samples. Lent *et al.* (1971) reported an average sample size of 68 in 406 validity studies. The *law of large numbers* states that *large* random samples will be highly representative of the population from which they are drawn. The *fallacy of small numbers* is to suppose that *small* random samples are also representative – as they are not. Salgado (1995) reported validity coefficients for five successive samples of Spanish Air Force pilots. Table 6.3

Table 6.3   Validity coefficient and significance of tests used to select pilots for the Spanish Air Force, in five samples.

Sample	Validity	Significance	n
1	0.30	NS	49
2	0.31	NS	45
3	0.41	$p < 0.05$	42
4	0.20	NS	41
5	0.68	$p < 0.01$	45

Source: Reproduced from Salgado (1995) by permission of the British Psychological Society.
Note: NS = non-significant; n = sample size.

shows how a test composite that 'works' in two groups did not 'work' with the other three. Perhaps each group of pilots differs, or perhaps the demands of training change subtly. More likely, however, as Salgado notes, the answer lies in the sample sizes (49, 45, 42, 41 and 45), which were too small to estimate accurately the true size of the correlation. Salgado (1998a) has reviewed recent validation research and found that the average sample size has increased from 68 to 113.

Analysis of US Postal Service data demonstrates conclusively how small sample correlations vary in the absence of any possible real cause. Schmidt *et al.* (1985b) randomly divided a large sample of 1,455 letter sorters into 63 smaller groups of 68 each (the average validation sample size reported by Lent *et al.*, 1971). The validity coefficient of a clerical test for the whole sample is 0.22. Figure 6.3 shows the distribution of validity coefficients for the 63 mini-samples – coefficients which can only vary because of sampling error. Figure 6.3 shows that correlations calculated on small samples are misleading, and that 68 is a small sample – *too* small. The validity of the test appears to range from −0.03 to 0.48. Less than a third of the coefficients were statistically significant, so the researcher using a small sample is more likely than not to 'miss' the link between test and work performance. If the 63 correlations in Figure 6.3 can vary so much just by chance, perhaps the 72 correlations for Ghiselli's clerical workers in Figure 6.2 vary as much by chance, too.

Schmidt, Gast-Rosenberg and Hunter (1980a) argued that sampling error accounts for most of the variation in validity, which has a historically interesting implication. Schmidt (1992) suggested that researchers could – and perhaps *should* – have concluded as long ago as the 1920s that tests of mental ability have generalised validity, and that validity only *appears* to vary from one study to another through sampling error. Why did industrial/organisational psychologists cling to the doctrine of situational specificity for so long? Perhaps

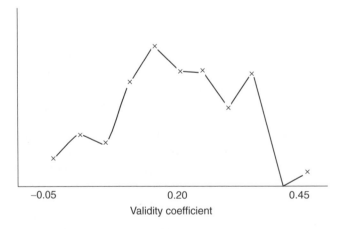

Figure 6.3 Distribution of validity coefficients for 63 subsamples, of 68 each, drawn randomly from a larger sample of 1,455 US postal workers. Data taken from Schmidt *et al.* (1985b)

they did not read their statistics books carefully enough and they overlooked sampling error. Perhaps they were reluctant to admit that studies on samples of 40 or 50 were not very useful, especially as it is often difficult to find larger numbers. Perhaps they just wanted to carry on selling employers local validity studies.

Sampling error explains why validity coefficients vary greatly (because sample sizes are too small) and why they are often statistically insignificant (small samples again), but not why validity coefficients are generally low.

Restricted range

The second limitation of the typical validity study is *restricted range* (*see* Figure 3.1, page 44). An ideal validation study tests every applicant, employs every applicant, and obtains work performance data from every applicant. During World War Two, the US Air Force did send an unselected sample of 1,143 men through pilot training, enabling Flanagan (1946) to calculate the validity of the test battery without restriction of range. The failure rate was high (77%), but so was the correlation between test scores and success (0.64). Flanagan's study showed how well mental ability tests can work, under ideal conditions. However, not many employers can afford to test and employ large unselected intakes, so the personnel researcher usually has to compromise and calculate validity from the *restricted range* of successful applicants. Restriction of range varies from one study to another. If the employer selects only one in five applicants and relies solely on test score, the range will be greatly restricted. If the employer selects two out of three applicants and prefers interview impression to test score, the range of test scores may not be greatly restricted.

Restricted range can account both for variability of validity coefficients (because restriction varies from one study to another) and for their generally low mean (because restriction limits validity).

Criterion reliability

Every validity study needs a criterion – that is, a quantifiable index of successful work performance (discussed in Chapter 11). Whatever criterion is used will be less than perfectly reliable. The most widely used criterion – supervisor rating – has poor reliability. Schmidt and Hunter's (1984) estimate is 0.60. The next most widely used criterion – training grades – is more reliable. Schmidt and Hunter's estimate is 0.80. Objective measures, such as output, achieve a reliability of 0.73 according to Hunter *et al.* (1990). An unreliable criterion is difficult to predict, and necessarily reduces the correlation between predictor and criterion, which cannot exceed the square root of criterion reliability. If criterion reliability is 0.60, validity cannot exceed $\sqrt{0.60}$, which is 0.77. Criterion reliability varies from one validity study to another, which will cause variations in the validity coefficients. Suppose that the criterion in study A has a reliability of 0.75, while the criterion in study B achieves a reliability of only 0.45 (because the raters in study B are not as conscientious, or as well trained, or are not using such a good rating system). The validity in study B cannot exceed $\sqrt{0.45}$ (i.e. 0.67), whereas in study A it could be as high as $\sqrt{0.75}$ (i.e. 0.86).

Criterion unreliability can account both for variability of validity coefficients (because unreliability varies from one study to another) and for their generally low mean (because criterion unreliability limits validity).

Test reliability

Validity is limited by test reliability, which also *varies from one study to another*, contributing a fourth source of variation in validity coefficients.

Test unreliability can account both for the variability of validity coefficients (because unreliability varies from one study to another) and for their generally low mean (because test unreliability limits validity).

Question 1. Why do validity coefficients vary so much?

All four limitations of the typical validity study increase error variance in validity coefficients. All four limitations themselves vary from one study to another, which means that the highest validity coefficient possible also varies. Suppose that the four sources of error in validity were sufficient to explain all of the variation about the mean. According to this argument, all of the variation in Ghiselli's distributions (*see* Figure 6.2) is effectively random error or noise, so trying to interpret it by moderator variables is futile. This argument also implies that in a series of ideal validation studies, the validity coefficient will remain constant.

Validity generalisation analysis (VGA) asks whether we can explain all of the variation in validity coefficients as noise in the system, or whether there is some real variation, even after we have allowed for noise. VGA compares *observed variance* with *estimated variance*. Observed variance is the extent to which validity varies, and is expressed as the SD of the validity coefficients. Estimated variance is the extent to which one would expect validity to vary, given what we know – or can estimate – about the sources of error.

VGA estimates how much variance in validity the four sources of error could account for (*estimated variance*), and then compares this estimate with the actual variance (*observed variance*) to see whether there is any variation (*residual variance*) left to explain. Sampling error can (usually) be calculated. Variations in range restriction and test and criterion reliability can sometimes be calculated if the authors of the study provide details, but VGA more often uses estimates of the likely distribution of restricted range, criterion reliability, etc. Pearlman, Schmidt and Hunter (1980) give computational details. *Zero residual variance* means that there is no variance left when the four sources of error have been subtracted from the observed variance. There is no true variation in validity. Validity is the same in every study included in the analysis, and only appears to vary because it is not measured accurately. If the residual variance is zero, the hypothesis of situational specificity can be rejected.

Table 6.4 Validity generalisation analysis of the data shown in Figure 6.2, based on data given by Schmidt and Hunter (1977).

Job	Mechanical repairman	Bench worker	Clerk	Machine tender
Test	Mechanical principles	Finger dexterity	General mental ability	Spatial relations
Number of validity coefficients	114	191	72	99
Raw median validity	0.39	0.25	0.36	0.11
Observed variance of validity	0.21	0.26	0.26	0.22
Estimated variance of validity	0.19	0.14	0.17	0.12
Observed minus estimated variance	0.02	0.12	0.09	0.10
Percentage of observed variance accounted for	90%	54%	65%	54%
Estimated mean true validity	0.78	0.39	0.67	0.05
90% credibility value	0.75	0.24	0.50	−0.03

Table 6.4 applies VGA to the four sets of Ghiselli's data in Figure 6.2. Table 6.4 shows that between 54% and 90% of the *observed variance* in validity can be accounted for by the four artefacts. In research on testing repairmen with tests of mechanical principles, 90% of the variation in size of correlations can be explained by the four limitations, which suggests that the correlation does not 'really' vary much. However, in research on testing bench workers with finger dexterity tests, only 50% of the variation in validity can be explained by the four limitations, which suggests that validity does 'really' vary.

Schmidt *et al.* (1980a) suggested that there are other sources of error besides the four described (e.g. careless mistakes by researchers) which could explain more variation in validity. They suggested that if the four main limitations can explain 75% of the observed variance, one could regard the remaining 25% as potentially explainable as well, and could conclude that validity does not really vary. Hermelin and Robertson (2001) noted other limitations of validation research that could lead to underestimation of validity, namely *indirect range restriction* and *range restriction in work performance measures*. Indirect restriction means that candidates are screened by some measure that correlates with the predictor. For example, it is common to require minimum educational qualifications, which tends to select out the less bright, creating indirect restriction of range of mental ability. Restriction of range of work performance occurs when the very good have been promoted, and the very poor have left (either voluntarily or at the organisation's insistence). Neither group then contributes to the validity coefficient, which would be higher if they were still present to be included.

The reader may wonder why it seems to matter so much whether the validity of tests 'really' varies, or does not 'really' vary. One reason is practical. If the correlation between mental ability and work performance is really always 0.50, then psychologists and human resource departments can use tests 'off the shelf', in the knowledge that they will work. The second reason may have more to do with the standing of psychology as a science. A true science states laws. For example, 'every schoolboy knows' Boyle's law in physics, that the pressure of a gas varies inversely with its volume. Psychology has always seemed to be short of such general laws with which to impress the lay person. Perhaps the Schmidt–Hunter law, that the correlation between mental ability and work performance is always 0.50, would fill this gap.

Question 2. Why do validity coefficients vary about such a low mean?

The traditional validity study underestimates validity, because range is restricted and because the criterion is unreliable. VGA corrects mean validity for criterion unreliability and restricted range, to find the *estimated mean true validity*. (This is not a new idea; both corrections were discussed, and sometimes made, long before VGA appeared. However, it was not usual to make *both* corrections to the same data, as VGA does.) Table 6.4 gives the estimated mean true validity for Ghiselli's four sets of data. The corrected estimates of mean validity, with one exception, are far higher than the uncorrected estimates presented by Ghiselli. As a rule of thumb, VGAs find that true validity is twice the uncorrected mean validity coefficient. The exception, namely spatial relations tests in machine tenders, shows that if validity is zero, twice zero still equals zero.

Some VGAs also correct for (un)reliability of the predictor (i.e. the ability test). Critics say that it is pointless to estimate how much more accurate selection would be if tests were perfectly reliable, because no test is perfectly reliable. Validity is necessarily limited by test reliability. For most purposes, including selection, this is true. However, researchers testing a theory of numerical ability and work performance may regard both as *constructs* that could ideally be measured perfectly reliably, and could legitimately correct for reliability of both before calculating the true correlation between the two. Some analyses distinguish between *estimated population correlation*, which is corrected for unreliability of test and criterion, and *operational validity*, which is corrected for criterion reliability only.

Some applications of validity generalisation

Nine general classes of work

Hunter and Hunter's (1984) re-analysis of Ghiselli's (1966b) database concludes that the combination of general ability, perceptual ability and psychomotor validity achieves true validities higher than 0.40 for all classes of work except sales assistants (*see* Table 6.5).

Table 6.5 Re-analysis by Hunter and Hunter (1984) of Ghiselli's (1966b) summary of estimated true validity coefficients for nine broad classes of job and three ability factors.

	General ability	Perceptual speed	Psychomotor	All three combined
Manager	0.53	0.43	0.26	0.53
Clerk	0.54	0.46	0.29	0.55
Salesperson	0.61	0.40	0.29	0.62
Protective professions	0.42	0.37	0.26	0.43
Service jobs	0.48	0.20	0.27	0.49
Trades and crafts	0.46	0.43	0.34	0.50
Elementary industrial	0.37	0.37	0.40	0.47
Vehicle operator	0.28	0.31	0.44	0.46
Sales assistants	0.27	0.22	0.17	0.28

Source: Reproduced from Hunter & Hunter (1984) by permission of the American Psychological Association © 1984.

Project A

During the 1980s, the American armed services carried out the world's largest and most expensive validation study, Project A, to re-validate the army's Armed Services Vocational Aptitude Battery (ASVAB) against five new composite criteria of military work performance (McHenry *et al.*, 1990). Project A data show that the two core job performance criteria, namely *technical proficiency* and *general soldiering proficiency*, are best predicted by general mental ability, which achieves true validities of 0.65 and 0.69, respectively. The other three criteria, namely *effort and leadership*, *personal discipline* and *fitness and military bearing*, are better predicted by personality measures (*see* Chapter 7).

Job knowledge tests

Dye, Reck and McDaniel (1993) reported a VGA for job knowledge tests, which shows an overall true validity of 0.45, rising to 0.62 where the test content is closely related to the job.

Psychomotor tests

Salgado (1994) reported a VGA of 15 Spanish studies on psychomotor tests (of dexterity and co-ordination) for pilots, mechanics and train and bus drivers, and documented an estimated mean true validity of 0.42. Two-thirds of the studies used a training-grade criterion; the other third used accident rate.

Craft jobs

Levine *et al.* (1996) analysed 167 studies, mostly in the electrical industry, and found an estimated mean true validity of 0.43. Validity was lower (0.31) for assembly jobs, which are simpler, and higher (around 0.50) for more complex jobs.

Some VGAs have failed to find a strong link between mental ability and work performance.

Achievement in science and technology

Funke *et al.* (1987) reported a VGA for various predictors of achievement in science and technology, and found that conventional mental ability tests were the poorest predictor (corrected $r = 0.13$), lagging behind creativity tests and biographical measures.

Police officers

A VGA of research on selecting police officers found that true validity was low (no more than 0.27). Hirsh, Northrop and Schmidt (1986) consider that finding an adequate criterion for police work is particularly problematic.

Pilots

Martinussen (1996) reviewed 66 European and American studies, and reported low mean validities for tests of general mental ability ($r = 0.16$) and of specific abilities ($r = 0.24$). Hunter and Burke (1994) reported a similar value ($r = 0.13$) for general mental ability, and also higher values for some specific abilities. However, neither study corrected for restricted range or criterion reliability, because the information needed was lacking. As with any pair of meta-analyses of the same body of research, one is uncertain how independent the two analyses are.

Sales ability

Two VGAs (Vinchur *et al.*, 1998; Farrell & Hakstian, 2001) both found that mental ability correlates with rated sales ability but not with actual sales figures. This is a worrying finding, because it suggests that mental ability may not predict actual work performance, but only perceived work performance.

European data

Most data on mental test validity, like most research in personnel selection, come from North America. People sometimes ask whether we can extrapolate from American research to other cultures whose approach to work may differ. Salgado and Anderson (2001) have started to address this issue with a VGA of Spanish and UK research. Table 6.6 shows that ability tests predict supervisor and training grade criteria in Europe as well as in the USA.

Incremental validity

Mental ability tests by and large predict work performance quite well. What other assessments are worth using alongside them that will give a better prediction still? Schmidt and Hunter (1998) reviewed data on validity of other predictors, and their correlation with mental ability, and concluded

Table 6.6 VGA of UK and Spanish research on mental ability tests: validity corrected for criterion reliability and restricted range but not for test reliability.

Criterion	UK		Spain	
	Supervisor rating	Training grade	Supervisor rating	Training grade
Number of samples	45	61	9	25
Total sample	7,283	20,305	1,239	2,405
Raw validity	0.18	0.34	0.36	0.35
Corrected validity	0.41	0.56	0.61	0.47

Note: Data taken from Salgado & Anderson (2001).

that personality tests, work samples and structured interviews will offer incremental validity on mental ability tests, whereas assessment centres or biodata will not. Note, however, that Schmidt and Hunter were not reviewing research which shows that, for example, personality tests *do* offer incremental validity, but research which implies that they *should*.

Different outcomes

The measure of success at work that is used in most research is supervisor rating. Supervisor ratings correlate poorly with measures of actual output where these exist (Bommer *et al.*, 1995). It is fairly easy to make a case that supervisor rating might be related to mental ability through paths other than good work. One could argue that brighter people will be less trouble to supervise, or that they will be more interesting and agreeable company, or that they will be better at seeming to do good work without actually doing so, etc. Meta-analyses of mental ability and selling show that mental ability correlates with supervisor rating but not with sales figures, which is consistent with this hypothesis (Vinchur *et al.*, 1998). It is therefore important to look more closely at how well mental ability predicts other aspects of work performance. Schmitt *et al.*'s (1984) review located some studies in which work performance was assessed by methods other than supervisor rating (*see* Table 6.7). Three

Table 6.7 Correlation of mental ability with four indices of work performance: validity corrected for restricted range and unreliability of work performance measure.

	Number of studies	Total n	Validity
Supervisor rating	25	3,597	0.32
Achievement/grades	5	888	0.44
Status change	9	21,190	0.28
Work sample	3	1,793	0.43

Note: Data taken from Schmitt *et al.* (1984).

studies using work samples, in which the worker performs key tasks and is observed by an expert, produced an average validity of 0.43. Five studies using achievement or training grades produced a similar correlation, but may suffer from shared method variance problems. Training grades have features in common with ability tests which tend to ensure a positive correlation, such as time limits, multiple-choice format and possible dependence on motivation. There is a gap in Schmitt *et al.*'s review, as there were not enough studies correlating mental output with countable output to allow a meta-analysis to be calculated.

Organisational performance

Gottfredson (1997) and Schmidt (2002) argue that organisations which employ large numbers of people of low ability will face major problems – and indeed that the American economy will suffer if large numbers of people of low mental ability are employed in important jobs. However, all of the available data on mental ability and work performance relate only to individuals. There are hundreds of studies which show that people of lower mental ability get poorer supervisor ratings or poorer training grades. This implies that organisations which employ many such people will tend to perform poorly. However, we lack any empirical demonstration of this. Gottfredson cites the Washington DC police force, which has been described in press articles as having very lax selection standards and as being very inefficient. Press reports are interesting, but they hardly constitute scientific evidence. We need detailed studies of the functioning of organisations that employ large numbers of less able people.

Another interesting line of research would be to follow through the work histories of able and less able individuals in similar jobs. If the less able on average get poorer ratings from supervisors, they will presumably be less likely to be promoted, and will possibly therefore be more likely to become less satisfied, and more likely to leave either willingly or unwillingly. It would also be useful to gain more insight into the way in which they work. Presumably the less able are more likely to make mistakes, and are possibly slower to complete a given task, etc. Hunter and Schmidt (1996) have speculated that the career of the low-ability worker will depend on their level of organisational citizenship – that is, their willingness to go beyond the letter of their job description. The less able worker who is however a good citizen will be tolerated by supervisors because he or she is obviously trying hard, and may be moved to easier work. The less able worker who is also a poor citizen is, they suggest, more likely to have their position terminated.

Moderator variables

VGA and meta-analysis allow researchers to check more systematically whether validity is moderated by gender, management style, etc. Each study is coded for gender, type of work, type of test, etc., and then the significance of differences in validity is checked by conventional statistical tests. The validity of mental ability tests does not seem to be moderated by other factors, except complexity of the job (see below). However, when VGA is applied to other selection methods (e.g. assessment centres; *see* Chapter 8), moderator variables are sometimes found.

Complexity

The US *Dictionary of Occupational Titles* includes ratings of the complexity of every job. Hunter and Hunter (1984) divided jobs into five complexity bands, and found a clear link with ability (*see* Figure 6.4). In highly complex jobs, such as those of doctor or lawyer, the correlation between mental ability and work performance is high. In less complex jobs, such as packing and handling, the correlation is much lower. Job complexity is therefore a true moderator of the validity of mental ability tests.

Credibility values

These are often used to estimate how well a selection method will work in practice. If 90% of true validity coefficients have values above 0.33, the test can be used with a nine in ten chance of achieving a true validity of at least 0.33, so 0.33 is the 90% credibility value. Table 6.4 gives 90% credibility values for the four test × job pairs analysed. Values for mechanical comprehension in repair workers and general mental ability in clerks are high, while the value for finger dexterity in bench workers is lower. Researchers often report that '90% credibility value exceeds zero', meaning that nine out of ten validity coefficients are greater than zero, so selectors can use the test with a reasonable certainty that it will predict something.

The job families argument

The situational specificity and local validity arguments held that every job was different, and so needed different selection tests. VGA makes it easy to test this

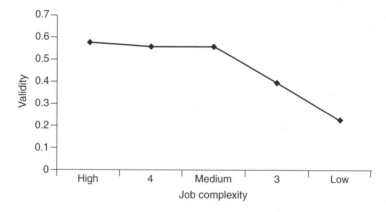

Figure 6.4 Estimated true validity of combined GATB general, verbal and numerical test composite with job performance, for five levels of job complexity. Data taken from Hunter & Hunter (1984)

hypothesis. If genuinely different jobs are grouped together in a VGA, then true residual variance will be found, indicating that test validity varies according to job type. Conversely, if grouping jobs together in a VGA does not result in true residual variance, then those jobs do not really differ in terms of how to select for them. VGA found no true residual variance, suggesting that the same tests can be used to select for all clerical jobs, from shorthand-typing, through bank clerk to mail-room staff. Similar analyses have been reported for several large sets of US military and public sector data (Schmidt & Hunter, 1978).

Implications of validity generalisation analysis

VGA has a number of very important implications, and changes the selector's perspective on a number of issues.

Mental ability tests can break the 0.30 barrier

Hunter and Hunter's (1984) re-analysis of Ghiselli's data concludes that the *mean true validity* of mental ability tests is much higher than 0.30. Their estimate averages around 0.50 for most types of work, which accounts for a quarter of the variance in work performance.

Mental ability tests are transportable

If the hypothesis of *situational specificity* is rejected, tests become *transportable*, and can be used without a local validity study. If the GATB selects good clerical workers in Washington DC, it can also select good clerical workers in Boston, San Francisco and very probably in London. Schmidt thinks that local validity studies are not very useful, and likens them to 'checking the accuracy of the powerful telescopes used in astronomy by looking at the night sky with the naked eye'.

Job analyses are not absolutely essential

Pearlman *et al.* (1980) reported that mental ability tests predict productivity equally well throughout a large hierarchical family of clerical jobs, which implies that job analysis need be no more elaborate than categorising the job as 'clerical'. (This does not mean that all job analyses are redundant. Chapter 2 lists many other uses as well as guiding the choice of measures in selection.)

Mental ability tests work for minorities

The hypothesis of *single group validity* states that tests work for majority (i.e. white) Americans, but not for minorities. The hypothesis of *differential validity* states that tests are more valid for majority than for minority individuals. Chapter 12 reviews the research in greater detail, and concludes that there is no evidence for single group validity or differential validity, which implies that tests can be used equally well for majority and minority persons in the USA.

Literature reviews are as important as empirical research

Schmidt (1992) argues that re-analyses of existing empirical research often change our view of what the research means, and so are a form of research in themselves and should not be dismissed – as they often are by some academics – as a second-class activity.

Criticisms of meta-analysis and validity generalisation

VGA has attracted its share of critics. Seymour (1988) contemptuously referred to it as the 'hydraulic' model of test validity – if your validity coefficient is not large enough, simply inflate it to the desired size by making corrections.

Reporting bias

Do meta-analyses of selection research push up average validities by leaving out studies which find that selection methods do not work? Bias can operate at the publication stage, where it is notoriously difficult to interest academic journals in 'negative' results. Most VGAs include unpublished studies, and make careful enquiries to locate them. Reporting bias could also suppress negative results well before the publication stage if researchers who find their results are inconclusive or confusing never write them up at all. Russell *et al.*'s (1994) meta-analysis showed that studies reported by academics find lower average validity than studies reported by authors employed in private industry. One possible explanation is that academics have no vested interest in showing that tests 'work'.

Researchers can estimate how likely it is that unreported studies could change conclusions about test validity. The File Drawer statistic calculates how many unreported studies with negative results would have to be hidden in researchers' file drawers in order to reduce the collective validity of the meta-analysed studies to insignificance. Callender and Osburn (1981) calculated File Drawer for their VGA of 38 validity studies in the American petroleum industry, and found that the number of unreported studies would have to be between 482 and 2,010 (i.e. improbably large). However, Ashworth *et al.* (1992) suggested that File Drawer is overly optimistic. Their proposed replacement – Null-K – gives far smaller estimates of the number of unincluded studies needed to render VGA conclusions insignificant (only 10 to 18 for the American petroleum industry).

Restricted range

How much allowance for restricted range should be made? The greater the allowance made, the greater the consequent increase in estimated true validity. Correcting for restricted range uses a formula based on the ratio of sample standard deviation to population standard deviation. The 'sample' means the successful applicants, for whom the researcher has the data to compute SD. The 'population' might mean all of the people who applied for the job, in which case it is easy to calculate that SD, too. However, often the 'population' is taken to mean everyone who *might have applied*, which makes it more difficult to find a value for their SD. One approach is to use normative data from the test's manual. Sackett and Ostgaard (1994) presented estimates of range restriction in the Wonderlic Personnel Test, comparing the SD of test scores for each of 80 jobs with the overall SD of the whole database. On average, SDs for particular jobs are 8.3% smaller than the overall SD. For 90% of jobs, restriction is less than 20%. For more complex jobs, range restriction is greater, whereas for simple jobs it is much less. Sackett and Ostgaard (1994) suggest that a mere 3% correction would be appropriate – far smaller than is implied by talking about using tests to select the best 1 in 5!

Hunter's analysis of GATB (Hunter, 1986) used a similar strategy, and also produced a fairly low estimate of range restriction, but has nevertheless proved controversial. Hunter used the SD of the whole GATB database, (i.e. of everyone who got a job in all 515 studies), as his estimate of population SD, which generates an estimate of restriction of 20%. Critics, such as Hartigan and Wigdor (1989), object to this. They argue that doctors and lawyers, at the 'top' of the GATB database, are unlikely to apply for the minimum-wage jobs at the 'bottom', while the people in minimum-wage jobs could not apply for 'top' jobs because they lack the necessary qualifications. Hartigan and Wigdor argue that the purpose of correcting validity coefficients is not to produce the largest possible correlation, but to give the test's user a realistic estimate of how well it will work in practice, avoiding underestimates that do not allow for known methodological limitations, and avoiding overestimates based on showing how efficiently the test could reject people who would never actually apply for the job.

Criterion reliability

How much allowance should be made for unreliability of the criterion measure? Again, the greater the allowance, the greater the resulting increase in estimated true validity, which creates the worrying paradox that the *less* reliable the criterion, the *higher* the true validity becomes. Assuming that the reliability of the supervisor rating criterion averages 0.60 (as Hunter's group do) increases the estimated validity by 29%. Hartigan and Wigdor prefer a more conservative assumption, that supervisor rating reliability averages 0.80, which increases raw-to-true validity by only 12%. The most recent meta-analysis (Viswesvaran, Ones & Schmidt, 1996) favours Hunter, reporting a value of only 0.52 for inter-rater reliability of supervisor ratings. Murphy and DeShon (2000) argue that the difference between supervisors should not be regarded as error, because different supervisors see different aspects of the worker's performance. Suppose that instead we used internal consistency reliability. This is much higher – 0.86 in the meta-analysis by Viswesvaran *et al.*, which will only increase validity by 8%.

Table 6.8   Two analyses of the GATB database, by Hunter (1986) and Hartigan & Wigdor (1989).

	Hunter's analysis	Hartigan & Wigdor's analysis
Number of studies	515	755
Number of subjects	38,000	76,000
Mean raw validity	0.25	0.19
Criterion reliability estimate used	0.60	0.80
Restricted range estimate used	0.80	1.00
Estimated mean true validity	0.47	0.22
Variance accounted for	22%	5%

Re-analysis of GATB data

Hartigan and Wigdor re-analysed the GATB database, making different assumptions to Hunter, and reached quite different conclusions (*see* Table 6.8). They assumed that criterion reliability was 0.80, not 0.60, and they did not correct for restricted range at all. These more conservative assumptions increased validity by only 12%, whereas Hunter's more generous assumptions increased it by 40%. Furthermore, Hartigan and Wigdor started from a different, *lower*, average raw validity. They used an extended GATB database, in which the extra later studies showed lower validity than the earlier studies used in Hunter's VGA. The combined effect of these three differences was to place their estimate of the GATB's true validity at only 0.22, compared with Hunter's value of 0.47. The smaller the GATB's true validity, the less loss to American national productivity results from not using it, and the more scope there is for using personnel selection for other ends, such as creating a representative workforce.

Low power to detect true difference

VGA analyses a set of validity coefficients to check whether there is any real difference in validity, or whether the apparent variation is simple noise produced by the limitations of selection research. Critics argue that VGA lacks the statistical power to detect true differences, and they rely on simulated data to make their point. For example, Sackett, Harris and Orr (1986) created an artificial data set in which real differences in validity of 0.10 or 0.20 were included, and then applied VGA to the data. VGA could detect a true difference of 0.20 if the number of studies and the total sample size were very large, but failed to detect a true difference in validity of 0.10 at all. This implies that if the validity of mental ability tests was higher for females than for males, or vice versa, VGA might fail to detect this, and might dismiss the variation in validity as noise.

True restriction of criterion range

If the test used has any validity, then the range of criterion scores will be restricted, because using the test will exclude some poor performers.

This leads to a genuine underestimate of the test's validity, a fact that was recognised long before VGA was devised. However, suppose that the range of criterion scores is restricted for some other reason, not because some less proficient workers are not included in the analysis. James *et al.* (1992) pointed to *restrictiveness of organisational climate*, where work is highly standardised and employees are allowed little autonomy because management does not trust them. This irons out individual differences in job performance, so that everyone performs at the same mediocre level, and range is restricted. In this case, correcting for restricted range is not appropriate, because the restriction is inherent to the way in which the organisation works, and has nothing to do with selection.

g or aptitude battery?

As far back as 1928, Hull argued that profiles of specific abilities will predict work performance better than tests of general mental ability, or *g*. American industrial psychology has always preferred multiple aptitude batteries. The earliest battery was Thurstone's Primary Mental Abilities, which measured seven abilities, namely verbal, reasoning, number, spatial, perceptual speed, memory and word fluency. The General Aptitude Test Battery (GATB) measures nine abilities (*see* Table 6.9), and is very widely used in the USA because it belongs to the US Employment Service (USES). The US military has used several successive generations of aptitude battery, from the Army General Classification Test (AGCT) to the Armed Services Vocational Aptitude Battery (ASVAB). The Differential Aptitude Test (DAT) measures seven abilities, and has UK normative data.

In theory, multiple aptitude batteries should give more accurate predictions, on the assumption that each job requires a different profile of abilities (accountants need to be numerate, architects need good spatial ability, etc.). The multiple aptitude battery can be used to generate regression equations (*see* Box 3.4, page 56) for different jobs, in which each aptitude score is given a

Table 6.9 The General Aptitude Test Battery, which measures nine abilities using eight paper-and-pencil and four apparatus tests.

	Ability	Test
G	General	Vocabulary, three-dimensional space, arithmetic reasoning
V	Verbal	Vocabulary
N	Numerical	Computation, arithmetic reasoning
S	Spatial	Three-dimensional space
P	Form perception	Tool matching, form matching
Q	Clerical perception	Name comparison
K	Motor co-ordination	Mark making
F	Finger dexterity	Assemble, disassemble
M	Manual dexterity	Place, turn

different weight according to how well it predicts performance. The American military have been using such equations to select for different specialised jobs since World War Two. However, during the late 1980s some American psychologists rediscovered g, and started to ask themselves whether the extra time needed to administer the whole of the GATB or the ASVAB added much to their predictions. Thorndike (1986) analysed three large sets of data, namely DAT predicting school grades, ACB predicting training grades in military specialities, and GATB occupational data. Thorndike concluded that the gain from using differential weighting was small for the DAT and ACB, and non-existent for the GATB. Treating the GATB like a single very long test of general mental ability, scored and weighted in exactly the same way for every occupation, predicts proficiency as accurately as using differently weighted combinations for each occupation.

Ree and Earles (1991) analysed ASVAB data for nearly 80,000 US Air Force personnel doing 82 different jobs, and concluded that although ASVAB's 10 tests included:

> some seemingly specific measures of automotive knowledge, shop infor-mation, word knowledge, reading, mathematics, mechanical principles, electronic and scientific facts, as well as clerical speed... its predictive power was derived from psychometric 'g'. The training courses prepared students for seemingly different job performance, such as handling police dogs, clerical filing, jet engine repair, administering injections, and fire fighting, yet a universal set of weights across all jobs was as good as a unique set of weights for each job.

Ree and colleagues reported similar results for pilot and navigator train-ing (Olea & Ree, 1994), and for work performance in various air force specialised jobs (Ree, Earles & Teachout, 1994). Schmidt-Atzert and Deter (1993) reported similar data for the German chemical industry. Interestingly, British military research in World War two (Vernon & Parry, 1949) had earlier made the same discovery:

> We would naturally have expected the verbal and educational tests to show relatively low validities in mechanical and spatial occupations, and the mechanical spatial tests to be of value only among mechanics. But such differentiation was conspicuously small.

Hunter (1986) argued that the American preference for aptitude batteries, and sets of weights carefully tailored to specific jobs, may be another exercise in trying to read meaning into error variance. A single study may 'find' by chance that sub-tests A, C and F predict success in a particular job, but the finding will not replicate. Hunter showed that using the wrong equation (e.g. selecting mechanics using the electricians' equation) gives just as good results as using the right equation.

VG-GATB

In 1980, the US Department of Labor contracted Hunter to re-analyse the large GATB database and devise a new way of using the GATB to place job applicants. Hunter (1986) concluded that only two GATB scores, namely *general intelligence* and *psychomotor ability* (dexterity and co-ordination), were needed to predict job performance. Jobs need only to be categorised by complexity using DOT ratings; more complex jobs need general intelligence, while less complex jobs need dexterity. The VG-GATB (VG stands for validity generalisation) system was intended to place Americans into all 12,000 jobs listed in the *Dictionary of Occupational Titles* (i.e. into virtually every job in the USA) on the basis of just two scores. Hunter claimed that if the VG-GATB had been used for all four million USES placements each year, US national productivity could have increased by $79 billion. In practice, the VG-GATB was adopted by only a minority of USES offices, and was shelved in 1986 after fair employment problems (*see* Chapter 12).

Criticisms of the g hypothesis

These take two lines. Some critics argue that specific abilities *are* required for some jobs. Research has provided two examples of specific abilities that predict success in work, with g held constant. Trainee military pilots with poor visuo-spatial ability tend to fail pilot training, regardless of g (Gordon & Leighty, 1988). Fuel-tanker drivers with poor selective attention make more mistakes, holding Progressive Matrices scores constant (Arthur, Barrett & Doverspike, 1990). Other critics argue that very broad analyses covering the entire range of mental ability and of work are not detailed enough to detect true differential profile validities. Baehr and Orban (1989) pointed out that Hunter's analysis lumps all managers together. They cite data which show that technical specialists and general managers, while having equal values of g, differ markedly in specific abilities.

Mental ability and the success of teams

Selection persists in assessing the individual's character and trying to relate it to the individual's success at work. Yet most work is done by teams of people, who often depend on each other to get the job done. So should selection not consider the team as a whole? Does a successful team consist of people who are all able? Or will a mixture of ability be sufficient, or even better? Can one person of low ability hold everyone back? Will one very able person be able to get the group moving forward, or will he or she be submerged and frustrated? Will some teams fail to function at all? It seems likely that the answers to these questions will depend on the nature of the work, suggesting a very fruitful area of research.

An early study (Tziner & Eden, 1985) found a simple relationship – units in the Israeli army with higher average mental ability performed better. A more recent study by Barrick *et al.* (1998) confirmed this with groups of assembly workers. The brighter the team overall, the more they produced, and the less likely the team was to fall apart. Barrick *et al.* found no link between output and the range of ability in the group, or the presence of extremes of high or low ability. On the other hand, O'Connell *et al.* (2001) found no effect of average ability in team performance in motor manufacturing, but did find poorer team performance linked to more variation in ability, and to the presence of low scorers. The smaller the group, the stronger the effect. These results are consistent with a 'weakest link' hypothesis – that a few low scorers, or even just one, can hold the whole team back. Research on team performance will undoubtedly be a growth area, and may uncover complex relationships. However, it will also prove laborious. For example, O'Connell *et al.* (2001) had to assess 917 individuals to obtain the data necessary to calculate a correlation for 97 teams.

Why mental ability tests predict productivity

Mental ability testing has never pretended to much in the way of systematic theory. Binet's first test was written to identify slow learners in French schools, and derived its items from the convenient fact that older children can solve problems that younger ones cannot. Mental ability tests ever since have mostly been written for specific practical purposes, not as part of a general theory of human mental abilities. A very large body of past research has shown that there is a definite link between mental ability and work performance. A smaller body of current research is beginning to throw some light on *why* this is so.

Occupational differences in mental ability level

Gottfredson (1997) has reviewed the Wonderlic database, which gives means and SDs for 72 varied occupations. The highest scoring occupations are lawyer, research analyst, editor and advertising manager, the closest to average are cashier, clerical worker, sales assistant and meter reader, and the lowest scoring are packer, material handler, caretaker (janitor) and warehouse worker. However, these data merely show that people in different jobs have different average ability levels. They do not prove that they *need* particular levels of mental ability in order to perform successfully.

Threshold hypothesis

A widely held 'common-sense' view claims that, above a certain minimum level, most people are capable of doing most jobs. All that tests can accomplish is to screen out the unfortunate minority of incompetents. This view implies a threshold or step in the relationship between test scores and job proficiency (*see* Figure 6.5). Thus Mls (1935) found a clear break in truck-driving proficiency at approximately IQ 80. Any Czech soldier with an IQ over 80 was equally

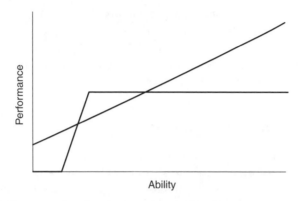

Figure 6.5   Linear vs. threshold models of the relationship between mental ability and work performance

competent to drive a truck, while all those whose IQ was below 80 were equally unfit to be trusted with an army vehicle.

Linearity hypothesis

Linearity means that work performance improves as test score increases, throughout the entire range of test scores, with no step or threshold. Several large analyses of test data show that test × performance relationships are generally linear, which implies that Mls's results with Czech army truck drivers were atypical (Waldman & Avolio, 1989; Coward & Sackett, 1990). The threshold vs. linearity issue has important implications for fair employment. Linearity implies that candidates should be placed in a strict rank order on the predictor, and selected in that order, because the higher the predictor score, the better their job performance. If the threshold hypothesis is true, all applicants in a broad band of scores will be equally suitable. The employer can then select to ensure a representative workforce without reducing overall efficiency.

Setting cut-off scores

Selectors are often asked whether a particular candidate is appointable – in other words, what is the minimum level of mental ability necessary to function in that job. Gottfredson (1988) stated that only 10–20% of the general population have enough general mental ability to achieve 'minimally acceptable performance' as a physician, whereas 80% have enough to function as a licensed practical nurse. The commonest approach to setting cut-offs is *distribution based* – do not appoint anyone who falls within the bottom one-third of existing post-holders, or more than one SD below the mean. The *contrasting groups* method nominates groups of definitely satisfactory and unsatisfactory employees, and hopes to find a cut-off that clearly distinguishes them. Strictly speaking, the idea of a fixed cut-off is simplistic. The relationship between test score and performance is linear and probabilistic – the *lower* the test score, the *poorer* the person's performance is *likely* to be. This implies that any cut-off must be arbitrary. If the employer has sufficiently good records, it may be possible to construct an expectancy table (*see* Figure 6.6) showing the level of work performance expected for people with different test score ranges. The employer can decide the level of performance required and then set the cut-off accordingly.

Necessary but not sufficient

Herrnstein (1973) argued that mental ability is *necessary but not sufficient* for good work performance. Table 6.10 shows that few accountants had IQs more than 15 points below the accountant average, whereas quite a few lumberjacks had IQs well *over* their average of 85. Assuming that the latter had not always wanted to be lumberjacks, the data imply that they either could not or did not

Test score	Appraisal rating				
	Very poor	Poor	Average	Good	Very good
Very good	7	15	20	37	21
Good	6	20	32	31	11
Average	11	18	44	20	7
Poor	13	36	33	15	3
Very poor	26	31	23	18	2

Figure 6.6 Expectancy table showing relationship between test score and work performance

Table 6.10 Average scores of accountants and lumberjacks conscripted into the US Army during World War Two, and 10th and 90th percentiles.

	10th percentile	Median	90th percentile
Accountants	114	129	143
Lumberjacks	60	85	116

use their mental ability to find more prestigious work. Perhaps they lacked some other important quality, such as energy, social skill, good adjustment or luck. Research shows that personality tests have *incremental validity* (*see* Chapter 7) over mental ability tests, which confirms Herrnstein's hypothesis that mental ability alone is not always sufficient for success.

Do we need both motivation and ability?

It is plausibly argued that people need both ability and motivation to succeed in work – lazy geniuses achieve little, while energetic but dim people are just a nuisance. Sackett, Gruys and Ellingson (1998) tested this theory with four separate sets of data, including 22 different jobs, and found no evidence for it – ability and motivation do not interact. Mount, Barrick and Strauss (1999) similarly found no evidence that ability and conscientiousness interact to predict performance.

Class and education

Sociologists argue that any apparent link between occupation and mental ability is a creation of the class system. Children from better-off homes get a better education, so do better on mental ability tests, which are in any case heavily biased towards the middle classes. Better-off children then go on to get better-paid jobs. According to this argument there is no true link between mental ability and work performance – psychological tests are merely class-laden rationing mechanisms.

The social class argument is undermined to some extent by Wilk and Sackett's (1996) longitudinal analysis of a large cohort of Americans. The ASVAB score in 1980 predicted whether people moved up or down the occupational ladder between 1982 and 1987. Brighter people tended to move up the ladder into work of greater complexity, while less able people tended to move down into work of lower complexity. This implies that the less mentally able find themselves less able to cope with complex work, and gravitate to work that is more within their intellectual grasp – something which would not happen if the ASVAB was just an arbitrary class-based way of keeping some people out of better jobs. Similarly, Barrick, Mount and Strauss (1994) found that lower mental ability correlates with poorer job rating, which in turn correlates with losing one's job during downsizing.

Box 6.5   Path analysis

This is essentially a correlational analysis in which the researcher is prepared to make some assumptions about direction of cause. To take an obvious example, height might affect success as a police officer, but it is virtually impossible to make any case for being successful as a police officer having any effect on one's height. Path analysis is generally calculated by structural equation modelling, which tests the fit of various models to the data.

Mental ability, job knowledge and work performance

Recent research uses *path analysis* to explore why mental ability tests predict work performance so well in such a wide range of jobs. Hunter (1983) found that general mental ability did not correlate directly with supervisor ratings, but did correlate with job knowledge and work sample performance, which in turn correlated with supervisor ratings. Figure 6.7 shows that more able people are better workers primarily because they learn more quickly what the job is about. In high-level work, this may mean learning scientific method, scientific techniques and a large body of knowledge. In low-level work it may only mean learning where to find the broom, and where to put the rubbish when you have swept it up. There is no direct path from mental ability to work performance. Ree, Carretta and Teachout (1995) presented a path analysis for mental ability, job knowledge and actual job performance. In US Air Force trainee pilots, *g* led to job knowledge, in the shape of better grades in navigation. Job knowledge in turn led (less strongly) to better ratings of their flying ability in check flights.

An unemployable minority?

Over 60 years ago, Cattell (1936) made some pessimistic comments about employment prospects for people with limited mental ability in a complex industrial society: 'the person of limited intelligence is not so cheap an employee as he at first appears. His accident proneness is high and he cannot adapt himself to changes in method'. More recently, Gottfredson (1997) has raised the same issue, arguing that the American armed services have three times made the experiment of employing low-aptitude recruits – once when short of recruits during World War Two, once as an idealistic experiment during the 1960s, and once by mistake in the early 1980s when they miscalculated their norms. Gottfredson notes that 'these men were very difficult and costly to train, could not learn certain specialities, and performed at a lower average level once on a job.' Low-aptitude recruits took between two and five times as long to train, and their training might need to be stripped of anything theoretical or abstract. Hunter and Schmidt (1996) suggested that the less able can only get minimum-wage jobs, which do not pay enough to raise a family, so

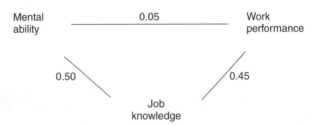

Figure 6.7   Schematic path diagram showing the paths from mental ability to work performance

are only suitable as short-term jobs for young people. What is the threshold of unemployability? Cattell estimated it to be IQ 85, while Gottfredson mentions an IQ of 80. However, there is no research on what proportion of people with limited mental ability are unemployed or unemployable. Many other commentators refer to an *underclass* of unemployed and disaffected individuals. However, only Herrnstein and Murray (1994) have specifically linked mental ability and the underclass.

Hunter and Schmidt (1996) suggested that America should consider a two-tier economy in ability and fair employment law. The first tier is international, where the country must be competitive, so employers must be free to select the most able. The second tier is the domestic economy, which is not subject to foreign competition, and here the reduced efficiency caused by employing the less able will cause less harm. What sectors fall within this second tier? Hunter and Schmidt only mention catering, insurance, hairdressing and cosmetology.

A problem with ability testing

In the USA, practice and coaching in ability tests are very widespread, and are provided on a commercial basis. Kulik, Bangert-Downs and Kulik's (1984) review showed that practice and coaching improved scores on mental ability tests to a modest extent (about half an SD on the same test and a quarter of an SD on similar tests). This is sufficient to affect selection decisions if some candidates have had practice and coaching and others have not. Barrett (1997) was more pessimistic, and said that American employers should not use a test more than once, for if they did, 'the only applicants who will not receive a near perfect score would be those who couldn't afford the $1,000 or more often charged for a "test-preparation seminar"'. Barrett was suggesting that some professionals in the USA will misuse their access to test material to give test takers an unfair advantage. Barrett also pointed out that a *closed* test (one used only by that employer and not accessible to outsiders) can still be compromised very easily. The first set of people to take the test conspire to reconstruct it, each person memorising seven items. They then give or sell their reconstruction to subsequent intakes.

Law, fairness and minorities

Mental ability tests create a major adverse impact on some sections of the American population. Roth *et al.* (2001) reported a meta-analysis which found a difference between white and African–Americans of 1.10 SDs, and between white and Hispanic Americans of 0.72 SDs. Other American minorities do not share this pattern. For example, Americans of Chinese or Japanese ancestry score better on ability tests than white Americans (Vernon, 1982). Avolio and Waldman (1994) analysed GATB scores for 30,000 people and reported very small age and gender differences. Hough, Oswald and Ployhart (2001) provided a detailed review of group differences in ability test scores. Differences between groups create major problems when using tests in selection, and many systems for using test scores have been proposed.

Top down

The higher the ability test score, the better the consequent work performance, which implies that employers should always choose the highest scorers to fill a vacancy (unless they have some other valid predictor). This is called *top-down* selection. However, in the USA, strict application of *top down* will greatly reduce the number of people from some ethnic minorities who are selected, and will virtually exclude them in some cases. This outcome is likely to prove politically unacceptable.

Top-down quota

The *top-down quota* is a possible compromise. The employer decides what proportion of people appointed shall come from ethnic minorities, and then selects the best minority applicants, even though their test scores may be lower than those of majority persons who are not appointed. This is effectively a formal quota for minorities, but one which selects the most able minority applicants.

Separate norms

The VG-GATB system employed separate norms for white and African–Americans. A raw score of 300 on the GATB translated into a percentile of 45 for white Americans, compared with a percentile of 83 for African–Americans. Separate norms have the advantage of avoiding setting a formal quota, which often proves to be a focus of discontent, but they do require adequate normative data for minority applicants.

Both top-down quota and separate norms represent an acceptable compromise between maximising productivity and achieving a representative workforce. However, both systems became unpopular in the USA because of allegations of reverse discrimination, and both were forbidden by the Civil Rights Act 1991. Neither system is formally prohibited in the UK, but both could be viewed as direct discrimination, so are considered to be unsafe.

Fixed bands

Score banding means that raw scores between, for example, 25 and 30 are regarded as equivalent. Some ability test manuals provide score bands, but the principle will be most familiar to American readers in the shape of college grades, and to UK readers in the shape of degree classes. Banding of scores makes them easier to describe, at the expense of loss of some information. The main limitation of score bands will also be familiar to American and UK readers. The difference between grade B and grade A, or a lower second and an upper second is one mark, which is bad luck for those who are short of that one mark.

Traditional bands are arbitrary, whereas present banding systems are based on error of measurement. The band is usually defined as two s.e.ds extending down from the highest scorer (Cascio *et al.*, 1991). The reasoning is that scores

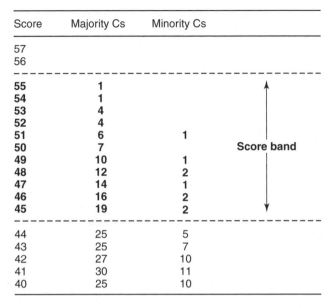

Score	Majority Cs	Minority Cs	
57			
56			
55	1		
54	1		
53	4		
52	4		
51	6	1	
50	7		Score band
49	10	1	
48	12	2	
47	14	1	
46	16	2	
45	19	2	
44	25	5	
43	25	7	
42	27	10	
41	30	11	
40	25	10	

Figure 6.8 Illustration of a score band. The first column represents scores on a selection test. The second column represents the number of white people achieving that score. The third column represents the number of minority people achieving that score

that do not differ by more than two s.e.ds do not differ significantly at the 5% level. In Figure 6.8, the highest scorer scores 55, and two s.e.ds cover 11 raw score points, so the band starts at 55 and extends down to include 45. Within this band all candidates are regarded as equal. If everyone within the band is defined as having an equal score, the employer can then give preference to minority persons without engaging in reverse discrimination. This is called *diversity-based referral.*

A number of criticisms of *banding* have been made.

- Banding fails to distinguish individual scores and average scores. It is true that candidates who score 55 and 54 are interchangeable in the sense that if they do the test again in a week's time, they could change places and score 54 and 55. However, it is also true that in a large enough sample, people who score 55 will perform significantly better on average than people who score 54. This follows necessarily from the fact that test and work performance are linearly related (Schmidt & Hunter, 1995).
- The two-s.e.d. criterion suggested by Cascio *et al.* (1991) creates a fairly broad band, amounting to nearly one SD in test scores in the example they presented.
- If the test is not very reliable, the size of the band can extend to cover most of the range of scores.
- Banding will not look very fair to an unsuccessful candidate who scores one point outside the band, with a score of 44, and who does not differ

significantly from most of those appointed, using exactly the same reasoning and calculation as are used to define the band.

Anguinis, Cortina and Goldberg (1998) argue that we should base bands on expected work performance, not on test scores. Given that most work performance measures are less reliable than most tests, and given that the relationship between test and work performance is far less than perfect, the effect of their suggestion would be to broaden bands still further, and so make selection even less selective.

Sliding band

This takes the error-of-measurement argument one stage further, by moving the boundaries of the band once the top scorers have been appointed. Figure 6.9 illustrates the method.

- The top scorer, who scores 55, is selected, whereupon the band slides so that its upper limit is now 54 and its lower limit is 44. The band now includes 30 new people scoring 44, who were previously one point outside it. Five of these are minority people who can benefit from diversity-based referral. The guiding principle is that one should not exclude candidates who do not differ reliably from those who are appointed.

Score	Majority Cs	Minority Cs	
57			
56			
			Original upper limit
55	1		
			New upper limit after 'sliding' once
54	1		
			New upper limit after 'sliding' twice
53	4	1	
52	4	1	
51	6	2	
50	7	2	
49	10	2	
48	12	3	
47	14	3	
46	16	4	
45	19	4	
			Original lower limit
44	25	5	
			New lower limit after 'sliding' once
43	25	7	
			New lower limit after 'sliding' twice
42	27	10	
41	30	11	
40	25	10	

Figure 6.9 Illustration of a sliding score band, showing the new boundaries of the score band after it has slid once, and then after a second time

- The employer selects the majority person who scores 54, so the band can slide down one more point, to include the 25 majority people and 7 minority people who score 43. The nearer to the mean the score band gets, the more people and the more minority people a change of one score point will bring into it.

Two criticisms of *sliding bands* have been made.

1. The score band tends to be fairly broad to start with. Sliding it a few times makes it even broader, and consequently makes selection that much less selective.
2. The top scorer(s) must be selected before the band can slide. This means that the successful applicants will tend to consist of majority people selected by *top down* because they are at the top of the sliding band, and minority people selected because they are minority people.

Bands, whether fixed or sliding, have been criticised as a 'fudge' – complicated and ingenious, but a fudge none the less. They are one way to try to achieve two apparently not very compatible goals, namely appointing the best while also creating a representative workforce. However, the legal position is uncertain (Campion *et al.*, 2001). Score banding is accepted by American courts, but giving preference to minority people within bands may not be legal.

A *dissenting voice*

Schmidt (2002) considers that the search for an ability test that does not create adverse impact on American minorities is mistaken, and doomed to failure. He notes that average differences in *work performance* are also found between majority and minority people. Meta-analyses of both supervisor rating (Kraiger & Ford, 1985) and objective criteria show differences of around half a standard deviation. This implies that a valid predictor of work performance must also find a difference between majority and minority. A predictor that did not find a difference would not reflect differences in work performance, and would therefore lack validity.

Ways of reducing adverse impact

The 'holy grail' of American selection psychologists is a test of intellectual ability that does not have an adverse impact. Many modifications to conventional tests have been tried in the hope of achieving this.

- Computer rather than paper administration reduces adverse impact (Carey, 1994).
- Video presentation of a situational judgement test creates much less adverse impact than the paper form (Chan & Schmitt, 1997). However, a video version of the Multistate Bar exam for lawyers did not reduce adverse impact at all (Sackett, 1998).

- Providing a social context to test items reduces adverse impact (DeShon *et al.*, 1998).
- Spoken rather than written responses may reduce adverse impact (Outtz, 1998).
- Adverse impact in a firefighters' test is reduced by changing from a conventional multiple-choice format to either writing in one's own response, or marking on a picture the best place to start fighting the fire. This makes scoring slower and slightly less reliable. Arthur, Edwards and Barrett (2002) suggest that dropping multiple choice reduces the length of the test, and thus reduces the amount of reading that is required.
- Lowering the reading level of a situational judgement test from 14th grade (approximately age 18 years) to 10th grade (approximately age 14 years) reduces adverse impact (Sacco *et al.*, 2000).
- It was discovered early on that 'culture-free' tests such as Raven's progressive matrices do not reduce adverse impact.
- Several studies that have been reviewed by Sackett *et al.* (2001) suggest that giving people more time to complete the test will not reduce adverse impact, and may even increase it.

Outside the USA

The adverse impact of mental ability tests has been documented in Israel, on Israelis of non-European origin (Zeidner, 1988), and in The Netherlands. te Nijenhuis and van der Flier (1997) have presented data for large samples of immigrant and native applicants for jobs on the Dutch railways, and found differences on most GATB sub-tests. The differences were greater on tests with a verbal element, but the data also showed substantial differences on tests that did not require a knowledge of Dutch. The immigrants came from a wide range of other countries in the Far East, the Near East and North Africa. Information about ethnic differences in test scores in the UK is conspicuous by its absence.

Other ways of assessing mental ability

Mental ability tests have the advantages of economy, reliability and validity. However, they also have problems of adverse impact and extreme unpopularity. Are there any other ways of assessing mental ability? Schmidt and Hunter's (1998) analysis of incremental validity indicates that there are. They argue that assessment centres, biodata and unstructured interviews all assess little else apart from mental ability. Work samples, structured interviews and job knowledge tests are highly correlated with mental ability, although they are also assessing something else. In the USA, *authentic assessment* is popular in education. Candidates are assessed from portfolios of intellectual achievements, on the topic of their choice, in the form of their choice. This approach is likely to be neither very reliable nor very useful for many selection decisions, because it is difficult to compare people.

Key points

In Chapter 6 you have learnt the following.

- Mental ability tests are the focus of much controversy.
- There are various types of ability test, some of which are more specialised while others are more general.
- There are various ways of presenting and interpreting test scores.
- Test scores are not perfectly reliable, and there are various ways of estimating reliability.
- Validation research has methodological limits, including small samples, unreliable work performance measures and restricted range, that create the impression of low validity. Research therefore needs to be analysed carefully.
- Validity generalisation analysis is intended to generate an accurate estimate of test validity. Validity generalisation analysis also suggests that validity of mental ability tests may be fairly constant, and that the true relationship between mental ability and work performance is stronger than it seems.
- Mental ability tests predict work performance fairly well – as well as any other method available. The relationship between mental ability and work performance is continuous and linear – the brighter someone is, the more likely their work performance is to be good.
- Research on mental ability and team (rather than individual) performance suggests the existence of more complex relationships. Low scorers may hold the whole team back.
- Research on why mental ability tests predict work performance is less well developed, but suggests that mental ability leads to improved job knowledge, which in turn leads to better work performance.
- Mental ability tests create a large adverse impact on some ethnic minorities in the USA. There is a dearth of information on this issue elsewhere.
- Attempts to solve the adverse impact problem in the USA include trying to identify features of mental ability testing that will reduce adverse impact.
- Attempts to deal with the adverse impact problem in the USA include score banding, which defines a range of scores as equivalent, thus allowing selection within the band to be based on achieving diversity.

Key references

Campion *et al.* (2001) answer questions about score banding in the use of mental ability tests.

Gottfredson (1997) argues that mental ability genuinely predicts work performance. She also presents data on occupational differences in the Wonderlic personnel test.

Hermelin and Robertson (2001) provide a critical review of validity generalisation analysis.

Hunter and Hunter (1984) present one of the earliest comprehensive meta-analytical reviews of selection method validity.

O'Connell *et al.* (2001) present data on mental ability in teamwork, suggesting that low scorers may hold back the entire team.

Ree and Earles (1991) present data which suggest that general mental ability predicts work performance as efficiently as differential aptitude batteries.

Ree *et al.* (1995) present a path analysis of mental ability and flying performance in US military pilots.

Roth *et al.* (2001) present an up-to-date account of ethnicity differences in mental ability in the USA.

Salgado and Ones (2001) present UK and Spanish data on the validity of mental ability tests.

Schmidt and Hunter (1981) argue forcefully for the predictive power of mental ability in the workplace.

Schmidt and Hunter (1998) analyse the likely incremental validity of various other selection tests over mental ability tests.

Schmidt *et al.* (1985a) answer 40 questions about validity generalisation analysis.

Seymour (1988) provides a critical account of validity generalisation analysis.

Useful websites

www.ase-solutions.co.uk. ASE, UK publisher of ability tests.
www.shl.com. Saville & Holdsworth Ltd, UK publisher of ability tests.
www.internationalmta.org. International Military Testing Association; includes conference proceedings.
www.psychcorp.com. The Psychological Corporation, US publisher of ability tests.

CHAPTER 7

Personality tests

Total awareness of bottom-line vitality

Defining personality

Advertisements for sales staff list the traits that are considered to be essential for selling – commitment, enthusiasm, smartness, discipline, dynamism, flair, drive, resilience, acumen, self-motivation, etc. One advert for the position of sales manager creates a series of bizarre, even indecent images by specifying 'thrusters – pro-active and professional in interpersonal skills – with total awareness of bottom-line vitality' (but neglects to say what the product is).

There are a number of different models of personality (Cook, 1993):

- trait – a set of 5 to 10 traits
- factor – 16 statistical abstractions
- social learning – bundles of habits
- motives – a profile of needs
- phenomenological – the way that the person sees the world
- self – the way that one sees oneself
- psychoanalytic – a system of defences
- constitutional – inherited neuropsychological differences.

Most industrial psychologists adopt, explicitly or implicitly, the trait or factor models. Personality traits are 'neuropsychic system[s]...with the capacity to render many stimuli functionally equivalent, and to initiate and guide consistent (equivalent) forms of adaptive and expressive behaviour' (Allport, 1937). Traits are mechanisms within individuals that shape the way in which they react to classes of event and occasion. A trait summarises past behaviour and predicts future behaviour. Factors have much in common with traits, but are derived by statistical analysis.

Mischel's criticisms

Is there anything there to define? In the late 1960s, many psychologists began to question the very existence of personality. Mischel (1968) reviewed evidence, much of it by no means new even then, which seemed to show that behaviour was not consistent enough to make general statements about personality meaningful. Consider the trait of honesty, which reference requests often ask about. Hartshorne and May's Character Education Inquiry, in the late 1920s, found that seven sets of measures of honesty correlated very poorly, which implies that it is not very informative to describe someone as 'honest' unless one specifies when, where, with what and with whom. Mischel reviewed similar evidence for other traits that often feature in job descriptions, namely extraversion, punctuality, curiosity, persistence, and attitude to authority. Mischel's critique was so influential that even now some psychologists tend to think personality research has been conclusively discredited. In fact, new research and re-analysis of old research dealt with most of Mischel's points.

- Hartshorne and May's tests of honesty, although very ingenious, were single-item tests, so it is not surprising that they intercorrelated poorly. Single-item tests are inherently unreliable and unlikely to predict much.
- One solution is *aggregation*. Epstein (1979) averaged measures of extraversion, forgetfulness, mood and carefulness across six days, and found that he obtained stable, useful measures, which implies that the answer may lie in collecting sufficient data.
- Industrial psychologists note that personality research shares many of the features of selection research, such as small samples, restricted range, unreliable tests and unreliable outcomes. What personality research does not share is the use of VGA to correct correlations for these defects, or much awareness of the dangers of doing correlational research with small samples. Meta-analysis and VGA tend to give a more consistent and (slightly) more positive view of the value of personality tests as predictors of behaviour, including work performance.

Measuring personality

There are many approaches to assessment of personality.

1. *Observation*. The Thought Police in Orwell's *1984* could watch everyone all the time by omnipresent CCTV: 'You had to live. . .in the assumption that every sound you made was overhead and, except in darkness, every movement scrutinised' (Orwell, 1949/1984, p. 158). Personnel managers have considerably less power, and can only observe a limited, carefully edited performance that lasts for between the 30 minutes of a typical interview and the 3 days of a long assessment centre. Nor can they observe applicants' thoughts and feelings. If continuous observation represents the ideal way of assessing personality, then all other methods could be regarded as short cuts.
2. *Situational/behavioural tests*. How does X behave in a particular situation? Waiting for behaviour to occur naturally is very time-consuming. The situational test saves time by contriving an occasion for significant behaviour to occur. The War Office Selection Board used *command tasks* which give candidates the opportunity to demonstrate leadership (*see* Chapter 8).
3. *Peer ratings and references*. What do other people think of X? Another short cut, already discussed in Chapter 4, is to ask someone who knows the

person well to describe him or her, in the form of references, ratings and checklists.

4. *Biodata and weighted application blanks*. Is X the sort of person who will stay with the company? Biographical methods, already discussed in Chapter 5, look for aspects of the person's background that can predict work behaviour.

5. *Projective tests*. What are X's motives, complexes and defences? People react to being observed, and may not tell the truth about themselves or others. Projective tests are intended to bypass these defences and make people reveal their personality despite themselves. Projective tests assume that people *project* their motives and complexes into what they see in drawings, how they complete stories, or how they interpret ambiguous material.

6. *Laboratory/physiological tests*. Can we assess X's personality without asking X or anyone else? Some purely physical tests of personality have been described, but few of them are practical propositions for selection work. For example, Hare's (1970) research on psychopathic personality showed that psychopaths do not react physically to the threat of an electric shock. Apart from the likely unpopularity of giving job applicants electric shocks, the method has a high false-positive rate, meaning that it would incorrectly identify as psychopaths many people who are not.

7. *Archive data*. What do the files say about X? When deciding whether it is safe to release violent offenders from prison, information from prison files about aggressive or threatening behaviour, and from school records about disruptive behaviour in childhood, help to make accurate predictions (Quinsey *et al.*, 1998). Concerns over privacy make it unlikely that this type of information could be used in selection decisions.

8. *Questionnaire/inventory*. What does X say about his or her own behaviour? Observation is time-consuming – it can easily take 15 minutes to observe a single act by a single person. A very good short cut is the questionnaire or inventory. Instead of watching the person to see if he or she talks to strangers, one asks 'Are you afraid of talking to strangers?'. Questionnaires are very economical. Within 15 minutes one can ask 100 questions of as many people as one can assemble. The questions can tap thoughts and feelings, as well as behaviour. For example, 'Do you often long for excitement?' or 'Are you sometimes troubled by unusual thoughts?'.

Method variance

Questionnaire measurements of different traits often correlate very well. Similarly, ratings of different traits often correlate very highly. This effect, known as *method variance*, means that assessors should ideally measure every trait by two *different* types of measure – *multi-trait, multi-method measurement*. This is not always easy in practice, nor does it always seem to work, as research on assessment centres (*see* Chapter 8) has found.

Personality inventories

Personality questionnaires, or inventories, are what most people think of as 'personality tests'. Inventories use various formats, different ways of interpreting scores, different ways of choosing the questions to ask, and different ways of deciding what aspects of personality to measure.

Item format

Table 7.1 illustrates three item formats. Some inventories use *endorsement* items, which are quicker and easier for subjects. However, more and more tests are using *rating* format. The *forced-choice* format equates the attractiveness of the alternatives, to try to limit faking. The Crippen/Ripper item in Table 7.1, said to come from a real inventory, offers subjects a difficult and unpleasant choice – *either* a poisoner *or* someone who mutilates people after murdering them, and both long dead. Forced choice may create correlations between the scales, which can give misleading results (see above).

Interpreting inventory scores

A raw score on a personality inventory, like a raw score on a mental ability test, means little. It must be related to a population – people in general, bank managers, bus drivers, students, etc. Good normative data are vital, and distinguish good tests from worthless imitations of a personality test. Several major inventories that are used in the UK have normative data based on large, representative cross-sections of the general population. Examples include the 16 Personality Factors (16 PF), the Occupational Personality Questionnaires (OPQ) and the California Psychological Inventory (CPI).

Table 7.1   Three personality inventory item formats.

Endorsement format items:		
I like meeting new people	True	False
I usually let other people decide what to do	True	False
Do you trust psychologists?	Yes	No
Forced-choice format items:		
On your day off would you rather paint a picture or paint your house?		
Would you rather be Dr Crippen or Jack the Ripper?		
Which of these words do you prefer?	Profit	Prophet

Rating Format:

I wait to find out what important people think before offering an opinion
    Never   5   4   3   2   1   Always
I spend my evenings at home watching television
    Never   5   4   3   2   1   Always
I feel tired at the end of the day
    Never   5   4   3   2   1   Always

Box 7.1 *T* scores

The *T* score is a form of standard score in which the mean is set at 50 and the SD is set at 10. A raw score is converted into a *T* score using the formula $T = 50 + [10 \times (\text{raw score} - \text{mean})/\text{SD}]$. For example, a raw score of 30 on CPI dominance converts into a *T* score of 67, using the UK national normative data in which the raw score mean is 18.78 and the SD is 6.54. *T* scores give the same information as *z* scores (*see* page 98) but avoid decimal points and minus signs.

Several variations on the *standard score* theme are used to interpret raw scores (*see* Figure 7.1). Many inventories (e.g. the CPI) use *T scores* (*see* Box 7.1). Cattell's 16 personality factors (16 PF) and the OPQ both use *sten scores* (*see* Box 7.2).

Box 7.2 sten scores

The sten is a form of standard score, in which the mean is set at 5.5 and the SD at 1.5. The effect is to divide the distribution into ten bands, each covering half a standard deviation.

Keying and validation

The way in which the items are chosen distinguishes a list of questions thrown together, like an 'Are you boring?' magazine quiz, from a proper personality

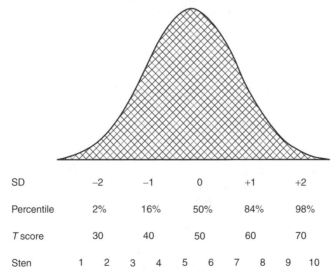

SD	−2	−1	0	+1	+2
Percentile	2%	16%	50%	84%	98%
T score	30	40	50	60	70
Sten	1 2	3 4	5 6	7 8	9 10

Figure 7.1 A normal distribution of personality test scores, illustrating *T* scores and stens

test. A proper personality test is carefully constructed, and is *validated*. There are five main ways of validating personality tests.

1. *Acceptance or face validity*. People accept the test's results as accurate. This is a very weak test of validity, because people are very easily taken in by all-purpose personality profiles – the so-called *Barnum* or *horoscope* effect.
2. *Content*. The inventory looks plausible. The first personality inventory, Woodworth's Personal Data Sheet of 1917, gathered questions from lists of symptoms in psychiatric textbooks to ensure that item *content* was plausible and relevant. The first stage in writing any inventory is choosing the questions, but a good inventory does not leave it there. The second stage, namely deciding which questions to keep, uses *empirical* or *factorial* validation.
3. *Empirical*. The questions are included because they predict. The inventory is *empirically keyed* using *criterion groups* of people of known characteristics. The California Psychological Inventory (CPI) developed its Dominance scale from answers that differentiated college students who were nominated as leaders or followers. Kline (1995) argues that empirical keying risks creating scales that may assess several different traits, and may lack psychological meaning. For example, the CPI Dominance scale reflects all of the various differences between leaders and followers, and 'need not be psychologically homogeneous, since it is unlikely that any two groups would differ only on one variable'.

Box 7.3   Item whole correlation

The response to a particular dominance scale item (e.g. 'I like telling other people what to do') is correlated with the total score for the dominance scale. A positive correlation means that the item relates to the common theme of the dominance scale, whereas a low or zero correlation suggests that the item is not contributing to the scale and should be discarded.

---

4. *Factorial*. The questions have a common theme. The author chooses questions that relate to a common theme, and tests their fit by correlation and factor analysis (*see* Box 2.1 on page 24). Factor analysis estimates how many themes underlie the questions in the inventory. Cattell (1965) found 16 factors in his 187 questions. Cattell's 16 PF research was one of the earlier uses of factorial validation. Some items will turn out not to relate to any theme, and are discarded because they are not contributing anything to the questionnaire. The main statistics used are *item whole correlation*, which checks that every item in the scale contributes to the total score, and *alpha coefficient*, which estimates the internal reliability of the scale. In practice, development of a new inventory will almost always include factor analysis, regardless of how the questions are chosen.

   Critics argue that the factorial approach encourages the development of very narrow scales, which may in some cases get close to asking the same question ten times, which ensures high item whole correlations, high alpha coefficient and one clear factor, but at the possible expense of any generality of meaning. Barrett and Paltiel (1996) argued that the scales of one well-known factorial measure – OPQ Concept 5.2 – are composed of items so similar in meaning that one can replace each 8-item OPQ scale with one single carefully chosen 11-point scale (e.g. 'I am at ease in social settings'). The technical term for factors that are obtained by asking the same or very similar questions is a *bloated specific*.

5. *Item parcels/homogeneous item composites (HICs)*. These are sets of between three and six items that are highly correlated, and relate to a common theme that is narrower than a conventional trait (e.g. confidence in social situations, or having high expectations of others). HICs have more psychological meaning and are more reliable than individual items, so may be a better way to generate new scales. The Hogan Personality Inventory is based on 41 HICs which can be assembled in different sub-sets to create special scales (e.g. stress tolerance or service orientation).

Eysenck (1957) pointed out that answers to inventory items should be regarded as *signs*, not *samples* or reports of behaviour. He gave the example of 'I suffer a lot from sleeplessness', which is answered 'true' more frequently by neurotics than by controls. It does not follow that neurotics sleep less well – it could be that they actually sleep more soundly than average, but are given to complaining more. If psychologists wanted precise information about the subject's sleep patterns, they would not use vague phrases such as 'a lot', but would ask them to keep a *sleep diary*. Psychologists want an answer to the statement 'I suffer a lot from sleeplessness' for what they can *infer* from it (high Neuroticism in Eysenck's example).

The big five

Recently the idea of the big five personality dimensions (*see* Table 7.2) has become very popular (Costa, 1996). It is argued that analyses of inventory data, rating data, and data on how people use trait words all reliably find not three, nor 16, but five separate personality factors. Five is the largest number of *uncorrelated* traits that can be found in rating or questionnaire data. If six or more factors are extracted, two or more will be correlated. The big five are said to emerge reliably in many different cultures, including the USA, the UK, Germany, The Netherlands, Israel, Russia, Japan and China. Most recent analyses of personality and work behaviour and most recently written personality questionnaires have used the big five framework.

Hierarchical models

Different inventories measure different numbers of traits. The Eysenck Personality Inventory measures only two, Cattell found 16 factors, while the OPQ concept model measures 30 factors. However, there is not necessarily

Table 7.2   The big five personality factors.

Big five factor	Alternative titles	Alternative titles (reversed)
Neuroticism	Anxiety Emotionality	Emotional stability Emotional control
Extraversion	Surgency Assertiveness	Introversion
Openness	Culture Intellect	Dogmatism Closedness
Agreeableness	Likeability Friendly compliance	Antagonism
Conscientiousness	Will to achieve	Negligence

any real disagreement between Eysenck and Cattell. Cattell's 16 factors inter-correlate to some extent. Factor analysis of the 16 factors reveals *higher-order factors* – exvia/invia and anxiety – which resemble Eysenck's Extraversion and Neuroticism (*see* Figure 7.2). Sixteen scores look more useful than two or three, and 16 PF is much more widely used for selection than Eysenck's measures. Some inventories explicitly adopt a hierarchical format. The short form of the NEO measures the big five factors, while the longer form also measures six *facets* within each factor, giving a 30-scale model. For example, the Conscientiousness factor has facets of competence, order, dutifulness, achievement striving, self-discipline and deliberation.

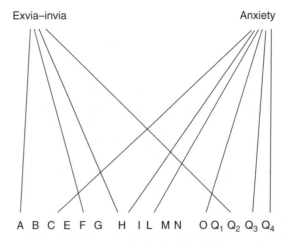

Figure 7.2   Higher-order factors, exvia-invia and anxiety, in Cattell's 16 personality factors (16 PF)

Reliability

Viswesvaran and Ones (2000) reported a meta-analysis of personality inventory reliability, which found average reliabilities of between 0.71 and 0.78. This level of reliability is consistent with some scores changing considerably over fairly short periods of time. Changes exceeding 0.5 SD (i.e. five T points or one whole sten) (*see* Figure 7.1) may be expected to occur in one in three re-tests. Changes exceeding 1 SD (i.e. ten T points or two whole stens) may be expected to occur in one in 20 re-tests.

Personality profiles and error of difference

Figure 7.3 shows a CPI profile. The score for *Do(minance)* is the highest, at one and a half SDs above the mean. The score for *So(cialisation)*, on the other hand, is nearly three SDs below the mean, indicating a person with a very low level of social maturity, integrity and rectitude. The combination of someone who is very keen to exert influence on others, and the lack of any maturity or moral standards, suggests someone who is liable to lapse into dishonesty.

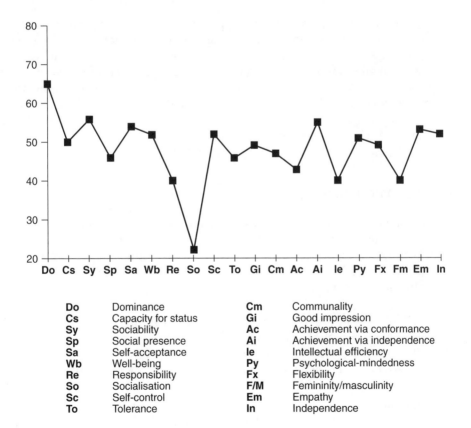

Do	Dominance	**Cm**	Communality
Cs	Capacity for status	**Gi**	Good impression
Sy	Sociability	**Ac**	Achievement via conformance
Sp	Social presence	**Ai**	Achievement via independence
Sa	Self-acceptance	**Ie**	Intellectual efficiency
Wb	Well-being	**Py**	Psychological-mindedness
Re	Responsibility	**Fx**	Flexibility
So	Socialisation	**F/M**	Femininity/masculinity
Sc	Self-control	**Em**	Empathy
To	Tolerance	**In**	Independence

Figure 7.3 CPI profile for 'John Smith'

The profile belongs to a person who ran a dating agency which was accused of taking money and failing to provide a worthwhile service in exchange.

Score profiles are a neat, quick way of presenting the data, but may encourage over-interpretation. The difference between two scores is doubly unreliable, so the difference between points on a CPI or 16 PF profile has to be quite large to merit interpretation (*see* Box 7.4).

Box 7.4   Standard error of difference (s.e.d.)

Using a multi-score personality measure often involves comparing pairs of scores. It is important to realise that the difference between two scores contains *two* sources of error. Taking 0.80 as a general estimate of CPI scale reliability gives a general estimate for s.e.d. for a pair of CPI scores of 6.3 *T* score points. This means that differences of more than 6.3 points will arise by chance in one in three comparisons, and differences of 12.6 points will arise by chance in one in 20 comparisons.

Contextualisation

Inventories such as the CPI assess personality in general, which may be a broader assessment than is needed in selection. We do not need to know what someone is like at home, and perhaps should not enquire. A general inventory may give misleading results in selection if the person describes how he or she behaves outside work. Robie *et al.* (2000) described a version of the NEO which provides a context, by inserting 'at work' into every item (e.g. 'I take great care with detail *at work*'. This might increase validity for selection, but it was also shown to raise scores – perhaps because people do behave more carefully at work – so new normative data will be needed for a contextualised NEO.

Using inventories in personnel selection

Opinion on the value of personality inventories in selection has shifted over time. In the 1960s and 1970s they were widely dismissed as useless. In the 1980s and 1990s they have grown steadily more popular, and more and more new measures have appeared. But does validation research justify this new optimism? Inventories answer four main questions.

1. Does the applicant have the right personality for the job?
2. Will the applicant be able to do the job?
3. How will the applicant behave in the workplace?
4. Does the applicant have any problems that will interfere with work?

Questions 1 and 2 look similar, but differ subtly. Question 1 is answered by comparing bank managers with people in general. Question 2 is answered by comparing successful and less successful bank managers.

Question 1. The right personality?

The Attraction Selection Attrition model argues that certain personalities are attracted to psychology (Attraction), certain personalities are selected to become psychologists (Selection) and certain personalities find that psychology does not suit them (Attrition). These three processes together may ensure that psychologists have particular personalities. Jordan, Herriot and Chalmers (1991) found that different types of British managers have different personalities, on average. R&D managers scored higher on 16 PF Conscientiousness, while finance managers scored higher on Astuteness. Schneider *et al.* (1998) analysed 142 organisations in the USA, and found differences in Myers Briggs Type Indicator types, especially Thinking/Feeling. Some organisations attract, select or retain people who base decisions on logic, while others are largely staffed by people who base decisions more on others' feelings. Some employers seem to want a book of perfect personality profiles for manager, salesman, engineer, etc. Test manuals meet this demand to some extent, by giving norms for different occupations. However, the perfect profile approach has several limitations.

- The sample sizes for occupational profiles are often too small, and cross-validation information is rarely available. Ideally, a perfect profile for a cost accountant will be based on two or more large, separate samples.
- Most perfect profiles derive from people doing the job, taking no account of how *well* they do it.
- A perfect profile may show how well people have adapted to the job's demands, not how well people with that profile will fit the job.
- The perfect profile approach may encourage *cloning* (i.e. selecting as managers only people who resemble as closely as possible existing managers). This may create great harmony and satisfaction within the organisation, but may make it difficult for the organisation to cope with any change.

Question 2. Will he or she be able to do the job?

The second, more important question is whether inventories can select people who will do their job well. A very early meta-analysis (Ghiselli & Barthol, 1953) was moderately favourable, reporting average correlations of up to 0.36 (*see* Table 7.3). Ghiselli and Barthol only included studies where they thought that the trait was relevant to the job. For example, sociability was considered relevant for sales staff but not for machinists. More reviews appeared in the 1960s and 1970s (Guion & Gottier, 1965; Lent *et al.*, 1971), which generally made depressing reading. Lent *et al.* found that only 12% of validity coefficients were significant, and Guion and Gottier found only 10%. Guion and Gottier did not systematically analyse correlation size, but of those they did cite as being significant, only half were greater than 0.30 and only 20% were greater than 0.40. However, these later reviews usually included all correlations, even where there was no reason to expect any relationship, which would tend to lower the correlation between personality and work performance. Such

Table 7.3 Validity of personality tests for selection for eight types of work.

Type of work	Number of correlations	Total sample	Correlation
Supervisor	8	518	0.14
Foreman	44	6,433	0.18
Clerical	22	1,069	0.25
Sales assistant	8	1,120	0.36
Salesperson	12	927	0.36
Protective	5	536	0.24
Service	6	385	0.16
Trades and crafts	8	511	0.29

Source: Reproduced from Ghiselli & Barthol (1953).

reviews, and Mischel's (1968) attack on the trait model, led to the general feeling that personality tests had no useful place in selection. Guion and Gottier concluded that 'it is difficult to advocate, with a clear conscience. the use of personality measures in most situations as a basis for making employment decisions'.

Subsequently, numerous *meta-analytic* reviews have been calculated, most also using *validity generalisation analysis*, and most fitting personality into a big five framework (Barrick & Mount, 1991; Tett, Jackson & Rothstein, 1991; Hough, 1992, 1998a; Ones, Viswesvaran & Schmidt, 1993; Salgado, 1997, 1998b; Vinchur *et al.*, 1998; Hurtz & Donovan, 2000). Salgado's analyses cover European research, which sometimes gets left out of American reviews. Hurtz and Donovan asked whether forcing scales that were not designed to assess the big five into a big five framework might underestimate validity, so limited their meta-analysis to true big five measures such as NEO. It turned out to make no difference to validity.

Barrick, Mount and Judge (2001) summarised all of these various meta-analyses in a meta-meta-analysis. Of the big five, Conscientiousness is most strongly associated with work performance, followed by (low) Neuroticism. The values for Extraversion, Openness and Agreeableness do not differ significantly from zero. At first sight, Table 7.4 makes depressing reading. Even making corrections for reliability and restricted range, personality tests do not predict work performance better than 0.23. They cannot even reach the 0.30 barrier, let alone break it. Barrick *et al.*'s results are no better than those reported by reviews in the 1960s and 1970s – results that made people despair of personality tests as useful predictors. However, more detailed analysis, distinguishing different types of work and examining other aspects of work behaviour, may find more encouraging results.

Different occupations

Barrick *et al.*'s meta-meta-analysis found some small differences between five broad classes of work.

Table 7.4   Meta-meta-analysis of the big five and job performance, overall and for five broad classes of work.

	Neuroticism r/ρ	Extraversion r/ρ	Openness r/ρ	Agreeableness r/ρ	Conscientiousness r/ρ
All	−0.06/−0.12	0.06/0.12	0.03/0.05	0.06/0.10	0.12/0.23
By different occupations					
Sales	−0.03/−0.05	0.07/0.09	−0.01/−0.02	0.01/0.01	0.11/0.21
Management	−0.05/−0.08	0.10/0.17	0.05/0.07	0.04/0.08	0.12/0.21
Professional	−0.04/−0.06	−0.05/−0.09	−0.05/−0.08	0.03/0.05	0.11/0.20
Police	−0.07/−0.11	0.06/0.10	0.02/0.02	0.06/0.10	0.13/0.22
Skilled	−0.08/−0.14	0.03/0.05	0.03/0.04	0.05/0.08	0.12/0.19

Note: Data taken from Barrick *et al.* (2001).
r, raw correlation; ρ, estimated mean true validity (i.e. corrected for restricted range and reliability of both test score and outcome measure).

- (Low) Neuroticism predicts success in police work and skilled/semi-skilled work.
- Extraversion predicts success in management and police work, but not in other areas. (The apparent negative relationship for professional work reported in Table 7.4 is based on only four studies totalling less than 500 subjects.)

Some individual meta-analyses also report occupational differences.

- Hough (1998a) and Vinchur *et al.* (1998) both found that Extraversion, as well as Conscientiousness, correlates with sales performance.
- Two meta-analyses suggest a role for Agreeableness in some types of work. Hurtz and Donovan's analysis found that Agreeableness and Openness correlate with performance more strongly for customer service work. Mount, Barrick and Stewart (1998) found that Agreeableness correlates better with performance in work where co-operation and teamwork are important, than in work which simply involves interacting with clients (e.g. hotel work).
- Hough (1998) found that (low) Neuroticism correlates with combat effectiveness, and Salgado (1998b) found that (low) Neuroticism correlated well (0.27) with performance in European military samples. Meta-analyses of Conscientiousness and combat effectiveness disagree. Mount and Barrick (1995) reported a correlation of 0.47 in 10 studies, whereas Hough reported much lower correlations between achievement and dependability and combat effectiveness.
- Although Barrick *et al.*'s analysis found no occupational differences for Conscientiousness, several experts have argued that high Conscientiousness could be a drawback in some jobs, encouraging indecision and bureaucracy. UK data reported by Robertson *et al.* (2000) found no correlation with rated performance in managers, and a negative correlation with rated promotability, which suggests that high Conscientiousness may not always be an asset.

Is the big five the best account?

Some researchers argue that specific traits give better predictions of work behaviour than the big five. Mershon and Gorsuch (1988) argued that Cattell's 16 personality factors give a better prediction of work behaviour than the big five. Both Hough (1992, 1998) and Vinchur *et al.* (1998) found it useful to divide Extraversion into *potency/ascendancy* and *affiliation*, and to divide Conscientiousness into *achievement* and *dependability*. Hough (1998) argued that Conscientiousness becomes a very broad factor indeed in some accounts of the big five, covering achievement, striving, competence, dutifulness, order, self-discipline and deliberation, and that it contains elements which are potentially opposites. Achievement suggests 'self-expansive striving and setting goals to alter the environment', whereas dependability suggests 'self-restrictive caution, conventionality, and adapting to goals set by others'. Hough's results for sales (*see* Table 7.5) seem to confirm this; achievement correlates quite well with sales, but dependability does not. Vinchur *et al.* (1998) found that this difference was especially marked for studies using sales figures, rather than ratings of sales ability.

Several meta-analyses have found that work proficiency is related to more specific traits.

- Judge and Bono (2001) found that work performance correlates with self-esteem (0.26) and locus of control (0.22).
- Sadri and Robertson (1993) reported that self-efficacy correlates by 0.34 (uncorrected) with work performance. Self-efficacy refers to 'people's judgements of their capabilities to organise and execute courses of action required to attain designated types of performances'.
- Frei and McDaniel (1998) meta-analysed 39 studies of customer service orientation, and reported an average raw validity of 0.24, which corrects to 0.49. Customer service orientation means being pleasant, courteous, co-operative

Table 7.5 The big five and sales performance (correlations are not corrected in any way).

Meta-analysis	Vinchur *et al.* (1998)	Hough (1998a)	
Criterion	Rating	Sales figures	Sales effectiveness
Neuroticism	−0.05	−0.07	−0.18
Extraversion	0.09	0.12	−
Affiliation	0.06	0.08	0.19
Potency	0.15	0.15	0.25
Openness	0.06	0.03	0.15
Agreeableness	0.03	−0.02	−
Conscientiousness	0.11	0.17	−
Achievement	0.14	0.23	0.27
Dependability	0.10	0.10	0.06

Note: Data from meta-analyses by Hough (1998a) and Vinchur *et al.* (1998).

and helpful in dealing with customers, and is considered to be an increasingly important attribute, given the importance of service industries.

Personality questionnaires are not very good at answering the question 'Will X be able to do this job well?'. Possibly questions about ability are better answered by mental ability tests, which Chapter 6 showed were good at answering Question 1.

Question 3. How will he or she behave at work?

So far we have reviewed research on personality and work performance – how well the person can do the job. However, there may be other aspects of work performance where personality is more relevant. Barrick *et al.*'s (2001) meta-meta-analysis compared four criteria of work performance, namely supervisor rating, objective criteria such as sales figures, rated teamwork and training criteria (*see* Table 7.6). Although Extraversion did not significantly predict overall work performance, it did predict rated teamwork (which might be expected) and training performance (which is surprising). Perhaps extraverts like new experiences, or meeting new people (or getting away from work for a day or two!). (Low) Neuroticism also predicted rated teamwork, as did high Agreeableness. Openness correlated with training performance, consistent with the hypothesis that open-minded people will welcome the opportunity to gain new knowledge and skills. Conscientiousness predicted supervisor rating, teamwork and training performance. Barrick *et al.* suggested that Conscientiousness may be 'the trait-oriented motivation variable that industrial–organisational psychologists have long searched for' – a good all-round predictor of work performance.

Leadership

In some sectors, especially management and the military, leadership is an important ability. Judge *et al.* (2002b) reported a meta-analysis of leadership and the big five for two sectors of employment and found modest estimated true correlations for (low) Neuroticism and Extraversion. In civilian management, Openness correlated positively, while in the military and government,

Table 7.6   Meta-meta-analysis of the big five and four aspects of work performance.

	Neuroticism	Extraversion	Openness	Agreeableness	Conscientiousness
	r/ρ	r/ρ	r/ρ	r/ρ	r/ρ
Supervisor rating	0.07/0.12	0.07/0.11	0.03/0.05	0.06/0.10	0.15/0.26
Objective criteria	0.05/0.09	0.06/0.11	0.02/0.02	0.07/0.13	0.10/0.19
Training criteria	0.05/0.08	0.13/0.23	0.14/0.24	0.07/0.11	0.13/0.23
Rated teamwork	0.13/0.20	0.08/0.13	0.08/0.12	0.17/0.27	0.15/0.23

Notes:
Data taken from Barrick *et al.* (2001).
r = average raw validity; ρ = average corrected validity, corrected for range restriction and reliability of both test score and outcome variable.

Table 7.7   The big five and leadership.

	N	E	O	A	C
Leadership – business[a]	−0.15	0.25	0.23	−0.04	0.05
Leadership – government and military[a]	−0.23	0.16	0.06	−0.04	0.17
Transformational leadership[b]	0.03	0.28	0.26	0.32	−0.06

Notes:
[a]Data from meta-analysis by Judge *et al.* (2002).
[b]Data from study ($n = 169$) by Judge and Bono (2000).
All correlations corrected for unreliability of both leadership and personality measures.

Conscientiousness correlated positively (*see* Table 7.7). These results suggest that personality inventories can throw some light on leadership. (There are inventories designed to measure leadership more directly, some of which collect information from people whom the candidate is leading, as well as from the leader him- or herself). Judge and Bono (2000) correlated the big five with transformational or charismatic leadership in a sample of community leaders. Extraversion, Openness and Agreeableness are related, but not Neuroticism and Conscientiousness.

Box 7.5   Transformational leadership (also known as charismatic leadership)

Transformational leaders inspire their followers and create a vision for them to follow. This can be very important in some types of managers.

Can do vs. will do

Most analyses from Ghiselli and Barthol (1953) through to Barrick *et al.* (2001) have looked at aspects of *proficiency* – what people *can do* at work, if they feel motivated to do so. Hough's (1992) meta-analysis also included three motivational or *will do* aspects.

1. *Commendable behaviour* is defined by 'letters of recommendation, letters of reprimand, disciplinary actions, demotions, involuntary terminations, ratings of effort, hard work'.
2. *Non-delinquency* means avoiding actual theft, conviction or imprisonment.
3. *Non-substance abuse* means not abusing alcohol and drugs.

These criteria are sometimes grouped together and called (absence of) *counter-productive behaviour* (Hough, 1998) or *employee reliability* (Mount & Barrick, 1995). Although inventories generally fail to predict *job proficiency* in Hough's meta-analysis, they predict *commendable behaviour* and *non-substance abuse* fairly well (0.20–0.39), and they predict *non-delinquency* very well (up to 0.52). Commendable behaviour and non-substance abuse correlate with dependability and achievement, the two aspects of Conscientiousness that

Hough distinguishes. Non-delinquency also correlates very well with potency and (low) Neuroticism. These correlations are not corrected for reliability or restricted range, and are based on very large pooled samples. These results indicate that personality inventories can be genuinely useful in selection. Several further researches and analyses confirm Hough's conclusions.

- Validation of the ABLE inventory in samples of seven or eight thousand soldiers (Hough *et al.*, 1990; McHenry *et al.*, 1990) showed that ABLE scales predict three 'will do' criteria, namely *effort and leadership, personal discipline* and *physical fitness and military bearing,* but not the two 'can-do' criteria, namely *technical proficiency* and *general soldiering proficiency.* The correlations are modest (0.03–0.29, median 0.16), but again have not been corrected for criterion reliability or restricted range.
- Ones, Viswesvaran and Schmidt's (1993) meta-analysis of honesty tests found a true validity of 0.32 for counter-productive behaviours, defined as breaking rules, being disciplined, being dismissed for theft or being rated as disruptive by one's supervisor.
- Mount and Barrick (1995) reported an extended meta-analysis for Conscientiousness, and found high true validities against a range of 'will do' criteria, namely *reliability* (0.41), *effort* (0.51) (defined as hard work, initiative, motivation, energy and persistence) and *quality* (0.44). Mount and Barrick pooled all of the 'will do' criteria and found an overall true validity of 0.45, compared with 0.22 for the pooled 'can do' criteria.
- Organisational citizenship means volunteering to do things that are not in the job description, helping others, following rules willingly, and publicly supporting the organisation, all of which are highly desirable behaviour in employees. Organ and Ryan (1995) reported a meta-analysis of 6 to 11 studies, and found modest correlations between citizenship and Extraversion, Agreeableness and Conscientiousness.

Although inventories do not seem to be very useful for predicting job proficiency, they do appear to have a useful role in selection, in predicting willingness to fit in, obey the rules, help others and refrain from antisocial or destructive behaviour.

Motivation, absence, job satisfaction and organisational citizenship

Motivation

Judge and Ilies (2002) reported a meta-analysis of the big five and work motivation (*see* Table 7.8). All three types of motivation correlated positively with Conscientiousness and negatively with Neuroticism. Relationships with the other three factors were less clear, possibly because there is less research to include in the meta-analysis. The results imply that employers can use personality measures to select people who are well motivated to work hard,

Table 7.8   The big five, motivation, job satisfaction and absence.

	N	E	O	A	C
Goal-setting motivation	−0.29	0.15	0.18	−0.29	0.28
Expectancy motivation	−0.29	0.10	−0.08	0.13	0.23
Self-efficacy motivation	−0.35	0.33	0.20	0.11	0.22
Absence	0.03	0.31	0.17	0.20	−0.24
Job satisfaction	−0.29	0.25	0.02	0.17	0.26
Organisational citizenship	−0.06	0.15	–	0.13	0.22

Notes:
Motivation data from meta-analysis by Judge & Ilies (2002): correlations corrected for reliability of both measures.
Job satisfaction data from meta-analysis by Judge, Heller & Mount (2002b): correlations corrected for reliability of both measures.
Absence data from study by Judge, Martocchio & Thorsen (1997): $n = 73$; correlations not corrected in any way.
Organisational data from Organ & Ryan (1995), corrected for reliability of both measures.

and throw some light on the link between personality and work performance. For example, Judge and Ilies suggest that Extraversion correlates with self-efficacy motivation, because extraverts have a more positive attitude, both in general and towards their own ability to perform.

Absence

Absence is a major problem for many employers, so the possibility of selecting people who are less likely to be absent is attractive. Earlier research was not promising, partly because absence can be difficult to define and quantify, and partly because research tended to use a shotgun approach. Judge, Martocchio and Thorsen (1997) used the big five to predict absence in university staff, and found that extraverts were absent more, consistent with their 'carefree, excitement-seeking, hedonistic nature', while conscientious employees were absent less, showing their 'dutiful, rule-bound and reliable nature'. The research covered only non-academic staff, because absence of academic staff was impossible to track.

Job satisfaction

Job satisfaction is weakly but positively related to job proficiency, so a satisfied worker will on average be slightly more productive than one who is dissatisfied. Satisfied workers also tend to be more committed and to stay longer which tends to be desirable from the employer's point of view. Keeping workers satisfied is largely achieved by managing them well and fairly, but Judge et al.'s meta-analysis suggests that personality, and so possibly selection, also plays a part. Table 7.8 shows that satisfied workers score higher on Extraversion, Agreeableness and Conscientiousness, but lower on Neuroticism.

Organisational citizenship

Organ and Ryan (1995) report a meta-analysis of studies of organisational citizenship and personality, finding low positive correlations with Conscientiousness, Extraversion and Agreeableness.

Teamwork

Earlier research, presented in Table 7.9 and discussed above, looked at rated teamwork in *individual* employees. The research discussed here relates *team* performance to team personality. Neuman and Wright (1999) studied human resource management teams in an American department-store chain. Team performance, assessed both by supervisor rating and by completing paperwork on time and accurately, related most strongly to team Agreeableness, then to team Conscientiousness, and not at all to team Neuroticism. Barrick *et al.* (1998) studied teams of assembly workers and found a different pattern of results. Teams with high average Conscientiousness scores performed better, as did teams with higher Agreeableness and lower Neuroticism scores. Barrick *et al.* also found some more complex relationships. Teams with no low scorers on Extraversion, Conscientiousness or Agreeableness performed better. This suggests that low Conscientiousness in particular is doubly problematic. Not only does the low scorer do less work, but he or she holds back the rest of the group as well. It is worth noting that relationships with Agreeableness and Neuroticism were found, although these were less clearly related to work performance at the individual level. Barrick *et al.* also found that high variance in Conscientiousness was related to lower performance, and suggested that very conscientious people find themselves having to spend time doing or redoing the work of less conscientious team members.

Other approaches to personality and teamwork argue that certain *combinations* of personalities create a more effective team. The Belbin Team Role Self-Perception Test assigns people to one of eight team roles (e.g. *shaper* or *company worker*), and argues that an effective team needs the right mix of roles.

Table 7.9 The big five and team performance.

	N	E	O	A	C
Assembly workers					
Team performance	−0.24	0.12	–	0.34	0.26
Team viability	−0.32	0.30	–	0.16	0.20
Human resource management teams					
Rated team task performance	0.12	0.06	−0.01	0.36	0.27
Rated interpersonal skills	0.14	0.01	0.19	0.39	−0.20
Objective team accuracy	0.03	−0.01	−0.16	0.14	0.31
Objective team performance	0.06	−0.17	−0.08	0.37	0.16

Notes:
Data for 51 teams of assembly workers from Barrick *et al.* (1998).
Data for 79 teams of human resource management workers from Neuman & Wright (1999).

If everyone wants to take charge and no one wants to be company worker, the team will fail. Senior (1997) showed that balanced teams were more effective. The Myers Briggs Type Indicator can be used in the same way.

Career success

Some research has linked the big five to career success in managers. Career success is defined by salary level or status (e.g. the number of rungs of the corporate ladder that separate the index person from the CEO or managing director). Career success reflects ability over a longer time span than conventional indices of job proficiency. Boudreau, Boswell and Judge (2000) reported a large cross-sectional study in America and Europe. Table 7.10 shows that career success in the USA correlates with low Neuroticism and low Agreeableness, but not with Conscientiousness. However, in Europe high Extraversion and low Agreeableness correlate with career success, but again Conscientiousness does not. Judge *et al.* (1999) used three California *cohort studies* to study career success longitudinally. Personality in childhood and adolescence was assessed using ratings made from detailed case histories rather than conventional self-report methods, and was then related to occupational status and income when the cohort had reached their fifties. Conscientious and extravert people were more successful, while anxious people tended to be less successful. The four factors combined correlated by 0.54 with career success, suggesting that personality is definitely important. Both cross-sectional and longitudinal studies found that less agreeable people were more successful, suggesting that perhaps it does not pay to be too nice to others if you want to get ahead. Both studies found that Openness was completely unrelated to career success. The studies differed with regard to the role of Conscientiousness in career success – the cross-sectional study found no link, whereas the longitudinal study found a strong link. Perhaps Conscientiousness is important at earlier stages of the manager's career.

Box 7.6   Cohort study

A group of people are studied early in life, and then followed up at intervals through their lives in order to see how, for example, upbringing relates to adult outcomes. Such studies are particularly valuable because they avoid some of the direction-of-cause problems that are often encountered in selection research. Judge *et al.*'s cohort was assessed long before they started employment, so we can exclude the possibility that being successful at work makes one more conscientious, or less anxious.

Incremental validity

Two meta-analyses both suggest that personality inventories will have considerable incremental validity over mental ability tests. They note that both Conscientiousness and mental ability are correlated with work performance,

Table 7.10 The big five and career success.

	Sample size	N	E	O	A	C	R
Income[a]	166	−0.21	0.27	−0.02	−0.32	0.44	0.54
Income – American[b]	1,885	−0.30	0.04	−0.02	−0.24	−0.07	
Income – European[b]	1,871	−0.05	0.26	−0.02	−0.11	−0.02	

Notes:
[a]Data taken from Judge *et al.* (1999): the values for the big five are beta weights in a multiple regression.
[b]Data taken from Boudreau *et al.* (2000).

but that they do not correlate with each other. They argue that it follows logically that Conscientiousness will have incremental validity over mental ability (and vice versa). Schmidt and Hunter (1998) estimated the incremental validity of the Conscientiousness factor to be 18%, and listed the combination as one of the four most useful. Salgado (1998b), in a review of European data, confirmed this and concluded that Neuroticism will also have incremental validity. Personality inventories have incremental validity in a second, broader sense. Military research shows that ABLE predicts aspects of soldiers' performance that are not predicted by mental ability tests (Hough *et al.*, 1990), so the combination of personality and aptitude measures gives a broader prediction of performance.

Other ways of analysing personality validity data

Multiple regression and correlation

The conventional validity study correlates predictor with criterion. When applied to 16 PF data, it performs this operation 16 times, which may not be the best way to analyse 16 PF data. 16 PF scales intercorrelate, so correlations between C (stability) and work performance and between O (Apprehension) and work performance might cover the same ground, given that C and O correlate by −0.58. Multiple regression (*see* Box 3.3, page 56) only adds new predictors if they both correlate with the criterion *and* add extra predictive power.

Moderator variables

Hochwarter, Witt and Kacmar (2000) found that the link between Conscientiousness and work performance was moderated by organisational politics. In some workplaces, people see a lot of favouritism, back-stabbing, pursuit of private agendas, etc., while in others they see things being done openly and fairly. Data from four fairly large and diverse samples found that Conscientiousness correlated with performance in people who experienced a lot of organisational politics, but not in people who did not. Hochwarter *et al.* suggested that in an open and fair environment everyone works conscientiously, but when such standards are lacking, only those who have their own internal standards are able to work effectively. Barrick and Mount (1993) suggested that autonomy may be a moderating variable, and reported that correlations with Conscientiousness, Extraversion and Agreeableness are all higher when the person is given greater autonomy in deciding how to do the job. Someone who is very closely supervised has less opportunity to bring individual differences into the workplace.

Interactions between personality factors

Even regression analyses may over-simplify the way in which different personality traits shape behaviour at work. Perhaps particular combinations of personality traits predict particular outcomes. Witt et al. (2002) postulated that Conscientiousness will predict work performance better in people who score high on Agreeableness. They argued that a conscientious but disagreeable person will not get on with colleagues, but be 'micromanaging, unreasonably demanding, inflexible, curt, and generally difficult to deal with'. Their hypothesis was confirmed for five of seven varied samples.

Cluster analysis

Gustafson and Mumford (1995) offered a classification approach to using information from the whole personality profile. They cluster-analysed scores on seven personality dimensions in US Navy personnel, yielding groups characterised as *anxious defensives, comfortable non-strivers* or *internally controlled rigids*. They could then relate membership of these personality groups to work behaviour. For example, the anxious defensive group scored low on both job satisfaction and work performance, whereas the non-anxious strivers scored higher on both.

Clinical interpretation of personality tests

The conventional validity study, either taken singly or combined in a meta-analysis, represents a mechanistic approach to personality tests. If CPI Dominance scores correlate with managerial performance, then the selector should logically use a top-down selection method (i.e. fill vacancies with the highest dominance scorers). However, personality tests are often used *clinically* – an expert uses the whole CPI profile to assess the person's fit with the job description. The expert can base an assessment of ability to influence others not just on dominance, but on social presence, empathy, tolerance, and on combinations of scores. High dominance and high good impression imply one approach to controlling others (being considerate and making an effort to carry them along), whereas high dominance and low good impression imply a more autocratic approach. On the positive side, the clinical approach can in theory make better use of the information, and avoid adverse impact problems because the expert takes into account gender differences. On the negative side, several studies (e.g. Ryan & Sackett, 1992) have shown that psychologists do not agree very well in their interpretations of profiles of test data.

Path models

A start has been made on tracing the paths from personality to work performance. Chapter 6 showed that the path from mental ability to work performance runs through job knowledge. Borman *et al.* (1991) added personality data to a path analysis of proficiency in American soldiers, and found that the path from ABLE Dependability to good supervisor rating runs through commendations for good work and absence of disciplinary proceedings for poor work (*see* Figure 11.5, page 236). Barrick, Mount and Strauss (1993) reported a path analysis for Conscientiousness and sales figures in wholesale appliance sales people. The conscientious salesperson sets his or her own goals and sticks to them, which secures both good sales figures and a good supervisor rating.

More unemployable minorities?

If there are reliable links between the big five and success in work, we encounter the same alarming possibility as with intellectual ability – a section of the population whose employment prospects will be rendered less promising by their having characteristics that few employers will want. Perhaps people with Conscientiousness scores below the 15% percentile will not find themselves in great demand. They will join the 15% or so whose low mental ability places them in the same position. And because there is no correlation between mental ability and Conscientiousness, they will largely be a different 15%. Suppose that they are then joined by high scorers on Neuroticism. An increasing proportion of humanity could turn out to be people whom employers are not very keen to employ. Yet most people view employment as a right, and most governments assume that everyone will be or should be employed.

Screening tests

Question 4. Does the applicant have any problems that will interfere with work?

Personality inventories can be used like the driving test – not to select the best, but to exclude the unacceptable. The use of personality measures to screen applicants has a long history. Anderson's (1929) survey of staff at Macy's department store in New York found that 20% of employees fell into the 'problem' category (cannot learn, suffer chronic ill-health, are in constant trouble with fellow employees, cannot adjust satisfactorily to their work). Culpin and Smith's (1930) survey of over 1,000 British postal workers found that 20–30% were suffering some measurable level of neurosis. These figures may seem improbably high, but are confirmed by *community surveys* of mental health. If psychologists go out looking for maladjusted people, instead of waiting for them to be referred, one in five is the sort of ratio they discover. Zickar (2001) has described an unfortunate episode in American work psychology in the 1930s and 1940s, when some employers tried to use personality tests to exclude workers who would join trades unions, working on the assumption that desire to join a union was a sign of maladjustment.

Military screening

Very large numbers of US service personnel were screened during World War Two. Some studies reported very high correlations (up to 0.80) between inventory scores and adjustment, while other studies reported cut-off points of amazing efficiency. For example, anyone scoring over 25 on the Cornell Selectee Index 'invariably fell into the category of severe psychoneurotics', while anyone with a score under 15 'could be almost as readily accepted for employment' (Ellis & Conrad, 1948).

Some military screening results were too good to be true. Military testing reached men that other test programmes never saw ('unemployables, tramps, loafers, "bums", alcoholics, frank neurotics'), so it suffered an unusual statistical problem, namely *excessive* (as opposed to *restricted*) *range*. There is a *wider* range of individual differences in conscript samples than in typical applicant samples, so the test can correlate better. It is useful to know how a test performs on a complete cross-section of American men, but it may not be all that relevant to civilian employers who are not interested in screening out people who would never apply anyway, or who would not get past reception if they did.

Police work

In the USA, personality inventories are often used to screen out candidates who are psychologically unfit for police work. The Minnesota Multiphasic Personality Inventory (MMPI) is the favourite test, the CPI and 16PF being the runners up. Sarchione et al. (1998) analysed CPIs that had previously been completed by 109 disciplinary cases and 109 controls, and found differences in Responsibility, Socialisation (reversed delinquency) and Self-control of around half a standard deviation. Note, however, that an average difference between two groups does not tell us what proportion of individuals are correctly identified as problem or non-problem recruits. Kelley, Jacobs and Farr (1994) reported that repeated testing with the MMPI tends to normalise initially deviant profiles, which implies that screening may become less effective over time.

Violence and negligent hiring

In 1979, the Avis car-rental company in the USA was sued when an employee raped a customer and was found to have previous convictions for similar offences. Avis should, it was claimed, have found out that the man was dangerous. Avis lost the case, and since then negligent hiring claims have become common in the USA (Ryan & Lasek, 1991). How can employers foresee crimes that employees might commit against customers? Several violence scales are now available in the USA (Ones & Viswesvaran, 2001). A meta-analysis of 11 studies suggests that they predict violent behaviour quite well, achieving a corrected validity of 0.48. However, they also predict counter-productive behaviour equally well, and general job performance almost as well, which strongly suggests that they do not predict violent behaviour specifically, but rather some more general pattern of poor adjustment. Ones and Viswesvaran found that violence scales correlate quite highly with Conscientiousness, Agreeableness and Neuroticism in that order, confirming that they assess very broad areas of personality, rather than one specific aspect, and suggesting that they will correlate highly with honesty tests. Connerley et al. (2002) argued that the prospective employee's workmates also have the right not to have their life at work made unpleasant by co-workers' disagreeable or disturbed behaviour. In any case, such behaviour is likely to prove expensive for the employer, through absence, reduced output, higher turnover, etc.

Stress tolerance

Several stress tolerance scales are used in the USA (Ones & Viswesvaran, 2001), but no research on their ability to predict coping with pressure has been reported.

Sexual abuse

Several cases have occurred in the UK in which children in children's homes were sexually abused by members of staff, sometimes over periods of many years. British Government reports, the Walner Report and the Waterhouse Report have recommended psychological testing to screen out applicants who may sexually abuse children. Personality inventories cannot specifically detect sexual interest in children, but could screen out maladjusted individuals who may be less able to resist deviant impulses. However, abusers are likely to try very hard to keep their preferences secret, so will probably fake good on questionnaires.

Honesty testing

Surveys indicate that employee theft is a widespread problem in the USA. It has even been suggested that it contributes to up to 30% of company failures. Honesty tests became popular in the USA after use of the polygraph was restricted in 1988. These tests use various approaches, including indirect questions which assume that dishonest people see crime as more frequent or as easier, or questions that present dishonesty as meriting less punishment, or as more easily justified (by low wages, etc.). Honesty tests have been validated against polygraph assessments, till shortages or even low takings, on the assumption that low takings means the person is stealing. Ones et al. (1993) reported a meta-analysis of 665 honesty test validity coefficients, covering no less than 576,460 individuals. The analysis produced some surprising results.

- Honesty tests work. They predict counter-productive behaviours very well, achieving an operational validity of 0.39.
- Honesty tests also predict general job proficiency very well, achieving a true validity of 0.41. Ones and Viswesvaran (2001) reported a further meta-analysis of integrity tests and other aspects of work behaviour, and found them to be surprisingly versatile – they can predict training performance, accidents at work, and even output.
- Mainstream psychological tests are no more successful than specialist honesty tests. These results are disturbing for professional psychologists, who have been warning the public for years that writing psychological tests is a specialised task that is best left to the experts (i.e. psychologists). Yet honesty tests written by non-psychologists seem to be very successful, not just for assessing honesty but also for judging general work performance.
- Honesty tests work for all levels of employee, not just for lower-paid workers as is sometimes supposed.

Honesty tests do not create adverse impact. Ones and Viswesvaran (1998a) analysed gender, age and ethnicity differences in another enormous meta-analysis, covering 725,000 individuals. They found that women, the over-40s, Hispanic-Americans and Native Americans are all slightly more honest. Another meta-analysis explored the construct validity of honesty tests (Marcus, Funke & Schuler, 1997) using a big five framework. They reported positive correlations with Conscientiousness (0.29) and Agreeableness (0.31), and negative correlations with Neuroticism (-0.28) and Openness (-0.15). This suggests that honesty tests are measuring an undifferentiated construct.

Sackett and Wanek (1996) have expressed some cautions about the validity of honesty testing.

- Many honesty tests are validated by including questions that ask subjects to admit past dishonesty, and using these questions as the criterion for the rest of the measure. This is obviously a very weak form of validation.
- The number of studies that use behavioural measures of dishonesty is considerably smaller than 665, and the number that use actual theft as the outcome is fewer still. Only seven studies, covering a total of 2500 individuals, used actual theft as the outcome predicted, and these achieved much poorer results (a corrected validity of only 0.13). (It could be argued that actual theft is not an ideal criterion either, since only some thieves are caught – possibly the less efficient ones – so a test that can identify *successful* thieves might be better.)
- Many studies of specialist honesty tests are carried out by the test's publisher, which tends to carry less weight than validation by independent persons.
- Although there are several dozen honesty tests on the market, the meta-analysis by Ones *et al.* (1993) is largely based on only six or seven tests, so the value of the rest is as yet unproven.

Problems with screening

False positives

Honesty testing, like the polygraph before it, generates a high rate of *false positives*. These are individuals described as dishonest by the test, who do not in fact commit any dishonest acts (*see* Figure 7.4). The other problem with screening is the *false negative* – that is, dishonest people whom the test fails to identify. Some critics consider that *false positives* are a strong argument for not using honesty tests, because a false positive means an honest person who is wrongly accused of dishonesty. False positives will always occur because no test will ever be perfectly valid. Martin and Terris (1991) argued that the false-positive issue is irrelevant. If the test has any validity, then using it will benefit the organisation by excluding some dishonest individuals. They also argue that *not* screening implies accepting more dishonest people, thereby excluding some honest individuals who might otherwise have got the job. According to this argument, screening by and large benefits honest applicants. Guastello and Rieke (1991) disagree with Martin and Terris, starting that a false positive on an honesty test means labelling someone as dishonest when he or she is not, and abridging that person's civil rights by implicitly accusing them of theft but denying them any opportunity to answer. Other critics argue that honesty tests may be unfair on certain groups of people. For example, a reformed criminal who admits to past dishonesty is likely to fail an honesty test and be deprived of employment. Honesty tests that reject people who look 'too good to be true' may unfairly reject people with very high moral and/or religious standards.

Base rate

Testing works best when people split more or less equally into suitable/unsuitable, honest/dishonest, etc. This does not always happen with screening. In screening for childcare work, one hopes that the base rate is low – that only a few applicants will have deviant sexual impulses. However, the lower the base rate, the less successful screening will be, and the more false-positives will result.

	Person who is really dishonest	Person who is really honest
Test predicts dishonest	True positive	False positive
Test predicts honest	False negative	True negative

Figure 7.4   Possible outcomes of screening for honesty

The problem of faking

Personality inventories are not *tests* but *self-reports*. A test has right and wrong answers, but a self-report does not. Many inventories look fairly transparent to critics, who argue that no one applying for a sales job is likely to say 'True' to 'I don't much like talking to strangers'. Personality inventories are usually fakable, in the sense that people who are directed to give the answers that they think will maximise their chances of getting a job do generate 'better' profiles. Viswesvaran and Ones (1999) reviewed 51 studies of *directed faking*, and found that all aspects of personality can be improved by between 0.54 and 0.93 SDs (*see* Figure 7.5). Conscientiousness, which of the big five predicts work performance best, can be improved by nearly one whole SD. Honesty tests also improve a lot (by 0.86 SD) in directed faking studies (Ones & Viswesvaran, 1998b).

However, there is some dispute about how large a problem faking good is in real selection. Some time ago, Dunnette *et al.* (1962) estimated that only one in seven applicants for sales jobs faked, and even they faked less than subjects in directed faking studies. Several other early studies reported similar results, but all of them, as Mount and Barrick (1995) have noted, were based on very small samples, which identifies this as an under-researched issue. Hough (1992) compared applicants, who were motivated to fake, with incumbents, who already had the job so did not need to fake. Applicants' dependability scores were 0.45 SD higher, whereas Conscientiousness scores are 1 SD higher in directed faking studies. This confirms that real-life faking is less than directed faking, but also shows that it is substantial. Some research has suggested that faking may change the factor structure of inventories (i.e. it may change what the inventory is measuring). Schmit and Ryan (1993) found that faked NEOs acquire a sixth 'ideal-employee' factor, while Ellingson, Sackett and Hough (1999) found that faking weakened the factor structure of ABLE. However,

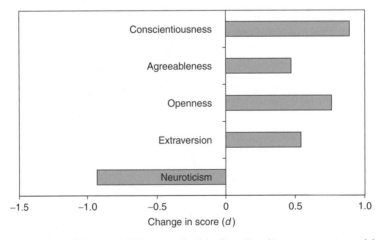

Figure 7.5   Effect of directed faking on the big five. Baseline represents unfaked big five. Data taken from meta-analysis by Viswesvaran and Ones (1999)

these were directed faking studies which generate larger effects. Ellingson, Smith and Sackett (2001) analysed four large data sets for real job applicants completing ABLE, CPI, 16PF and the Hogan Personality Inventory, and found no difference in the factor structure for any measure.

There are many lines of defence against faking. Some of them try to modify the way in which the test is administered.

1. *Rapport*. The tester can try to persuade the subjects that it is not in their interests to fake, because getting a job for which one's personality is not really suited may ultimately result in unhappiness, failure, etc. This argument may have limited appeal to those who do not have any job, ideal or otherwise.
2. *Faking verboten*. At the other extreme, military testers have been known to warn their subjects that faking, if detected, will be severely punished.
3. *Faking will be found out*. Goffin and Woods (1995) reported that faking can be reduced by telling people that it will be detected and this may prevent them getting the job. They also note that this strategy would create problems if it was used in routine selection.
4. *Faking will be challenged*. Doll (1971) told candidates that they would be required to defend their answers in a subsequent interview, and found that this dramatically reduced faking. If the selection procedure really does include such an interview, no unethical deception is involved. If the inventory is part of an assessment centre, candidates could be warned that they will be expected to exhibit the behaviour that they describe on the inventory. Some employers might think that this approach looks rather coercive.
5. *Administer by computer*. It is sometimes claimed that people are more honest about their health when giving information to a computer rather than a person. Richman *et al.* (1999) found that this does not apply to personality tests, where computer administration does not reduce faking good.

Other approaches alter the way in which the test is written, to try to reduce faking.

1. *Subtle questions*. The question 'Do you like meeting strangers?' clearly seems to suggest a 'right' answer in the context of selecting door-to-door sales staff. Is it possible to find subtler questions? Authors of empirically keyed inventories like to think so. Critics say that inventory questions can be divided into the unsubtle that work, and the subtle that do not.
2. *Forced choice*. Questions can be equated for desirability so that the subject must choose between pairs of equally flattering or unflattering statements:

> I am very good at making friends with people.
> I am respected by all my colleagues.
>
> I lose my temper occasionally.
> I am sometimes late for appointments.

Two recent studies suggest that forced choice may solve the faking good problem. Jackson, Wroblewski and Ashton (2000) found that forced choice reduces faking in a simulated selection exercise. Martin, Bowen and Hunt (2002) compared the forced-choice format OPQ 4.2 with the more conventional rating format OPQ 5.2. Students can fake a junior manager profile on the rating form but not on the forced-choice form.

The forced-choice format usually creates *interdependence* between scales, which can make interpretation difficult. Consider the Allport–Vernon–Lindzey Study of Values (AVL). On the AVL, the six scores must total 180. The test's instructions advise using this as a check on accuracy of scoring. However, if all six scores must total 180, the person who wants to express a strong preference for one value must express less interest in one or more others – it is impossible to obtain six very high scores or six very low scores on the AVL (whereas this is perfectly possible on, for example, the 16PF). This happens because within each forced choice, one answer scores for, say, e.g. social interest, while the other scores for, say, aesthetic interest. Interdependence in forced-choice questionnaires can make it difficult to use them *normatively*. The typical forced-choice measure can conclude that a person is more interested in dominating others than in helping others (an *ipsative* comparison). Forced-choice measures cannot usually conclude that person A is more interested in dominating others than is person B, but this is the comparison that selectors usually want to make. Jackson *et al.* (2000) avoided interdependence by using an elaborate quartet format, where people select *most like me* and *least like me* from sets of four items in which two items are equally desirable and the other two are equally undesirable. Two items in each set of four relate to, say, dependability, while the other two are not scored at all but serve simply to create the forced choice. This avoids interdependence but it makes the inventory very lengthy, as four items are needed to generate a single data point. Saville and Willson (1991) have argued that interdependence is not really a problem when a measure has a large number of scales.

3. *Control keys*. Many inventories contain *lie scales* or *faking good* scales, which are more politely known as *social desirability* scales. Lie scales are lists of items that deny common faults or claim uncommon virtues. A high score alerts testers to the possibility of less than total candour, but then presents them with a difficult decision – either to discard the applicant altogether or to rely on other evidence. It is not always possible to discard applicants in practice. Hurtz and Alliger (2002) reported the particularly worrying discovery that coaching helps people to avoid being detected by faking good scales.

4. *Correcting for defensiveness*. Some inventories have *correction keys*, which assess faking good and then reduce other scores proportionately. The MMPI's K key assesses defensiveness, and then adds varying proportions of K to other scores to estimate the shortcomings that people would have admitted if they had been more frank. Cronbach (1984) expressed scepticism

about this: "If the subject lies to the tester there is no way to convert the lies into truth'.

5. *Change the questionnaire into a real test.* Cattell's Motivation Analysis Test uses several novel question formats, some of which are probably quite hard to fake. For example, the *Information* subtest consists of factual questions, with right and wrong answers, and works on the principle that people know more about things that matter to them. For example, an aggressive person is more likely to know which of the following *is not* a type of firearm: Gatling, Sterling, Gresley, Enfield, FN.

Does faking affect validity?

It seems intuitively obvious that untrue answers will not predict work performance, but it has been claimed that faking does not reduce validity. Hough *et al.* (1990) analysed the moderating effect of faking good on ABLE, using very large samples, and found that validity coefficients in recruits who faked ABLE were no lower than those in subjects who did not. Hough (1998b) confirmed this in large samples of telecommunications workers, state troopers and police officers. However, two recent studies cast doubt on this comforting conclusion. Rosse *et al.* (1998) showed that some applicants fake a little, some fake a lot, and some do not fake at all, so faking good does not constitute a simple constant error that can be subtracted, leaving scores valid again. Where only a small proportion of applicants are appointed, they tend to be the ones who faked good a lot. Ellingson, Sackett and Hough (1999) asked a sample of US paratroopers to complete ABLE twice, once honestly and once faking good. They then used the unfaked ABLEs to decide who ought to get the job, and the faked ABLEs to see who actually got the job. Where one in three subjects faked and one in three were appointed, 40% of those who 'ought to have' got the job did not, and it went to someone who faked good instead. Faking may make a big difference to who is appointed.

Can correction keys restore validity?

Ellingson *et al.* (1999) had faked and unfaked ABLEs from the same sample of US paratroopers, so could answer the question 'Do correction keys succeed in turning lies back into truth?'. At one level the answer was 'yes'. Faked ABLEs were about half an SD 'better' than unfaked ones on average, but the corrected faked ABLEs were no 'better' than the unfaked ones. However, at another level the answer was 'no'. Faking changed the rank order of candidates (compared with a rank order based on unfaked completion), and so changed who 'got the job'. Correcting for faking did not change the rank order back, so did not ensure that the 'right' people were appointed after all. Hough (1998) confirmed this in three large samples of real applicants – corrected faked scores did not generate the same selection decisions as uncorrected scores.

Faking bad

People who are being assessed on conscription to the army might be motivated to fake bad if they hope to avoid military service. Otherwise, faking bad is unlikely to be a problem in selection. Hough *et al.* (1990) found that faking bad on ABLE did not reduce validity coefficients.

Infrequency keys

Some inventories contain sets of questions for which only one answer should be possible for almost any respondent. For example, consider the statement 'I have never seen a live animal'. Who might answer *true* to this? The possibilities include people answering too quickly, people who do not speak English very well or who cannot read very well, and people who are trying to sabotage the assessment. A high infrequency score means that the whole assessment must be discarded or redone. High infrequency scores do reduce the validity of ABLE (Hough *et al.*, 1990).

Inventories and the law

Inventories have encountered surprisingly little trouble with the law, at least compared with ability tests.

Gender differences

Until 1966, the Strong Interest Inventory had separate male and female question books, appropriately printed on blue or pink paper. Two Civil Rights Acts later, gender differences still create potential problems for the occupational tester. There are gender differences in many inventory scores (Sackett & Wilk, 1994; Hough, Oswald & Ployhart, 2001). Figure 7.6 shows the male–female differences in CPI scores in the UK standardisation data (Cook, Leigh & McHenry, 1997). Males score higher on scales assessing forcefulness, while females score higher on scales assessing responsibility. Similar differences are found in many other inventories, both in the UK and in the USA. Gender differences create a dilemma for the occupational tester. Using separate norm tables for men and women is prohibited in the USA by the Civil Rights Act of 1991, and is considered to be inadvisable in the UK, because calculating scores differently for men and women could be regarded as direct discrimination. On the other hand, using pooled gender norms may create adverse impact. For example, using a cut-off score of 60 on CPI Dominance to select managers would exclude more women than men. However, as Sackett and Wilk have noted, there have been few complaints against personality tests in the USA on the grounds of adverse impact, partly because the male–female differences are small compared with majority–minority differences in ability tests, and partly because personality tests are not usually used with mechanistic cut-off points.

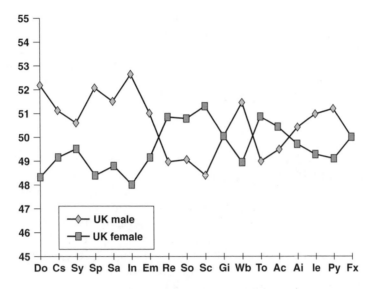

Figure 7.6   Male and female average CPI profiles from the UK standardisation data

Ethnicity

Analyses of differences between black and white groups in the USA suggest that personality tests will not create the major adverse impact problems that are found with tests of mental ability. Project A research (White *et al.*, 1993) using very large numbers found that black Americans score higher than whites on ABLE scales of dependability, achievement and adjustment (which means that there is no adverse impact problem). More recently, Collins and Gleaves (1998) examined big five data for white and African American job applicants, using more sophisticated analyses, and found no differences in factor structure or mean scores. Some European data are now available. te Nijenhuis, van der Flier and van Leeuwen (1997) found quite large differences in Neuroticism and Extraversion in some immigrant groups in The Netherlands. Ones and Anderson (2002) reported data on Afro-Caribbean, Asian and Chinese college students in the UK, and found few white–African differences, while Asian and Chinese differences generally favoured the minorities, showing them to be more conscientious.

Age

The UK standardisation of the CPI has found quite large age differences in some scales, including *self-control* (higher in older people), *flexibility* (lower in older people) and desire to create a *good impression* (higher in older people).

Disability

The Americans with Disabilities Act (ADA) of 1990 prohibits health-related enquiries before a job offer is made (i.e. as part of the conventional selection process). This can have two effects on personality questionnaires. First, items that could be interpreted as health-related enquiries (e.g. 'Do you suffer from sleeplessness?') have been deleted from some scales. Secondly, health includes mental health, so scales with psychiatric-sounding names, such as NEO's Neuroticism factor, become suspect for selection use (whereas reversed Neuroticism, which is called Emotional Stability, creates less of a problem).

Privacy

In the *Soroka v Dayton-Hudson* case, a job applicant claimed that the combined MMPI and CPI inventory contained intrusive questions about politics and religion, contrary to the Constitution of the State of California (Merenda, 1995). The case was settled out of court, so no definitive ruling emerged. Another Californian case, *Staples et al. v Rent-a-Center*, also complained of intrusive questions in the MMPI, and about computer-generated reports that made 'gross and unfounded generalisations' (e.g. '[the candidate] tends to be restless and impatient, should reduce caffeine and nicotine consumption and drink more water') (Sullivan & Arnold, 2000).

The potential danger of multi-score inventories

Most questionnaires come as fixed packages. The Sixteen Personality Factor Questionnaire (16PF) assesses all 16 factors every time it is used. One cannot decide to use only dominance, ego strength and shrewdness, or to leave out suspicion and guilt proneness. This is just an inconvenience to the researcher, but a far more serious problem to the selector. Suppose that your job analysis has identified dominance, ego strength and shrewdness as the (only) personality characteristics that are needed for the job. The other 13 factors are not job related, and should not be used to make the decision. However, having the other 13 scores in front of them, the selection team may well use them anyway, which will create problems for the employer later on. Someone objects to the selection procedure, and it becomes apparent that scores were used which were not job related, so the employer cannot justify their use or offer any defence against the claim. Inventories that describe people's weakness and poor adjustment can be particularly dangerous. For example, someone applying for a clerical job will be justifiably annoyed if they find that their sexual orientation or level of fantasy aggression has been assessed.

Survey of (some) inventories

Inventories are listed and reviewed in the *Mental Measurements Yearbooks (MMY)* (Buros, 1970). MMY reviews discuss the size and adequacy of the standardisation sample, reliability, validity, and whether the manual is adequate. MMY reviews are very critical, even of major tests. The British Psychological Society also publishes reviews of personality tests that are used in selection (Lindley, 2001).

Minnesota Multiphasic Personality Inventory (MMPI)

The first major multi-score inventory, dating from the late 1930s, the MMPI contains 550 questions, assesses nine psychiatric syndromes, and was the first inventory to be empirically keyed against clinical groups. The MMPI has been widely used to screen police officers in the USA for problem personalities, but may now face difficulties with disability discrimination laws. A new form of the MMPI, known as the MMPI-2, was published in 1990, which removes potentially offensive items and which has been re-normed.

16PF (16 Personality Factors)

Cattell originally referred to his 16 factors by letter and neologism, to emphasise that his factor analysis yielded an entirely new account of human personality, but he eventually had to compromise and give 'plain English' descriptions. Factor I was originally called *premsia*, meaning *projected emotional sensitivity*, but was later renamed *sensitivity*. The 16PF does not fit within the big five framework. The current edition of the 16PF, namely the 16PF5, has good internal and re-test reliability, as well as good normative data (Conn & Rieke, 1994).

California Psychological Inventory (CPI)

The CPI includes 434 endorsement format questions and measures 20 main personality traits. The CPI can also be scored for three *vectors*, which are similar to broad underlying factors but are not derived from factor analysis. The CPI contains about half of the MMPI (the less intrusive questions), and is sometimes called the 'sane person's MMPI'. It does not fit within the big five framework. The CPI has recent UK normative data (Cook, Leigh & McHenry, 1997).

Occupational Personality Questionnaires (OPQ)

This is a family of inventories that vary in *length* and *format*. The longest version (OPQ32) measures 32 aspects of personality, and the shorter *Factor, Octagon* and *Pentagon* versions measure 14, 8 and 5 aspects, respectively. The OPQ uses three formats, namely endorsement, forced choice and five-point rating, and it has recent UK normative data.

NEO

The short NEO-FFI (Five-Factor Inventory) measures the big five, using 12 items per factor with a five-point rating format. The longer NEO-PI (Personality Inventory) also measures six *facets* within each main factor, and contains 240 items. Costa (1996) has reported several studies that used the NEO to predict work performance, while Cellar *et al.* (1996) found modest correlations (0.10–0.20) with training ratings for flight attendants.

Assessment of Background and Life Experiences (ABLE)

ABLE was written for the US armed forces as part of Project A. It has 205 items, and measures six temperament constructs, namely surgency, adjustment, agreeableness, dependability, intellectance and affiliation, based on the big five. ABLE also has four control scales, namely random responding, social desirability, poor impression and self-knowledge (Hough *et al.*, 1990).

Hogan Personality Inventory (HPI)

The HPI has 206 endorsement-format items. It uses an extended big five model that divides Extraversion and Openness into two factors each.

Global Personality Inventory (GPI)

The GPI measures the big five and 32 facets. GPI was simultaneously written in 14 countries (the USA, UK, France, Belgium, Sweden, Germany, Spain, Norway, China, Japan, Singapore, Korea, Argentina and Colombia) to ensure that its item content was truly pan-cultural. The main item analyses were performed in parallel in English, Spanish and Chinese (Schmit, Kihm & Robie, 2000).

Goldberg's Item Bank

Goldberg offers a bank of personality questionnaire items that can be combined in different sets to assess the big five or to provide analogues to many popular inventories. Goldberg's Item Bank has an unusual feature – it is in the public domain, and can be used without restriction or payment by anyone. An item bank enables the selector to assess only those attributes that are identified as relevant by job analysis. Goldberg's item bank is accessible through his IPIP (International Personality Item Pool) website.

Alternatives to the inventory

Projective tests

Kinslinger's (1966) review covered projective tests that are widely used in US personnel research, including the Rorschach ink blot, the Thematic Apperception Test (TAT) and sentence completion tests. The TAT is a set of pictures that have been carefully chosen both for their suggestive content and for their vagueness. (*see* Figure 7.7). The subject describes 'what led up to the event shown in the picture, what is happening, what the characters are thinking and feeling, and what the outcome will be', and is supposed to project into the story his or her own 'dominant drives, emotions, sentiments, complexes and conflicts'. Early studies, which have been described by Dorcus and Jones (1950), considered the TAT and the Rorschach ink blot to be the ideal way to

Figure 7.7   Drawing similar to those used in the Thematic Apperception test (TAT)

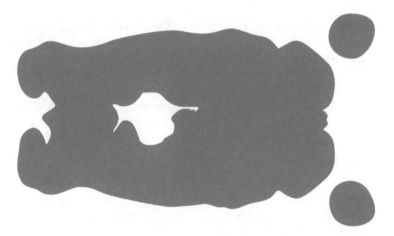

Figure 7.8   Ink blot similar to those used in the Rorschach test

predict turnover or accident proneness in tram (streetcar) drivers in Southern California, but obtained disappointing results. Other studies reviewed by Kinslinger (1966) similarly failed to demonstrate that the Rorschach ink blot (*see* Figure 7.8) predicted any aspect of work performance. Sentence completion tests are more structured and easier to score, but are not necessarily very subtle. For example:

My last boss was . . .

I don't like people who . . .

The Miner Sentence Completion Scale is written for selecting managers. It assesses attitude to authority, competitive motivation, masculine role, etc.

In Europe, one projective test has been used quite extensively – and apparently successfully – for selecting pilots. The *Defence Mechanism Test (DMT)* uses a picture showing a hero figure and a hideous face, made more ambiguous by being shown at first for only a fraction of a second. Various defence mechanisms can be inferred from responses to the DMT. For example, seeing the hideous face as an inanimate object is coded as repression, because the person is pushing emotion out of the picture. The rationale for using the test to select pilots is that defence mechanisms bind psychic energy, which is thus unavailable for coping with reality in an emergency. Martinussen and Torjussen (1993) meta-analysed 15 studies of the DMT, mainly in military pilot selection, and reported an uncorrected validity of 0.20, which is very promising. However, they did discover one worrying moderator variable. The DMT works in Scandinavia but not in the UK or The Netherlands. Martinussen and Torjussen consider that the test may be administered or scored differently in different countries. A test becomes very much less useful if one is not sure how to use it.

DNA

Research has shown that personality, as assessed by inventory, has a substantial heritable element (Cook, 1993). This implies that research will eventually identify particular genes associated with the differences between people which we describe as personality, and that it may eventually be possible to assess personality by DNA testing of skin or saliva. It will be interesting to see whether a DNA account of personality will bear any resemblance to the big five, or the 16PF, or any other current model.

Key points

In Chapter 7 you have learnt the following.

- Personality is a vaguer and more diffuse concept than ability, and there are many models of personality.
- Personality is most conveniently assessed by inventory or questionnaire. It can also be assessed by interview, assessment centre, references or peer ratings.
- Personality inventories are written by a variety of methods which generally overlap to some extent, including internal analysis by statistics, and external analysis comparing groups of people with known characteristics.
- The big five factor model is widely accepted, but may not give the best prediction of work behaviour. Other models exist.
- Personality inventories have limited value in predicting how well a person can do a job.
- Personality inventories may be more successful in predicting effort, citizenship, leadership, motivation or career success.

- Personality inventories may also be more successful in predicting avoidance of deviant or problematic behaviour at work.
- Preliminary results suggest that the relationship between team personality and team performance may be complex, and that low scorers may be able to hold back the entire group.
- Personality inventories are self-reports and not tests, and can be faked. Faking appears to affect the outcome of selection.
- Personality tests are also widely used to screen out people with problem characteristics, such as violent tendencies, deviant sexual impulses or dishonesty.
- Screening tests for employee honesty are surprisingly successful.
- Gender differences are often found with personality tests, but ethnicity differences do not seem to be a problem.
- Personality inventories have been criticised on the grounds that some of their questions are unduly intrusive.

Key references

Barrick *et al.* (2001) present a meta-meta-analysis of personality inventory validity.

Cook (1993) gives a general introduction to personality theory and research.

Costa (1996) describes the big five model.

Ellingson *et al.* (1999) examine how faking affects selection decisions and whether correction keys can solve the problem.

Frei and McDaniel (1998) summarise research on personality and customer service orientation.

Guion and Gottier (1965) present an early and not very optimistic review of personality test validity.

Hough (1998a) presents a meta-analysis of personality inventory validity against a range of work behaviours.

Hough *et al.* (1990) describe research on the validity of the American armed services personality test, ABLE.

Jackson *et al.* (2000) describe the use of the forced-choice format to limit faking.

Judge *et al.* (1999) describe a longitudinal study of career success in which success as an adult is predicted by personality and mental ability in childhood.

Ones *et al.* (1993) present a review of honesty testing.

Sackett and Wanek (1996) express some cautions about honesty testing.

Salgado (1997) reviews the European evidence on the validity of personality questionnaires.

Zickar (2001) describes the use of personality measures to screen out 'thugs and agitators'.

Useful websites

http://ipip.ori/ipip Goldberg's personality item bank

www.reidlondonhouse.com. Leading US publisher of honesty tests.

www.opp.co.uk. Oxford Psychologists Press, UK publisher of personality tests.

www.parinc.com. Psychological Assessment Resources Inc, US publisher of personality tests.

CHAPTER 8

Assessment centres

Does your face fit?

Introduction

The assessment centre was invented during World War Two, on both sides of the Atlantic more or less simultaneously. The British Army set up the War Office Selection Board (WOSB) to select its officers. Soon afterwards the UK Civil Service devised a civilian version – the Civil Service Selection Board (CSSB). In the USA, psychologists led by Henry Murray were advising the Office of Strategic Services (OSS), forerunner of the CIA, how to select spies. Murray's team identified nine dimensions to effective spying, including practical intelligence, emotional stability, and maintenance of cover. Maintenance of cover required each candidate to pretend to be someone else throughout the assessment; the OSS programme must be unique in regarding systematic lying as a virtue. In the early 1950s, AT&T's Management Progress Study (MPS) included a business game, leaderless group discussion, in-basket test, two-hour interview, autobiographical essay and personal history questionnaire, projective tests, personality inventories and a high-level mental ability test. The original MPS assessed over 400 candidates who were followed up five to seven years later. AC ratings predicted success in management with an accuracy that came as a welcome surprise to psychologists who were finding most other methods very fallible (Bray & Grant, 1966). ACs can be used for selection, or for deciding who to promote. They are also often used for *development* – assessing the individual's profile of strengths and weaknesses and planning what further training he or she needs.

The present shape of assessment centres

ACs work on the principle of *multi-trait, multi-method* assessment. Any single assessment method may give misleading results – some people interview well, while others are good at tests, whereas a person who shows ability to influence in both interview and inventory is more likely really to be able to influence others. The key feature of the true AC is the *dimension × assessment method matrix* (*see* Figure 8.1). Having decided what dimensions of work performance are to be assessed, the AC planners include at least two qualitatively different methods of assessing each dimension. In Figure 8.1, ability to influence is

	Influence	Numeracy	Delegation
Exercise A	XXX		XXX
Exercise B		XXX	
Test C	XXX	XXX	
Test D		XXX	XXX
In-tray			XXX

Figure 8.1   The dimension × predictor conceptual matrix underlying every assessment centre. XXX indicates that influence is assessed by exercise A

assessed by group exercise and personality inventory, while numerical ability is assessed by financial case study and timed numerical reasoning test. An assessment centre that does not have a matrix plan like that shown in Figure 8.1 is not a real AC, just a superstitious imitation of one. Unfortunately, one still sometimes encounters people whose idea of an AC is any old collection of tests and exercises – begged, borrowed or stolen – included because they are available, not because they are accurate measures of important dimensions of work performance.

Components of the AC

An AC includes whatever assessment methods are needed to assess each dimension twice. Sometimes the measures can be taken 'off the shelf', but often they are devised specially. ACs use *group*, *individual* and *written* exercises. Group exercises include the following:

- *leaderless group discussions*, in which the group has to discuss a given topic and reach a consensus, but where no one is appointed as chairman
- *revealed difference technique discussions*, in which each candidate first records his or her own priorities (e.g. survival aids in the desert) and then joins in a discussion to establish the group's agreed priorities
- *assigned role exercises*, in which each person has an individual brief, competing for a share of a budget, or trying to push his or her candidate for a job
- *command exercises*, often used in military ACs, simulate the task of controlling a group of candidates who are solving a practical problem. The OSS programme included the 'Buster' and 'Kippy' command task in which candidates tried to erect a prefabricated structure using two specially trained 'assistants', one of whom was aggressive and critical, while the other was sluggish and incompetent
- *business simulations*, often using computers, in which decisions must be made rapidly, with incomplete information, under constantly changing conditions
- *team exercises*, in which half of the group collectively advocates one side of a case, and the other half takes the opposing viewpoint.

Individual exercises can be divided into the following:

- *role play*, in which the candidate handles a visit or phone call from a dissatisfied customer, or from an employee with a grievance. The OSS programme included an exercise in which the candidate tried to explain why he had been found in Government offices late at night searching secret files, and was aggressively cross-examined by a trial lawyer and police detective
- *sales presentation*, in which the candidate tries to sell goods/services to an assessor who has been briefed to be challenging, sceptical, unsure that the product is necessary, etc.
- *presentation*, in which the candidate makes a short presentation on a topic on which he or she is an expert, or on a general knowledge topic
- *interview* – some ACs contain one or more interviews.

Written exercises can be divided into the following:

- *in-basket (or in-tray) exercises*, in which the candidate deals with a set of letters, memos, etc. (*see* Chapter 9). Candidates can be interviewed about their actions and asked to account for them
- *biographies*, which can take various forms, and are occasionally slightly macabre, as when the candidate is informed that he or she has just died, and should write his or her own obituary
- *psychological tests* of mental ability or personality.

The most recent survey of US employers (Spychalski *et al.*, 1997) found leaderless group discussions and in-tray exercises being used in most ACs, presentations and interviews being used in about half, tests of skill or ability used in one in three, and peer assessments used in only one in five. Woehr and Arthur (in press) reported that the average number of dimensions rated in ACs is between 10 and 11.

Reliability

AC reliability is a complex issue. One can calculate the reliability of the entire process, of its component parts, or of the assessors' ratings. Most elements of the AC (group exercises, role plays, in-tray exercises, simulation) are rated by assessors. Ratings of group discussions achieve fair to good inter-rater reliability. An early review by Hinrichs and Haanpera (1976) found generally good agreement in the short term. Research on overall AC reliability is mostly very old. Wilson (1948) reported a fairly good re-test reliability for the CSSB as a whole, based on candidates who exercised their right to try the CSSB twice. Morris (1949) gave details of two re-test reliability studies with the WOSB. In the first study, two parallel WOSBs were set up specifically to test inter-WOSB agreement, and two batches of candidates attended both WOSBs. There were 'major disagreements' over 25% of candidates. In the second study, two parallel boards simultaneously but independently observed and evaluated the same 200 candidates. The parallel WOSBs agreed very well overall, as did their respective presidents, psychiatrists, psychologists and military testing officers. Later, Moses (1973) compared 85 candidates who attended long and short ACs and were evaluated by different staff. Overall ratings from the two ACs correlated well, and ratings on parallel dimensions were also highly correlated.

Assessors' conference

The final stage of the AC is the assessors' conference, when all of the information about each candidate is collated (*see* Figure 8.2). The assessors resolve disagreements in ratings of group exercises, and then review all of the ratings in the matrix in order to determine a final set of ratings for each candidate. The final ratings define the candidate's *development needs* in a developmental AC, or who is successful in a selection AC. American ACs sometimes use the AT&T model, in which assessors only observe and record behaviour during the AC, but do not make any evaluations until all of the exercises are complete.

Centre for Occupational Research Ltd
Assessment Centre for Health Service Management
Candidate Summary Rating form

CANDIDATE: RECOMMENDATION:

DIMENSION	UIN	UFG	VIS	INF	AWA	ENG	TIM
Personality (CPI)	XXX	XXX					
Ability (GMA-N)	XXX		XXX	XXX	XXX	XXX	
Tests (GMA-V)		XXX	XXX	XXX	XXX	XXX	XXX
In-tray exercise		XXX		XXX			
Group ('access')	XXX	XXX			XXX	XXX	XXX
Exercises ('home')			XXX		XXX		
Presentation	XXX	XXX	XXX			XXX	
SUM							
AVERAGE							
FINAL							
	UIN	UFG	VIS	INF	AWA	ENG	TIM

UIN	understanding information	AWA	awareness of others
UFG	understanding figures	ENG	energy
VIS	strategic vision	TIM	time management
INF	influence		

Figure 8.2   Example of summary sheet used to record assessment centre data for one person

The assessors' conference may fail to make the best use of the wealth of information collected. ACs that are used for selecting senior police officers in the UK contain 13 components, including leaderless group discussion, committee exercise, written 'appreciation', drafting a letter, peer nomination, mental ability tests, and a panel interview. The assessors' conference uses the 13 components to generate an *overall assessment rating (OAR)*. Feltham (1988b) analysed the data statistically and found that only four of the 13 components were needed to predict the five criteria. Moreover, a weighted average of the four successful predictors predicted the criteria *better* than the OAR. This clearly implies that the assessors' conference is not doing an efficient job of processing the information that the AC generates, and that their discussion might usefully be complemented by a statistical analysis of the data. However, Spychalski *et al.* (1997) found that only 14% of American ACs used statistical analysis in the assessors' conference. Anderson *et al.* (1994) reported that assessors give much more weight to ratings of performance in group discussions than to ability test data when arriving at their OARs. However, it would be wrong to suggest that the assessors' conference could be replaced by a simple numerical model. Jones *et al.* (1991) consider it unlikely that anyone would agree to act as an assessor if the AC used a formula or model to reach decisions. Without line managers to act as assessors, the AC risks losing much of its credibility.

Validity of assessment centres

Like the interview, the AC is a *method* of assessment that can in theory assess whatever the organisation is interested in. Therefore one should logically ask about the validity of the AC for assessing, say, delegation, not about its validity in general. In practice the AC, like the interview, is often used to assess general suitability for the job, and its validity is computed against management's estimates, also of general suitability. When the AC tries to assess specific attributes, there is some question about whether it succeeds in doing so.

AT&T's Management Progress Study (MPS)

This achieved impressively good predictive validity. The candidates were originally assessed in 1957. Table 8.1 shows that on follow-up eight years later the MPS identified 82% of the college group and 75% of the non-graduates who had reached middle management (a predictive validity of 0.44 for college-educated subjects and 0.71 for non-college-educated subjects). The AC also identified 88% of the college group and 95% of the others who did not reach middle-manager level. It identified successful and unsuccessful managers equally accurately (Bray & Grant, 1966).

Civil Service Selection Board (UK)

The most senior ranks of the UK Civil Service have been selected since 1945 by a two-day AC, whose elements currently include group discussions, written

Table 8.1   Results of the AT&T Management Progress Study.

AC ratings	n	Achieved rank		
		First line	Second line	Middle
Potential middle manager	103	4%	53%	46%
Not potential middle manager	166	68%	86%	12%

Source: From Bray & Grant (1966).

Table 8.2   Predictive validity of the CSSB and its components after two years: correlations have been corrected for restricted range.

	Observer	Psychologist	Chairman
First discussion	0.26	0.34	0.36
Appreciation	–	–	0.31
Committee	0.42	0.34	0.41
Individual problem	0.35	0.36	0.42
Short talk	0.40	–	0.47
Interview	0.42	0.42	0.48
Second discussion	0.32	–	–
Final mark	0.44	0.49	0.49

Source: Reproduced from Vernon (1950) by permission of the British Psychological Society.

exercises and interviews, preceded by biodata and mental ability tests. Vernon (1950) reported a follow-up study in the CSSB's early years. Table 8.2 shows that the CSSB achieved good predictive validity, correcting for restricted range. Anstey (1977) continued to follow up Vernon's sample until the mid-1970s, when many of those selected were nearing retirement. Using achieved rank as criterion, Anstey reported an eventual predictive validity, after 30 years, that was very good (0.66, corrected for restricted range). All but 21 of 301 CSSB graduates in Anstey's analysis achieved Assistant Secretary rank, showing that they made the grade as senior Civil Servants. Only three left because of 'definite inefficiency'.

Police officers

ACs, described as 'extended interviews', are used for selecting senior police officers in the UK (Feltham, 1988a). Validity has been very disappointing. Assessors' conference rating correlated at best by 0.18 (uncorrected) with supervisor rating and training criteria, although Feltham's re-analysis (see above) suggested that more efficient use of the information could have achieved better results. American research using ACs for entry-level police officer selection has also reported poor results (Pynes & Bernardin, 1989), suggesting that selection for police work may present unusual difficulties.

Netherlands postal workers

Jansen and Stoop (2001) reported a seven-year follow-up, using career progress as outcome, which achieved an overall validity of 0.39.

Reviews and meta-analyses

Reviews (Cohen, Moses & Byham, 1974; Schmitt *et al.*, 1984; Gaugler *et al.*, 1987) distinguish between different criteria of success, such as performance ratings, promotion, rated potential for further promotion, achievement/grades, status change and wages (*see* Table 8.3). Hunter and Hunter (1984) corrected Cohen *et al.*'s median for performance ratings for attenuation, increasing it to 0.43. UK data, especially from the CSSB, suggest that ACs have good predictive validity in selection as well. Schmitt *et al.* corrected for sampling error, but not for criterion reliability. The third review (Gaugler *et al.*, 1987) is a validity generalisation analysis covering 50 studies. The authors reported a median raw validity of 0.29 and an estimated true validity of 0.37. Where the criterion was rated potential, validity was higher, as in earlier reviews. Gaugler *et al.*'s VGA uncovered several factors that moderated AC validity, as well as finding that several other factors which might be thought to affect validity did not in fact do so. AC validity was higher when:

- more assessments were included
- psychologists rather than managers were used as assessors
- peer evaluations were used
- more candidates were female.

Table 8.3   Summary of four analyses of assessment centre validity.

	Reviewer			
	Cohen	Schmitt	Gaugler	Arthur
Criterion				
Performance	0.33	0.43	0.37	0.35
Promotion	0.40	0.41	0.36	
'Potential'	0.63	0.53		
Achievement		0.31		
Wages		0.24		
Training			0.35	
AC dimension				
Communication				0.32
Consideration				0.24
Drive				0.32
Influence				0.38
Organising/planning				0.39
Problem solving				0.36
Tolerance of stress/uncertainty				0.20

Note: Data from Cohen *et al.* (1974), Schmitt *et al.* (1984), Gaugler *et al.* (1987), and Arthur *et al.* (in press).

AC validity was not affected by the following:

- ratio of candidates to assessors
- amount of assessor training
- how long the assessors spent integrating the information.

The most recent review (Arthur *et al.*, in press) only covered studies that reported validity for AC dimensions separately, so does not represent a complete updating.

Maintaining and improving AC validity

The nature of the AC method makes it especially vulnerable to loss of validity by careless practice. Schmitt, Schneider and Cohen (1990) analysed data from ACs for school administrators, centrally planned but locally implemented in 16 separate sites. A VGA across the sites found true residual variance, showing that validity was higher in ACs that served several school districts rather than just one, but lower where assessors had worked with the candidates. Both results suggested that impartiality improves validity. Jones *et al.* (1991) discussed ways of improving the validity of the Admiralty Interview Board. They reduced eight dimensions to four, they required assessors to announce ratings for specific dimensions before announcing their overall suitability rating, and they introduced nine-point ratings with indications of what percentage of ratings should fall within each category. Gaugler and Thornton (1989) confirmed that using fewer dimensions gives more accurate ratings. Ryan *et al.* (1995) investigated the use of video-recording, which should in theory make assessors' ratings more reliable and accurate, because they can watch key events more than once to make quite sure who said what, and how each person reacted. Use of video-recording resulted in more accurate observations of group discussions, but did not improve the accuracy of ratings. Watching video-recordings is also very time-consuming, and time tends to be limited in most ACs.

Reservations about AC validity

Ipsativity

One person's performance in a group exercise depends on how the others in the group behave. A fairly dominant person in a group of extremely dominant subjects may appear weak and ineffective by comparison. Gaugler and Rudolph (1992) showed that the way in which one candidate in a group is rated depends on how the others behave. Candidates who performed poorly in an otherwise good group obtained lower ratings than a poor candidate in a generally poor group. Gaugler and Rudolph also found that assessors' ratings were more accurate when candidates differed a lot, suggesting that assessors compare candidates with each other rather than with an external standard.

The *ipsativity* problem can be reduced to some extent by recombining groups, and by introducing *normative* data from psychological tests.

Criterion contamination

This can be a blatant self-fulfilling prophecy, which the uncritical observer might take for proof of validity. For example, Smith returns from the AC with a good rating (predictor) and so gets promoted (criterion). A high correlation between AC rating and promotion is therefore found, but proves little. Criterion contamination can be subtler. For example, candidates who have done well at the AC are deemed suitable for more challenging tasks, develop greater self-confidence, acquire more skills and consequently get promoted. Many ACs suffer from criterion contamination, because employers naturally want to act on the results of the assessment. The AT&T Management Progress Study is one of the very few studies that kept AC results secret until the validity coefficient has been calculated, thereby avoiding contamination. However, the VGA of Gaugler *et al.* (1987) casts doubt on the extent of the criterion contamination problem. Criterion contamination will result in spuriously high validity coefficients, but Gaugler *et al.* found no evidence that criterion contamination increases validity. A follow-up of developmental ACs (Jones & Whitmore, 1995) showed that those who attended, and a naturally occurring control group (who had been selected to go, but for whom there was no space), displayed no difference in career advancement subsequently.

'Face fits'

Early on critics commented on the 'curious homogeneity in the criteria used', namely 'salary growth or progress (often corrected for starting salary), promotions above first level, management level achieved and supervisor's ratings of potential' (Klimoski & Strickland, 1977). These criteria 'may have less to do with managerial effectiveness than managerial adaptation and survival'. Klimoski and Strickland suggested that ACs pick up the personal mannerisms that top management use in promotion, which may not have much to do with actual effectiveness. According to this argument, ACs answer the question 'Does his/her face fit?', not the question 'Can he/she do the job well?'. Klimoski and Strickland complained that few studies use less suspect criteria.

The review by Cohen *et al.* (1974) found that AC ratings predicted *actual job performance* moderately well, but predicted *higher management ratings of management potential* much better (*see* Table 8.3). On the other hand, later reviews by Schmitt *et al.* (1984) and Gaugler *et al.* (1989) found less difference between promotion/potential criteria and performance criteria. Schmitt *et al.*'s review does strongly confirm Klimoski and Strickland's argument that 'face fits' criteria are more popular for ACs. A total of 12 coefficients, based on 14,662 subjects, used status change and wages criteria, whereas only six coefficients, based on a mere 394 subjects, used performance ratings. However, in a sense all of these studies are irrelevant to Klimoski and Strickland's criticism, because 'performance' criteria in AC research are still ratings (i.e. management's opinion of the candidate).

Klimoski and Strickland (1977) are really addressing a much more fundamental problem in selection research, namely the *criterion*, discussed in Chapter 11. The general class of supervisor rating criterion can be viewed as answering the question 'Does Smith make a good impression on management?'. Klimoski and Strickland argue that the AC – more than other selection tests – addresses the same question, which makes its high validity less surprising, and perhaps even trivial. The solution lies in validating ACs against objective criteria, such as sales or output, not against different wordings ('potential'/'performance') of the general 'favourable-impression-on-management' criterion. Very few studies of ACs have used objective criteria. Gaugler *et al.*'s meta-analysis distinguishes five broad classes and 12 narrower classes of criterion, all of which appear to involve, somewhere, management's opinion of the candidate. For example, *training* is 'performance of manager in training programme', which is presumably rated by some manager higher up. Two studies (McEvoy & Beatty, 1989; Atkins & Wood, 2002) have used peer and subordinate ratings as the criterion, and found that these agree with AC ratings as well as conventional ratings from above. This suggests either that Klimoski and Strickland's criticism is unfounded, or that the peer and subordinate ratings also assess image rather than substance. Only one study has used a truly objective criterion. Russell and Domm (1995) reported that AC rating correlated by 0.32 with net store profit, and by 0.28 with supervisor rating, in retail store managers. This single study suggests that Klimoski and Strickland's criticism is unfounded, but more research on AC validity is needed using objective criteria. The problem is that ACs are most commonly used to assess managers, who often do not do anything or produce anything that can be counted.

The exercise/attribute problem

The logic of the AC method implies that assessors should rate candidates on *dimensions*. However, research strongly suggests that assessors often assess candidates on *exercises*. In Figure 8.3 there are three types of correlations.

1. Those at AAA are for the same dimension rated in different exercises (monotrait heteromethod correlations), which 'ought' to be high. This is *convergent validity*.
2. Those at bbb are for different dimensions rated in the same exercise (heterotrait monomethod correlations), which 'ought' to be lower. This is *discriminant validity*. However, note that many AC dimensions are conceptually related and so are likely to be positively correlated. Thus zero correlations are not necessarily to be expected at bbb.
3. Those at ccc are for different attributes rated in different exercises (heterotrait heteromethod correlations), which 'ought' to be very low or zero.

	Exercise A			Exercise B		
Dimensions	1	2	3	1	2	3
Exercise A						
Dimension 1 Dimension 2 Dimension 3	 bbb bbb	 bbb				
Exercise B						
Dimension 1 Dimension 2 Dimension 3	AAA ccc ccc	ccc AAA ccc	ccc ccc AAA	 bbb bbb	 bbb	

Figure 8.3   Three types of correlation in an AC with three dimensions (1 to 3) rated in each of two exercises (A and B)

However, in real ACs what 'ought' to happen rarely does. Early research (Sackett & Dreher, 1982) found that ratings of different dimensions in the same exercise (bbb correlations in Figure 8.3) correlated very highly, showing a lack of *discriminant validity*, while ratings of the same trait in different exercises (AAA correlations) hardly correlated at all, showing a lack of *convergent validity*. The ACs were not measuring general decisiveness across a range of management tasks – they were measuring general performance on each of a series of tasks. However, if decisiveness in task A does not generalise to decisiveness in task B, how can one be sure that it will generalise to decisiveness on the job? Two meta-analyses of AC multitrait multimethod correlations have been published (Born, Kolk & van der Flier, 2000; Woehr & Arthur, in press). They report near identical averages for convergent validity (0.34 and 0.33) and divergent validity (0.55 and 0.58). A more complex analysis by Lievens and Conway (2001) concluded that on average exercise and attribute each account for the same proportion of variation in ratings, but with very wide variations between the 34 studies.

Factor analysis

If an AC is intended to assess four main attributes, then factor analysis of AC ratings 'ought' to find four corresponding factors. However, what frequently emerges from conventional or *exploratory* factor analysis is a set of factors corresponding to the exercises, not the attributes. Recent research uses *confirmatory factor analysis (CFA)*, which tests how well different factorial models fit the data. For an AC with five dimensions and four exercises, four models might describe the data:

1. five correlated dimension factors
2. four correlated exercise factors
3. five correlated dimension factors, and four correlated exercise factors

4. five correlated dimensions factors, with 'correlated uniquenesses' corresponding to the four exercises.

Model 1 is what 'ought' to be found – the ratings ought to reflect dimensions. Model 2 is what actually seems to occur in many sets of AC ratings – the ratings reflect exercises rather than dimensions. Models 3 and 4 include both attribute and exercise as sources of variance. Lievens and Conway (2001) analysed 34 sets of AC data and concluded that model 4, which includes both dimensions and exercises, seems to fit best. Attempts to fit models that include only attributes fail completely.

Explaining the exercise effect

Various explanations have been offered for the exercise effect. Some imply that the problem will be solved fairly easily by changing the way in which the AC is run.

Overload

When assessors are given too many people to watch or too many dimensions to rate, information overload forces them to simplify the task by rating overall performance rather than aspects of it.

Rating the unratable

Asking assessors to rate a dimension that is not manifested in observable behaviour encourages global ratings (i.e. an exercise effect).

Incomplete design

Most ACs use an incomplete experimental design. It is rarely the case that every rater rates every candidate on every dimension in every exercise, but this is what is needed to unravel the exercise/attribute problem. Poor correlations between exercises may result because different raters are used. Within-exercise correlations may be higher because the ratings are made by the same raters.

Transparency

Kleinmann, Kuptsch and Koller (1996) suggested that transparency will reduce the exercise effect. If the candidates know what is being assessed, and even more so if they make a conscious effort to exhibit that behaviour, then ratings will organise themselves more around dimensions and less around exercises.

Mis-specification

ACs do not assess the attributes that they were designed to assess, but something else, which happens fortunately to be related to job performance. The assessors are actually assessing this 'something else', which is why their ratings of attributes A, B and C are highly correlated. Using a method that works, but not in the way one intends it to, is worrying, and could create problems with regard to justifying its use when challenged. There might be a quicker, cheaper and better way of assessing whatever it is that ACs assess. Candidates for what ACs 'really' assess include mental ability and self-monitoring (Arthur & Tubre, in press) – that is, the ability to present oneself well.

Attributes do not exist

Social learning theorists such as Mischel (1968) would expect to find exercise effects. They do not believe in broad traits that shape behaviour consistently, but they do believe that behaviour is to a large extent shaped by the situation in which people find themselves (i.e. by the particular demands of the exercises).

Solving the exercise effect problem

Three recent analyses (Born et al., 2000; Lievens & Conway, 2001; Woehr & Arthur, in press) have assessed the effectiveness of various attempted solutions to the exercise effect.

- Convergent validity is higher when assessors have fewer dimensions to rate, consistent with the overload hypothesis.
- Psychologists and human resource specialists show more convergent validity than line managers or students.
- Analysis of length of training yields inconsistent results. Lievens and Conway (2001) reported that more than one day of training *reduced* convergent validity, whereas one might expect more training to improve it. Woehr and Arthur (in press) found that more than one day of training increased convergent validity, but that more than five days (represented by only one study) decreased it again.
- Lievens (2001a) argued that type of training is also important. *Frame of reference (FoR)* training seeks to give all assessors the same view of what behaviour counts as, for example, decision making. FoR training improves convergent validity more than training in observation skills. Schleicher et al. (2002) confirmed that FoR training improves reliability, convergent validity and criterion validity of an AC.
- Woehr and Arthur found that six studies in which assessors rated at the end of the AC yielded higher convergent validity than the larger number that followed the more usual practice of rating after each exercise. In a long AC this might not be practicable – assessors might find it difficult to rate behaviour that they saw two days and six exercises ago.
- Born et al. (2000) found seven studies where the same assessor rated both halves of the convergent validity correlation, which raised the convergent validity considerably to 0.64. Born et al. thought that this might reflect halo (i.e. not be a true solution to the problem).

- Lievens and Conway (2001) found that giving assessors behavioural checklists increased convergent validity, but not significantly.
- Haaland and Christianse (2002) confirmed that ensuring the behaviour to be rated would be visible in the exercise increased convergent validity.

However, other factors made no difference.

- The purpose of the AC – selection or development – makes no difference, although it is more important to achieve convergent validity in a developmental AC, where the profile of ratings is used to plan each person's training and development programme.
- The ratio of candidates to assessors makes no difference. However, the studies reviewed all have fairly low ratios (two or three candidates per assessor), so probably did not suffer overload.
- Transparency – that is, telling candidates what is being assessed so that they can exhibit it more clearly – does not increase convergent validity.

Two recent articles offer radically different perspectives on the exercise effect problem.

Lance et al. (2000b) argued that ACs have never worked in the way they were meant to: 'assessors form overall judgements of performance in each exercise. . .[then] produce separate post-exercise trait ratings because they are required to do so'. If assessors are 'working backwards' in this way, it is not surprising that traits within exercises correlate highly. ACs work if the right exercises have been included (i.e. those that 'replicate important job behaviors'). According to this argument, the AC becomes a collection of work sample tests, and we should abandon the trait/attribute/dimension framework, which just creates needless confusion for both assessor and researcher.

By contrast, Lievens (2001b) reported data which suggest that there may not really be an exercise/attribute problem. He noted that all previous research has used real ACs with real candidates, whose real behaviour is not known. Perhaps they do behave in the way that assessors describe (i.e. consistent within exercises, but not across them). Lievens prepared video recordings in which candidates showed high levels of some traits over all exercises, and low levels of other traits across all exercises (i.e. the candidates behaved in the way that the logic of the AC would expect). Psychologists and managers who rated these tapes correctly reported what they saw, so they generated strong attribute effects in their ratings. This proves that observers *can* make ratings that show convergent validity, but it does not explain why they *do not* make them in most real ACs.

Construct validity

Two meta-analyses (Scholz & Schuler, 1993; Collins et al., 2001) have compared AC overall assessment ratings with ability and personality tests, with interesting results.

- Both found a fairly large correlation with mental ability, to some extent confirming the suggestion that the AC may be an elaborate and very expensive way of assessing intellectual ability.
- In most studies the assessors have the mental ability test results in front of them when they are making their ratings, so the ratings could be influenced by the test data. However, Scholz and Schuler's analysis found four studies in which the assessors did not see the test data, and where the overall correlation was not significantly lower.
- Better overall AC ratings tend to be linked to Extraversion and (low) Neuroticism, but not to Conscientiousness, which is surprising, as Conscientiousness is the personality factor that is most closely associated with work performance. Surprisingly, however, few correlations with Conscientiousness have been reported.
- Scholz and Schuler (1993) found that correlations with the big five were fairly small, while correlations for some more specific traits (e.g. self-confidence) were greater.

It could be plausibly argued that some components will correlate more with mental ability (e.g. in-tray exercises), while others will correlate more with personality (e.g. performance in group discussions). Collins *et al.* (2001) also tried to estimate the construct validity of AC components. Unfortunately, too few studies reported a correlation between tests and AC components to permit a meta-analysis. However, the results did find that mental ability correlates highly with both in-tray (0.57) and group discussion (0.55). As Collins *et al.* note, it is unlikely that personality will correlate better than 0.55 with group exercise ratings. This tends to confirm the 'elaborate intelligence test' view of ACs, and also fails to provide evidence of discriminant validity.

Incremental validity

Schmidt and Hunter (1998) cited Collins' estimate of the 0.65 correlation between AC ratings and mental ability (*see* Table 8.4), and argued that the incremental validity of ACs over mental ability tests would be negligible. However, several empirical studies have shown that ACs achieve better validity than psychological tests. Vernon (1950) found that the CSSB's test battery had poor predictive validity. Similarly, the British Admiralty Interview Board found that tests alone gave poorer predictions (Gardner & Williams, 1973). Goffin, Rothstein and Johnston (1996) found that a personality test gives considerable incremental validity over an assessment centre. Dayan, Kasten and Fox (2002) reported data for the Israeli police force which do show incremental validity of a very thorough AC over mental ability tests. They suggested that Schmidt and Hunter's pessimistic conclusions may only apply to management, not to entry-level selection, and may not apply either to work where dealing with people under very difficult circumstances is crucial.

Table 8.4 Summary of two meta-analyses of AC construct validity: Scholz & Schuler (1993) correct for reliability of both test and AC rating; Collins *et al.* (2001) correct for restricted range and AC rating reliability, but not test reliability.

	Collins *et al.* (2001)	Scholz & Schuler (1993)
Mental ability	0.65	0.43
Neuroticism	−0.34	−0.15
Extraversion	0.47	0.14
Openness	0.23	0.09
Agreeableness	0.16	−0.07
Conscientiousness	−	−0.06
Dominance		0.30
Achievement motivation		0.40
Social competence		0.41
Self-confidence		0.32

Fairness and the assessment centre

The AC is often regarded as fair or even 'EEOC-proof', meaning that it creates no *adverse impact* on women or minorities. ACs have been recommended, or even ordered, by courts as alternatives to mental ability tests or educational requirements. Critics note that ACs are most often used for management, at which level adverse impact on minorities is less of an issue. The AC has high *face* or *content validity* (*see* Chapters 11 and 12), which probably accounts for much of its popularity, and also probably gives it a measure of protection against claims of unfairness. Fighting one's case in a committee, chairing a meeting, answering an in-tray or leading a squad all have obvious and easily defended job relevance.

Gender

ACs do not seem to create *adverse impact* – as many women as men get good ratings. A large-scale follow-up of 1,600 female entry-level managers in Bell Telephone found that ratings of middle-management potential predicted achieved rank seven years later as well as AT&T's study of male managers (Ritchie & Moses, 1983). Walsh *et al.* (1987) analysed data for 1,035 applicants for financial services sales posts, and reported that women got better assessments, but only from all-male assessor panels, which suggests that there was an inverted bias at work. Shore (1992) found that women got better ratings in an AC, but on follow-up 5–10 years later had not advanced any further up the organisation than men, which again suggested a bias at work, but not during the AC itself. Lievens (2001a) reviewed Dutch, German and North American research that found either no gender differences in AC ratings, or a slight tendency for women to get better ratings.

Race

Hoffman and Thornton (1997) compared data from ACs and from a test of mental abilities, for white and non-white Americans. The test had slightly higher (uncorrected) validity (0.30 vs. 0.26) and was very much cheaper ($50 per head vs. $500). However, it also created very much more adverse impact on non-white candidates, so much in Hoffman's view as to make its use politically impossible. The AC could be used to choose the best 50% of candidates without creating any adverse impact, whereas the test started to create adverse impact when only the bottom 20% of candidates were excluded. Lievens (2001c) noted that white/minority differences are sometimes found in US research, but not always, and suggested that this depended on the mix of components in the AC. Goldstein, *et al.* (2001) found that AC exercises which correlated more with mental ability created larger white/Afro-American differences. Partialling out mental ability removed the ethnicity differences without removing the AC's validity.

Age

AC ratings sometimes show small negative correlations with age, which may create problems in the USA, where discrimination on grounds of age is prohibited by the Age Discrimination in Employment Act.

Key points

In Chapter 8 you have learned the following.

- Assessment centres (ACs) are tailor-made, so they can assess a range of attributes by a range of methods.
- ACs should have a conceptual matrix linking attributes that are assessed to assessment methods that are included.
- ACs have good validity, although their validity may decay with careless usage.
- AC validity may have an element of circularity, because it tends to assess what management think of the applicants during the AC with what management thinks of the candidate subsequently 'on the job'.
- ACs are intended to assess competences as exhibited in a number of exercises (convergent validity), but appear to assess global proficiency in a series of exercises.
- AC construct validity has been researched, showing that ACs correlate quite strongly with mental ability.
- ACs create less adverse impact and encounter fewer legal problems.

Key references

Anstey (1977) describes a long-term follow-up of the British CSSB.

Arthur *et al.* (in press) present the most recent review of AC validity.

Bray and Grant (1966) describe the classic AT&T Management Progress Study.

Feltham (1988a) describes a British assessment centre for selecting senior police officers.

Gaugler *et al.* (1987) present a meta-analysis and VGA of assessment centre validity.

Lievens and Conway (2001c) present a detailed structural equation modelling account of the assessment centre convergent/discriminant validity problem.

Spychalski *et al.* (1997) describe a survey of current American assessment centre practice.

Woehr and Arthur (in press) discuss ways of solving the discriminant/convergent validity problem.

CHAPTER 9

Work samples and other methods

Education, work samples, physique, in trays, T & E ratings, drug use testing and self-ratings

Introduction

There are seven classes of miscellaneous selection test that do not fit neatly into any other main category, namely education, work samples, in tray, Training and Education (T & E) ratings, self-assessments, physical tests and drug use testing. Education is probably the oldest of these, having been in use in Imperial China for many centuries to select public officials. Work samples can be traced back to Munsterburg's work in 1913. In-tray tests date back to 1957. T & E ratings and self-assessments are slightly more recent. Formal physical tests have replaced more casual physical assessments since the 1970s to conform with fair employment legislation. Drug use testing is the most recent, and most controversial, of the seven classes of test.

Education

Employers in the UK often specify a requirement for so many GCSE or A-Level passes, and professional training schemes almost always do. American employers used to require high-school graduation, but most no longer do so. Common sense suggests that people who do well at school are more able, mature and highly motivated, so they fit into work more easily. It is a lot easier and cheaper to ask how well someone did at school than to try to assess their ability, maturity and motivation.

Early analyses of American college-grade-point averages (marks from exams and course work) found weak relationships with work performance (Reilly and Chao, 1982; Vineberg and Joyner, 1982). Baird's (1985) review reported low positive correlations between school or college achievements and various indices of occupational success, such as scientific output, performance as a physician, or success in management. More recently, Roth *et al.* (1996) meta-analysed 71 studies relating grades to work performance, and found a corrected validity of 0.33. However, validity decays very rapidly, falling from 0.45 one year after graduation to 0.11 six years after.

Education tests have fallen foul of American fair employment laws in a big way. Some US minorities do less well at school, so more fail to complete high school. Roth and Bobko (2000) reported an analysis of ethnicity differences in grade-point average for 7,000 students at an American university, and found a large difference that would create major adverse impact. The difference increases sharply from the first to the third year, where it amounts to 0.78 of an SD. Adverse impact means that the employer has to prove the job really needs the educational level or qualifications specified. This has usually proved difficult. Meritt-Haston and Wexley's (1983) review of 83 US court cases found that educational requirements were generally ruled unlawful for skilled or craft jobs, supervisors and management trainees, but were accepted for police and academics.

Work sample tests

Work-sample tests used not to be very highly thought of; Guion's (1965) book on personnel testing devoted just over three pages to them. However, they have become very much more popular since then. Work-sample tests are justified by *behavioural consistency* theory which states two principles: 'past behaviour is the best predictor of future behaviour' and 'like predicts like'. Close correspondence between predictor and criterion will ensure higher validity, as well as less scope for legal challenge. Mental ability tests assess the applicant's general suitability and make an intermediate inference – 'this person is intelligent so he/she will be good at widget-stamping'. Testing the employee with a real or simulated widget-stamper makes no such inference (nor is widget-stamping ability quite such an emotive issue as general mental ability).

Campion (1972) described a typical set of work-sample tests for maintenance mechanics. After a thorough job analysis, he selected four tasks, namely installing pulleys and belts, disassembling and repairing a gear box, installing and aligning a motor, and pressing a bush into a sprocket and reaming it to fit a shaft. Campion compared the work-sample test with a battery of paper-and-pencil tests, namely Bennett Mechanical Comprehension, Wonderlic, and Short Employment Tests (Verbal, Numerical and Clerical Aptitude). The work samples predicted three supervisor rating criteria fairly well, whereas the paper-and-pencil tests predicted very poorly. Campion described a classic work-sample test of the type used in Europe and Britain in the 1920s and 1930s, and applied on a large scale in wartime testing programmes. The meaning and scope of the term 'work sample' has been widened somewhat in the last 20 to 25 years. Robertson and Kandola (1982) distinguished four classes of work sample:

Class of work sample	Example
psychomotor	typing, sewing, using tools
individual decision making	in-tray exercise
job-related information tests	
group discussions/decisions.	

The *psychomotor* category covers the classic work sample. *In-trays* and *group exercises* extend the principle to jobs which do not need motor skills. 'Job-related information test' is another name for *trade* or *job knowledge* test, and does not have much in common with a true work sample.

Cascio and Phillips (1979) described 21 work samples for municipal employees in Miami Beach, covering a wide range of manual, clerical and administrative jobs, from electrician's helper to parking-meter technician, and from library assistant to concession attendant. Cascio and Philips argued that the tests were very convincing to the applicants. If applicants for the job of electrician had completed the wiring test correctly, the lights lit up, but if the wiring was incorrect, the bulbs did not light, and the applicant could not deny that he or she had made a mistake. Some of the tests had a *realistic job preview* (*see* Chapter 1) built in; quite a few would-be sewer mechanics withdrew after being tested in an underground sewage chamber. The US military also favour work samples, known as *hands-on performance tests* (Carey, 1991), but sometimes use them as *criterion* as well as using them as *predictor*.

Scoring

Work samples are observed and rated. Sometimes a global rating is made, and sometimes ratings of various aspects of task completion are made and possibly averaged. Often the rater will be provided with checklists (*see* Figure 9.1). Work samples can usually achieve good inter-rater reliability. For example, Lance *et al.* (2000a) quote values of 0.81 to 0.98. Lance *et al.* also analysed the validity of work-sample rating by comparing it with the checklist. They found that the rating was very largely shaped by the checklist, and was not affected by irrelevant factors such as ethnicity.

Validity

Several reviews all conclude that work samples achieve good validity. Schmitt *et al.* (1984) reported a *true validity* (corrected for sampling error only) of 0.38, one of the higher true validities that they report. Dunnette's (1972) analysis of

> • Remove inner tube
> • Inflate and submerge in water to detect (all) punctures
> • Mark (all) punctures
> • Deflate tube and dry thoroughly
> • Roughen tube with abrasive
> • Spread adhesive and wait 30 seconds
> • Peel cover off patch
> • Line up carefully and press firmly on to puncture
> • Dust with talc
> • Do not check whether patch is firmly stuck down
> • Check outer cover for damage or continued presence of nail, etc.

Figure 9.1   Part of checklist for work-sample test on repairing a puncture

tests in the American petroleum industry found that work samples achieved similar validities for operating and processing, maintenance and clerical jobs. Hunter and Hunter (1984) found work samples to be the best test (0.54) by a short head for promotion decisions, although all tests give fairly good results for the latter.

Robertson and Kandola (1982) reviewed the validity of work samples from a wider body of research, taking in US wartime studies and UK research. The median validity for *psychomotor* work samples is quite good (0.39), although it has a very wide range. Robertson and Kandola did not calculate a validity generalisation analysis, nor did they correct for any source of error, so their median was likely to be an underestimate of true validity. Median validities for job knowledge tests, group exercises and in-tray exercises were comparable to *psychomotor* work samples, although *job knowledge tests* predicted training grades much better than work performance.

Incremental validity

Schmidt and Hunter (1998) noted that work samples correlate by 0.38 with mental ability, and concluded that the incremental validity of work-sample tests over tests of mental ability will be high (0.12), one of the highest values that they cite. The combination of work sample and mental ability tests is one of the three that Schmidt and Hunter recommend employers to consider using.

Domain validity

Work samples achieve domain validity in some circumstances. If the employer can list every task that employees need to be able to do, and can devise work samples for every task, they can then make statements along the lines of 'X has mastered 80% of the job's demands'. X is being compared here with what the job requires, not with other candidates (as is usually the case in selection). This avoids many of the problems of validation. The employer does not need large samples from which to calculate a reliable correlation. X may be the one and only person who does that job, but we can still say that X has mastered 80% of it. If X has only mastered 60%, we can send X on more training courses until he or she has mastered enough of the job to be allowed to start work on it. We might still face adverse impact problems, but approaching validity from the perspective of how much of the job the person can competently do will probably be a lot easier to defend in court than conventional statistical validation. The problems with the domain approach are expense and practicality. Few employers can afford to describe their jobs in sufficient detail, and a very large number of jobs do not lend themselves to such detailed and specific descriptions. The American military has listed the critical tasks that US Marines have to do, and devised work samples to assess them (Carey, 1994).

Trainability tests

True work samples can only be used if the person has already mastered the job's skills – it is clearly pointless giving a typing test to someone who cannot type. (In contrast, in-tray and group exercises do not presuppose any special knowledge, skill or experience.) Trainability tests are a sub-type of work sample that assess how well the applicant can learn a new skill. They are widely used in Skillcentres run by the (British) Manpower Services Commission (Robertson and Downs, 1979). The instructor gives standardised instructions and a demonstration, and then rates the trainee's efforts using a checklist (does not tighten chuck sufficiently, does not use coolant, does not set calibrations to zero, etc.). Robertson and Downs reported good results for bricklaying, carpentry, welding, machine sewing, forklift truck driving, fitting, machining and even dentistry. In the USA, Reilly and Israelski (1988) used trainability tests, called *minicourses*, to select staff for AT&T's new technology training, and reported good correlations with training performance (0.55) and job performance (0.50), correcting for criterion reliability. A meta-analysis of trainability test validity (Robertson and Downs, 1989) found that they predicted training success much better (0.39–0.57, uncorrected) than job performance (0.20–0.24). The high correlation with training success almost certainly reflects the similarity between test and criterion. Robertson and Downs (1989) also found that trainability test validity fell off quite markedly over time.

People who are doing trainability tests can assess their own performance, even though they are not told the results. Applicants for machine sewing jobs in effect selected themselves for the job (*see* Figure 9.2). Scores on a sewing machine trainability test were not used to select, but high scorers took up sewing jobs, whereas low scorers generally did not (Downs, Farr and Colbeck, 1978).

Limitations of work-sample tests

Work samples are necessarily job specific, so a tramway system – like the Boston, Massachusetts network that used the first work sample – will need different work samples for drivers, inspectors, mechanics, electricians, etc., which will prove expensive. Work samples are best for specific concrete skills, and do not work so well if the work is diverse or abstract or involves other people. Work samples usually have to be administered one to one, which also makes them expensive. Carey (1991) evaluated various less expensive substitutes for true work samples and found that only job knowledge tests give the same results; training grades and various types of ratings do not. Hedge and Teachout (1992) found that *interview work samples* give as valid results as hands-on work samples, and are much cheaper and safer. Instead of driving a real tank from A to B, the candidate stands by a simulator and explains how to drive the tank.

Critics (Barrett, 1992) argue that work-sample tests are profoundly unin-formative, unlikely to retain validity over time, and difficult to modify in order to regain lost validity. A motor mechanic work sample 'may combine knowledge of carburettors, skill in using small tools, and...reasoning ability'. The work sample does not separate these abilities. If car engines change (e.g. adopting fuel injection), the work sample loses validity, but once devised the

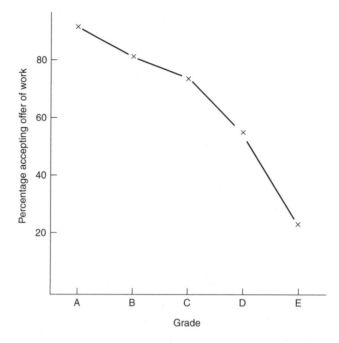

Figure 9.2   Proportion of applicants who accepted a job offer, after taking a trainability test, for each of five grades obtained on the test. Note that applicants were not told the test scores, nor were the test scores used to decide to whom to make offers. Data taken from Downs *et al.* (1978)

work sample is difficult to modify because there is no information about the contribution of different elements to the whole (whereas paper-and-pencil tests can be analysed item by item, and items that change meaning can be omitted or changed). The same difficulty arises if the work sample creates adverse impact. The test's users do not know what to alter in order to eliminate the adverse impact. Callinan and Robertson (2000) implicitly agree with Barrett's criticisms, noting that we know little about the work sample's construct validity. Schmidt and Hunter (1998) reported a correlation of 0.38 with general mental ability.

Law, fairness and work sample tests

Work samples became popular as alternatives to legally risky mental ability tests. Work samples have validity as high as that of mental ability tests, but create much less adverse impact. For example, Cascio and Phillips's (1979) Miami Beach work samples created no adverse impact on Afro- and Hispanic-Americans, unlike paper-and-pencil ability tests. Schmitt, Clause and Pulakos (1996) meta-analysed studies of adverse impact in the USA and found that work samples create far smaller differences than paper-and-pencil ability tests (a d statistic of 0.37 for Afro-Americans and zero for Hispanic Americans). Work samples are readily accepted by candidates (Steiner and Gilliland, 1996).

They are also less often the subject of litigation in the USA (Terpstra *et al.*, 1999), and even less often the subject of successful litigation.

In-tray exercises

The in-tray is a management work sample. Candidates deal with a set of letters, memos, notes, reports and phone messages (*see* Figure 9.3). They are instructed to act on the items, not write about them, but are limited to written replies by the assumption that it is Sunday, and that they will be departing shortly for a week's holiday or business trip abroad. The in-tray does not need mastery of specific skills, so can be used for graduate recruitment. The candidate's performance is usually rated both overall and item by item. The overall evaluation checks whether the candidate sorts the items into high and low priority, and notices any connections between items. Some scoring methods are more or less objective (e.g. counting how many decisions the candidate makes), while others require judgements by the scorer, and focus on stylistic aspects.

In-tray exercises can be scored with acceptable reliability by trained assessors (Schippmann *et al.*, 1990). Robertson and Kandola (1982) summarised 53 validity coefficients for individual, decision-making tests, which included an

---

IBT/1

From: V Wordy MICE CEMH FIME
                 (Engineering Director)

To: I Prior
                 (Assistant General Manager)

I am in receipt of your memorandum of 15th November concerning the necessity for more rapid progress on the revised layout of Number 4 component assembly area and am fully cognisant of the urgency of this matter myself. My strenuous efforts in this respect are not however being assisted by the calibre of some of the personnel allocated to myself for this purpose. A particular obstacle with which I am currently faced lies in the persistent absenteeism of certain members of the workforce who appear to have little interest in contributing an effort commensurate with their present rates of pay. The designated complement of shop-floor workers for Assembly Area 4 under the new establishment of 5th October is just adequate for the Area's requisites on the strict understanding that the full complement are in fact present and available for work as opposed to, for example, absenting themselves for lengthy smoking breaks in the male toilet facilities. Efforts on the part of myself and my foreman to instil a sense of purpose and discipline into a workforce sadly lacking any semblance of either attribute have not so far, I am sorry to say, received what I would consider adequate backing from the management. I would like to bring to your attention for your immediate executive action a particularly blatant case which fully merits in my estimation the immediate dismissal of the employee concerned. Yesterday our revised November schedule called for us to be securing the transfer of Number 111 lathe from its former position to its new location.

Figure 9.3   A sample item from an in-tray test

unspecified number of in-trays. The median validity, uncorrected for restricted range or limited reliability, was 0.28. Schippmann *et al.* reviewed 22 validity studies which they found to be too diverse to permit a meta-analysis. They concluded that criterion validity is generally good enough to justify using in-trays. Several studies (e.g. Bray and Grant, 1966) have reported that in-trays have *incremental validity* – that is, they add new information and do not just cover the same ground as tests of verbal or general mental ability. However, Brannick, Michaels and Baker (1989) reported that in-tray exercises show the same feature as the assessment centres of which they often form a part. Factor analysis of scores yields exercise-based factors, not factors corresponding to the dimensions that the exercise is supposed to be assessing. The in-tray's main shortcomings arise from the 'Sunday afternoon' assumption; writing replies in a deserted office may be quite unlike dealing with the same issues face to face or by telephone on a hectic Monday morning. Tests that require people to *write* things that they normally *say* to others have been criticised by fair employment agencies on both sides of the Atlantic.

Training and experience ratings

Training and Experience (T & E) ratings seek to quantify applicants' training and experience, instead of relying on possibly arbitrary judgements by application sifters about suitability. T & E ratings are widely used in the public sector in the USA, especially for jobs that require specialised backgrounds, such as engineering, science and research. T & E ratings would be useful for selecting academics, but are not used in the UK. They are also useful for trade jobs, where written tests unfairly weight verbal skills. T & E ratings are not suitable for entry-level jobs where no prior training and skill are required. Several systems are used. Applications are assigned points for years of training/education, or else applicants are asked for self-ratings of the amount and quality of their experience. In the *behavioural consistency* method, areas that reveal the largest differences between good and poor workers are identified by the *critical incident technique* (*see* Chapter 2). Applicants describe their major achievements in these areas, and their accounts are rated by the selectors using *behaviourally anchored rating scales* (*see* Chapter 4).

Validity

Hunter and Hunter's (1984) VGA included 65 validity coefficients for T & E ratings, and reported a mean true validity of 0.13. McDaniel, Schmidt and Hunter (1988) confirmed that T & E ratings achieve an overall fairly low validity (0.09). However, it is arguably more appropriate to compare the validity of T & E ratings with the 'validity' of sifting applications haphazardly, which is likely to be near zero. McDaniel *et al.* also concluded that some types of T & E ratings achieve higher validity than others – the *behavioural consistency* method does best (0.25). T & E ratings may create adverse impact on women and non-whites who lack training and experience, but otherwise are rarely the subject of fair employment complaints.

Self-assessments

Allport once said 'If you want to know about someone, why not ask him? He might tell you.' Self-assessments ask people for a direct estimate of their potential. The CPI Dominance scale infers dominance from the answers that people give to 36 questions. A self-assessment gets straight to the point ('How dominant are you?' – on a seven-point scale). A typing test takes half an hour to test typing skill, whereas a self-assessment simply asks 'How good a typist are you?'.

Validity

Ash (1980) compared a standard typing test with typists' ratings of their own skill. Ash's best result (0.59) suggested that Allport was right – people are quite good judges of their own abilities. However, Ash's other correlations, for typing letters, tables, figures and revisions, were nowhere near so promising. Levine *et al.* (1977) found that self-assessments of spelling, reading speed, comprehension, grammar, etc. correlated poorly with supervisor rating. DeNisi and Shaw (1977) measured 10 cognitive abilities (mechanical comprehension, spatial orientation, visual pursuit, etc.) and compared test scores with self-assessments. The correlations were very low, suggesting that self-assessments could not be substituted for tests.

Reilly and Chao (1982) found that the overall validity of self-assessments was very low (0.15). Mabe and West (1982) analysed 43 studies and reported a much higher true validity (0.42), partly because they corrected for predictor and criterion reliability. They concluded that self-assessments had highest validity when:

- they were given anonymously – not a lot of use in selection!
- people were told that self-assessments would be compared with objective tests, which means either giving a test or lying to the candidates
- subjects were comparing themselves with fellow workers, which again tends to make them impractical for selection.

Harris and Schaubroek (1988) reported a meta-analysis of self, supervisor and peer ratings of work performance. Self-ratings agreed fairly poorly with others' ratings (0.35 with supervisor, 0.36 with peer). The level of agreement was higher in blue-collar workers (0.40 and 0.42, respectively) and lower in managers (0.27 and 0.31, respectively), suggesting that egocentric bias in rating work performance is greater in work that has less in the way of visible output.

Although self-assessments have been shown to predict performance quite well, hardly anyone has used them for real decisions. Levine *et al.* (1977) suggested that self-assessments are not used because employers suppose that people either cannot or will not give accurate estimates of their abilities. They tested the faking hypothesis by comparing self-assessments of people who knew that their typing ability would be tested with those of people who had no such expectation. The two sets of self-assessments did not differ, implying that people were not faking. However, other studies (Ash, 1980) found that people over-estimated their abilities. Fox and Dinur (1988) tried telling subjects their self-assessments would be checked against other data; predictive accuracy was not affected by this.

Physical tests

Some jobs require strength, agility or endurance. Others require, or are felt to require, physical size. Some jobs require dexterity, and for some jobs an attractive appearance is (explicitly or implicitly) a requirement. Hunter and Burke's (1994) meta-analysis of pilot training included seven studies of reaction time and reported an uncorrected predictive validity of 0.28.

Strength

Tests of physique or strength are sometimes used in the UK, often in a fairly arbitrary or haphazard way. Fire brigades require applicants to climb a ladder while carrying a weight. Other employers rely on the company medical check-up, or an 'eyeball' test by a personnel manager or supervisor. North American employers use physical tests much more systematically. The American gas industry uses four isometric strength tests (arm, grip, shoulder and lower torso) for jobs with high- or medium-strength requirements (Hoffman, 1999). Armco Inc. uses a battery of physical work-sample tests for labourers, and has extensive data on norms, correlations and sex differences (Arnold *et al.*, 1982). Pole-climbing is an essential part of many AT&T engineering jobs. The company has developed a battery of three tests, namely *balance*, *static strength* (pulling on a rope) and *higher body density* (less fat and more muscle) (Reilly, Zedeck & Tenopyr, 1979).

Dimensions of physical ability

Measures of physique and physical performance often inter-correlate very highly. Fleishman and Mumford (1991) factor-analysed a very wide range of physical tasks and concluded that there are nine factors underlying physical proficiency (*see* Table 9.1). Fleishman developed *Physical Abilities Analysis*, a profile of the physical abilities that are needed for a job. Subsequently, Hogan (1991) re-analysed data on tests of physical proficiency, and concluded that there are only three main factors, namely *strength*, *endurance* and *movement quality*, of which *movement quality* is more important in sport than in work.

Validity

Schmitt *et al.*'s (1984) VGA yielded a true validity of 0.32 for physical tests. Hogan (1991) reviewed 14 studies which mostly found positive correlations with work performance, but did not calculate meta-analysis or VGA. Physical tests also predict whether the employee can cope with the job without finding it too demanding, or even suffering injury. Chaffin (1974) found that the greater

Table 9.1   The nine factors underlying human physical ability.

Dynamic strength	Ability to exert muscular force repeatedly or continuously. Useful for doing push-ups, climbing a rope
Trunk strength	Ability to exert muscular force repeatedly or continuously using trunk or abdominal muscles. Useful for leg-lifts or sit-ups
Static strength	The force that an individual can exert against external objects for a brief period. Useful for lifting heavy objects, pulling heavy equipment
Explosive strength	Ability to expend a maximum of energy in one act or a series of acts. Useful for long jump, high jump, 50-metre race
Extent flexibility	Ability to flex or extend trunk and back muscles as far as possible in any direction. Useful for continual bending, reaching, stretching
Dynamic flexibility	Ability to flex or extend trunk and back repeatedly. Useful for continual bending, reaching, stretching
Gross body co-ordination	Also known as agility
Balance	Ability to stand or walk on narrow ledges
Stamina	Also known as cardiovascular endurance, the ability to engage in prolonged maximum exertion. Useful for long-distance running

the discrepancy between a worker's strength and the physical demands of the job, the more likely the worker is to suffer a back injury (a notorious source of lost output in industry). Furthermore, the relationship is continuous and linear, and does not have a threshold, so an employer who wants to minimise the risk of back injury should choose the strongest applicant, all other things being equal. AT&T's battery of pole-climbing tests identified people who were more likely to last in the job for at least six months. Hogan (1985) found that three physical tests (one-mile run, sit-and-reach test and arm ergometer muscle endurance) considerably reduced the very high dropout rate in underwater bomb disposal training in the US Navy.

Adverse impact

Physical tests create a very substantial adverse impact on women, who are on average lighter and less strong than men. In North America, some ethnic groups also vary in physical strength. Disability discrimination laws also make it essential to consider very carefully whether a job really requires particular physical strengths. A review by Terpstra *et al.* (1999) of fair employment cases in the USA found that physical tests featured three or four times as often as would be expected from their estimated frequency of use. Thus physical tests need to be carefully chosen and validated. Requiring applicants for police work to run a mile was ruled unfair because job analysis revealed that most police pursuits on foot were only for short distances (Hogan and Quigley, 1986).

Hoffman (1999) has described a careful programme of physical testing within the American gas industry. 'Marker' jobs such as that of construction crew assistant were used to show that isometric strength tests were valid predictors of the ability to do work that involved carrying 80-pound bags of sand or wrestling with rusted-up bolts. However, many jobs had too few people doing them for conventional validation to be possible. Hoffman used the PAQ (*see* Chapter 2) to cluster-analyse jobs into construction, customer service, clerical, etc., and to indicate the likely physical requirements of each cluster. Physical requirements for construction and warehousing were high, those for customer service were medium, those for clerical work were low, etc. Included in some clusters were the 'marker' jobs. This enabled Hoffman to argue that 'this job is similar in PAQ profile to the construction assistant job, for which we have a validity study, so it's reasonable to expect physical tests to be valid for this post, too'. Hoffman recommends that employers do not rely solely on the PAQ, but arrange to have the physical requirements of each job reviewed by in-house job analysts and experienced supervisors.

Rayson, Holliman and Belyavin (2000) described a physical testing programme in the British Army, which wants to recruit women into all branches, but also sets demanding physical standards. They first listed the main generic physical tasks that the infantry soldier must be able to master. These include the 'single lift' (lifting a 44-kilogram box of ammunition from the ground to the back of a truck), and the 'loaded march' (covering 13 kilometres as quickly as possible while carrying a pack weighing 25 kilograms). However, the core tasks could not be used as actual work samples, on the grounds of both safety (suppose a candidate dropped the ammunition box on his or her foot) and practicality (the tests will be used in city-centre recruiting offices, while route marches require open country and take too long). Accordingly, tests of muscle strength, muscle endurance, body size, aerobic fitness and fat-free mass were devised which were safe and practical, and which would predict ability to complete the core tasks. Some were successful at predicting core task performance, while others were less so. Some showed *differential validity* – they worked well for men but not for women, which of course meant that they could not be used. The British Army programme shows how difficult it can be to devise physical tests that are practical, valid and fair.

Height

'Common sense' suggests that police officers need to be big, in order to overcome violent offenders and command respect. Police forces in the UK still specify minimum heights. American police forces used to set minimum heights, but have been challenged frequently under fair employment legislation. Women are less tall on average than men, and some ethnic minorities in the USA are also less tall, so minimum height tests create *adverse impact* by excluding many women and some minorities. Therefore minimum height tests must be shown to be *job related*. 'Common sense' is surprised to learn that American research has been unable to demonstrate a link between height and any criterion of effectiveness in police officers, so height requirements cannot be justified.

Dexterity

Dexterity can be divided into *arm and hand* or *gross* dexterity, and *finger and wrist* or *fine* dexterity. Dexterity is needed for assembly work, which is generally semi-skilled or unskilled. It is also needed for some professional jobs, notably dentistry and surgery. The General Aptitude Test Battery (*see* Chapter 6) includes both gross and fine dexterity tests. Many work sample and trainability tests also assess dexterity. Ghiselli's (1966b) meta-analysis reported moderate validities of dexterity tests for vehicle operation, trades and crafts, and industrial work. Re-analysis of the GATB database (Hunter, 1986) showed that dexterity became more important as the job became less complex. Hartigan and Wigdor (1989) suggested that the GATB data actually show that dexterity predicts success only at the lowest of five levels of complexity (cannery workers, shrimp pickers or cornhusking-machine operators).

Appearance and attractiveness

Attractiveness used to be dismissed as irrelevant, because 'beauty is in the eye of the beholder'. However, extensive research on physical attractiveness since 1970 has reached different conclusions. There is a broad consensus about who is and who is not attractive. Attractiveness is an important individual difference, and not just in sexual encounters. Research on interviewing (*see* Chapter 3) shows that appearance and attractiveness often affect selectors' decisions. But is appearance or attractiveness a *legitimate* part of the *person specification* for many jobs? For acting and modelling it certainly is. Appearance or attractiveness is often an implicit requirement for receptionists (many advertisements specify 'smart appearance', 'pleasant manner', etc.). Appearance, shading into 'charisma', is probably also important for selling, persuading and influencing jobs.

Drug-use testing

The 1990 (American) National Household Survey reports that 7% of adult employees use illegal drugs (while 6.8% drink alcohol heavily). In the USA, testing applicants for illegal drug use (marijuana, cocaine, heroin) is both popular and controversial. Alcohol testing is also used in the USA for pre-employment testing of truck drivers. Surveys of US companies have produced estimates of just over 40% of employers using drug testing (Murphy and Thornton, 1992). The most widely used method is chemical analysis of urine samples. Alternatives include paper-and-pencil tests, co-ordination tests to detect impairment, and analysis of hair samples. Hair samples have the advantages that they are easier to collect, transport and store, and they can reveal drug use over a period of months, making it more difficult to evade the test by not using drugs for a short period before it (Harris and Trusty, 1997).

Validity

Research on the validity of drug testing as a selection method tends to focus on absence, turnover and accidents rather than on more conventional measures of work performance. Two large separate studies in the US Postal Service (Normand, Salyards & Mahoney, 1990; Zwerling, Ryan & Orav, 1990) found that drug users are more likely to be absent, or to suffer *involuntary turnover*. The implication is that not employing drug users will increase productivity. The Postal Service studies, and other research reviewed by Normand, Lempert & O'Brien (1994), found that the relationship with accidents was less clear. One study (Lehman and Simpson, 1992) found that drug users were more likely to get into arguments with colleagues at work. Register and Williams (1992) reported that drugs users are paid *more*, which suggested that they work *harder*. Register and Williams suggest that this may be because marijuana reduces stress. The Postal Service studies yielded conflicting results on the issue of whether different drugs have different effects. One study found marijuana use to be more closely linked with problems at work than cocaine use, but the other study found the opposite results.

Critics have argued that the link between drug use and work performance is extremely tenuous. In correlational terms, the relationships that were found in the US Postal Service studies were very small (0.08 at best), and accounted for minute amounts of variance (0.6% at best). Critics argue that this is nowhere near enough to justify the intrusion on the applicant's privacy and civil rights. Both Postal Service studies report utility analyses, based on reduced absenteeism, and put a value of four or five million dollars a year on drug testing, albeit spread across the entire American postal workforce. Other critics suggest that many employers adopt drug-testing programmes not to increase productivity, but to retain an image of control, or to project an image of corporate responsibility and concern about social problems.

Mediation

Critics have also argued that the link between drug use and work performance is mediated by some third factor. However, the Postal Service data show that the link is not mediated by race, as some had alleged. The link may also be mediated by *general deviance*. People who do not wish to fit into American society use drugs, and behave differently at work, but do not necessarily behave differently at work *because* they use drugs. According to this argument, drug use is a convenient cue for employers who wish to avoid employing 'dropouts'.

Drug-use testing is legal in the USA, although there is the risk of detecting drugs taken for legitimate medical reasons, in which case refusing employment might violate the Americans with Disabilities Act. Research on the acceptability of drug testing gives conflicting results. Acceptability depends on perceptions of danger (Murphy, Thornton & Prue, 1991), so people regard drug testing as fair for surgeons, police officers or airline pilots, but as unjustified for janitors, farm workers or clerks.

Key points

In Chapter 9 you have learnt the following.

- Educational achievement predicts work performance in the short term but not in the long term.
- Educational achievement requirements create adverse impact in the USA.
- Work-sample tests assess work performance directly and avoid inferences based on abilities or personality traits.
- Work samples have good validity and are acceptable to candidates, but tend to be limited to fairly specific skills.
- Self-assessments can be valid indicators of performance, but probably not in most selection contexts.
- Training and Experience (T & E) ratings can be a good way of sifting applications.
- Physical ability tests will create quite a large adverse impact for gender, but can be used if they are carefully constructed, validated and normed.
- Drug-use testing needs to be thought about carefully. Who will be excluded, how and why? What will people think of it?
- In-tray tests are useful for management.

Key references

Callinan and Robertson (2000) provide an up-to-date review of work-sample research.

Carey (1991) describes the use of work samples by the US armed services.

Cascio and Philips (1979) describe a classic set of work samples devised for Miami City.

Harris and Trusty (1997) give a review of recent research on drug-use testing.

Mabe and West (1982) review early research on self-assessments.

McDaniel *et al.* (1988) review the validity of training and experience ratings.

Meritt-Haston and Wexley (1983) review earlier legal cases concerning educational requirements in the USA.

Rayson *et al.* (2000) describe the problems faced by the British Army in devising physical tests for infantry soldiers.

Roth *et al.* (1996) present a meta-analysis of the validity of educational requirements and work performance.

Schippmann *et al.* (1990) present a narrative review of in-basket test validity.

CHAPTER 10

Validity

How do you know it works?

Introduction

A *valid* test is one that works – that measures what it claims to measure, and that predicts something useful. Dunnette (1966) defined validity more elaborately as learning more about the meaning of a test. A valid test is backed by research and development. Anyone can string together a few dozen questions about assertiveness, but it takes years of patient research, studying large groups of people and collecting follow-up data, to turn the list of questions into a valid psychological test.

The earliest psychological tests were validated against external criteria. Binet's intelligence test used teacher ratings and age (the average 10-year-old can solve problems that the average 6-year-old cannot). Woodworth's Personal Data Sheet selected its questions from psychiatric texts and cases, and checked them against diagnostic status. Since then, validating tests has become a major industry, subject to intense legal scrutiny (*see* Chapter 12).

Types of validity

Many different types of validity can be distinguished. They differ in terms of how convincing they are, how suitable they are for different sample sizes, and their legal acceptability.

Faith validity

The person who sold me the test was very plausible.

The lay person is easily impressed by expensively printed tests, smooth-talking salespeople and sub-psychodynamic nonsense. However, plausibility does not guarantee validity, and money spent on glossy presentation and well-dressed sales staff is all too often money not spent on research and development.

Face validity

The test looks plausible.

Some people are persuaded that a test measures dominance if it is called 'Dominance Test', or if the questions all concern behaving dominantly. Early personality inventories mostly relied on *face validity*. Allport's A(scendance)–S(ubmission) Reaction Study asked questions about rebuking queue-jumpers, asking the first question at seminars, etc. Face validity is never sufficient in itself, but is desirable to the extent that it makes the test more acceptable to employer and employee.

Content validity

The test looks plausible to experts.

Experts analyse the job, choose relevant questions and put together the test. Content validation was borrowed from educational testing, where it makes sense to ask if a test covers the curriculum, and to seek answers from *subject-matter experts*. Content validation regards test items as *samples* of things that workers need to know, not as *signs* of what the workers are like. A *content-valid* test is almost always face valid, but a face valid test is not necessarily content valid. Content validity depends on job analysis (*see* Chapter 2). Distefano, Pryer and Erffmeyer (1983) described four stages in content-validating a test for psychiatric aides.

1. Psychiatric aides, nurses and psychologists write an initial pool of basic work behaviour items.
2. Personnel, training staff and nurses review and modify the items to ensure that they deal with observable behaviour and apply to all six hospitals.
3. Items are rated by 20 psychiatric aides and 18 aide supervisors with regard to how often the task is performed and how essential it is.
4. The 78 surviving items are rewritten in BARS format (*see* Chapter 4). Physically assists patients with bathing, dressing, grooming and related personal hygiene tasks as needed:
   - seldom performs correctly according to standards expected, and requires constant supervision
   - performs below acceptable level, below standards expected, and requires frequent instructions
   - performs consistently above acceptable level, greatly exceeds standards expected, and almost never requires instructions.

Content validation was poorly thought of before the law started taking such a keen interest in selection. Dunnette (1966) said that 'this armchair approach to test validation is, at best, only a starting point'. However, content validation has several advantages. It is plausible to candidates and the public, and easy to defend because the method ensures that the selection procedure is visibly related to the job. It does not require a large sample of people who are currently doing the job, unlike criterion validity. Arthur, Doverspike and Barrett (1996) described a procedure for using several content-valid tests and giving them weights according to the relative importance of different aspects of the job.

Content validation also has limitations. It is only suitable for jobs that involve a limited number of fairly specific tasks. Because it requires people to possess particular skills or particular knowledge, it is more suitable for promotion than for selection. Content-valid tests take a long time to write, and themselves are often very long. The (US) Equal Employment Opportunity Commission (EEOC) *Guidelines* on selection procedures say:

> a selection procedure based upon inferences about mental processes cannot be supported solely or primarily on the basis of content validity. Thus a content strategy is not appropriate for demonstrating the validity of selection procedures which purport to measure traits or constructs, such as mental ability, aptitude, personality, common-sense, judgement, leadership and spatial ability.

This ought to limit content validation to work-sample tests, but employers who are desperate to find fair and valid tests sometimes try to stretch content validation to 'traits and constructs'.

Criterion validity

The test predicts productivity.

Criterion validation is the traditional validation paradigm, favoured by psychologists since 1917. The traditional paradigm looks for evidence that people who score highly on the test are more productive – no matter what the test is called, what the questions are, how they are selected, how plausible the test looks, or how plausible the test's author sounds. What matters is the *criterion*, namely productivity. Criterion validity has three forms: *predictive, concurrent* and *retrospective*.

Predictive validity

The test predicts who *will* produce more.

This is the most convincing demonstration of a test's validity, because it parallels real-life selection – select *today*, and find out *later* if you made the right choice. However, the same time lag makes predictive validation slow and expensive. Predictive validity is also referred to as *follow-up* or *longitudinal* validity.

Concurrent validity

The test 'predicts' who *is* producing more.

Test and criterion data are collected at the same time, (i.e. concurrently). Concurrent validation is quicker and easier than predictive validation. It is also referred to as *present-employee* or *cross-sectional* validity.

Retrospective validity

Past tests 'predict' present productivity.

Retrospective validity is also known as *shelf research*, because employers who are trying to validate tests take data from the office shelf, obtained when employees were recruited, but not necessarily collected for selection purposes. Retrospective studies are usually untidy because the research has to be fitted to the data, not the data to the research.

However, criterion validation has some disadvantages. It requires predictor and criterion information from a large number of people who are currently doing the job in question, quite possibly a larger number than actually exist. Unless the researcher has very large numbers to work with, sampling error may render the results inconclusive.

Researchers usually report *correlations*, which can be misleading for one of four reasons.

1. *Non-linearity.* Figure 10.1 illustrates a *non-linear* relationship between predictor and criterion. Very dim subjects make poor bottle-washers, moderately bright people make good bottle-washers, and very bright people are as poor at bottle-washing as the very dim. This example is *fictional* because reliable examples of non-linear relationships between predictor and criterion are scarce.

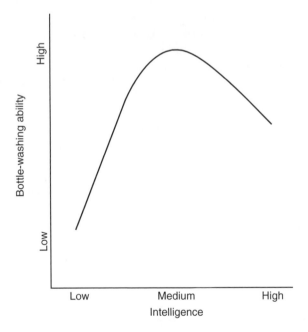

Figure 10.1 A fictional example of a non-linear relationship between a predictor (mental ability) and a criterion (bottle-washing ability)

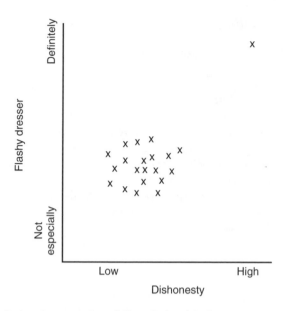

Figure 10.2   A fictional scatterplot of the relationship between two variables (being a flashy dresser and being dishonest) in occupational psychologists, illustrating an *outlier* (top right) that could create a spuriously high correlation and cause people to think that all flashily dressed psychologists are dishonest

2. *Non-homoscedascity*. Lack of *homoscedasticity* means that the variability of scores differs in different parts of the distribution. Figure 5.3 (*see* page 85) illustrates a *non-homoscedastic* relationship; low scores on the American insurance industry's Aptitude Index Battery (*see* Chapter 5) predict failure, but high scores do not predict success.

3. *Leverage by outliers*. A *scatterplot* (*see* Figure 10.2) identifies non-linear or non-homoscedastic data, and also identifies *leverage*, where an apparently large and highly significant correlation turns out to result mostly from a single *outlier* – that is, one subject whose scores on the predictor and criterion deviate from everyone else's.

4. *Suppressor variables*. Collins and Schmidt (1997) compared white-collar criminals with matched controls, using the California Psychological Inventory (CPI) (*see* Table 10.1). Three CPI scales, namely Socialisation (So), Responsibility (Re) and Tolerance (To), distinguish criminals from controls, with correlations of 0.40 to 0.45. Three more CPI scales, namely Well-being (Wb), Self-control (Sc) and Intellectual efficiency (Ie), do not distinguish criminals from controls, but do generate significant negative weights in a discriminant function analysis. White-collar crime is predicted by low So, Re and To, and by high Ie, Wb and Sc, even though criminals and controls do not differ in Ie, Wb and Sc. How can this be? The answer is because Wb, Sc and Ie suppress irrelevant variance from other predictors. Some *aspects* of So, Re and To do not predict white-collar crime, even though the total scores do. High scorers on Wb, Sc and Ie lack these aspects of So,

Table 10.1 Suppressor variables in personality and criminal behaviour.

	SDF weight[a]	Correlation[b]
Socialisation	0.53	0.61
Responsibility	0.42	0.40
Tolerance	0.43	0.42
Anxiety	−0.26	−0.18
Well-being	−0.43	0.11
Self-control	−0.29	0.18
Intellectual efficiency	−0.40	0.07
Social presence	0.23	−0.07

Notes:
Data taken from Collins & Schmidt (1997).
[a] SDF weight shows how the scales enter an equation to predict criminality from CPI profile.
[b] Correlation between CPI score and criminality, scored 0 = offender, 1 = non-offender.

Re and To, thereby improving the overall prediction. Collins and Schmidt have a large sample and show that the suppressor effect cross-validates from one half of the sample to the other. Suppressor effects had been discussed as a theoretical possibility for 60 years, and were occasionally found but rarely replicated. Collins and Schmidt consider that previous research failed to find replicable suppressor variables because they looked at mental ability measures, which correlate so highly that there is little scope for suppressor variables.

Rational validity

Experts can make a fairly accurate estimate of what the test's predictive validity will be.

For many years no self-respecting occupational psychologist would commit him- or herself to advising an employer that 'the best tests for this job are X, Y and Z'. Instead, the psychologist always recommended a local validation study. However, the local validation study can rarely include enough subjects to give a meaningful estimate of the test's validity. So might the psychologist's experience or knowledge of the literature on test validity not enable him or her to select an appropriate test? Schmidt *et al.* (1983) asked 20 occupational psychologists to predict the validity of six sub-tests of the Navy Basic Test Battery for nine navy jobs. They then compared estimates with the actual (but unpublished) validities based on samples of 3,000 to 14,000. The pooled judgement of any four experts gave a fairly accurate estimate of validity – as accurate as could be obtained by actually testing a sample of 173 subjects. In other words, asking four experts what test to use gives as good an answer as actually doing a local validation study on a sizeable sample.

Construct validity

The test measures something meaningful.

Construct validity can focus on a *test*, or on a *trait* or *ability*.

Test-centred construct validity

Cronbach (1984) discussed the construct validity of the Bennett Mechanical Comprehension Test (MCT).

1. *Experience.* The MCT assumes that subjects have seen, used or even repaired machinery, so it may be unsuitable for people in developing countries who have less experience of machinery.
2. *Gender.* Women tend to get lower scores on the MCT, perhaps because they have less experience of machinery.
3. *Education.* People who have studied physics get higher MCT scores.
4. *General ability.* MCT scores correlate well with general mental ability.
5. *Specific knowledge.* Cronbach once postulated that the MCT measured knowledge of a few specific mechanical principles (gears, levers, etc.). When he tested his hypothesis, he found it to be incorrect – the MCT does measure *general* acquaintance with mechanical principles.
6. *Dexterity.* MCT scores correlate poorly with manual dexterity and motor mechanic work-sample tests.

These various findings suggest that the Bennett test reflects general mental ability more than being *good with one's hands* or with real machinery. On the other hand, Bennett scores may be influenced by experience and education in ways that are not found in pure tests of general mental ability.

Trait/ability-centred construct validity

Need for achievement is what made America and the West get where they are today. Need for achievement, abbreviated to 'nAch', is ambition to make money and build a business empire (Cook, 1993). Research on the construct validation of nAch follows five main lines.

1. *Performance.* Measures of nAch predict who will perform better on a task, because ambitious people are more efficient.
2. *Level of aspiration.* Achievement motivation predicts who chooses more difficult tasks, suggesting that ambitious people welcome a challenge.
3. *Upbringing.* McClelland (1971) reported research on children building castles with toy bricks while their parents watched their efforts. Parents of high achievers were warm, encouraging, and physically affectionate, whereas parents of low achievers kept finding fault and telling the child what to do next.

4. *Psychohistory*. McClelland (1971) presented some very challenging data, showing for example that literature full of achievement themes preceded, and therefore possibly *caused*, expansion of ancient Greek trade, as measured by the dispersion throughout the Mediterranean of Greek wine jars.
5. *Creating an achieving society*. McClelland (1971) considers that culture also shapes achievement motivation, so changing culture should make a whole society achieve more. McClelland went to India and tried to do just that, with mixed results.

Opinions about construct validation differ widely. Guion (1978) argued that all test validation is necessarily construct validation, because the test writer always has a theory about what he or she is trying to measure. Ebel (1977) took a much narrower view, that constructs are 'a few internal forces of personality' which he thinks do not exist anyway. So 'why do we continue to talk about construct validation as if it were something we all understand and have found useful?'. Certainly examples of constructs, in Ebel's narrow sense, are hard to find. There is some evidence that aggressiveness operates as an internal force, present in the aggressive person but not always directly affecting his or her behaviour (Cook, 1993). Otherwise, evidence of internal forces in personality remains sketchy and inconsistent.

Factorial validity

The test measures two things but gives them 16 different labels.

Factor analysis is a useful component of validation, but insufficient in itself. Knowing *how many* factors a test measures does not tell you *what* they are, or what they can predict.

Synthetic validity

The test measures component traits and abilities that predict productivity.

The employer tells the psychologist 'I need people who are good with figures, who are sociable and outgoing, and who can type'. The psychologist uses tests of numerical ability, extraversion and typing skill, whose validities have been *separately* proved. The separate validities of the three tests are *synthesised* to yield a compound validity.

Synthetic validation employs two principles. The first is familiar – job analysis to identify underlying themes in diverse jobs and select tests corresponding to each theme. The second principle holds that validity, once demonstrated for a combination of theme × test across the workforce as a whole, can be inferred for sub-sets of the workers, *including sets that are too small for a conventional validation exercise*. Table 10.2 illustrates the principle with *fictional* data. A city employs 1,500 people in 300 different jobs. Some jobs (e.g. local tax clerk)

Table 10.2   Illustration of synthetic validation in a local authority (city) workforce of 1,500.

Attribute ⇒	n	Ability to influence	Attention to detail	Numeracy
Test		CPI-Do	CPI-Re	GMA-N
Job				
1. Local tax clerk	100	–	XX	XX
2. Refuse collection supervisor	25	XX	XX	XX
3. Crematorium attendant	1	XX	XX	–
etc.				
Total *n* involved		430	520	350
Validity		0.30	0.25	0.27

Note: CPI-Do = Dominance scale of California Psychological Inventory (CPI); CPI-Re = Responsibility scale of CPI; GMA-N = Graduate and Managerial Assessment – Numerical

employ enough people to calculate a conventional validity coefficient. Other jobs (e.g. refuse collection supervisor) employ too few for a conventional local validity study to be worth undertaking. Some jobs employ only one person, rendering any statistical analysis impossible. Job analysis identifies a number of themes underlying all 300 jobs, and suitable tests for each theme are selected. The validity of the Dominance scale of the California Psychological Inventory for the 25 refuse collection supervisors is inferred from its validity for all of the 430 people throughout the workforce whose work requires *ability to influence others*. It is even possible to prove the validity of the CPI Responsibility scale for the one and only crematorium supervisor, by pooling that individual's predictor and criterion data with the 520 others for whom *attention to detail* is important.

The combination of the Position Analysis Questionnaire (PAQ) (*see* Chapter 2) and the General Aptitude Test Battery (GATB) (*see* Chapter 6) is well suited to synthetic validation. McCormick, Jeanneret and Mecham (1972) have shown that PAQ scores correlate with GATB *scores* very well, and with GATB *validity* fairly well. This implies that PAQ job analysis can predict what profile of GATB scores will be found in people who are doing a job *successfully*.

The PAQ can generate *job component validity* (JCV) coefficients, which represent a different approach to synthetic validity. Rather than identifying a single test for each competency, as in Table 10.2, JCV uses the PAQ database to generate a regression equation that indicates which tests to use for a job and what weight to give each of them, based on the competencies that the PAQ lists for that job. Hoffman and McPhail (1998) compared JCV estimates for clerical jobs in the US gas industry analysed by the PAQ with meta-analytical estimates of validity, and found that the two agree very well, which justifies the use of JCV. Hoffman, Holden and Gale (2000) used JCV estimates to create test batteries for the many jobs in the gas industry that have too few incumbents to allow conventional validation.

Aspects of validation

Predictive vs. concurrent validity

For many years, received wisdom held predictive validity to be superior to concurrent validity. Guion (1965) even said that the 'present employee method is clearly a violation of scientific principles'. Why?

1. *Missing persons.* In concurrent studies, people who were rejected or who left or were dismissed are not available for study, nor are people who proved so competent that they have been promoted. Williams and Livingstone (1994) reported a meta-analysis that found a low negative correlation (-0.26) between turnover and job performance, confirming that poor performers are more likely to leave. In concurrent validation, both ends of the distribution of productivity may be missing, so range may be restricted.
2. *Unrepresentative samples.* Present employees may not be typical of applicants (actual or possible). The applicant sample is often younger than the employee sample. The workforce may be all white and/or all male when applicants include – or ought to include – women and non-whites.
3. *Direction of cause.* Present employees may have changed to meet the job's demands. Indeed, they have often been *trained* to meet the job's demands. Thus it may be trivial to find that successful managers are dominant, because managers learn to command influence and respect, whereas showing that dominant applicants *become* good managers is more convincing.
4. *Faking.* Present employees are less likely to fake personality inventories than applicants, because they have already got the job and so have no need to describe themselves as better than they are.

The first two arguments imply that concurrent validation will yield smaller validity coefficients, but reviews of research on mental ability testing conclude that the two methods of measuring validity yielded much the same results (Lent *et al.*, 1971; Barrett, Phillips & Alexander, 1981).

Concurrent validity also presents direction-of-cause problems. Suppose that a concurrent study shows that unsuccessful teachers are anxious. Are they poor teachers because they are anxious? Or are they anxious because they are beginning to realise that they are poor teachers? Brousseau and Prince (1981) tested 176 employees twice with the Guilford Zimmerman Temperament Survey (GZTS) at average intervals of seven years, and found that *changes* in GZTS scores correlated with aspects of their work measured by the Job Diagnostic Survey. People doing work with high *task identity* (doing a job from start to finish with a visible outcome) increased their scores on seven GZTS scales. Brousseau and Prince's data showed how work can cause systematic changes in personality, and suggested that doubts about concurrent validation of personality inventories may be justified.

The direction-of-cause argument implies that concurrent validity coefficients for personality measures will be lower. If people change in order to adapt to their work, their personality profiles will become more similar, which will reduce variance in personality scores and lower the correlation. Comparisons of predictive and concurrent validation of personality tests could logically report three results, namely higher predictive validity, higher concurrent validity, or no difference between the two. Two meta-analyses between them do report all three results:

- predictive validity higher than concurrent validity (Tett *et al.*, 1991)
- predictive validity lower than concurrent validity for honesty tests on employee samples (Ones *et al.*, 1993)
- predictive validity not different from concurrent validity for honesty tests on applicant samples (Ones *et al.*, 1993).

These results are not easy to explain, but suggest that caution is needed when using concurrent validation with personality tests.

Is direction of cause a problem with ability tests? Test users assume that it is not, whereas the lay person regards it as self-evident that a year spent working with figures will improve performance on a numerical test. The tester cites high re-test reliabilities as proof that cognitive abilities are stable, even fixed (but subjects in re-test reliability studies do not usually have intensive practice between their two tests). A review by Barrett *et al.* (1981) could find only two studies proving that cognitive ability test scores are 'probably resistant to the effects of work experience'. Anastasi (1981) reviewed research on practice and coaching effects with ability tests, and concluded that they exist but are small enough to be disregarded. However, all of the research dealt with coaching and practice for school and college tests, like the American Scholastic Aptitude Test or the British 'Eleven Plus', and did not address the question of the effects of long experience.

Cross-validation

This means checking the validity of a test a second time, on a second sample. Cross-validation is always desirable, and becomes absolutely essential when keys are empirically constructed, when regression equations are calculated, or when multiple cut-offs are used, because these methods are particularly likely to capitalise on chance. Locke (1961) gave a very striking demonstration of the hazards of not cross-validating. He found that students with long surnames (seven or more letters) were less charming, stimulating, gay, happy-go-lucky and impulsive, liked vodka but did not smoke, and had more fillings in their teeth. Locke's results sound quite plausible in places, but needless to say they completely failed to cross-validate.

Stability of validity over time

Most people assume that validity is stable over time, so that a test which predicts performance after one year in the job will predict performance after three years equally well. Utility analyses often explicitly assume that test validity remains constant over seven years (representing the length of time

easier, reducing staff costs, reducing absence and turnover, improving flexibility and creativity, improving customer service, creating a better public
image, increasing sales to minority customers, improving problem solving,
etc. Kandola (1995) notes that many of these benefits have not been proved to
occur, and suggests that the assumption that a diverse workforce will prove
more creative and innovative mistakenly confounds diversity of personality
and ability with diversity of background. Gottfredson sees more sinister trends
and suggests that diversity means:

> denigrat[ing] any traditional merit standards that women and minorities
> fail to meet: educational credentials, training and experience, objective
> tests. These standards are all suspect. . .because they were created by and
> for white European males.

Job-related tests

If the test creates adverse impact and the employer wants to continue using it,
the employer must prove that the test is *job related*, or valid. This is an area where
psychologists ought to be able to make a really useful contribution. However,
early court cases showed that lawyers and psychologists had different ideas
about test validity. Two events made the 1970s a very bad decade for selection
in general, and psychological tests in particular. These were the 1971 Supreme
Court ruling on *Griggs v Duke Power Company*, and the EEOC's 1970 *Guidelines
on Employee Selection Procedures*.

Griggs v Duke Power Company

Before the Civil Rights Act, the Duke Power Company in North Carolina did
not employ non-whites except as labourers. When the CRA came into effect, the
company changed its rules. Non-labouring jobs needed a high-school diploma
or national high-school graduate average scores on the Wonderlic Personnel
and Bennett Mechanical Comprehension Tests, which 58% of white employees
passed but only 6% of non-whites passed. In 1967, 13 employees sued the
company, and the case began its slow progress through the American legal
system, eventually reaching the Supreme Court in 1971. The Supreme Court
ruled that the company's new tests discriminated, although not necessarily
intentionally. The Court's ruling attributed non-whites' low scores on the
Wonderlic and Bennett tests to inferior education in segregated schools. The
Court said that 'The touchstone is business necessity. If an employment
practice which operates to exclude negroes cannot be shown to be related
to job performance, the practice is prohibited.' The ruling argued that high-
school education and high test scores were not necessary, because existing
white employees with neither continued to perform quite satisfactorily. The
Court concluded by saying that 'any tests used must measure the person for
the job and not the person in the abstract'. The Court also considered the
EEOC's 1970 *Guidelines* 'entitled to great deference' – giving the legal seal of
approval to a set of very demanding standards.

It is difficult to over-emphasise the importance of the *Griggs* case.

- *Griggs* established the principles of adverse impact and indirect discrimination. An employer could be proved guilty of discriminating by setting standards that made no reference to race or sex, and that were often well-established, 'common-sense' practice. *Griggs* objected to high-school diplomas and ability tests because they excluded more blacks than whites.
- *Griggs* objected to the assessment of people *in the abstract*, and insisted that all assessment be job related. This implicitly extended the scope of the act – employers cannot demand that employees be literate, or honest, or ex-army, or good-looking, just because that is the type of person they want working for them.
- Tests of mental ability clearly assess people in the abstract, so many employers stopped using them.
- *business necessity* means job-relatedness, which means validity. The Duke Power Company had introduced new selection methods, but had done nothing to prove that they were valid.

The *Griggs* case illustrates another important point about law and selection. Although the Civil Rights Act was passed in 1964, it was not until 1971 that its full implications became apparent. The ways in which a particular law will affect selection cannot be determined simply from a knowledge of the law's content. What is crucial – and takes a long time to emerge – is how the courts will interpret the law.

EEOC 1970 Guidelines on Employee Selection Procedures

The American Psychological Association (APA) had previously published its *Standards for Educational and Psychological Tests*, which described ways of proving that selection procedures were valid. When the EEOC drew up the 1970 *Guidelines*, the APA persuaded them to recognise its *Standards*. It seemed a good idea at the time, but went badly wrong. The APA's *ideal standards* for validation became the EEOC's *minimum acceptable standards*, which made proving that selection methods were valid very difficult.

Albemarle Paper Co. v Moody

Four years after *Griggs*, another court case examined a 'hastily assembled validation study that did not meet professional standards' (Cronbach, 1980), and did not like it. Albemarle used the Wonderlic Personnel Test and a modern version of Army Beta, and validated them concurrently against supervisor ratings. The court made a number of criticisms of the study's methodology.

- The supervisor ratings were unsatisfactory: 'there is no way of knowing precisely what criterion of job performance the supervisors were considering, whether each of the supervisors was considering the same criterion, or whether, indeed, any of the supervisors actually applied a focused and stable body of criteria of any kind.'

- Only senior staff were rated, whereas the tests were being used to select for junior posts.
- Only white staff were rated, whereas applicants included non-whites.
- The results were an 'odd patchwork'. Sometimes Form A of the Wonderlic test predicted, where the supposedly equivalent Form B did not. Local validation studies with relatively small sample sizes usually obtain 'patchy' results. Occupational psychologists accept this, but *Albemarle* showed that outsiders expected tests to do better.

Risk

Business necessity allows some employers to use selection methods that create AI without having to prove their validity exhaustively, if 'the risks involved in hiring an unqualified applicant are staggering'. The case of *Spurlock v United Airlines* showed that America's enthusiasm for equality stopped short of being flown by inexperienced pilots. The court even agreed that pilots must be graduates, 'to cope with the initial training program and the unending series of refresher courses'.

Bona fide occupational qualification (BFOQ)

This is known in the UK as *genuine* OQ. When Congress was debating the Civil Rights Act, a Congressman waxed lyrical about a hypothetical elderly woman who wanted a *female* nurse (white, black, oriental – but female), so Congress added the concept of the BFOQ – that for some jobs, being male, or female, is essential. The agencies interpreted BFOQs very narrowly. Early on, airlines found that they could not insist that flight attendants be female as a BFOQ – nor would the elderly woman have been allowed to insist on her female nurse. The scope of the BFOQ is limited in practice to actors and lavatory attendants.

Ward's Cove Packing Co. v Antonio

The Ward's Cove case of 1989 was also a landmark – but pointing in the opposite direction to the *Griggs* decision of 20 years earlier (Varca & Pattison, 1993). The Supreme Court diluted the business necessity principle of *Griggs*, implying that in future employers might not have to prove to such high standards that their selection methods were valid.

Civil Rights Act 1991

The (US) Civil Rights Act of 1991 was intended in part to undo the effect of the *Ward's Cove* case, and to specify that if a test creates AI, it must have 'substantial and demonstrable relationship to effective job performance'. The 1991 Act also apparently transferred the onus of proving validity back to the employer. Critics characterise the 1991 Act as unclear and a hasty compromise between opposing viewpoints.

Proving that selection is valid

We have discussed this issue previously, in Chapter 10, from an exclusively psychological point of view. Now it is necessary to consider it again, adding a lawyer's perspective, and using the three types of validation – content criterion, and construct – mentioned by the American Psychological Association's *Standards* and the EEOC's *Guidelines*. The 1970 *Guidelines* expressed a preference for criterion validation.

Criterion validation

Miner and Miner (1979) described an ideal criterion validation study, in which the employer should:

- test a large number of candidates
- but not use the test scores in deciding who to employ
- ensure that there is a wide range of scores on the test
- wait for as long as necessary, and then collect criterion data
- not use a concurrent design in which test data and criterion data are collected at the same time.

It sounds quite easy, but there are five reasons why it is difficult, time-consuming and expensive in practice.

1. *Criterion*. This 'must represent major or critical work behavior as revealed by careful job analysis' (1970 *Guidelines*). Rating criteria may be accused of bias, especially if non-whites or women get lower ratings. BARS formats (*see* Chapter 4) are more acceptable than vague graphic scales or highly generalised personality traits. Training criteria are least likely to prove acceptable, and may themselves be ruled to need validation against job performance.
2. *Sample size*. The correlation between predictor and criterion must be significant at the 5% level – yet the typical local validation study rarely has enough subjects to be sure of achieving this (*see* Chapter 6). The EEOC helps to ensure that the sample size is too small by insisting that differential validities for minorities be calculated, and by insisting that every job be treated separately.
3. *Concurrent/predictive validity*. The *Uniform Guidelines* favour predictive validity, which takes longer and costs more. An employer facing EEOC investigation may not have time to conduct a predictive validation study.
4. *Representative sampling and differential validity*. A representative sample contains the right proportion of non-whites and women. The hypothesis of *differential validity* postulates that tests can be valid for whites or men but

not for non-whites or women. An employer with an all-white and/or all-male workforce cannot prove that there is no differential validity without employing women and/or non-whites, making this the 'Catch 22' of the *Guidelines*.

5. *Adverse impact*. Mental ability tests create so much AI on some minorities that the agencies, the courts and the minorities are unlikely ever to accept them, no matter what proof of their predictive validity is produced.

Kleiman and Faley (1985) reviewed 12 court cases on criterion validity, since the publication of the *Uniform Guidelines* in 1978. Their review was not very encouraging for any employers thinking of relying on proving that their selection procedures actually predict productivity.

- Courts often appeared to suppose that some tests had been completely discredited and could never be valid – notably the Wonderlic Personnel Test.
- Courts often examined item content or format even though this is irrelevant when assessing predictive validity.
- Courts often objected to coefficients being corrected for restricted range.
- Courts' decisions were inconsistent and unpredictable.
- Courts often ignored or avoided technical issues, or took a common-sense approach to issues such as sample size, where common sense is generally wrong.
- Only five of the 12 employers won their cases.

Critics may say that psychologists have just been hoist with their own petard. They always claimed that their tests were the best way to select staff. They were always ready to dismiss other people's methods as invalid. They always insisted that validating tests was a highly technical business, best left to the experts. However, when American fair employment agencies took them at their word, the psychologists could not deliver an acceptable validity study. Their 50-year-old bluff had been called. In fact, fair employment legislation has done occupational psychologists a service by forcing them to prove more thoroughly that tests are valid and worth using, by *validity generalisation analysis (see* Chapter 6), *utility analysis (see* Chapter 13) and *differential validity research* (see below).

Content validation

In 1964, when the Civil Rights Act was passed, *content validity* was virtually unheard of, and not very highly regarded. Guion (1965) said that 'Content validity is of extremely limited utility as a concept for employment tests. ... [it] comes uncomfortably close to the idea of face validity unless judges are especially precise in their judgements'. Guion (1978) later said that content validation was added to the 1970 *Guidelines* as an afterthought, for occasions when criterion validation was not feasible. Content validation became the favourite validation strategy after the *Guidelines* and the *Griggs* case, because criterion validation was impossibly difficult (see above), and the courts could not understand construct validation (see below). Content validation has four big advantages.

1. No criterion is required, so it cannot be unsatisfactory. The test is its own justification.
2. There is no time interval between testing and validation. The test is validated before it is used.
3. Differential validity cannot exist because there is no criterion.
4. Content-valid tests are easy to defend in court. Every item of the test is clearly relevant to the job.

Content validation requires careful job analysis to prove that the test 'is a representative sample of the content of the job' (*Uniform Guidelines*). Test content must reflect *every* aspect of the job, in the *correct proportions*. If 10% of the job consists of writing reports, report writing must not account for 50% of the test. It is easy to prove job-relatedness for simple concrete jobs, such as typing tests for typists. However, content validation is much more difficult when the job is complex, yet the demands of the *Guidelines* caused many American employers to try content validation, where the problem really needed criterion or construct validation. The public sector in the USA, especially police and fire brigades, have repeatedly developed content-valid selection procedures and seen them ruled unfair. For example, the St Louis Fire Brigade devised a test for promotion to fire captain, in which firefighters viewed slides of fires and *wrote* the commands that they would give, which was ruled to over-emphasise verbal ability (Bersoff, 1981). Nearly 50% of the fire captain's job is supervision, which the tests did not cover at all (the Brigade planned to assess supervisory ability during a subsequent probationary period).

Construct validation

> A demonstration that (a) a selection procedure measures a construct (something believed to be an underlying human trait or characteristic, such as honesty) and (b) the construct is important for successful job performance.
>
> (*Uniform Guidelines*)

Cronbach (1980) cites the example of high-school graduation. A narrow approach might conclude that employees do not need to write essays or do sums or even be able to read, so graduation is not job related. The broader construct validity approach argues that it is a reasonable supposition that people who do well at school differ from those who do not, in something more than just academic ability or even mental ability. Cronbach calls the 'something' *motivation* and *dependability*. Thus an employer who does not want lazy, undependable employees could hope to exclude them by requiring a high-school diploma. Cronbach's example shows very clearly why construct validation is not a promising approach. The constructs *motivation* and *dependability* are exactly the type of abstractions that are difficult to define, difficult to measure and difficult to defend in court. In fact, general education requirements are rarely accepted by American courts (*see* Chapter 9).

The fate of PACE

Ironically, fair employment legislation created the biggest problems for state and federal governments, because they must appoint *by merit*. Before the Civil Rights Act, private employers could select who they liked, how they liked. The public sector had to advertise every post, check every application, use the same tests for every candidate, and select the best. The weight of numbers made written tests essential. The US public sector still has to select the best, but has also to 'get its numbers right'. After all, if the government does not set an example, it can hardly expect private employers to spend time and money ensuring fairness.

The Professional and Administrative Career Examination (PACE) was devised in order to select college-level entrants to fill 118 varied US Federal Government occupations (including internal revenue officer, customs inspector and criminal investigator). PACE consisted primarily of an ability test (Test 500), with bonus points for special experience or achievements. It was validated against five criteria, for four of the 118 jobs, and achieved a composite validity coefficient of 0.60 (Olian & Wilcox, 1982). PACE had both content and criterion validity. However, it created massive AI on African– and Hispanic–Americans. Applicants had to achieve a score of 70 in order to be eligible for selection – which 42% of whites achieved, but only 5% of blacks and 13% of Hispanics. PACE also illustrates well the principle that the higher the passmark, the greater the resulting AI. If the passmark was to be set at 90, 8.5% of whites but only 0.3% of blacks and 1.5% of Hispanics would be accepted.

PACE was challenged because only 27 of the 118 occupations were included in the job analysis (and only four were included in the validation study), because validation was concurrent, not predictive, and because the Office of Personnel Management (OPM) had not tried to find an alternative test that did not create AI. The OPM was prepared to fight the case by citing validity generalisation research, citing research showing that concurrent validities do not differ from predictive validities, citing differential validity research, and reviewing every possible alternative test. However, the case never came to court because the government abandoned PACE.

Cut-off scores

Despite the arbitrary nature of many test cut-off scores, they have created surprisingly little legal difficulty. Cut-offs are accepted, sometimes at levels that would exclude a proportion of the existing workforce, on the grounds that not all existing employees are necessarily competent, or that the employer can seek to raise standards. American courts frequently refer to 'unacceptable standards' or 'safe and efficient' performance, apparently subscribing to the simplistic view that performance is good *or* bad, rather than distributed on a continuum.

Validity generalisation analysis (VGA)

VGAs for mental ability tests imply that local validity studies are pointless, that differential validity probably does not exist, and that mental ability tests are valid predictors for every type of work. Accepting these conclusions would leave little or no scope for fair employment cases involving mental ability tests, so it is not surprising that American civil rights lawyers are not keen to accept VGA (Seymour, 1988). Sharf (1988) has described four cases in which American courts did accept that validity data collected elsewhere could be used to establish validity.

Alternative tests

The 1970 *Guidelines* required employers to prove that no alternative test existed that *did not* create AI before they used valid tests that *did* create AI. *Albemarle Paper Company v Moody* over-ruled this in 1975 on the grounds that employers could not prove a negative, but in 1978 the *Uniform Guidelines* placed the obligation to prove a negative back on the employer.

Some time ago, Reilly and Chao (1982) and Hunter and Hunter (1984) reviewed a range of *alternative* tests, and concluded that none of them achieved the same validity for selection as ability tests, except for biodata and job try-outs. Job try-outs can only be used where applicants have been trained for the job. However, for promotion a range of alternative tests are as valid as ability tests – for example, work samples, peer ratings, job knowledge tests and assessment centres. Culture-free tests, such the Raven Progressive Matrices, create as much adverse impact as any other ability tests.

Arvey (1979b) summarised evidence on AI of different methods (*see* Table 12.4). Every method excluded too many of one protected group or another, usually in at least one way that would be difficult to cure.

Table 12.4 Summary of adverse impact of five selection tests on four minorities.

	Blacks	Females	Elderly	Disabled
Mental ability and verbal tests	AI	+	ai	?
Work samples	+	NE	NE	NE
Interviews	+	AI	ai	ai
Educational requirement	AI	+	ai	?
Physical tests	+	AI	?	AI

Source: From Arvey (1979b).
Note: AI = major adverse impact; ai = minor adverse impact; ? = no proof of adverse impact, but likely to exist; + = no adverse impact; NE = no evidence.

Table 12.5 Bobko and Roth's meta-analytic matrix of (uncorrected) validity and ethnicity differences for four selection methods.

	Validity	D (white/African–American)
Mental ability	0.30	1.00
Structured interview	0.30	0.23
Conscientiousness factor	0.18	0.09
Biodata	0.28	0.33

Source: Reproduced from Bobko and Roth (1999) with permission.

- The law cannot make women as tall and strong as men.
- The EEOC cannot prevent intellectual efficiency falling off with age.
- Forty years of controversy have not closed the gap in test scores and educational achievement between white and non-white Americans.

On the other hand, Table 12.4 does suggest that discrimination against women should be easier to avoid for most jobs. Bias against women mostly emerges in the interview, from which it could be removed by careful practice. More recently, Bobko and Roth (1999) provided a *meta-analytic matrix* of validity and American ethnicity differences for four selection methods. Their matrix included two methods that are widely supposed to avoid adverse impact problems. Their findings indicated that structured interviews and biodata do not entirely avoid the problem. The Conscientiousness factor of the big five does avoid it, but at the expense of lower validity (*see* Table 12.5).

UK practice

The *Code* of the Commission for Racial Equality (CRE) recommends employers to keep detailed records in order to compare the actual and ideal composition of their applicant pool and workforce. They have adopted the adverse impact principle, sometimes referred to as the *disproportionate effect*, and offer the four-fifths principle as guidance while admitting that it has no statutory force. The CRE *Code* recommends that 'selection criteria and tests are examined to ensure that they are related to job requirements and are not unlawfully discriminatory' (Para 1.13). The Equal Opportunity Commission (EOC) *Code* similarly states that 'selection tests. . .should specifically relate to job requirements'. The CRE's *Code* is particularly concerned that employers do not require better command of English or higher educational qualifications than the job needs. The CRE's earlier formal *Inquiries* dealt with employers who were sufficiently ignorant or unsubtle to say things like '[we don't employ West Indians because they are] too slow, too sly, too much mouth and they skive off' (Commission for Racial Equality, 1984), than with employers whose recruitment methods appeared to keep out minorities, usually by recruiting through existing staff.

Towards the end of the 1980s, the first cases involving psychological tests began to appear. London Underground appointed 160 middle managers in such a rush that they did not have time to include all of the tests that psychologists had recommended, or to pre-test the ones that they did use (Commission for Racial Equality, 1990). The tests used (numerical and verbal reasoning and an interview) created adverse impact on minority applicants. However, race was confounded with age and education – the Afro-Caribbean applicants were much older than the white applicants and had less formal education. In 1990, another case involving tests came to trial – the 'Paddington Guards' case (Commission for Racial Equality, 1996). British Rail guards (conductors) seeking promotion to driver were tested with verbal reasoning, numerical reasoning and clerical tests. A group of guards of Asian origin alleged unfair discrimination because the tests were not clearly job related, but were more difficult for people whose first language was not English. A striking feature of the case was that British Rail already had a job analysis for train drivers, done by Netherlands Railways, but disregarded it and did not match the tests to the job's needs. Both cases were settled out of court, and did not give rise to any legal rulings about test use in the UK.

Subsequently, the CRE issued a series of recommendations about psychological tests (Commission for Racial Equality, 1992). Some of them are sound.

- Conduct a job analysis and use it to choose selection tests.
- Allow candidates enough time to absorb the instructions and do the practice examples.
- Avoid English-language tests on candidates whose first language is not English.

Some are less realistic.

- Do not use time limits (most mental ability tests are timed, and cannot be used untimed without being restandardised).

Other recommendations seek to send UK human resource HR managers and psychologists down paths already travelled in the USA.

- If the test creates adverse impact, do not use it, or else validate it on at least 100 people in each minority group.
- Do not assume that a test which has been proved valid for one job will be valid for another.

Current thinking in the USA sees local validity studies as a waste of time (*see* Chapter 6), because the validity of mental ability tests generalises widely, and regards differential validity as non-existent (see below).

Fair employment laws have not had the impact in the UK that they had in the USA. The UK government has not introduced *contract compliance*, although some local authorities have. English law does not provide for *class actions*, in which one person's test case can be used to enforce the rights of a whole class of others (e.g. female employees). This can be enormously expensive for the employer. In the State Farm Insurance case the employer was found guilty of gender discrimination and had to pay $193,000 not just to the plaintiff, but to each of 812 other women as well.

European law

Most European countries have laws to prohibit gender discrimination in employment, but seem more concerned with issues of equal pay than with those of fairness in selection. Few European countries appear to express much concern about discrimination in employment based on ethnicity, according to the Price-Waterhouse–Cranfield Survey (Hegewisch & Mayne, 1994). 'European law' has a second meaning, in the shape of laws passed by the European Community rather than individual European countries. The Community's Social Charter – which the British government for a long time refused to accept – includes concerns with equal opportunities in employment, and for people 'excluded' from employment by disability or for other reasons (Teague, 1994). The European Court has accepted the idea of adverse impact as *discrimination by results*, and several European countries (Italy, Ireland, and The Netherlands) have incorporated the concept into their legislation (Higuera, 2001).

Disability

The Americans with Disabilities Act (ADA) was passed in 1990 and came into effect in 1992, to prohibit discrimination on grounds of disability. Disability is defined very broadly, to cover mental retardation, specific learning disabilities (e.g. dyslexia), emotional or mental illness, AIDS/HIV and severe obesity, as well as physical disability, blindness and deafness. However, ADA does not cover mild obesity, gambling, sexual deviations (e.g. paedophilia), short-term illnesses or injuries, pregnancy or common personality traits. Current (illegal) drug use is also excluded, but rehabilitated former drug users are covered. Alcoholism is covered by ADA, but employers can require that employees are sober during working hours. Simon and Noonan (1994) consider that ADA may prevent employers refusing to hire applicants who smoke, because nicotine is a legal drug, and smoking is a form of addiction. Discrimination against someone you think has a disability (e.g. HIV/AIDS), but who in fact has not, also counts as discrimination. So far the commonest disabilities mentioned in ADA cases have been back trouble and emotional/psychiatric problems (Coil & Shapiro, 1996). The same survey found that over 50% of all complaints concerned termination, while only 9% concerned hiring.

Job analysis

ADA makes a distinction between *essential* and *marginal* job functions. Ability to drive is an essential function for a bus driver, but may be marginal for an office worker. If a disabled person cannot perform essential functions, the employer may refuse to make an offer. Employers may ask if an applicant could perform an essential function, and may ask applicants to demonstrate their ability. However, employers must not refuse to employ a disabled person solely because they cannot perform a marginal function. This means that careful job analysis is vital. ADA also implies that person specifications may need to be more detailed. For example, if the job is stressful, and therefore might not suit someone who cannot handle stress well, the person specification should make this clear (Edwards, 1992). (However, the employer should *not* assume that anyone with a history of mental illness cannot handle stress well; an individual assessment of resilience would be required.)

Medical examinations

Employers can only carry out medical examinations on people who have been offered a job. Employers may not enquire about disability or carry out medical examinations as part of the selection process, which rules out some selection tests. Personality traits are excluded from the scope of ADA, but mental illness is definitely included. For example, employers can use a personality test to exclude candidates with poor self-control, but not to exclude psychopaths. The Minnesota Multiphasic Personality Inventory (MMPI), which has been widely used to screen candidates for police work in the USA, was originally keyed to psychiatric diagnosis and gives its scales psychiatric names, such as Schizophrenia, which tends to make it look very like a medical examination. Physical tests of strength or stamina may count as medical checks if they include measures of blood pressure or heart rate.

Accommodation

Employers must make *reasonable accommodation* to disabled people, both as employees and as candidates for employment. This means adapting selection methods by providing large-print question books, Braille question books, tape format, or someone to help the candidate (Nester, 1993; Baron, 1995). Time limits are sometimes changed to accommodate dyslexic applicants, or to allow for changes in format slowing down candidates. However, changing the time limit for a timed test – and most ability tests are timed – tends to invalidate the norms, and so makes the results very hard to interpret. Research on educational testing reviewed by Geisinger, Boodoo and Noble (2002) suggests that allowing extra time in entrance tests sometimes results in *over-predicting* subsequent college performance (i.e. students do not do as well as expected from the test results – possibly they were given too much extra time). There is no workplace research on this issue. Given the diversity of disability, and the large sample sizes that are needed to compare validity coefficients, no workplace research seems likely to be forthcoming, so employers will never know if allowing 50% or 100% or 200% extra time for a particular disability will make the test 'the same as for' someone without that disability. Guion (1998) has expressed pessimism about the practicalities of adapting ability tests: 'We have no clue how to maintain standardisation while accommodating people who are disabled'. One implication of ADA may be a need for more untimed tests.

Disability discrimination legislation may force employers to look carefully at some long-established selection procedures. Before ADA was passed, American police forces routinely required good eyesight (20/40 vision) *without glasses*, on the argument that glasses could be lost in a struggle, leaving the officer unable to see what weapon an assailant might be carrying (or find the missing glasses). Good, Maisel and Kriska (1998) found that 20/40 vision was an unnecessarily strict criterion, and that officers with poorer sight could see well enough to function effectively. The relaxed criterion excludes only 5% of applicants on grounds of eyesight, instead of 14%.

ADA has the usual collection of vague, but crucial phrases, such as *'reasonable* accommodation' or *'undue* hardship', whose meaning for employers will only become apparent after a series of court cases. ADA differs from the Civil Rights Act in one key respect – cases cannot be brought on the basis of adverse impact. The fact that an organisation employs few or no disabled people is not in itself grounds for complaint.

The UK has again followed American practice, with the 1995 Disability Discrimination Act (DDA), which came into force in December 1996. DDA covers selection, and requires employers to make reasonable accommodation for disabled employees. DDA excludes addiction to any drug, including nicotine and alcohol, unless the drug is medically prescribed, and only covers mental illness if 'recognised by a respected body of medical opinion'. DDA may have more impact on selection in the UK than the Race Relations Act, given that 17% of the population describe themselves as having some form of disability (Cook, Leigh & McHenry, 1997), whereas only 6% describe themselves as belonging to an ethnic minority.

Differential validity and test fairness

Differential validity

Critics often claim that tests are valid for the white majority but not for non-whites. There are two linked hypotheses:

1. *single group validity* – tests are valid for one group but not (at all) for others
2. *differential validity* – tests are valid for both groups, but are more valid for one group than for the other.

Critics generally assume that tests have lower (or no) validity for non-whites, because of differences in their culture, education, etc. The issue gets complex statistically.

Early research

Kirkpatrick *et al.*'s (1968) data on the Pre-Nursing and Guidance Examination were once cited as proof that tests are not fair for minorities. Validity coefficients for whites tended to be higher, or more statistically significant, than those for non-whites. Kirkpatrick *et al.* reported a *local validation* study, which is not capable of demonstrating differential validity. In most comparisons the minority sample was smaller than the white sample, so the correlation was more likely to be insignificant. Many of the samples – white or non-white – were too small to prove anything.

Meta-analysis

Single studies of differential validity will always prove inconclusive, because the samples will almost always be too small. Pooling the results of many studies by meta-analysis is needed to give conclusive answers. Schmidt, Berner and Hunter (1973) reviewed 410 pairs of non-white/white validity coefficients. In 75 pairs the correlation was significant for whites but not for non-whites, while in 34 pairs it was significant for non-whites but not for whites. At first sight this is weak confirmation of the hypothesis that tests are more likely to be valid for whites than for non-whites. However, the average non-white sample was only half the size ($n = 49$) of the average white sample ($n = 100$), which obviously makes non-white correlations less likely to achieve significance. Schmidt *et al.* calculated how often the patterns (white significant and non-white insignificant, and white insignificant and non-white significant) would appear by chance, given the sample sizes. The values calculated (76 and 37, respectively) were almost identical to those observed. Schmidt *et al.* concluded that single-group validity is 'probably illusory'.

If white and non-white sample sizes are the same, the pattern of *white correlation significant but black correlation insignificant* ought to occur as often as *white insignificant but black significant*. O'Connor, Wexley and Alexander (1975) analysed only studies where the numbers of white and non-white people were the same, and found 25 white-significant and black-insignificant pairs and 17 white-insignificant and black-significant pairs, which does not prove a trend. Other early meta-analyses also found no evidence of differential validity. Boehm (1972) found that only seven pairs of correlations from a total of 160 showed differential validity. Most pairs showed that the test failed to predict significantly for white *or* non-white. Boehm (1977) later analysed 538 pairs of white and non-white validities, and found differential validity in only 8%. Boehm concluded that differential validity was more likely to be found by methodologically inferior studies; neither single-group validity nor differential validity was found by any study in which both white and non-white samples exceeded 100.

Sets of correlations

Boehm's (1977) analysis may be misleading. Most validation studies use more than one test and more than one criterion. The tests usually intercorrelate to some degree, and so do the criteria. Therefore each correlation between test and criterion is not an independent observation. Suppose that a validation study used Forms A and B of the Watson Glaser Critical Thinking Appraisal (WGCTA), and found that both correlated well with ratings of intellectual

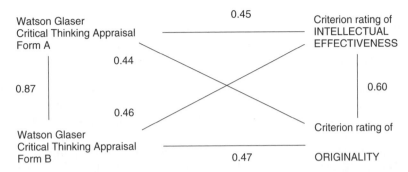

Figure 12.1 Fictional set of predictor–criterion relationships, showing fictional correlations between criterion ratings, actual correlation between Forms A and B of the Watson Glaser Critical Thinking Appraisal (WGCTA), and fictional correlations between WGCTA and criterion ratings

effectiveness and of originality (*see* Figure 12.1). Does the study report four relationships, or two, or only one? Hunter and Schmidt argue that including all 538 pairs of correlations in Boehm's calculation is conceptually the same as including the same correlation several times over – it makes the results look more consistent and more significant than they really are. Katzell and Dyer (1977) analysed the same 31 studies, but first identified sets of correlated predictors and criteria like the one illustrated in Figure 12.1, and then chose *one* pair of correlations at random from each set, so that each of the 64 pairs was an independent observation. Ten of the 64 pairs (19%) showed a significant white vs. non-white difference. A second random sample of correlation pairs found 31% yielded a significant white vs. non-white difference. Katzell and Dyer's re-analysis implies that Boehm had allowed true differential validity to be masked, by including pairs of correlations that found no differential validity over and over again under different names.

Exclude insignificant correlations?

Hunter and Schmidt (1978) argued that *both* analyses, by Boehm (1977) and Katzell and Dyer (1977), are seriously flawed. They both excluded pairs where neither correlation was significant, on the grounds that a test that failed to predict for either race cannot demonstrate differential validity. Hunter and Schmidt argued that this was a mistake. Validity coefficients often fail to achieve significance because the sample is too small, or range is restricted, or the criterion is unreliable (*see* Chapter 6). Thus excluding pairs where the correlations were small or insignificant excludes some pairs where there was true validity, and also excludes some pairs where white and non-white validities were identical. Three subsequent studies that avoided this error found differential validity occurring at only chance levels (Bartlett *et al.*, 1978; Hunter, Schmidt & Hunter, 1979; Schmidt, Pearlman & Hunter, 1980b). More recently, Hartigan and Wigdor (1989) pointed to 72 studies using the GATB with at least 50 black and 50 white subjects, in which the GATB's composite validity was lower for blacks (0.12) than for whites (0.19).

Shared bias

Rotundo and Sackett (1999) noted a potential flaw with differential validity research, namely the possibility of shared bias. The criterion in most selection research is supervisor rating, and most supervisors are white, so suppose that some of them are consciously or unconsciously prejudiced towards African Americans and give them lower work ratings. According to the shared bias argument, the ability tests are also biased against minority Americans, so this bias combines with the supervisors' bias to give an appearance of tests predicting work performance in both majority and minority, but with different averages for the two groups. Some earlier studies (Gael, Grant & Ritchie, 1975) had used criteria of work performance that depended less on someone's opinion, such as work samples or training grades, and still found differential validity. Rotundo and Sackett searched the GATB database to find 1,212 cases where black workers had been rated by a black supervisor, who might be expected to show less bias, if supervisor bias is a problem. The data again contained no evidence of predictive bias against black employees.

On balance, the hypothesis of differential validity has been disproved. Ability tests can be used equally validly for white and non-white Americans. Humphreys (1973) suggests reversing perspective in a way that he thinks many psychologists will find hard to accept:

> [the hypothesis of differential validity implies] Minorities probably do not belong to the same biological species as the majority; but if they do, the environmental differences have been so profound and have produced such huge cultural differences that the same principles of human behaviour do not apply to both groups.

All of the research reviewed so far is American, and deals with white, African and Hispanic Americans. We cannot assume that the finding of no differential validity in the USA implies there is none in other societies, if only because different sets of ethnic groups are involved. Te Nijenhuis and van der Flier (1999, 2000) reported data for various immigrant groups in The Netherlands, and found little evidence of differential validity of ability tests. There are no published data on this important issue for the UK.

Gender

Rothstein and McDaniel (1992) presented a meta-analysis of 59 studies where validity coefficients for males and females could be compared. Overall there was no difference. However, the results also suggest that where the work is usually done by one gender (e.g. most machinists are male), validity is higher for the majority gender. This trend is particularly marked for low-complexity jobs, where female validity for 'female' jobs was higher by 0.20 than male validity. Rothstein and McDaniel suggested that the result may reflect a bias in the supervisor rating criterion. Men who enter a low-level, traditionally female occupation may be viewed by the (mostly female) supervisors as being somehow out of the ordinary. Saad and Sackett (2002) analysed ABLE data for nine US Army specialist jobs and found that the relationship between personality and work performance was the same for males and females.

Test fairness

Critics often claim that tests are not 'fair', meaning that non-whites do not score as well as whites. The technical meaning of *test fairness* is quite different. The term *unfair* means that the test does not predict the minority's productivity as accurately as it predicts the majority's productivity. Several models of test fairness have been proposed. The most widely accepted one is Cleary's model, which is based on regression lines. The EEOC accepts Cleary's model of test fairness. Figure 12.2 shows the first type of unfair test, where there is true differential validity. When regression lines are fitted to the majority and minority distributions, the *slopes* of the lines differ. A slope difference means that the test predicts productivity more accurately for one group than for the other. Bartlett *et al.*'s (1978) review found that a black vs. white difference in

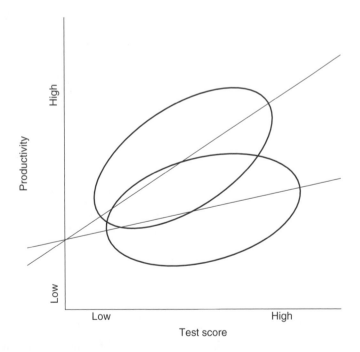

Figure 12.2 An unfair test, showing a *slope* difference. The correlation between test and productivity is higher for majority applicants than for minority applicants

slope occurred at chance frequency. Schmidt *et al.* (1980b) reported the same finding for Hispanic Americans.

Figure 12.3 shows the second type of unfair test. Minority and majority applicants differ in test score but do not differ in productivity. When regression lines are fitted to the majority and minority distributions, they *intercept* the vertical axis at different points. In Figure 12.3, test scores *under-predict* minority applicants' work performance – minority applicants do better work than the test predicted, Sometimes the opposite occurs. In Ruch's unpublished review (see Schmidt *et al.*, 1980b), nine out of 20 studies found that tests *over*-predicted non-white productivity (i.e. gave a more favourable view of minority productivity than they should have).

Figure 12.4 shows a test which is fair, even though majority and minority averages differ. A regression line fitted to the two distributions has the same slope and the same intercept, which means that it is one continuous straight line. Test scores predict productivity regardless of minority or majority group membership. Schmidt *et al.* (1980b) reviewed eight studies which show that tests do not under-predict non-whites' productivity.

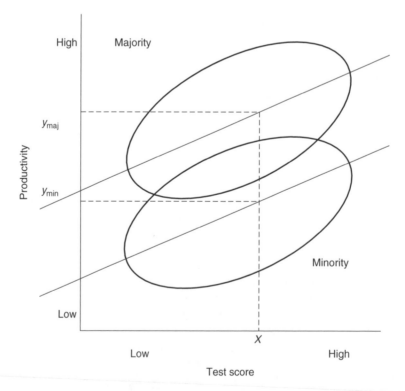

Figure 12.3 An unfair test, showing an *intercept* difference. A given test's score (x) predicts lower productivity (y_{min}) for minority applicants than for majority applicants (y_{maj})

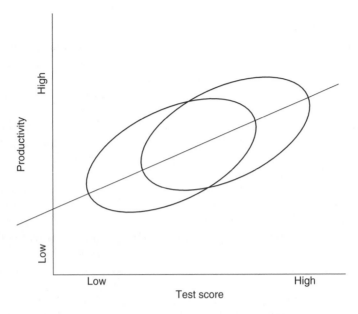

Figure 12.4   A fair test, in which test scores predict productivity equally accurately for minority and majority applicants

Schmidt and Hunter (1981) suggested that everyone should accept that tests are fair:

> that average ability and cognitive skill differences between groups are directly reflected in test performance and thus are *real*. We do not know what all the causes of these differences are, how long they will persist, or how best to eliminate them. ... [They conclude] it is not intellectually honest, in the face of empirical evidence to the contrary, to postulate that the problem [of AI] is biased and/or unfair employment tests.

Alternative fairness models

Although the Cleary model is generally accepted, other models have been proposed, notably the Thorndike model. Chung-yan and Cronshaw (2002) noted that a higher scorer is more likely to be accepted but also to prove to be a less successful employee, whereas a low scorer is more likely to be rejected even though he or she would have been a more successful employee. This happens because the correlation between score and work performance is far from perfect. Where higher scorers are mostly white Americans and low scorers are mostly minority Americans, this creates a problem. Thorndike (1986) suggests setting cut-offs for the two groups so that if, for example, 30% of minority applicants would turn out to be successful employees, then 30% would be accepted.

Conclusions

Fair employment legislation is needed, because discrimination in employment on the grounds of gender and ethnicity is clearly unacceptable, and would probably be rejected by most people these days. However, fair employment law has not primarily concerned itself with overt discrimination, but with adverse impact. In the USA, adverse impact places the burden of proof on employers, effectively requiring them to prove that they are not discriminating if there are not 50% female employees and X% ethnic minority employees throughout the entire workforce. It is less immediately obvious that this is entirely reasonable, or what the average person wants.

The effect of new fair employment laws typically takes some years to become apparent, and does not always seems to be quite what was intended. This creates prolonged periods of uncertainty, and costs employers large amounts. The Civil Rights Act has often, only half-jokingly, been called 'the occupational psychologists' charter'. Lawyers have also done very well from it. However, fair employment legislation was not meant to benefit psychologists and lawyers – it was intended to help minorities.

There are still sections of the population who are not covered by fair employment legislation, but would like to be. A law limiting age discrimination in employment has been suggested for the UK, but is not on the legislative programme at present. A high proportion of homosexual men and women in America report discrimination in employment (Croteau, 1996). In the UK, homosexuality is still grounds for exclusion from the armed services. Applying the model of the Civil Rights Act to sexual orientation would have interesting implications (such as potentially requiring every employee to declare his or her sexual preferences, to allow adverse impact to be calculated).

Although it is true that fair employment laws have been a burden to American employers, it could also be argued that they have indirectly helped industrial psychology, by forcing the profession to look much harder at issues such as utility, validity and differential validity, to devise new techniques such as validity generalisation or rational estimates, and to devise better selection methods.

Key points

In Chapter 12 you have learnt the following.

- Fair employment law covers gender, ethnicity, disability, religion and age (in the USA).
- Most fair employment selection cases involve adverse impact, not direct discrimination. Adverse impact means that fewer minority applicants are successful. If the success rate for minority applicants is less than four-fifths that of the majority, adverse impact is established.
- Getting the numbers right (i.e. ensuring that there are the right proportions of women and minorities in the workforce) can be difficult, as there are legal restrictions on how employers can achieve this.

- A selection method that creates adverse impact must be proved – in court – to be valid, which is expensive and uncertain.
- If the test is proved valid, the employer must also show that there is no possible alternative that is equally valid but which will not create adverse impact.
- American researchers are trying combinations of tests to try to find one that will prove valid but create no adverse impact
- Differential validity means that a test has different validity for minority and majority people. North American research has not found evidence of differential validity. Virtually no research has been reported on this issue outside North America.
- Disability discrimination legislation affects selection in different ways. Adverse impact claims cannot be made. The employer must not use any health-related enquiries as part of the selection process, and must try to adapt selection tests to disabled applicants.
- In the UK far fewer unfair selection cases have been brought, and the position is still much more open.
- Other countries, in Europe and elsewhere, have adopted the same basic adverse impact model.

Key references

Baron (1995) discusses how to adapt psychological tests for people with disabilities.

Bobko and Roth (1999) review the validity and ethnicity differences of four commonly used selection tests.

Coil and Shapiro (1996) describe the operation of the Americans with Disabilities Act.

The Commission for Racial Equality (1990) describes the Centurion Managers case, one of the few fair employment cases involving psychological tests to have been tried in the UK.

Gottfredson (1994) is critical of the 'diversity' movement in the USA.

Higuera (2001) provides a European perspective on fair employment.

Hough *et al.* (2001) provide a detailed review of gender and ethnicity differences in a range of selection tests.

Hunter and Schmidt (1978) present a meta-analysis of research on differential validity.

Kleiman and Faley (1985) review early attempts by American employers to prove in court that their selection tests were valid.

te Nijenhuis and van der Flier (2000) present data on the differential validity of psychological tests in The Netherlands.

Olian and Wilcox (1982) describe the fate of an American government test (PACE) in the 1970s.

Saad and Sackett (2002) present data on differential validity by gender in American military testing.

Terpstra *et al*. (1999) give a survey of US fair employment cases between 1978 and 1997.

Varca and Pattison (1993) are critical of the US 1991 Civil Rights Act.

Useful websites

www.usdoj.gov/crt/ada. Official Americans with Disabilities Act site.
www.eeoc.gov. US government fair employment agency.
www.cre.org.uk. UK government fair employment agency for ethnicity.
www.eoc.org.uk. UK government fair employment agency for gender.
www.hrhero.com/q&a. Interesting question-and-answer site on US fair employment.
www.jan.wvu.edu/links/adalink.htm. A wealth of information on the Americans with Disabilities Act.

The value of good employees

The best is twice as good as the worst

Introduction

In an ideal world, two people doing the same job under the same conditions will produce exactly the same amount. In the real world, some employees produce more than others. This poses two questions.

1. How much do workers vary in productivity?
2. How much are these differences worth?

The short answer to both questions is 'a lot'. The answer to the first question is that good workers do twice as much work as poor workers. The answer to the second question is that the difference in value between a good worker and a poor one is roughly equal to the salary that they are paid.

How much does worker productivity vary?

Hull (1928) described ratios of output of best to worst performers in a variety of occupations. He reported that the best spoon polishers polished five times as many spoons as the worst. Ratios were less extreme for other occupations – between 1.5:1 and 2:1 for weaving and shoe-making jobs. (Unfortunately, Hull does not answer several fascinating questions. For example, how many spoon polishers were studied? And did they polish spoons full-time?) Tiffin (1943) drew graphs of the *distribution* of output for various jobs, including hosiery loopers, who gather together the loops of thread at the bottom of a stocking to close the opening left in the toe (*see* Figure 13.1). Most workers fall between the extremes to form a roughly *normal* distribution of output. If the distribution is normal, it can be summarised by its mean (mean$_p$) and standard deviation (SD$_p$). The standard deviation of the data in Figure 13.1 is the SD$_p$ of hosiery looping.

Judiesch and Schmidt (2000) reviewed research on SD$_p$. For 95 samples of unskilled workers, SD$_p$ is 18% of average output, indicating a substantial difference between good and poor performers. If we define 'the best' as two SDs above the mean, and 'the worst' as two SDs below the mean, Judiesch and Schmidt's 18% average for SD$_p$ confirms neatly that the best, at 136%, is twice the worst, at 64%. Earlier analyses had suggested that paying people

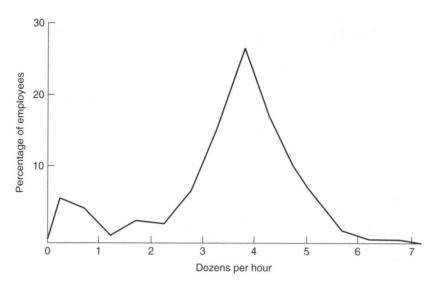

Figure 13.1   Distribution of productivity for 199 hosiery loopers. From Tiffin (1943)

piece-rate, as is common in blue-collar jobs, compressed the distribution of output, but making allowance for error of measurement, Judiesch and Schmidt concluded that this does not happen. SD_p for low-level jobs is 18% whether people are paid by the hour or by output. SD_p is slightly higher for white-collar jobs, being 20–24% for low-level clerical jobs. SD_p is considerably higher for more complex work, being 27% for skilled craft jobs, 35% for clerical jobs that involve making decisions, and 46% for professional jobs. This implies that the best/worst ratio in higher-level work will be much greater. However, few clerical and professional jobs have been analysed, probably because it is far easier to count the output of soap wrappers or bicycle-chain assemblers than it is to measure the output of office workers or managers. It is also worth noting that many of the studies that Judiesch and Schmidt analysed are very old, and the jobs involved may no longer exist in the same form, if at all.

How much is a productive worker worth?

If some workers produce more than others, an employer who succeeds in selecting them will make more money – but how much more? For many years, accepted wisdom held that the financial benefit of employing good staff could not be directly calculated. Thus the psychologist could not tell employers 'my selection method can save you so many thousand pounds or dollars or euros per year'. A lot of ingenious effort has gone into trying to put a cash value on the productive worker. Accountants tried first and were not very successful, which left the field open to psychologists. Accountants can, at least in theory, calculate the value of each individual worker (so many units produced, selling at so much each, less the worker's wage costs, and a proportion of the company's overheads). In practice, such calculations proved very difficult.

Roche (1965) tried to quantify the value of individual radial drill operators, but his detailed calculations were criticised as over-simplified. The drill operators machined a great variety of different components, but the company's figures did not record output per operator, *per type of component* – pooled estimates had to be used. However, if accountants cannot put a precise value on an individual production worker's output, how can they hope to do so for a manager, a supervisor or a personnel director?

Rational estimates

In the late 1970s, psychologists devised a technique for putting a cash value on the people doing any job, no matter how varied and complex its demands, or how intangible its end-products. *Rational estimate (RE)* technique was invented by Schmidt and Hunter, who argued that people who are supervising a particular grade of employee 'have the best opportunities to observe actual performance and output differences between employees on a day-to-day basis' (Schmidt *et al.*, 1979). Thus the best way to put a value on a good employee is simply to ask supervisors to judge that employee's worth. REs are collected using the following instructions:

> Based on your experience with [widget press operators] we would like you to estimate the yearly value to your company of the products and services provided by the average operator. Consider the quality and quantity of output typical of the average operator and the value of this output.…In placing a cash value on this output, it may help to consider what the cost would be of having an outside firm provide these products and services.

Similar estimates are made for a good operator and for a poor one. 'Good' is defined as an operator at the 85th percentile – one whose performance is better than that of 85% of his or her fellows. 'Poor' is defined as an operator at the 15th percentile. Why 15% and 85%? The answer is because these values correspond roughly to one *standard deviation* either side of the mean. Therefore, assuming that the value of operators is normally distributed, the three estimates – 15th percentile, mean and 85th percentile – can be used to calculate the standard deviation of operator productivity, referred to as SD_y. SD_y summarises the distribution in value to the employer of differences in output between employees (*see* Figure 13.2). SD_y tells the employer how much the workers' work varies in value. SD_y is a vital term in the equation for estimating the return on a selection programme. The smaller SD_y is, the less point there is in putting a lot of effort and expense into selecting staff, because there is less difference in value between good and poor staff.

A large number of supervisors make rational estimates, and then averages are calculated. Schmidt and Hunter first obtained estimates by 62 supervisors of the value of average and good budget analysts, and found a mean difference

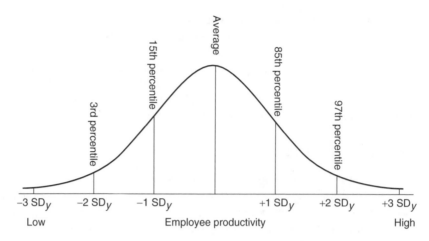

Figure 13.2   The distribution of employee productivity, showing the percentile points used in rational estimate technique to measure it

between average and good of $11,327 a year. This means that a good budget analyst is rated as worth $11,000 a year more than an average one. The study of budget analysts only made estimates for the average and the 85th percentile, so could not prove that value to the organisation is normally distributed. Schmidt and Hunter's second study made REs for good, average and poor computer programmers (Schmidt, Gast-Rosenberg & Hunter, 1980a). The differences between average and good, and average and poor were both around $10,000, and did not differ significantly, which confirms that the distribution is normal.

Bobko, Shetzer and Russell (1991) reported an estimate of SD_y for college professor (university lecturer) of $55,600, although the value varied greatly according to the way in which it was elicited. Yoo and Muchinsky (1998) generated estimates for 24 very varied jobs, and obtained a range of SD_y estimates from a low of $5.8K for window cleaners and toll collectors to highs of $84K and $62K for stockbrokers and industrial/organisational psychologists, respectively. They found that the more complex the job, in terms of either data analysis or interaction with other people, the greater SD_y was, confirming Judiesch and Schmidt's finding for SD_p.

Variations on the rational estimate theme

A number of other approaches to estimating the distribution of employee value have been proposed.

- Eaton, Wing and Mitchell (1985) devised the *superior equivalents technique*, in which commanders estimate how many tanks with superior (85th percentile) crews would be the match in battle of a standard company of 17 tanks with average crews. Estimates converged on a figure of nine. An elite tank company need number only nine to be the match of an average company, neatly confirming Schmidt and Hunter's estimate that the best is twice as good as the worst.

- Cascio (1982) described a more complex way of calculating differences in productivity – CREPID (Cascio Ramos Estimate of Performance In Dollars). The job is divided into different components (e.g. teaching, research and administration), the relative importance of each is rated (e.g. research is more important), and the value of the worker's contribution to each area is estimated, multiplied by its weighting, and then summed. CREPID is better suited for jobs which involve a range of activities that might not be done equally efficiently.

- Judiesch (2001) varied RE technique by asking supervisors for estimates of output and staffing levels for average, good and poor performers. If an average nurse can look after three patients adequately, how many could a good nurse look after? If the unit needs three average nurses, how many poor nurses would be needed to get the same work done to the same standard? Supervisors found these estimates easier to make. They also translate more directly into savings in staffing levels (and thus money).

- Raju, Burke and Normand (1990) proposed a different utility model, that does not require estimation of SD_y. Instead, they use A (average total compensation per employee, covering salary, benefits, bonuses and direct overheads) to put a figure on costs, and SD_r, the standard deviation of performance ratings for employees, to put a figure on differences between employees. This presupposes that the organisation has a performance appraisal system, which most American employers do have, but not all employers in other countries. It also presupposes that the performance appraisal system accurately describes differences between workers, which is not always true. Leniency – giving undeservedly good ratings – is a pervasive problem of performance appraisal in practice (Murphy & Cleveland, 1995), which would undermine Raju et al.'s method.

The 40–70% rule

SD_y for budget analysts worked out at 66% of salary; SD_y for computer programmers worked out at 55%. These values prompted Schmidt et al. (1979) to propose a *rule of thumb*:

SD_y is between 40% and 70% of salary.

Good and poor workers are each one SD_y from the average, so the difference between the best and the worst is *two* SD_ys. If SD_y is 40% to 70% of salary, the difference between good and poor is between 80% and 140% of salary, which generates another *rule of thumb*:

The value of a good employee minus the value of a poor employee is roughly equal to the salary paid for the job.

If the salary for the job in question is £30,000, the difference in value between the best and the worst worker is roughly £30,000, too. Recall also that 'good'

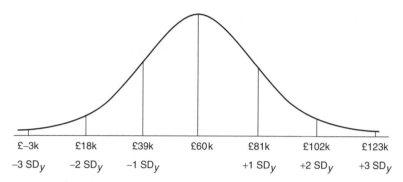

Figure 13.3 Distribution of productivity where average employee value is £60,000 and SD$_y$ is £21,000

and 'poor', at the 85th percentile and 15th percentile, are far from being the extremes.

The 'worse than useless' worker?

It is self-evident that the average value of each worker's output must exceed average salary. Otherwise the organisation will lose money and go out of business or require a subsidy. Schmidt *et al.* (1979) proposed another *rule of thumb*:

The yearly value of output of the average worker is about twice his or her salary.

Certain combinations of values of the two ratios – productivity/salary and SD$_y$/salary – have alarming implications for employers. Suppose that salary is £30,000. The first rule of thumb implies that SD$_y$ could be as high as £21,000 (70% of salary). The third rule of thumb implies that average productivity is about £60,000 (twice salary). Consider a worker whose productivity is *three* SD$_y$ below the mean. That worker is worth £60,000 less £21,000 × 3, i.e. *minus* £3,000 (*see* Figure 13.3). The goods and services that this employee provides would not cost anything to buy in from outside, because they are not worth anything. In fact, that employee actually loses the employer £3,000, on top of the cost of his or her salary of £30,000. Only one or two in a thousand employees fall three SDs below the mean, so 'worse than useless' employees are probably scarce, although some commentators feel that they could nominate organisations where 'worse than useless' workers proliferate.

Are rational estimates valid?

Some critics think that REs are dangerously subjective. Schmidt *et al.* disagree; the instructions specify estimating the cost of employing an outside firm to do the work, which provides a 'relatively concrete standard'. Furthermore, 'the idiosyncratic tendencies, biases and random errors of individual judges can be controlled by averaging across a large number of judges'. In any case, they argue, cost-accounting calculations are often fairly subjective, too, involving 'many estimates and arbitrary allocations'. Some research suggests that REs are valid.

- Blankenship, Cesare and Giannetto (1995) reported that rational estimates made by people doing the job agree well with estimates made by supervisors.
- Bobko and Karren (1982) compared rational estimates for 92 insurance sales-people with their actual sales figures, and found very similar values of SD_y.
- Cesare, Blankenship and Giannetto (1994) found that rational estimates agreed with conventional supervisor ratings very well ($r = 0.67$), although it is not clear whether the same supervisors generated both sets of data.

However, other studies have cast some doubt on the validity of REs. Bobko *et al.* (1991) found that relatively minor changes in the wording of the instructions, or the order of presentation (85th percentile estimate, then 50th percentile, or vice versa) generate a very wide range of SD_y estimates, from as low as $29K to as high as $101K. Another study asked supervisors to explain how they generated REs (Mathieu & Tannenbaum, 1989) and found that most – especially the more experienced – based their estimates on salary. This makes some of Schmidt and Hunter's rules of thumb look suspiciously circular. If rational estimates of SD_y are based on salary, it is not surprising to find that they are closely related to salary.

Is productivity normally distributed?

Psychologists like normal distributions, if only to justify the statistical an-alyses that they use. Schmidt *et al.* (1980a) produced evidence that value to the organisation is normally distributed. Subsequently, however, Yoo and Muchinsky (1998) found that value was not normally distributed for 15 of the 24 occupations they studied. In every case the above-average estimate (50–85) was higher than the below-average estimate. This is consistent with there being more high performers than would be found in a true distribution. However, it should be noted that they used the same panel to estimate for all 24 jobs, so shared rating bias could explain their results.

Calculating the return on selection

It is fairly easy to calculate the cost of selection, although many employers only think of doing so when asked to introduce new methods. They rarely work out how much existing methods, such as day-long panel interviews, cost. It is more difficult to calculate the *return* on selection. The formula was first stated by Brogden in 1950, but for many years had only academic interest because a crucial term within it could not be measured – SD_y, the standard deviation of employee productivity. Until rational estimate technique was devised, there was no way of measuring how much more good employees are worth.
   Brogden's equation states:

$$\text{saving per employee per year} = (r \times SD_y \times z) - (C/P)$$

where r is the validity of the selection procedure (expressed as a correlation coefficient), SD_y is the standard deviation of employee productivity in pounds, dollars or euros, z is the calibre of recruits (expressed as their standard score on the selection test used), C is the cost of selection per applicant and P is the proportion of applicants selected.

To put it in plain English, the amount that an employer can save per employee recruited per year is:

VALIDITY of the test

times

CALIBRE of recruits

times

Sd_y

minus

COST of selection

divided by

PROPORTION of applicants selected.

Here is a worked example.

1. The employer is recruiting in the salary range £30,000 pa, so SD_y can be estimated – by the 40% rule of thumb – at £12,000.
2. The employer is using a test of mental ability whose validity is 0.45, so r is 0.45.
3. The people recruited score on average 1 SD above the mean (for present employees), so z is 1. This assumes that the employer succeeds in recruiting high-calibre people.
4. The employer uses a consultancy, who charge £650 per candidate.
5. Of 10 applicants, four are appointed, so P is 0.40.

The SAVING per employee per year is:

$$(0.45 \times £12,000 \times 1) - (£650/0.40) = £5,400 - £1,625 = £3,775$$

Each employee selected is worth nearly £4,000 a year more to the employer than one recruited at random. The four employees recruited will be worth in all £15,100 more to the employer each year. The larger the organisation, the greater the total sum that can be saved by effective selection – hence the estimate given in Chapter 1 of $18 million for the Philadelphia police force, with 5,000 employees.

Selection pays off better when:

- the calibre of recruits is high
- employees differ widely in worth to the organisation (i.e. when SD_y is high)
- selection procedure has high validity.

Selection pays off less well when:

- recruits are uniformly mediocre
- SD_y is low (i.e. workers do not vary much in value)
- the selection procedure has low validity.

Employers should have no difficulty attracting good recruits in periods of high unemployment (unless pay or conditions are poor). Rational estimate and other research shows that SD_y is rarely low. The third condition – zero validity – is all too likely to apply, given that many employers still use very poor selection methods. However, if any of the three terms are zero, their product – the value of selection – is necessarily zero, too. Only the right-hand side of the equation – the cost of selection – is never zero. In the worked example, even using a fairly expensive selection procedure the cost per employee selected is less than a fifth of the increased value per employee per year. In this example, selection pays for itself six times over in the first year. By contrast, failure to select the right employee goes on costing the employer money year after year.

Utility analysis in practice

Other authors have pointed out that some utility theory estimates of savings achieved by good selection are over-optimistic.

- Increased productivity is not all 'money in the bank'. Increased production means increased costs (raw materials, overheads, commission, etc.). It also means increased taxes. Moreover, the costs of selection are incurred before the savings are made, so interest charges need to be included. Correcting for these omissions reduces estimates of savings by 67% (Boudreau, 1983).
- Brogden's equation overestimates the return on selection, because it assumes that everyone who is offered a job will accept it. In practice, some applicants, especially the better ones, reject the employer's offer, so the calibre of the new employees (z in the Brogden equation) is reduced (Murphy, 1986).
- Roth and Bobko (1997) argued that the cash value of increased productivity is not the only basis for assessing the success of selection. Diversity, legal exposure and organisational image are also important. A selection procedure that maximises output, at the expense of excluding minorities, resulting in lawsuits and creating bad publicity, may not be very successful.

- At a more individual level, selecting the most capable may have hidden costs, if such individuals turn out to be divisive, verbally abusive, bullying, etc. This might reduce others' job satisfaction or even output, and result in people leaving the organisation and perhaps even suing the company.
- Vance and Colella (1990) commented that utility theory makes the simplistic assumption that every worker works in isolation, whereas in reality much work is done by teams, where 'superhumans' performing at the 95% percentile will be held back by slower mortals performing at the 50th percentile. Organisations in the Soviet Union discovered this in the 1930s. They held up as a model a coal miner called Alexei Stakhanov, who exceeded his quota of coal many times over, and encouraged other workers to try to achieve enormous outputs. Some 'Stakhanovites' proved a liability. Either they produced far more of their product than was actually needed, or else the organisation had to provide extra workers to bring in extra raw materials and carry away the Stakhanovite's output.

Do utility estimates impress management?

Macan and Highhouse (1994) reported that 46% of industrial psychologists and personnel managers say they use utility argument to sell projects to managers. By contrast, Latham and Whyte (1994), who admit to being sceptical about utility theory, reported a study which showed that managers are less likely to buy a selection package from an occupational psychologist on the strength of utility estimates. If Latham is right, occupational psychologists are using the wrong tactics to sell their services to management. Hazer and Highhouse (1997) found that accounts of utility based on the '40% rule' are more convincing to managers than those based on more complex ways of estimating SD_y, suggesting that simple accounts are better. Carson, Becker and Henderson (1998) found that a more 'user-friendly' exposition of utility gained more acceptance. Evidently a difficult concept needs to be explained in fairly simple terms.

Proving that selection really adds value

Critics of utility theory dismiss it as just another set of meaningless estimates along the lines of 'traffic congestion costs £30 million a day'. Vance and Colella (1990) complained that savings that dwarf the national debt are postulated, but no real savings from selection have been demonstrated. Such critics are asking for proof that using good selection methods actually improves the organisation's performance. Recently some studies have provided such proof, although it is probably still not as specific and definite as the critics would like. Huselid, Jackson and Schuler (1997) correlated general human resource (HR) effectiveness and capability with employee productivity (defined as net sales per employee), return on assets and profitability across 293 organisations. They reported weak (0.10–0.16) significant correlations between HR effectiveness and capability, and return on assets and profitability, but not with employee productivity. However, their measures of HR effectiveness and capability were very global, including only a few specific references to selection and recruitment in a 41-item list.

| £–3k | £18k | £39k | £60k | £81k | £102k | £123k |
| –3 SD$_y$ | –2 SD$_y$ | –1 SD$_y$ | | +1 SD$_y$ | +2 SD$_y$ | +3 SD$_y$ |

Perhaps the most convincing data have been provided by Terpstra and Rozell (1993) who correlated HR practices with performance across 201 organisations, and showed that organisations which use five particular selection and recruitment practices have higher annual profits, more profit growth and more sales growth. The selection methods in question are structured interviews, mental ability tests, biodata, analysis of recruiting source and validation of selection methods. The relationship is very strong (0.70–0.80) in sectors that arguably depend crucially on the calibre of their staff, such as service industry and the financial sector, but it is insignificant in sectors where capital equipment is possibly more important, such as manufacturing. However, Terpstra and Rozell's data could be interpreted as showing that better-run companies are more profitable and also use better selection methods. It does not follow that better selection creates greater profitability. To prove that we will need a longitudinal study, in which increased profitability follows changes in selection.

Key points

In Chapter 13 you have learnt the following.

- Utility theory deals with the cost-effectiveness of selection.
- People vary in the amount of work they do, and in the value of their work to the organisation.
- It is possible to estimate how people vary by various techniques, including rational estimates.
- Estimates of how much people vary can be used to determine when selection is cost-effective, and when it is not.
- Estimates of how people vary can also be used to estimate the return on selection programmes.
- Utility estimates do not seem to impress managers all that much.
- Some preliminary evidence suggests that good selection may improve an organisation's profitability.

Key references

Bobko *et al.* (1991) present data on the distribution of value of American academic staff.

Judiesch and Schmidt (2000) review research on individual differences in productivity.

Schmidt *et al.* (1979) report the first application of rational estimate technique to budget analysts.

Terpstra and Rozell (1993) present data which show that better selection may be linked to increased profitability.

Vance and Colella (1990) criticise utility theory estimates as being unrealistic.

Yoo and Muchinsky (1998) present estimates of distribution of value to the organisation for 24 varied jobs.

CHAPTER 14

Conclusions

Calculating the cost of smugness

Introduction

> We find everywhere a type of organisation (administrative, commercial or academic) in which the higher officials are plodding and dull, those less senior are active only in intrigue. . .and the junior men are frustrated and frivolous. Little is being attempted, nothing is being achieved.
>
> (C. Northcote Parkinson, 1958)

In some organisations the costs of selecting ineffective staff mount indefinitely, because the organisation lacks the mechanism or the will to dispense with their services. Naturally morale in such organisations suffers, driving out the remaining efficient workers until only the incompetent remain, creating the state of terminal sickness that was so graphically described by Northcote Parkinson. Staff wander aimlessly about, 'giggling feebly', losing important documents, coming alive only to block the advancement of anyone more able, 'until the central administration gradually fills up with people stupider than the chairman'. Other diagnostics include surly porters and telephonists, out-of-order lifts, a proliferation of out-of-date notices, and smugness – especially smugness. The organisation is doing a good job, in its own modest way, and anyone who disagrees is a troublemaker who would probably be happier somewhere else. Parkinson advises that smugness is most easily diagnosed in the organisation's refectory. The terminally smug do not just consume an 'uneatable, nameless mess' – they congratulate themselves on having catering staff who can provide it at such reasonable cost, 'smugness made absolute'.

Selectors sometimes see their task as avoiding mistakes and minimising error. They bring in psychologists as the final check that the candidate is 'safe'. So long as the year has gone by with no obvious disasters and no complaints, the human resource department has done its job. This negative approach to selection is wrong. Chapter 13 showed that productivity is normally distributed. There is a continuous distribution of productivity from the very best to the very worst. Selection is not as simple as avoiding mistakes – not employing a small minority of obvious incompetents or troublemakers. The employer who succeeds in employing *average* staff has not succeeded in employing *good* staff, and the employer who finds *good* staff has not found *excellent* staff. To take this argument to its logical limit, any employer who has not got the world's 100 best programmers filling 100 programmer vacancies has not maximised productivity. The world's 100 best programmers clearly are not a realistic target, but programmers in the top 15% perhaps might be, at least for some employers.

How to select

There are six criteria for judging selection tests.

1. *Validity* is the most important criterion. Unless a test can predict productivity, there is little point in using it.
2. *Cost* tends to be accorded far too much weight by selectors. Cost is not an important consideration, so long as the test has *validity*. A valid test, even the most elaborate and expensive, is almost always worth using.
3. *Practicality* is a negative criterion – reason for *not* using a test.
4. *Generality* simply means how many types of employees the test can be used for.
5. *Acceptability* to candidates is important, especially in times of full employment.
6. *Legality* is another negative criterion – a reason for *not* using something. It is often hard to evaluate, as the legal position on many tests is obscure or confused.

Validity

Table 14.1 collates the results of the various meta-analyses and VGAs discussed in earlier chapters. The earlier analyses, by Dunnette (1972), Vineberg and Joyner (1982), Schmitt *et al.* (1984), Reilly and Chao (1982) and Hunter and Hunter (1984), remain in some cases the main source of information. For example, no one since has analysed the letter of reference as a selection method, probably because little new research has appeared. Dunnette's review derived entirely from the American petroleum industry. Vineberg and Joyner's review derived entirely from the American armed services. Schmitt *et al.*'s analysis covered only studies published in *Personnel Psychology* and the *Journal of Applied Psychology*. Hunter and Hunter's VGA mainly used unpublished US government data.

Later meta-analyses and VGAs, for graphology, interviewing, biographical measures, psychomotor tests, job-knowledge tests, personality testing, projective tests, assessment centres, T & E ratings, and work-sample and trainability tests, generally confirm the conclusions of the earlier meta-analyses, with two exceptions.

1. Research on interviewing indicates that *structured* interviewing achieves far higher validity than interviewing in general.
2. Research on personality tests confirms that they generally predict job proficiency very poorly, but other research (not included in Table 14.1)

Table 14.1 Summary of the validity of different selection tests for work performance.

	Early analyses					Later analyses						Reference
	D	R&C	V&J	H&H	S	W&C	H&A	Mcd	B&R			
Graphology	16	'None'		14								21/00[a] Neter & Ben-Shakhar (1989)
Interview												
Unstructured IV		19				47	37	47				
Structured IV						31	20	33				
Empirical IV						62	57	44	30*			40 Schmidt & Rader (1999)
Situational IV												46 Latham & Sue-Chan (1999)
	D	R&C	V&J	H&H	S	Blies	Drak	Vetal	B&R			
References		18		26								
Peer ratings		35		49								
Biodata	34		24	37	24	30*	21*	52	30*			47 Funke et al. (1987)
	D	R&C	V&J	H&H	S	Vetal	B&R					
General mental ability	45			53	25	40	30*					
Perceptual	34											
Psychomotor	35											42 Salgado (1997)
Aptitude			28	48	27							
Job knowledge	51											45 Dye et al. (1993)
Common sense												53 McDaniel et al. (2001)
Craft jobs												43 Levine et al. (1996)
	D	R&C	V&J	H&H	S	B&M	Tett	Vetal	Sal	BMJ	B&R	
Personality inventory	08											
Neuroticism						−07	−22	−05	−13	−12		
Extraversion						10	16	09	08	12		
Openness						−03	27	06	06	05		
Agreeableness						06	33	03	01	10		
Conscientiousness						23	18	11	15	23	18*	

	D	R&C	V&J	H&H	S	Gau	Art	
Honesty tests	'Little'							41 Ones et al. (1993)
Customer service								50 Frei & McDaniel (1998)
Projective tests								22 Martinussen & Torjussen (1993)
Assessment centre				43	41	37	35	33 Roth et al. (1996)
Education		14	25	10				39* Robertson & Kandola (1982)
Work-sample test				54	38			
Trainability test								20–24* Robertson & Downs (1989)
In-tray test								28* Robertson & Kandola (1982)
T & E rating			13					17/45^b McDaniel et al. (1988)
Self-assessment								08–45 Mabe & West (1982)
Physical test				32				

Notes:
D = Dunnette (1972); R&C = Reilly & Chao (1982); V&J = Vineberg & Joyner (1982); H&H = Hunter & Hunter (1984); S = Schmitt et al. (1984); B&M = Barrick & Mount (1991); Tett = Tett et al. (1991); Sal = Salgado (1997); BMJ = Barrick et al. (2001); B&R = Bobko & Roth (1999); Vetal = Vinchur et al. (1998); W&C = Wiesner & Cronshaw (1988); H&A = Huffcutt & Arthur (1994); McD = McDaniel et al. (1994); Blies = Bliesener (1996); Funk = Funke et al. (1987); Drak = Drakeley, in Gunter et al. (1993); Gau = Gaugler et al. (1989); Art = Arthur et al. (in press).
* Uncorrected validity.
^{a} 0.21 overall, zero for content-free text.
^{b} 0.17 overall, 0.45 for behaviour consistency method.

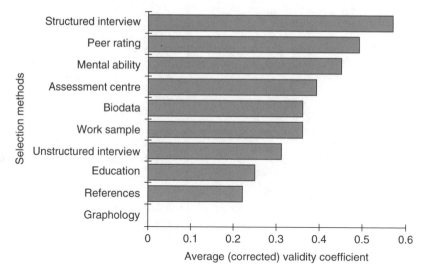

Figure 14.1   Schematic summary of validity of different selection tests, based on data from Table 14.1

shows that personality tests can predict honesty, effort, organisational citizenship, leadership and motivation more successfully.

Figure 14.1 shows that selection tests vary very widely in validity, from a high point of 0.53 to a low point of zero. Moreover, the distribution of validity is *skewed* towards the low end – there are a lot of tests with very limited validity. Selectors should therefore choose their tests carefully. As noted previously, the mere fact that a selection measure is widely used does not prove that it has any validity.

Table 14.2 summarises the relative merits of 10 selection methods against the six criteria, namely validity, cost, practicality, generality, acceptability and legality.

Cost

Interview costs are given as medium/low, because interviews vary so much, and because they are so much taken for granted that few estimates of their cost have been made. Structured interview costs are high, because the system has to be tailor-made and requires a full job analysis. Biodata costs are given as high or low; the cost is high if the inventory has to be specially written for the employer, but it might be low if a 'ready-made' consortium biodata could be used. The cost of using educational qualifications is given as nil, because the information is routinely collected through application forms. Checking that someone really has a first-class maths degree from Idontgoto State University will cost a small amount, but many UK employers do not take this precaution.

Table 14.2 Summary of 12 selection tests by six criteria.

Selection test	VAL	COST	PRAC	GEN	ACC	LEGAL
Interview	Low	Medium/Low	High	High	High	Uncertain
Structured interview	High	High	?Limited	High	Untested	No problems
References	Moderate	Very low	High	High	Medium	Some doubts
Peer rating	High	Very low	Very limited	Very limited	Low	Untested
Biodata	High	High/Low	High	High	Low	Some doubts
Ability	High	Low	High	High	Low	Major problems
Psychomotor test	High	Low	Moderate	Limited	Untested	Untested
Job knowledge	High	Low	High	Limited	Untested	Some doubts
Personality	Variable	Low	High	High	Low	Some doubts
Assessment	High	Very high	Fair	Fair	High	No problems
Work sample	High	High	Limited	Limited	High	No problems
Education	Moderate	Nil	High	High	Untested	Major doubts

Note: VAL = validity, COST = cost, PRAC = practicality, GEN = generality, ACC = acceptability, LEGAL = legality.

Practicality

This means that the test is not difficult to introduce, because it fits into the selection process easily. Ability and personality tests are very practical because they can be given when candidates come for interview, and they generally permit group testing. References are very practical because everyone is used to giving them. Assessment centres are only fairly practical, because they need a lot of organising, and do not fit into the conventional timetable of selection procedures. Peer assessments are highly impractical because they require applicants to spend a long time with each other. Structured interviews may have limited practicality, because managers may resist the loss of autonomy involved. Work-sample and psychomotor tests have limited practicality, because candidates have to be tested individually, not in groups.

Generality

Most selection tests can be used for any category of worker, but true work samples and job knowledge tests can only be used where there is a specific body of knowledge or skill to test, which in practice means skilled manual jobs. Psychomotor tests are only useful for jobs that require dexterity or good motor control. Peer ratings can probably only be used in uniformed disciplined services. Assessment centres tend to be restricted to managers, probably on grounds of cost, although they have been used for humbler posts.

Acceptability

This is based on the surveys of Ryan and Ployhart (2000) and Steiner and Gilliland (1996), described in Chapter 1.

Legality

This is largely rated on American experience, Chapter 12 argued that many other countries' fair employment agencies tend to model themselves on American practice, so American experience may be a useful guide to the shape of things to come elsewhere. Assessment centres, work samples and structured interviews probably do not cause legal problems, but educational qualifications and mental ability tests most certainly do. The position on other measures, such as biodata, remains uncertain. As time passes, selection methods tend to acquire poorer ratings under this heading. For example, personality tests were listed as 'untested' in the second edition of this book, but are now listed as 'some doubts', because the American *Soroka* case has raised – not settled – the issue of invasion of privacy. Bobko and Roth (1999) have challenged the generally accepted view that structured interviews and biodata cause no adverse impact, so these measures may in time become legally problematic. It may be necessary to distinguish the letter and spirit of the law. Hoffman and Thornton (1997) argued that tests which create large adverse impact probably cannot be used in practice in the USA, even if they do meet the letter of the law by demonstrating business necessity (i.e. validity). American courts have proved to have fairly wide discretion in how they interpret fair employment law, possibly because the law is often rather vague.

Taking *validity* as the over-riding consideration, there are seven classes of test with high *validity*, namely peer ratings, biodata, structured interviews, ability tests, assessment centres, work-sample tests and job-knowledge tests. Three of these have very limited *generality*, which leaves biodata, structured interviews, ability tests and assessment centres.

- *Biodata* do not achieve quite such good validity as ability tests, and are not as transportable, which makes them more expensive.
- *Structured interviews* have excellent validity but limited transportability, and are expensive to set up.
- *Ability tests* have excellent validity, can be used for all types of jobs, are readily transportable, and are cheap and easy to use, but fall foul of the law in the USA.
- *Assessment centres* have excellent validity, can be used for most grades of staff and are legally fairly safe, but are difficult to install, and expensive.
- *Work samples* have excellent validity, are easy to use and are generally quite safe legally, but are expensive, because they are necessarily specific to the job.
- *Job-knowledge tests* have good validity, are easy to use, and are cheap because they are commercially available, but they are more likely to cause legal problems because they are usually paper-and-pencil tests.

Most of the other tests in Tables 14.1 and 14.2 have lower validity – but not zero validity. Tests with validities below 0.20–0.30 are commonly written off as a waste of time, but in fact can be worth using if they are cheap, or if they contribute new information. Thus the only test in Table 14.1 that can definitely be dismissed as never worth using is graphology.

- *Personality inventories* achieve poor validity for predicting job proficiency, but can prove more useful for predicting how well the individual will conform to the job's norms and rules.
- *References* have only moderate validity, but are cheap to use. However, legal cautions are tending to limit their value.

Incremental validity

The big gap in present knowledge is the validity of *combinations* of tests. Schmidt and Hunter (1998) made predictions based on intercorrelations of predictors, and argued that many other tests add little to mental ability tests. Empirical research on actual incremental validity is as yet relatively scarce. Chapter 7 shows that personality tests do contribute incremental validity when used with mental ability tests. Chapter 9 shows that in-tray exercises contribute incremental validity to tests of mental ability. On the other hand, tests of mental ability are unlikely to add much to tests of job knowledge. However, there remain a large number of possible combinations of selection methods for which no information about incremental validity is available. Do reference checks improve on personality inventories? Is there anything to be gained by adding peer ratings to work samples and mental ability tests? What combination of the methods listed in Tables 14.1 and 14.2 will give the best results, and how good will that 'best' be?

Conclusions

The illusion of selection

Bad selection is not just a waste of time – it costs employers a lot of money, year after year. Robertson and Makin (1986) concluded pessimistically from their survey of major UK employers that 'the frequency of a method's use is inversely related to its known validity'. Bad selection methods are still very popular, especially the unstructured interview. The interview has survived 60 years of mounting criticism from psychologists, while ability tests, which are very good predictors of productivity, have been practically forced out of business in the USA. Why is this?

'Summing other people up' is an activity that people like to think they are good at, like driving a car or making love. Thus people are not receptive to the suggestion that their task could be done quicker and better by ability test or biodata inventory. One wonders if the popularity of assessment centres derives as much from the elaborate opportunities they provide to 'sum people up' as from their high validity.

Incompetence + jealousy = 'injelitance'?

The discussion has assumed that all employers genuinely want the best applicants. Northcote Parkinson thinks this is very naive: 'If the head of an organisation is second-rate, he will see to it that his immediate staff are all third-rate, and they will in turn see to it that their subordinates are fourth-rate'. Such organisations suffer *injelitance* – 'a disease of induced inferiority', compounded equally of *incompetence* and *jealousy*. The 'injelitant' organisation does not fill up with stupid people accidentally. Dull smug people at its core deliberately recruit even duller smugger people, to protect their own positions. And what better way is there to perpetuate incompetence than the traditional interview? Mediocrities can be selected and promoted, using the code words 'soundness', 'teamwork' and 'judgement'. And what greater threat to injelitant organisations can there be than objective tests of ability which might introduce unwelcome, disruptive, 'clever' people? Parkinson thinks that injelitance is a terminal illness of organisations, which can only be cured by dismissing all of the staff and burning the buildings to the ground. However, he does suggest that 'infected personnel' might be 'dispatched with a warm testimonial to such rival institutions as are regarded with particular hostility'.

Cook's law

An important principle of selection is that the more important the decision, the longer the time that must be spent making it, and *the more time that must be seen to be spent making it*. Work samples and simple aptitude tests are good enough for shop-floor workers. Clerical tests are good enough for lowly office workers. But selecting anyone 'important' requires longer, more elaborate selection procedures that take many man-hours. Panel interviews in the UK public sector show Cook's law to advantage – a panel of 10 people spends all day interviewing candidates, at vast expense. Usually all the time is spent interviewing – the *visible* part of selection – while far too little time is spent in preparation and analysis. Cook's law has a corollary, which is very comforting to occupational psychologists – the more important the selection, the more the employer is willing to pay. It is no more difficult or time-consuming to assess a potential Managing Director (Company President) than to assess a line manager, but most consultancies charge more, and most employers pay willingly.

Creating an underclass?

An employer who succeeds in recruiting able, productive workers needs fewer of them. If all employers use highly accurate tests to select productive workers, the number of jobs will shrink, creating more unemployment. If every employer uses highly accurate tests, people of low ability will find it hard to get work. If employers started to exchange information, the ungifted would find themselves never even being shortlisted. The result would be a steadily growing, unemployed, disillusioned and resentful *underclass*. This is not a new idea – Cattell saw it coming 65 years ago (Cattell, 1936).

Burning the candle at both ends?

At the other end of the distribution of ability, a shrinking workforce of more able people works harder and longer to maximise productivity. In the process, they wear themselves out and have no time left to enjoy life. Many managers are already seeing this happening to themselves. If fewer and fewer people produce more and more, who is going to buy it? How are they going to pay for it?

Is productivity the only end?

This book started life as a title in a series on *Psychology and Productivity*, so it reviews what psychologists know about selecting people who produce more. This does not mean that psychologists think all employers ought to work like that all the time. A world run by cost accountants would be a very dreary place.

Work serves other purposes besides producing goods and services. Work fulfils workers, work absorbs unemployment, work is good for people, work keeps people out of bars, work fills up the day, work brings people together, work prevents urban riots.

References

Aamodt M G, Bryan D A & Whitcomb A J (1993) Predicting performance with letters of recommendation. *Public Personnel Management*, **22**, 81–90.

Aamodt M G, Nagy M S & Thompson N (1998) *Employment references: who are we talking about?* Paper presented to annual meeting of the International Personnel Management Association Assessment Council, Chicago, IL, 22nd June.

Ackerman P L (1988) Determinants of individual differences during skill acquisition: cognitive abilities and information processing. *Journal of Experimental Psychology: General*, **117**, 288–313.

Aiello J R & Kolb K J (1995) Electronic performance monitoring and social context: impact on productivity and stress. *Journal of Applied Psychology*, **80**, 339–353.

Allport G W (1937) *Personality: a Psychological Interpretation*. Holt, New York.

Amir Y, Kovarsky Y & Sharan S (1970) Peer nominations as a predictor of multistage promotions in a ramified organisation. *Journal of Applied Psychology*, **54**, 462–469.

Anastasi A (1981) Coaching, test sophistication and developed abilities. *American Psychologist*, **36**, 1086–1093.

Anderson N & Shackleton V (1990) Decision making in the graduate selection interview: a field study. *Journal of Occupational Psychology*, **63**, 63–76.

Anderson N, Payne T, Ferguson E & Smith T (1994) Assessor decision making, information processing and assessor decision strategies in a British assessment centre. *Personnel Review*, **23**, 52–62.

Anderson V V (1929) *Psychiatry in Industry*. Holt, New York.

Andrews L G (1922) A grading system for picking men. *Sales Management*, **4**, 143–144.

Anguinis H, Cortina J M & Goldberg E (1998) A new procedure for computing equivalence bands in personnel selection. *Human Performance*, **11**, 351–365.

Anstey E (1977) A 30-year follow-up of the CSSB procedure, with lessons for the future. *Journal of Occupational Psychology*, **50**, 149–159.

Arnold J D, Rauschenberger J M, Soubel W G & Guion R G (1982) Validation and utility of strength tests for selecting steelworkers. *Journal of Applied Psychology*, **67**, 588–604.

Arthur W & Tubre T (in press) The assessment center construct-related validity paradox: a case of construct mis-specification. *Journal of Applied Social Psychology*.

Arthur W, Barrett G V & Doverspike D (1990) Validation of an information-processing-based test battery for the prediction of handling accidents among petroleum transport drivers. *Journal of Applied Psychology*, **75**, 621–626.

Arthur W, Doverspike D & Barrett G V (1996) Development of a job-analysis-based procedure for weighting and combining content-related tests into a single battery score. *Personnel Psychology*, **49**, 971–985.

Arthur W, Edwards B D & Barrett G V (2002) Multiple choice and constructed response tests of ability: race-based subgroup performance differences on alternative paper-and-pencil tests. *Personnel Psychology*, **55**, 985–1009.

Arthur W, Day E A, McNelly T L & Edens P S (in press) The criterion-related validity of assessment center dimensions: distinguishing between methods and constructs. *Personnel Psychology*.

Arthur W, Woehr D J, Akande A & Strong M H (1995) Human resource management in West Africa: practices and perceptions. *International Journal of Human Resource Management*, **6**, 347–367.

Arvey R D (1979a) Unfair discrimination in the employment interview: legal and psychological aspects. *Psychological Bulletin*, **86**, 736–765.

Arvey R D (1979b) *Fairness in Selecting Employees*. Addison Wesley, Reading, MA.

Arvey R D & Begalla M E (1975) Analysing the homemaker job using the Position Analysis Questionnaire. *Journal of Applied Psychology*, **60**, 513–517.

Arvey R D, Gordon M, Massengill O & Mussio S (1975) Differential dropout rates of minority and majority job candidates due to 'time lags' between selection procedures. *Personnel Psychology*, **28**, 175–180.

Ash R A (1980) Self-assessments of five types of typing ability. *Personnel Psychology*, **33**, 273–282.

Ashworth S D, Osburn H G, Callender J C & Boyle K A (1992) The effects of unrepresented studies on the robustness of validity generalisation results. *Personnel Psychology*, **45**, 341–361.

Atkins P W B & Wood R E (2002) Self- versus others' ratings as predictors of assessment center ratings: validation evidence from 360-degree feedback programs. *Personnel Psychology*, **55**, 871–904.

Austin J T & Villanova P (1992) The criterion problem: 1917–1992. *Journal of Applied Psychology*, **77**, 836–874.

Avis J M, Kudisch J D & Fortunato V J (2002) Examining the incremental validity and adverse impact of cognitive ability and conscientiousness on job performance. *Journal of Business and Psychology*, **17**, 82–105.

Avolio B J & Waldman D A (1994) Variations in cognitive, perceptual and psychomotor abilities across the working life span: examining the effects of race, sex, experience, education and occupational type. *Psychology and Ageing*, **9**, 430–442.

Baehr M E & Orban J A (1989) The role of intellectual abilities and personality characteristics in determining success in higher-level positions. *Journal of Vocational Behavior*, **35**, 270–287.

Baird L L (1985) Do grades and tests predict adult accomplishment? *Research in Higher Education*, **23**, 3–85.

Banks M H, Jackson P R, Stafford E M & Warr P B (1983) The Job Components Inventory and the analysis of jobs requiring limited skill. *Personnel Psychology*, **36**, 57–66.

Barclay J M (2001) Improving selection interviews with structure: organisations' use of "behavioural" interviews. *Personnel Review*, **30**, 81–101.

Barge B N & Hough L M (1986) Utility of biographical data for predicting job performance. In: L M Hough (ed.) *Utility of Temperament, Biodata and Interest Assessment for Predicting Job Performance: a Review of the Literature*. Army Research Institute, Alexandria, VA.

Baron H (1995) Occupational testing of people with disabilities: what have we learnt? *International Journal of Selection and Assessment*, **3**, 207–213.

Baron R A (1983) 'Sweet smell of success'? The impact of pleasant artificial scents of evaluations of job applicants. *Journal of Applied Psychology*, **68**, 709–713.

Barrett G V (1992) Clarifying construct validity: definitions, processes and models. *Human Performance*, **5**, 13–58.

Barrett G V (1997) An historical perspective on the Nassau County Police entrance examination: Arnold v Ballard (1975) revisited. The *Industrial/Organisational Psychologist*; www.siop.org/tip/backissues/tipoct97/BARRET~1.htm.

Barrett G V, Alexander R A & Doverspike D (1992) The implications for personnel selection of apparent declines in predictive validities over time: a critique of Hulin, Henry and Noon. *Personnel Psychology*, **45**, 601–617.

Barrett G V, Caldwell M S & Alexander R A (1985) The concept of dynamic criteria: a critical reanalysis. *Personnel Psychology*, **38**, 41–56.

Barrett G V, Phillips J S & Alexander R A (1981) Concurrent and predictive validity designs: a critical reanalysis. *Journal of Applied Psychology*, **66**, 1–6.

Barrett P & Paltiel L (1996) Can a single item replace an entire scale? POP vs. the OPQ 5.2. *Selection and Development Review*, **12**, 1–4.

Barrick M R & Mount M K (1991) The big five personality dimensions and job performance: a meta-analysis. *Personnel Psychology*, **44**, 1–26.

Barrick M R & Mount M K (1993) Autonomy as a moderator of the relationships between the big five personality dimensions and job performance. *Journal of Applied Psychology*, **78**, 111–118.

Barrick M R, Mount M K & Judge T A (2001) Personality and performance at the beginning of the new millennium: what do we know and where do we go next? *International Journal of Selection and Assessment*, **9**, 9–30.

Barrick M R, Mount M K & Strauss J P (1993) Conscientiousness and performance of sales representatives: test of the mediating effects of goal setting. *Journal of Applied Psychology*, **78**, 715–722.

Barrick M R, Mount M K & Strauss J P (1994) Antecedents of involuntary turnover due to reduction in force. *Personnel Psychology*, **47**, 515–535.

Barrick M R, Stewart G L, Neubert M J & Mount M K (1998) Relating member ability and personality to work team processes and effectiveness. *Journal of Applied Psychology*, **83**, 377–391.

Bartlett C J, Bobko P, Mosier S B & Hannan R (1978) Testing for fairness with a modified multiple regression strategy: an alternative to differential analysis. *Personnel Psychology*, **31**, 233–241.

Bartram D (2000) Internet recruitment and selection: kissing frogs to find princes. *International Journal of Selection and Assessment*, **8**, 261–274.

Bartram D, Lindley P A, Marshall L & Foster J (1995) The recruitment and selection of young people by small businesses. *Journal of Occupational and Organizational Psychology*, **68**, 339–358.

Baxter J C, Brock B, Hill P C, & Rozelle R M (1981) Letters of recommendation: a question of value. *Journal of Applied Psychology*, **66**, 296–301.

Becker T E & Colquitt A L (1992) Potential versus actual faking of a biodata form: an analysis along several dimensions of item type. *Personnel Psychology*, **45**, 389–406.

Bennett R J & Robinson S L (2000) Development of a measure of workplace deviance. *Journal of Applied Psychology*, **85**, 349–360.

Bersoff D N (1981) Testing and the law. *American Psychologist*, **36**, 1047–1056.

Bingham W V & Freyd M (1926) *Procedures in Employment Psychology.* Shaw, Chicago.

Blankenship M H, Cesare S J, & Giannetto P W (1995) A comparison of supervisor and incumbent estimates of SD$_y$. *Journal of Business and Psychology*, **9**, 415–425.

Bliesener T (1996) Methodological moderators in validating biographical data in personnel selection. *Journal of Occupational and Organizational Psychology*, **69**, 107–120.

Bobko P & Karren R (1982) The estimation of standard deviation in utility analysis. *Proceedings of the Academy of Management*, **42**, 272–276.

Bobko P & Roth P L (1999) Derivation and implications of a meta-analytic matrix incorporating cognitive ability, alternative predictors and job performance. *Personnel Psychology*, **52**, 561–589.

Bobko P, Shetzer L & Russell C (1991) Estimating the standard deviation of professors' worth: the effects of frame of reference and presentation order in utility analysis. *Journal of Psychology*, **64**, 179–188.

Boehm V R (1972) Negro–white differences in validity of employment and training selection procedures: summary of research evidence. *Journal of Applied Psychology*, **56**, 33–39.

Boehm V R (1977) Differential prediction: a methodological artifact. *Journal of Applied Psychology*, **62**, 146–154.

Bommer W H, Johnson J L, Rich G A, Podsakoff P M & MacKenzie S B (1995) On the interchangeability of objective and subjective measures of employee performance: a meta-analysis. *Personnel Psychology*, **48**, 587–605.

Borman W C (1979) Format and training effects on rating accuracy and rater errors. *Journal of Applied Psychology*, **64**, 410–421.

Borman W C, White L A & Dorsey D W (1995) Effects of ratee task performance and interpersonal factors on supervisor and peer performance ratings. *Journal of Applied Psychology*, **80**, 168–177.

Borman W C, White L A, Pulakos E D & Oppler S H (1991) Models of supervisory job performance ratings. *Journal of Applied Psychology*, **76**, 863–872.

Born M P, Kolk N J & van der Flier H (2000) *A meta-analytic study of assessment center construct validity.* Paper given at Fifteenth Annual Conference of the Society for Industrial and Organizational Psychology, New Orleans, 14–16 April.

Boudreau J W (1983) Economic considerations in estimating the utility of human resource productivity improvement programs. *Personnel Psychology*, **36**, 551–576.

Boudreau J W, Boswell W R & Judge T A (2000) Effects of personality on executive career success in the United States and Europe. *Journal of Vocational Behavior*, **58**, 53–81.

Bowen C C, Swim J K & Jacobs R R (2000) Evaluating gender biases on actual job performance of real people: a meta-analysis. *Journal of Applied Social Psychology*, **30**, 2194–2215.

Brannick M T, Michaels C E & Baker D P (1989) Construct validity of in-basket scores. *Journal of Applied Psychology*, **74**, 957–963.

Bray D W & Grant D L (1966) The assessment center in the measurement of potential for business management. *Psychological Monographs*, **80** (17, whole of No. 625).

Bretz R D & Judge T A (1998) Realistic job previews: a test of the adverse self-selection hypothesis. *Personnel Psychology*, **83**, 330–337.

Brogden H E (1950) When testing pays off. *Personnel Psychology*, **2**, 171–183.

Brousseau K R & Prince J B (1981) Job–person dynamics: an extension of longitudinal research. *Journal of Applied Psychology*, **66**, 59–62.

Brown S H (1981) Validity generalisation and situational moderation in the life insurance industry. *Journal of Applied Psychology*, **66**, 664–670.

Brtek M D & Motowidlo S J (2002) Effects of procedure and outcome accountability on interview validity. *Journal of Applied Psychology*, **87**, 185–191.

Brush D H & Owens W A (1979) Implementation and evaluation of an assessment classification model for manpower utilisation. *Personnel Psychology*, **32**, 369–383.

Buel W D (1964) Voluntary female clerical turnover: the concurrent and predictive validity of a weighted application blank. *Journal of Applied Psychology*, **48**, 180–182.

Burnett J R, Fan C, Motowidlo S J & Degroot T (1998) Interview notes and validity. *Personnel Psychology*, **51**, 375–396.

Buros O K (1970) *Personality Tests and Reviews.* Gryphon Press, Highland Park, NJ.

Cable D M & Judge T A (1997) Interviewers' perceptions of person–organisation fit and organizational selection decisions. *Journal of Applied Psychology*, **82**, 546–561.

Callender J C & Osburn H G (1981) Testing the constancy of validity with computer-generated sampling distributions of the multiplicative model variance estimate: results for petroleum industry validation research. *Journal of Applied Psychology*, **66**, 274–281.

Callinan M & Robertson I T (2000) Work sample testing. *International Journal of Selection and Assessment*, **8**, 248–260.

Campbell C C, Ford P, Rumsey M G *et al.* (1990) Development of multiple job performance measures in a representative sample of jobs. *Personnel Psychology*, **43**, 277–300.

Campion J E (1972) Work sampling for personnel selection. *Journal of Applied Psychology*, **56**, 40–44.

Campion M A, Palmer D K & Campion J E (1997) A review of structure in the selection interview. *Personnel Psychology*, **50**, 655–702.

Campion M A, Pursell E D & Brown B K (1988) Structured interviewing: raising the psychometric qualities of the employment interview. *Personnel Psychology*, **41**, 25–42.

Campion M A, Outtz J L, Zedeck S *et al.* (2001) The controversy over score banding in personnel selection: answers to 10 key questions. *Personnel Psychology*, **54**, 149–185.

Carey N B (1991) Setting standards and diagnosing training needs with surrogate job performance measures. *Military Psychology*, **3**, 135–150.

Carey N B (1994) Computer predictors of mechanical job performance: Marine Corps findings. *Military Psychology*, **6**, 1–30.

Carlson K D, Scullen S E, Schmidt F L, Rothstein H & Erwin F (1999) Generalizable biographical data validity can be achieved without multi-organizational development and keying. *Personnel Psychology*, **52**, 731–753.

Carroll S J & Nash A N (1972) Effectiveness of a forced-choice reference check. *Personnel Administration*, **35**, 42–146.

Carson K P, Becker J S & Henderson J A (1998) Is utility really futile? A failure to replicate and an extension. *Journal of Applied Psychology*, **83**, 84–96.

Cascio W F (1975) Accuracy of verifiable biographical information blank responses. *Journal of Applied Psychology*, **60**, 767–769.

Cascio W F (1982) *Costing Human Resources: the Financial Impact of Behavior in Organisations*. Kent, Boston, MA.

Cascio W & Phillips N F (1979) Performance testing: a rose among thorns? *Personnel Psychology*, **32**, 751–766.

Cascio W F, Outtz J, Zedeck S & Goldstein I L (1991) Statistical implications of six methods of test score use in personnel selection. *Human Performance*, **4**, 233–264.

Cattell R B (1936) *The Fight for Our National Intelligence*. P S King, London.

Cattell R B (1965) *The Scientific Analysis of Personality*. Penguin, Harmondsworth.

Cellar D F, Miller M L, Doverspike D D & Klawsky J D (1996) Comparison of factor structures and criterion-related validity of two measures of personality based on the five factor model. *Journal of Applied Psychology*, **81**, 694–704.

Cesare S J, Blankenship M H & Giannetto P W (1994) A dual focus of SD_y estimations: a test of the linearity assumption and multivariate application. *Human Performance*, **7**, 235–255.

Chaffin D B (1974) Human strength capability and low back pain. *Journal of Occupational Medicine*, **16**, 248–254.

Chan D & Schmitt N (1997) Video-based versus paper-and-pencil method of assessment in situational judgement tests: subgroup differences in test performance and face validity perceptions. *Journal of Applied Psychology*, **82**, 143–159.

Chung-yan G A & Cronshaw S F (2002) A critical re-examination and analysis of cognitive ability tests using the Thorndike model of fairness. *Journal of Occupational and Organizational Psychology*, **75**, 489–510.

Clark T (1992) Management selection by executive recruitment consultancies. *Journal of Managerial Psychology*, **7**, 3–10.

Clevenger J, Pereira G M, Wiechmann D, Schmitt N & Harvey V S (2001) Incremental validity of situational judgement tests. *Journal of Applied Psychology*, **86**, 410–417.

Cohen B M, Moses J L & Byham W C (1974) *The Validity of Assessment Centers: a Literature Review*. Development Dimensions Press, Pittsburgh.

Coil J H & Shapiro L J (1996) The ADA at three years: a statute in flux. *Employee Relations Law Journal*, **21**, 5–38.

Colarelli S M, Hechanova-Alampay R & Canali K G (2002) Letters of recommendation: an evolutionary perspective. *Human Relations*, **55**, 315–344.

Collins J M & Gleaves D H (1998) Race, job applicants, and the big five model of personality: implications for black psychology, industrial/organisational psychology, and the five-factor theory. *Journal of Applied Psychology*, **83**, 531–544.

Collins J M & Schmidt F L (1997) Can suppressor variables enhance criterion-related validity in the personality domain? *Educational and Psychological Measurement*, **57**, 924–936.

Collins J M, Schmidt F L, Sanchez-Ku M, Thomas L, McDaniel M A & Le H (2001) *Can Basic Individual Differences Shed Light on the Construct Meaning of Assessment Center Dimensions?* Unpublished paper.

Commission for Racial Equality (CRE) (1984) *St Chads' Hospital: Report of a Formal Investigation*. CRE, London.

Commission for Racial Equality (CRE) (1990) *Lines of Progress: an Enquiry into Selection and Equal Opportunities in London Underground*. CRE, London.

Commission for Racial Equality (CRE) (1992) *Psychometric Tests and Racial Equality*. CRE, London.

Commission for Racial Equality (CRE) (1996) *A Fair Test? Selecting Train Drivers at British Rail*. CRE, London.

Conn S R & Rieke M L (1994) *The 16PF Fifth Edition Technical Manual*. Institute for Personality and Ability Testing, Inc., Champaign, IL.

Connerley M L, Arvey R D, Gilliland S W, Mael F A, Paetzold R L & Sackett P T (2002) Selection in the workplace: whose rights prevail? *Employee Responsibilities and Rights Journal*, **13**, 1–13.

Conway J M (1999) Additional construct validity evidence for the task-contextual performance distinction. *Journal of Applied Psychology*, **84**, 3–13.

Conway J M, Jako R A & Goodman D F (1995) A meta-analysis of inter-rater and internal consistency reliability of selection interviews. *Journal of Applied Psychology*, **80**, 565–579.

Cook M (1993) *Levels of Personality*, 2nd edn. Cassell, London.

Cook M (1995) Performance appraisal and true performance. *Journal of Managerial Psychology*, **10**, 3–7.

Cook M, Leigh V & McHenry R (1997) *UK Data Supplement to CPI-434 Manual*. Oxford Psychologists Press, Oxford.

Cornelius E T, DeNisi A S & Blencoe A G (1984) Expert and naive raters using the PAQ: does it matter? *Personnel Psychology*, **37**, 453–464.

Cortina J M, Goldstein N B, Payne S C, Davison H K & Gilliland S W (2000) The incremental validity of interview scores over and above cognitive ability and conscientiousness scores. *Personnel Psychology*, **53**, 325–352.

Costa P T (1996) Work and personality: use of the NEO-PI-R in industrial/organisational psychology. *Applied Psychology: An International Review*, **45**, 225–241.

Coward W M & Sackett P R (1990) Linearity of ability–performance relationships: a reconfirmation. *Journal of Applied Psychology*, **75**, 297–300.

Crites J O (1969) *Vocational Psychology*. McGraw Hill, New York.

Cronbach L J (1980) Selection theory for a political world. *Public Personnel Management Journal*, **9**, 37–50.

Cronbach L J (1984) *Essentials of Psychological Testing*, 4th edn. Harper and Row, New York.

Croteau J M (1996) Research on the work experience of lesbian, gay and bisexual people: an integrative review of methodology and findings. *Journal of Vocational Behavior*, **48**, 195–209.

Culpin M & Smith M (1930) *The Nervous Temperament*. Medical Research Council, Industrial Health Research Board, London.

Dalessio A T (1994) Predicting insurance agent turnover using a video-based situational judgment test. *Journal of Business and Psychology*, **9**, 23–32.

Dany F & Torchy V (1994) Recruitment and selection in Europe: policies, practices and methods. In: C Brewster & A Hegewisch (eds) *Policy and Practice in European Human Resource Management: the Price-Waterhouse–Cranfield Survey*. Routledge, London.

Davies M, Stankov L & Roberts R D (1998) Emotional intelligence: in search of an elusive construct. *Journal of Personality and Social Psychology*, **75**, 989–1015.

Davison H K & Burke M J (2000) Sex discrimination in simulated employment contexts: a meta-analytic investigation. *Journal of Vocational Behavior*, **56**, 225–248.

Day D V, Schleicher D J, Unckless A L & Hiller N J (2002) Self-monitoring personality at work: a meta-analytic investigation of construct validity. *Journal of Applied Psychology*, **87**, 390–401.

Dayan K, Kasten R & Fox S (2002) Entry-level police candidate assessment center: an efficient tool or a hammer to kill a fly? *Personnel Psychology*, **55**, 827–849.

DeNisi A S & Shaw J B (1977) Investigation of the uses of self-reports of abilities. *Journal of Applied Psychology*, **62**, 641–644.

DeShon R P, Smith M R, Chan D & Schmitt N (1998) Can racial differences in cognitive test performance be reduced by presenting problems in a social context? *Journal of Applied Psychology*, **83**, 438–451.

Devlin S E, Abrahams N M & Edwards J E (1992) Empirical keying of biographical data: cross-validity as a function of scaling procedure and sample size. *Military Psychology*, **4**, 119–136.

Di Milia D, Smith P & Brown D F (1994) Management selection in Australia: a comparison with British and French findings. *International Journal of Selection and Assessment*, **2**, 80–90.

Dipboye R L, Gaugler B B, Hayes T L & Parker D (2001) The validity of the unstructured panel interview: more than meets the eye? *Journal of Business and Psychology*, **16**, 35–49.

Distefano M K, Pryer M W & Erffmeyer R C (1983) Application of content validity methods to the development of a job-related performance rating criterion. *Personnel Psychology*, **36**, 621–631.

Doll R E (1971) Item susceptibility to attempted faking as related to item characteristics and adopted fake set. *Journal of Psychology*, **77**, 9–16.

Dorcus R M & Jones M H (1950) *Handbook of Employee Selection*. McGraw-Hill, New York.

Dougherty T W, Ebert R J & Callender J C (1986) Policy capturing in the employment interview. *Journal of Applied Psychology*, **71**, 9–15.

Downs S, Farr R M & Colbeck L (1978) Self-appraisal: a convergence of selection and guidance. *Journal of Occupational Psychology*, **51**, 271–278.

Dreher G F, Ash R A & Hancock P (1988) The role of the traditional research design in underestimating the validity of the employment interview. *Personnel Psychology*, **41**, 315–327.

Dubois C L Z, Sackett P R, Zedeck S & Fogli L (1993) Further exploration of typical and maximum performance criteria: definitional issues, prediction, and white–black differences. *Journal of Applied Psychology*, **78**, 205–211.

Dulewicz S V (1994) Personal competencies, personality and responsibilities of middle managers. *Journal of Competency*, **1**, 20–29.

Dulewicz S V & Higgs M (2000) Emotional intelligence. *Journal of Managerial Psychology*, **15**, 341–372.

Dulewicz S V & Keenay G A (1979) A practically oriented and objective method for classifying and assigning senior jobs. *Journal of Occupational Psychology*, **52**, 155–166.

Dunnette M D (1966) *Personnel Selection and Placement*. Tavistock, London.

Dunnette M D (1972) *Validity Study Results for Jobs Relevant to the Petroleum Refining Industry*. American Petroleum Institute, Washington, DC.

Dunnette M D & Maetzold J (1955) Use of a weighted application blank in hiring seasonal employees. *Journal of Applied Psychology*, **39**, 308–310.

Dunnette M D, McCartney J, Carlson H C & Kirchner W K (1962) A study of faking behavior on a forced-choice self-description checklist. *Personnel Psychology*, **15**, 13–24.

Dye D A, Reck M & McDaniel M A (1993) The validity of job knowledge measures. *International Journal of Selection and Assessment*, **1**, 153–157.

Eaton N K, Wing H & Mitchell K J (1985) Alternate methods of estimating the dollar value of performance. *Personnel Psychology*, **38**, 27–40.

Ebel R L (1977) Comments on some problems of employment testing. *Personnel Psychology*, **30**, 55–63.

Edwards M H (1992) The ADA and the employment of individuals with mental disabilities. *Employee Relations Law Journal*, **18**, 347–389.

Ekman P & O'Sullivan M (1991) Who can catch a liar? *American Psychologist*, **46**, 913–920.

Ellingson J E, Sackett P R & Hough L M (1999) Social desirability corrections in personality measurement: issues of applicant comparison and construct validity. *Journal of Applied Psychology*, **84**, 155–166.

Ellingson J E, Smith D B & Sackett P R (2001) Investigating the influence of social desirability on personality factor structure. *Journal of Applied Psychology*, **86**, 122–133.

Ellis A & Conrad H S (1948) The validity of personality inventories in military practice. *Psychological Bulletin*, **45**, 385–426.

Epstein S (1979) The stability of behavior. I. On predicting most of the people much of the time. *Journal of Personality and Social Psychology*, **37**, 1097–1126.

Eysenck H J (1957) *Sense and Nonsense in Psychology*. Penguin Harmondsworth.

Facteau J D & Craig S B (2001) Are performance appraisal ratings from different rating sources comparable? *Journal of Applied Psychology*, **86**, 215–227.

Farh J, Werbel J D & Bedeian A G (1988) An empirical investigation of self-appraisal-based performance evaluation. *Personnel Psychology*, **41**, 141–156.

Farrell J N & McDaniel M A (2001) The stability of validity coefficient over time: Ackerman's (1988) model and the General Aptitude Test Battery. *Journal of Applied Psychology*, **86**, 60–79.

Farrell S & Hakstian A R (2001) Improving salesforce performance: a meta-analytic investigation of the effectiveness and utility of personnel selection procedures and training interventions. *Psychology and Marketing*, **18**, 281–316.

Feltham R (1988a) Validity of a police assessment centre: a 1–19-year follow-up. *Journal of Psychology*, **61**, 129–144.

Feltham R (1988b) Assessment centre decision making: judgemental vs. mechanical. *Journal of Psychology*, **61**, 237–241.

Fine S A & Cronshaw S (1994) The role of job analysis in establishing the validity of biodata. In: G S Stokes, M D Mumford & W A Owens (eds) *Biodata Handbook: Theory, Research and Use of Biographical Information in Selection and Performance Prediction*. CPP Press, Inc., Palo Alto, CA.

Finkelstein L M, Burke M J & Raju N S (1995) Age discrimination in simulated interview contexts. *Journal of Applied Psychology*, **80**, 652–663.

Flanagan J C (1946) The experimental validation of a selection procedure. *Educational and Psychological Measurement*, **6**, 445–466.

Flanagan J C (1954) The critical incident technique. *Psychological Bulletin*, **51**, 327–358.

Fleishman E A & Mumford M D (1991) Evaluating classifications of job behavior: a construct validation of the ability requirement scales. *Personnel Psychology*, **44**, 523–575.

Fletcher C (1997) *Appraisal: Routes to Improved Performance*, 2nd edn. Institute for Personnel Development, London.

Ford J K & Kraiger K (1984) *The study of race differences in objective indices and subjective evaluations of performance: a meta-analysis of performance criteria*. Paper presented at American Psychological Association Convention, Toronto, Canada, August 1984.

Ford J K, Kraiger K & Schechtman S L (1986) Study of race effects in objective indices and subjective evaluations of performance: a meta-analysis of performance criteria. *Psychological Bulletin*, **99**, 330–337.

Forsythe S, Drake M F & Cox C E (1985) Influence of applicant's dress on interviewer's selection decisions. *Journal of Applied Psychology*, **70**, 374–378.

Foster J J, Wilkie D & Moss B (1996) Selecting university lecturers: what is and should be done. *International Journal of Selection and Assessment*, **4**, 122–128.

Fox S & Dinur Y (1988) Validity of self-assessment: a field evaluation. *Personnel Psychology*, **41**, 581–592.

Frei R L & McDaniel M A (1998) Validity of customer service measures in personnel selection: a review of criterion and construct evidence. *Human Performance*, **11**, 1–27.

Funke U, Krauss J, Schuler H & Stapf K H (1987) Zur Prognostizierbarkeit wissenschaftlich-technischer Leistungen mittels Personvariablen: eine Metaanalyse der Validitat diagnosticher Verfahren im Bereich Forschung und Entwicklung. *Gruppendynamik*, **18**, 407–428.

Gael S, Grant D L & Ritchie R J (1975) Employment test validation for minority and non-minority clerks with work sample criteria. *Journal of Applied Psychology*, **60**, 420–426.

Gandy J A, Outerbridge A N, Sharf J C & Dye D A (1989) *Development and Initial Validation of the Individual Achievement Record*. Office of Personnel Management, Washington, DC.

Gardner K E & Williams A P O (1973) A twenty-five year follow-up of an extended interview selection procedure in the Royal Navy. *Occupational Psychology*, **47**, 1–13.

Gaugler B B & Rudolph A S (1992) The influence of assessee performance variation on assessors' judgements. *Personnel Psychology*, **45**, 77–98.

Gaugler B B & Thornton G C (1989) Number of assessment center dimensions as a determinant of assessor accuracy. *Journal of Applied Psychology*, **74**, 611–618.

Gaugler B B, Rosenthal D B, Thornton G C & Bentson C (1987) Meta-analysis of assessment center validity. *Journal of Applied Psychology*, **72**, 493–511.

Geisinger K F, Boodoo G & Noble J P (2002) The psychometrics of testing individuals with disabilities. In: R B Ekstrom & D K Smith (eds) *Assessing Individuals with Disabilities in Educational, Employment and Counseling Settings*. American Psychological Association, Washington, DC.

Ghiselli E E (1966a) The validity of a personnel interview. *Personnel Psychology*, **19**, 389–394.

Ghiselli E E (1966b) *The Validity of Occupational Aptitude Tests*. John Wiley & Sons, New York.

Ghiselli E E & Barthol P P (1953) The validity of personality inventories in the selection of employees. *Journal of Applied Psychology*, **37**, 18–20.

Ghiselli E E & Haire M (1960) The validation of selection tests in the light of the dynamic character of criteria. *Personnel Psychology*, **13**, 225–231.

Glennon J R, Albright L E & Owens W A (1963) *A Catalog of Life History Items*. American Psychological Association, Chicago.

Goffin R D & Woods D M (1995) Using personality testing for personnel selection: faking and test-taking inductions. *International Journal of Selection and Assessment*, **3**, 227–236.

Goffin R D, Rothstein M G & Johnston N G (1996) Personality testing and the assessment center: incremental validity for managerial selection. *Journal of Applied Psychology*, **81**, 746–756.

Goldsmith D B (1922) The use of a personal history blank as a salesmanship test. *Journal of Applied Psychology*, **6**, 149–155.

Goldstein H W, Yusko K P, Braverman E P, Smith D B & Chung B (2001) The role of cognitive ability in the subgroup differences and incremental validity of assessment center exercises. *Personnel Psychology*, **31**, 357–374.

Goldstein I L (1971) The application blank: how honest are the responses? *Journal of Applied Psychology*, **55**, 491–492.

Goleman D (1995) *Emotional Intelligence*. Bloomsbury, London.

Good G W, Maisel S C & Kriska S D (1998) Setting an uncorrected visual acuity standard for police officer applicants. *Journal of Applied Psychology*, **83**, 817–824.

Gordon H W & Leighty R (1988) Importance of specialised cognitive functions in the selection of military pilots. *Journal of Applied Psychology*, **73**, 38–45.

Gottfredson L S (1988) Reconsidering fairness: a matter of social and ethical priorities. *Journal of Vocational Behavior*, **33**, 293–319.

Gottfredson L S (1994) From the ashes of affirmative action. *The World and I*, **November issue**, 365–377.

Gottfredson L S (1997) Why g matters: the complexity of everyday life. *Intelligence*, **24**, 79–132.

Graham K E, McDaniel M A, Douglas E F & Snell A E (2002) Biodata validity decay and score inflation with faking: do other attributes explain variance across items? *Journal of Business and Psychology*, **16**, 573–592.

Graves L M & Karren R J (1992) Interviewer decision processes and effectiveness: an experimental policy-capturing investigation. *Personnel Psychology*, **45**, 313–340.

Grote C L, Robiner W N & Haut A (2001) Disclosure of negative information in the letter of recommendation: writers' intentions and readers' experience. *Professional Psychology – Research and Practice*, **32**, 655–661.

Guastello S J & Rieke M L (1991) A review and critique of honesty testing. *Behavioral Sciences and the Law*, **9**, 501–523.

Guion R M (1965) *Personnel Testing*. McGraw-Hill, New York.

Guion R M (1978) 'Content validity' in moderation. *Personnel Psychology*, **31**, 205–213.

Guion R M (1998) Jumping the gun at the starting gate: when fads become trends and trends become traditions. In: M Hakel (ed.) *Beyond Multiple Choice: Evaluating Alternatives to Traditional Testing for Selection*. Erlbaum, Mahwah, NJ.

Guion R M & Gottier R F (1965) Validity of personality measures in personnel selection. *Personnel Psychology*, **18**, 135–164.

Gunter B, Furnham A & Drakeley R (1993) *Biodata: Biographical Indicators of Business Performance*. Routledge, London.

Gustafson S B & Mumford M D (1995) Personal style and person–environment fit: a pattern approach. *Journal of Vocational Behavior*, **46**, 163–188.

Gutenberg R L, Arvey R D, Osburn H G & Jeanneret P R (1983) Moderating effects of decision-making/information-processing job dimensions on test validities. *Journal of Applied Psychology*, **68**, 602–608.

Haaland S & Christianse N D (2002) Implications of trait-activation theory for evaluating the construct validity of assessment center ratings. *Personnel Psychology*, **55**, 137–164.

Hare R D (1970) *Psychopathy: Theory and Research*. John Wiley & Sons, New York.

Harris M M & Schaubroek J (1988) A meta-analysis of self–supervisor, self–peer and peer–supervisor ratings. *Personnel Psychology*, **41**, 43–62.

Harris M M & Trusty M L (1997) Drug and alcohol programs in the workplace: a review of recent literature. In: I Robertson & C Cooper (eds) *International Review of Industrial and Organisational Psychology*. John Wiley & Sons, Chichester.

Harris M M, Dworkin J B & Park J (1990) Pre-employment screening procedures: how human resource managers perceive them. *Journal of Business and Psychology*, **4**, 279–292.

Harris M M, Smith D E & Champagne D (1995) A field study of performance appraisal purpose: research versus administrative-based rating. *Personnel Psychology*, **48**, 151–160.

Hartigan J A & Wigdor A K (1989) *Fairness in Employment Testing*. National Academy Press, Washington, DC.

Harvey-Cook J E & Taffler R J (2000) Biodata in professional entry-level selection: statistical scoring of common format applications. *Journal of Occupational and Organizational Psychology*, **73**, 103–118.

Hattrup K, Rock J & Scalia C (1997) The effects of varying conceptualisations of job performance on adverse impact, minority hiring and predicted performance. *Journal of Applied Psychology*, **82**, 656–664.

Hazer J T & Highhouse S (1997) Factors influencing managers' reactions to utility analysis: effects of SD_y method, information frame and focal intervention. *Journal of Applied Psychology*, **82**, 104–112.

Hedge J W & Teachout M S (1992) An interview approach to work sample criterion measurement. *Journal of Applied Psychology*, **77**, 453–456.

Hegewisch A & Mayne L (1994) Equal opportunities policies in Europe. In: C Brewster & A Hegewisch (eds) *Policy and Practice in European Human Resource Management*. Routledge, London.

Hemphill J K & Sechrest L B (1952) A comparison of three criteria of aircrew effectiveness in combat over Korea. *Journal of Applied Psychology*, **36**, 323–327.

Hermelin E & Robertson I T (2001) A critique and standardisation of meta-analytic validity coefficients in personnel selection. *Journal of Occupational and Organizational Psychology*, **74**, 253–277.

Herrnstein R J (1973) *IQ in the Meritocracy*. Allen Lane, London.

Herrnstein R J & Murray C (1994) *The Bell Curve: Intelligence and Class Structure in American Life*. Free Press, New York.

Higgins C A, Judge T A & Ferris G R (2000) *Influence Tactics and Work Outcomes: a Meta-Analysis*. Unpublished paper.

Higuera L A (2001) Adverse impact in personnel selection: the legal framework and test bias. *European Psychologist*, **6**, 103–111.

Hinrichs J R & Haanpera S (1976) Reliability of measurement in situational exercises: an assessment of the assessment center method. *Personnel Psychology*, **29**, 31–40.

Hirsh H R, Northrop L C & Schmidt F L (1986) Validity generalisation results for law enforcement occupations. *Personnel Psychology*, **39**, 399–420.

Hitt M A & Barr S H (1989) Managerial selection decision models: examination of configural cue processing. *Journal of Applied Psychology*, **74**, 53–61.

Hochwarter W A, Witt L A & Kacmar K M (2000) Perceptions of organizational politics as a moderator of the relationship between conscientiousness and job performance. *Journal of Applied Psychology*, **85**, 472–478.

Hodgkinson G P, Daley N & Payne R L (1995) Knowledge of, and attitudes towards, the demographic time bomb. *International Journal of Manpower*, **16**, 59–76.

Hoffman C C (1999) Generalizing physical ability test validity: a case study using test transportability, validity generalisation, and construct-related validation evidence. *Personnel Psychology*, **52**, 1019–1041.

Hoffman C C & McPhail S M (1998) Exploring options for supporting test use in situations precluding local validation. *Personnel Psychology*, **51**, 987–1003.

Hoffman C C & Thornton G C (1997) Examining selection utility where competing predictors differ in adverse impact. *Personnel Psychology*, **50**, 455–470.

Hoffman C C, Holden L M & Gale K (2000) So many jobs, so little 'n': applying expanded validation models to support generalisation of cognitive test validity. *Personnel Psychology*, **53**, 955–991.

Hoffman C C, Nathan B R & Holden L M (1991) A comparison of validation criteria: objective versus subjective performance and self- versus supervisor ratings. *Personnel Psychology*, **44**, 601–619.

Hoffman D A, Jacobs R & Baratta J E (1993) Dynamic criteria and the measurement of change. *Journal of Applied Psychology*, **78**, 194–204.

Hogan J (1985) Tests for success in diver training. *Journal of Applied Psychology*, **70**, 219–224.

Hogan J (1991) Physical abilities. In: M D Dunnette & L M Hough (eds) *Handbook of Industrial–Organisational Psychology*. Consulting Psychologists Press, Palo Alto, CA.

Hogan J & Quigley A M (1986) Physical standards for employment and the courts. *American Psychologist*, **41**, 1193–1217.

Hoque K & Noon M (1999) Racial discrimination in speculative applications: new optimism six years on? *Human Resource Management Journal*, **9**, 71–83.

Hough L M (1992) The "big five" personality variables – construct confusion: description versus prediction. *Human Performance*, **5**, 139–155.

Hough L M (1998a) Personality at work: issues and evidence. In: M Hakel (ed.) *Beyond Multiple Choice: Evaluating Alternatives to Traditional Testing for Selection*. Erlbaum, Mahwah, NJ.

Hough L M (1998b) Effects of intentional distortion in personality measurement and evaluation of suggested palliatives. *Human Performance*, **11**, 209–244.

Hough L M & Paullin C (1994) *Construct-oriented scale construction: the rational approach*. In: G S Stokes, M D Mumford & W A Owens (eds) *Biodata Handbook: Theory, Research and Use of Biographical Information in Selection and Performance Prediction*. CPP Books, Palo Alto, CA.

Hough L M, Oswald F L & Ployhart R E (2001) Determinants, detection and amelioration of adverse impact in personnel selection procedures: issues, evidence and lessons learned. *International Journal of Selection and Assessment*, **9**, 152–194.

Hough L M, Eaton N K, Dunnette M D, Kamp J D & McCloy R A (1990) Criterion-related validities of personality constructs and the effect of response distortion on those validities. *Journal of Applied Psychology*, **75**, 581–595.

Huffcutt A I & Arthur W (1994) Hunter and Hunter (1984) revisited: interview validity for entry-level jobs. *Journal of Applied Psychology*, **79**, 184–190.

Huffcutt A I & Woehr D J (1999) Further analyses of employment interview validity: a quantitative evaluation of interviewer-related structuring methods. *Journal of Organizational Bahaviour*, **20**, 549–560.

Huffcutt A I, Roth P L & McDaniel M A (1996) A meta-analytic investigation of cognitive ability in employment interview evaluations: moderating characteristics and implications for incremental validity. *Journal of Applied Psychology*, **81**, 459–473.

Huffcutt A I, Conway J M, Roth P L & Klehe U C (2002) *Evaluation and Comparison of Situational and Behavior Description Interviews*. Unpublished paper.

Huffcutt A I, Conway J M, Roth P L & Stone N J (2001) Identification and meta-analytic assessment of psychological constructs measured in employment interviews. *Journal of Applied Psychology*, **86**, 897–913.

Hughes J F, Dunn J F & Baxter B (1956) The validity of selection instruments under operating conditions. *Personnel Psychology*, **9**, 321–423.

Hulin C L, Henry R A & Noon S L (1990) Adding a dimension: time as a factor in the generalisability of predictive relationships. *Psychological Bulletin*, **107**, 328–340.

Hull C L (1928) *Aptitude Testing*. Harrap, London.

Humphreys L G (1973) Statistical definitions of test validity for minority groups. *Journal of Applied Psychology*, **58**, 1–4.

Hunt S T (1996) Generic work behavior: an investigation into the dimensions of entry-level, hourly job performance. *Personnel Psychology*, **49**, 51–83.

Hunter D R & Burke E F (1994) Predicting aircraft pilot training success: a meta-analysis of published research. *International Journal of Aviation Psychology*, **4**, 297–313.

Hunter J E (1983) A causal analysis of cognitive ability, job knowledge and supervisory ratings. In: F Landy, S Zedeck & J Cleveland (eds) *Performance Measurement and Theory*. Erlbaum, Hillsdale, NJ.

Hunter J E (1986) Cognitive ability, cognitive aptitudes, job knowledge and job performance. *Journal of Vocational Behavior*, **29**, 340–362.

Hunter J E & Hunter R F (1984) Validity and utility of alternate predictors of job performance. *Psychological Bulletin*, **96**, 72–98.

Hunter J E & Schmidt F L (1978) Differential and single-group validity of employment tests by race: a critical analysis of three recent studies. *Journal of Applied Psychology*, **63**, 1–11.

Hunter J E & Schmidt F L (1996) Intelligence and job performance: economic and social implications. *Psychology, Public Policy and Law*, **2**, 447–472.

Hunter J E, Schmidt J E & Hunter R (1979) Differential validity of employment tests by race: a comprehensive review and analysis. *Psychological Bulletin*, **86**, 721–735.

Hunter J E, Schmidt F L & Judiesch M K (1990) Individual differences in output variability as a function of job complexity. *Journal of Applied Psychology*, **75**, 28–42.

Hurtz G M & Alliger G M (2002) Influence of coaching on integrity test performance and unlikely virtues scale scores. *Human Performance*, **15**, 255–273.

Hurtz G M & Donovan J J (2000) Personality and job performance: the big five revisited. *Journal of Applied Psychology*, **85**, 869–879.

Huselid M A, Jackson S E & Schuler R S (1997) Technical and strategic human resource management effectiveness as determinants of firm performance. *Academy of Management Journal*, **40**, 171–188.

Jackson D N, Wroblewski V R & Ashton M C (2000) The impact of faking on employment tests: does forced choice offer a solution? *Human Performance*, **13**, 371–388.

Jacobs R (1989) Getting the measure of management competence. *Personnel Management*, **September issue**, 32–37.

James L R, Demaree R G, Mulaik S A & Ladd R T (1992) Validity generalisation in the context of situational models. *Journal of Applied Psychology*, **77**, 3–14.

Jansen P G W & Stoop B A M (2001) The dynamics of assessment center validity: results of a 7-year study. *Journal of Applied Psychology*, **86**, 741–753.

Janz T (1982) Initial comparisons of patterned behavior description interviews versus unstructured interviews. *Journal of Applied Psychology*, **67**, 577–580.

Jawahar I M & Williams C R (1997) Where all the children are above average: the performance appraisal purpose effect. *Personnel Psychology*, **50**, 905–925.

Jeanneret P R (1992) Application of job component/synthetic validity to construct validity. *Human Performance*, **5**, 81–96.

Jensen A R (1969) *Genetics and Education*. Methuen, London.

Jones A & Harrison E (1982) Prediction of performance in initial officer training using reference reports. *Journal of Occupational Psychology*, **55**, 35–42.

Jones A, Herriot P, Long B & Drakeley R (1991) Attempting to improve the validity of a well-established assessment centre. *Journal of Psychology*, **64**, 1–21.

Jones R G & Whitmore M D (1995) Evaluating developmental assessment centers as interventions. *Personnel Psychology*, **48**, 377–388.

Jones R G, Sanchez J I, Parameswaran G *et al.* (2001) Selection or training? A twofold test of the validity of job-analytic ratings of trainability. *Journal of Business and Psychology*, **15**, 363–389.

Jordan M, Herriot P & Chalmers C (1991) Testing Schneider's ASA theory. *Applied Psychology: an International Review*, **40**, 47–53.

Judge T A & Higgins C A (1998) Affective disposition and the letter of reference. *Organizational Behavior and Human Decision Processes*, **75**, 207–221.

Judge T A & Bono J E (2000) Five-factor model of personality and transformational leadership. *Journal of Applied Psychology*, **85**, 751–765.

Judge T A & Bono J E (2001) Relationship of core self-evaluation traits – self-esteem, generalised self-efficacy, locus of control, and emotional stability – with job satisfaction and job performance: a meta-analysis. *Journal of Applied Psychology*, **86**, 80–92.

Judge T A & Ilies R (2002) Relationship of personality to performance motivation: a meta-analytic review. *Journal of Applied Psychology*, **87**, 797–807.

Judge T A, Heller D & Mount M K (2002b) Five-factor model of personality and job satisfaction: a meta-analysis. *Journal of Applied Psychology*, **87**, 530–541.

Judge T A, Martocchio J J & Thorsen C J (1997) Five-factor model of personality and employee absence. *Journal of Applied Psychology*, **82**, 745–755.

Judge T A, Bono J E, Ilies R & Gerhardt M W (2002a) Personality and leadership: a qualitative and quantitative review. *Journal of Applied Psychology*, **87**, 765–780.

Judge T A, Higgins C A, Thoresen C J & Barrick M R (1999) The big five personality traits, general mental ability, and career success across the life span. *Personnel Psychology*, **52**, 621–652.

Judiesch M K (2001) Using estimates of the output productivity ratio to improve the accuracy and managerial acceptance of utility analysis estimates. *Journal of Business and Psychology*, **16**, 165–176.

Judiesch M K & Schmidt F L (2000) Between-worker variability in output under piece-rate versus hourly pay systems. *Journal of Business and Psychology*, **14**, 529–551.

Kalin R & Rayko D S (1978) Discrimination in evaluation against foreign-accented job candidates. *Psychological Reports*, **43**, 1203–1209.

Kandola B (1995) Selecting for diversity. *International Journal of Selection and Assessment*, **3**, 162–167.

Kane J S & Lawler E E (1978) Methods of peer assessment. *Psychological Bulletin*, **85**, 555–586.

Katz D & Kahn R L (1966) *The Social Psychology of Organisations*. John Wiley & Sons, New York.

Katzell R A & Dyer F J (1977) Differential validity revived. *Journal of Applied Psychology*, **62**, 137–145.

Keenan T (1995) Graduate recruitment in Britain: a survey of selection methods used by organizations. *Journal of Organizational Behavior*, **16**, 303–317.

Keenan T (1997) Selection for potential: the case of graduate recruitment. In: N Anderson & P Herriott (eds) *International Handbook of Selection and Appraisal*. John Wiley & Sons, Chichester.

Kelley P L, Jacobs R R & Farr J L (1994) Effects of multiple administrations of the MMPI for employee screening. *Personnel Psychology*, **47**, 575–591.

Kinslinger H J (1966) Application of projective techniques in personnel psychology since 1940. *Psychological Bulletin*, **66**, 134–150.

Kirkpatrick J J, Ewen R B, Barrett R S & Katzell R A (1968) *Testing and Fair Employment*. New York University Press, New York.

Kleiman L S & Faley R H (1985) The implications of professional and legal guidelines for court decisions involving criterion-related validity: a review and analysis. *Personnel Psychology*, **38**, 803–833.

Kleiman L S & Faley R H (1990) A comparative analysis of the empirical validity of past- and present-oriented biographical items. *Journal of Business and Psychology*, **4**, 431–437.

Kleinmann M, Kuptsch K & Koller O (1996) Transparency: a necessary requirement for the construct validity of assessment centres. *Applied Psychology: an International Review*, **45**, 67–84.

Klimoski R J & Rafaeli A (1983) Inferring personal qualities through handwriting analysis. *Journal of Occupational Psychology*, **56**, 191–202.

Klimoski R J & Strickland W J (1977) Assessment centers – valid or merely prescient? *Personnel Psychology*, **30**, 353–361.

Kline P (1995) Models and personality traits in occupational psychological testing. *International Journal of Selection and Assessment*, **3**, 186–190.

Kluger A N, Reilly R R & Russell C J (1991) Faking biodata tests: are option-keyed instruments more resistant? *Journal of Applied Psychology*, **76**, 889–896.

Knapp D J, Campbell C H, Borman W C, Pulakos E D & Hanson M A (2001) Performance assessment for a population of jobs. In: J P Campbell & D J Knapp (eds) *Exploring the Limits of Personnel Selection and Classification*. Erlbaum, Mahwah, NJ.

Kraiger K & Ford J K (1985) A meta-analysis of ratee race effects in performance ratings. *Journal of Applied Psychology*, **70**, 56–65.

Krzystofiak F, Newman J M & Anderson G (1979) A quantified approach to measurement of job content: procedures and payoffs. *Personnel Psychology*, **32**, 341–357.

Kulik J A Bangert-Downs R K & Kulik C C (1984) Effectiveness of coaching for aptitude tests. *Psychological Bulletin*, **95**, 179–188.

Kumar K & Beyerlein M (1991) Construction and validation of an instrument for measuring ingratiatory behaviors in organisational settings. *Journal of Applied Psychology*, **76**, 619–627.

Lance C E, Johnson C D, Douthitt S S, Bennett W & Harville G L (2000a) Good news: work sample administrators' global performance judgements are (about) as valid as we've suspected. *Human Performance*, **13**, 253–277.

Lance C E, Newbolt W H, Gatewood R D, Foster M S, French N R & Smith D E (2000b) Assessment center exercise factors represent cross-situational specificity, not method bias. *Human Performance*, **12**, 323–353.

Landis R S, Fogli L & Goldberg E (1998) Future-oriented job analysis: a description of the process and its organisational implications. *International Journal of Selection and Assessment*, **6**, 192–197.

Latham G P & Skarlicki D P (1995) Criterion-related validity of the situational and patterned behavior description interviews with organisational citizenship behavior. *Human Performance*, **8**, 67–80.

Latham G P & Sue-Chan C (1999) A meta-analysis of the incremental validity of the situational interview: an enumerative review of the reasons for its validity. *Canadian Psychology*, **40**, 56–67.

Latham G P & Wexley K N (1981) *Increasing Productivity Through Performance Appraisal*. Addison Wesley, Reading, MA.

Latham G P & Whyte G (1994) The futility of utility analysis. *Personnel Psychology*, **47**, 31–46.

Latham G P, Saari L M, Pursell E D & Campion M A (1980) The situational interview. *Journal of Applied Psychology*, **65**, 422–427.

Laurent H (1970) Cross-cultural cross-validation of empirically validated tests. *Journal of Applied Psychology*, **54**, 417–423.

Lautenschlager G J (1994) Accuracy and faking of background data. In: G S Stokes, M D Mumford & W A Owens (eds) *Biodata Handbook: Theory, Research, and Use of Biographical Information in Selection and Performance Prediction*. CPP Books, Palo Alto, CA.

Lehman W E K & Simpson D D (1992) Employee substance abuse and on-the-job behaviours. *Journal of Applied Psychology*, **77**, 309–321.

Lent R H, Aurbach H A & Levin L S (1971) Predictors, criteria and significant results. *Personnel Psychology*, **24**, 519–533.

LePine J A & Van Dyne L (2001) Voice and co-operative behavior as contrasting forms of contextual performance: evidence of differential relationships with big five personality characteristics and cognitive ability. *Journal of Applied Psychology*, **86**, 326–336.

LePine J A, Erez A & Johnson D W (2002) The nature and dimensionality of organisational citizenship behavior: a critical review and meta-analysis. *Journal of Applied Psychology*, **87**, 52–65.

Levin H M (1988) Issues of agreement and contention in employment testing. *Journal of Vocational Behavior*, **33**, 398–403.

Levine E L, Flory A & Ash R A (1977) Self-assessment in personnel selection. *Journal of Applied Psychology*, **62**, 428–435.

Levine E L, Maye D M, Ulm R A & Gordon T R (1997) A methodology for developing and validating minimum qualifications (MQs). *Personnel Psychology*, **50**, 1009–1023.

Levine E L, Spector P E, Menon S, Narayan L & Cannon-Bowers J (1996) Validity generalisation for cognitive, psychomotor and perceptual tests for craft jobs in the utility industry. *Human Performance*, **9**, 1–22.

Lewin A Y & Zwany A (1976) Peer nominations: a model, literature critique and a paradigm for research. *Personnel Psychology*, **29**, 423–447.

Lievens F (2001a) Assessor training strategies and their effects on accuracy, interrater reliability and discriminant validity. *Journal of Applied Psychology*, **86**, 255–264.

Lievens F (2001b) Assessors and use of assessment center dimensions: a fresh look at a troubling issue. *Journal of Organizational Behavior*, **22**, 203–221.

Lievens F (2001c) Understanding the assessment centre process: where are we now? *International Review of Industrial and Organisational Psychology*, **16**, 246–286.

Lievens F & Conway J M (2001) Dimension and exercise variance in assessment center scores: a large-scale evaluation of multitrait–multimethods studies. *Journal of Applied Psychology*, **86**, 1202–1222.

Lindley P (2001) *Review of Personality Assessment Instruments (Level B) for Use in Occupational Settings*, 2nd edn. British Psychological Society, Leicester.

Link H C (1918) An experiment in employment psychology. *Psychological Review*, **25**, 116–127.

Little B L & Sipes D (2000) Betwixt and between: the dilemma of employee references. *Employee Responsibilities and Rights Journal*, **12**, 1–8.

Locke E L (1961) What's in a name? *American Psychologist*, **16**, 607.

Loher B T, Hazer J T, Tsai A, Tilton K, & James J (1997) Letters of reference: a process approach. *Journal of Business and Psychology*, **11**, 339–355.

Longenecker C O, Sims H P & Goia D A (1987) Behind the mask: the politics of employee appraisal. *Academy of Management Executive*, **1**, 183–193.

Lynch F (1991) *Invisible Victims*. Greenwood, London.

Mabe P A & West S G (1982) Validity of self-evaluation of ability: a review and meta-analysis. *Journal of Applied Psychology*, **67**, 280–296.

McCarthy J M & Goffin R D (2001) Improving the validity of letters of recommendation: an investigation of three standardised reference forms. *Military Psychology*, **13**, 199–222.

McClelland D C (1971) *The Achieving Society*. Van Nostrand, Princeton, NJ.

McCormick E J, DeNisi A S & Shaw J B (1979) Use of the Position Analysis Questionnaire for establishing the job component validity of tests. *Journal of Applied Psychology*, **64**, 51–56.

McCormick E J, Jeanneret P R & Mecham R C (1972) A study of job characteristics and job dimensions as based on the Position Analysis Questionnaire (PAQ). *Journal of Applied Psychology*, **56**, 347–368.

McDaniel M A & Nguyen N T (2001) Situational judgement tests: a review of practice and constructs assessed. *International Journal of Selection and Assessment*, **9**, 103–113.

McDaniel M A, Schmidt F L & Hunter J E (1988) A meta-analysis of the validity of methods for rating training and education in personnel selection. *Personnel Psychology*, **41**, 283–314.

McDaniel M A, Morgeson F P, Finnegan E B, Campion M A & Braverman E P (2001) Use of situational judgement tests to predict job performance: a clarification of the literature. *Journal of Applied Psychology*, **86**, 730–740.

McDaniel M A, Whetzel D L, Schmidt F L & Maurer S (1994) The validity of employment interviews: a comprehensive review and meta-analysis. *Journal of Applied Psychology*, **79**, 599–616.

McEvoy G M & Beatty R W (1989) Assessment centers and subordinate appraisals of managers: a seven-year examination of predictive validity. *Personnel Psychology*, **42**, 37–52.

McEvoy G M & Buller P F (1987) User acceptance of peer appraisals in an industrial setting. *Personnel Psychology*, **40**, 785–797.

McHenry J J, Hough L M, Toquam J L, Hanson M A & Ashworth S (1990) Project A validity results: the relationship between predictor and criterion domains. *Personnel Psychology*, **43**, 335–354.

McManus M A & Brown S H (1995) Adjusting sales results measures for use as criteria. *Personnel Psychology*, **48**, 391–400.

McManus M A & Kelly M L (1999) Personality measures and biodata: evidence regarding their incremental predictive value in the life insurance industry. *Personnel Psychology*, **52**, 137–148.

Macan T H & Highhouse S (1994) Communicating the utility of human resource activities: a survey of I/O and HR professionals. *Journal of Business and Psychology*, **8**, 425–436.

Machwirth U, Schuler H & Moser K (1996) Entscheidungsprozesse bei der Analyse von Bewerbungsunterlagen. *Diagnostica*, **42**, 220–241.

Mael F A (1991) A conceptual rationale for the domain and attributes of biodata. *Personnel Psychology*, **44**, 763–792.

Mael F A & Ashworth B E (1995) Loyal from day one: biodata, organisational identification, and turnover among newcomers. *Personnel Psychology*, **48**, 309–333.

Mael F A & Hirsch A C (1993) Rainforest empiricism and quasi-rationality: two approaches to objective biodata. *Personnel Psychology*, **46**, 719–738.

Marcus B, Funke U & Schuler H (1997) Integrity Tests als spezielle Gruppe eignungsdiagnostischer Verfahren: Literaturuberblick und metaanalytische Befunde zur Konstruktvaliditat. *Zeitschrift fur Arbeits- und Organisationspsychologie*, **41**, 2–17.

Marlowe C M, Schneider S L & Nelson C E (1996) Gender and attractiveness in hiring decisions – are more experienced managers less biased? *Journal of Applied Psychology*, **81**, 11–21.

Martin B A, Bowen C C & Hunt S T (2002) How effective are people at faking personality questionnaires? *Personality and Individual Differences*, **32**, 247–256.

Martin S L & Terris W (1991) Predicting infrequent behavior: clarifying the impact on false-positive rates. *Journal of Applied Psychology*, **76**, 484–487.

Martinussen M (1996) Psychological measures as predictors of pilot performance: a meta-analysis. *International Journal of Aviation Psychology*, **6**, 1–20.

Martinussen M & Torjussen T (1993) Does DMT (Defense Mechanism Test) predict pilot performance only in Scandinavia? In: R S Jensen and D Neumeister (eds) *Proceedings of the Seventh International Symposium on Aviation Psychology*. Avebury Aviation, Aldershot.

Mathieu J E & Tannenbaum S I (1989) A process-tracing approach toward understanding supervisors' SD$_y$ estimates: results from five job classes. *Journal of Psychology*, **62**, 249–256.

Maurer T J, Solamon J M & Troxtel D D (1998) Relations of coaching with performance in situational employment interviews. *Journal of Applied Psychology*, **83**, 128–136.

Maurer T J, Solamon J M, Andrews K D & Troxtel D D (2001) Interviewee coaching, preparation strategies and response strategies in relation to performance in situational employment interviews: an extension of Maurer, Solamon and Troxtel (1998). *Journal of Applied Psychology*, **86**, 709–717.

Meehl P E (1954) *Clinical Versus Statistical Prediction*. University of Minnesota Press, Minneapolis, MN.

Merenda P F (1995) Substantive issues in the Soroka v. Dayton-Hudson case. *Psychological Reports*, **77**, 595–606.

Meritt-Haston R & Wexley K N (1983) Educational requirements: legality and validity. *Personnel Psychology*, **36**, 743–753.

Mershon B & Gorsuch R L (1988) Number of factors in the personality sphere: does increase in factors increase predictability of real life criteria? *Journal of Personality and Social Psychology*, **55**, 675–680.

Middendorf C H & Macan T (2002) Note-taking in the employment interview: effects on recall and judgements. *Journal of Applied Psychology*, **87**, 293–303.

Miner, J B (1971) Personality tests as predictors of consulting success. *Personal Psychology*, **24** 191–204.

Miner M G & Miner J B (1979) *Employee Selection Within the Law*. Bureau of National Affairs, Washington, DC.

Mischel W (1968) *Personality and Assessment*. John Wiley & Sons, New York.

Mitchell T W & Klimoski R J (1982) Is it rational to be empirical? A test of methods for scoring biographical data. *Journal of Applied Psychology*, **67**, 411–418.

Mls J (1935) Intelligenz und fahigkeit zum kraftwagenlenken. In: *Proceedings of the Eight International Conference of Psychotechnics*, Prague.

Morgeson F P & Campion M A (1997) Social and cognitive sources of potential inaccuracy in job analysis. *Journal of Applied Psychology*, **82**, 627–655.

Morris B S (1949) Officer selection in the British Army 1942–1945. *Occupational Psychology*, **23**, 219–234.

Mosel J N (1952) Prediction of department store sales performance from personal data. *Journal of Applied Psychology*, **36**, 8–10.

Mosel J N & Goheen H W (1958) The validity of the Employment Recommendation Questionnaire in personnel selection. I. Skilled trades. *Personnel Psychology*, **11**, 481–490.

Mosel J N & Goheen H W (1959) The validity of the Employment Recommendation Questionnaire. III. Validity of different types of references. *Personnel Psychology*, **12**, 469–477.

Moser K & Reuter N (2001) Wird durch die Aggregation von Interviewer daten die Validitat von Einstellungsinterviews underschatzt? Eine Primarstudie und Monte-Carlo-Analysen. *Zeitschrift fur Arbeits- und Organisationspsychologie*, **45**, 188–201.

Moser K & Rhyssen D (2001) Referenzen als eignungsdiagnostische Methode. *Zeitschrift fur Arbeits- und Organisationspsychologie*, **45**, 40–46.

Moses J L (1973) The development of an assessment center for the early identification of supervisory talent. *Personnel Psychology*, **26**, 569–580.

Motowidlo S J & van Scotter J R (1994) Evidence that task performance should be distinguished from contextual performance. *Journal of Applied Psychology*, **79**, 475–480.

Motowidlo S J, Carter G W, Dunnette M D *et al.* (1992) Studies of the structured behavioural interview. *Journal of Applied Psychology*, **77**, 571–587.

Mount M K & Barrick M R (1995) The big five personality dimensions: implications for research and practice in human resources management. *Research in Personnel and Human Resources Management*, **13**, 153–200.

Mount M K, Barrick M R & Stewart G L (1998) Five-factor model of personality and performance in jobs involving interpersonal interaction. *Human Performance*, **11**, 145–165.

Mount M K, Barrick M R & Strauss J P (1994) Validity of observer ratings of the big five personality factors. *Journal of Applied Psychology*, **79**, 272–280.

Mount M K, Barrick M R & Strauss J P (1999) The joint relationship of conscientiousness and ability with performance: test of the interaction hypothesis. *Journal of Management*, **25**, 707–721.

Mount M K, Witt L A & Barrick M R (2000) Incremental validity of empirically keyed biodata scales over GMA and the five factor personality constructs. *Personnel Psychology*, **53**, 299–323.

Mount M K, Sytsma M R, Hazucha J F & Holt K E (1997) Rater–ratee race effects in developmental performance ratings of managers. *Personnel Psychology*, **50**, 51–69.

Mumford M D & Owens W A (1987) Methodology review: principles, procedures and findings in the applications of background data measures. *Applied Psychological Measurement*, **11**, 1–31.

Murphy K R (1986) When your top choice turns you down. *Psychological Bulletin*, **99**, 133–138.

Murphy K R (1989) Is the relationship between cognitive ability and job performance stable over time? *Human Performance*, **2**, 183–200.

Murphy K R & Cleveland J N (1995) *Understanding Performance Appraisal: Social, Organisational and Goal-Based Perspectives.* Sage, Thousand Oaks, CA.

Murphy K R & Davidshofer C O (2000) *Psychological testing: principles and applications*, 5th edn. Prentice Hall, Upper Saddle River, NJ.

Murphy K R & DeShon R (2000) Inter-rater correlations do not estimate the reliability of job performance ratings. *Personnel Psychology*, **53**, 873–900.

Murphy K R and Thornton G C (1992) Characteristics of employee drug testing policies. *Journal of Business and Psychology*, **6**, 295–309.

Murphy K R, Jako R A & Anhalt R L (1993) Nature and consequences of halo error: a critical analysis. *Journal of Applied Psychology*, **78**, 218–225.

Murphy K R, Thornton G C & Prue K (1991) Influence of job characteristics on the acceptability of employee drug testing. *Journal of Applied Psychology*, **76**, 447–453.

Nathan B R & Alexander R A (1988) A comparison of criteria for test validation: a meta-analytic investigation. *Personnel Psychology*, **41**, 517–535.

Nathan B R & Tippins N (1990) The consequences of 'halo error' in performance ratings: a field study of the moderating effect of halo on test validation results. *Journal of Applied Psychology*, **75**, 290–296.

Nester M A (1993) Psychometric testing and reasonable accommodation for persons with disabilities. *Rehabilitation Psychology*, **38**, 75–85.

Neter E & Ben-Shakhar G (1989) The predictive validity of graphological inferences: a meta-analytic approach. *Personality and Individual Differences*, **10**, 737–745.

Neuman G A & Wright J (1999) Team effectiveness: beyond skills and cognitive ability. *Journal of Applied Psychology*, **84**, 376–389.

te Nijenhuis J & van der Flier H (1997) Comparability of GATB scores for immigrants and majority group members: some Dutch findings. *Journal of Applied Psychology*, **82**, 675–687.

te Nijenhuis J & van der Flier H (1999) Bias research in The Netherlands: review and implications. *European Journal of Psychological Assessment*, **15**, 165–175.

te Nijenhuis J & van der Flier H (2000) Differential prediction of immigrant versus majority group training performance using cognitive and personality measures. *International Journal of Selection and Assessment*, **8**, 54–60.

te Nijenhuis J, van der Flier H & van Leeuwen L (1997) Comparability of personality test scores for immigrants and majority group members: some Dutch findings. *Personality and Individual Differences*, **23**, 849–859.

Normand J, Lempert R O & O'Brien C P (1994) *Under the Influence? Drugs and the American Work Force*. National Academy Press, Washington, DC.

Normand J, Salyards S D & Mahoney J J (1990) An evaluation of pre-employment drug testing. *Journal of Applied Psychology*, **75**, 629–639.

O'Connell M S, Doverspike D, Cober A B & Philips J (2001) Forging work teams: effects of the distribution of cognitive ability on team performance. *Applied HRM Research*, **6**, 115–128.

O'Connor E J, Wexley K N & Alexander R A (1975) Single-group validity: fact or fallacy? *Journal of Applied Psychology*, **60**, 352–355.

Olea M M & Ree M J (1994) Predicting pilot and navigator criteria: not much more than g. *Journal of Applied Psychology*, **79**, 845–851.

Olian J D & Wilcox J C (1982) The controversy over PACE: an examination of the evidence and implications of the Luevano consent decree for employment testing. *Personnel Psychology*, **35**, 659–676.

Olian J D, Schwab D P & Haberfeld Y (1988) The impact of applicant gender compared to qualifications on hiring recommendations: a meta-analysis of experimental studies. *Organisational Behavior and Human Decision Processes*, **41**, 180–195.

Ones D S & Anderson N (2002) Gender and ethnic group differences on personality scales in selection: some British data. *Journal of Occupational and Organizational Psychology*, **75**, 255–277.

Ones D S & Viswesvaran C (1998a) Gender, age and race differences on overt integrity tests: results across four large-scale applicant datasets. *Journal of Applied Psychology*, **83**, 35–42.

Ones D S & Viswesvaran C (1998b) The effects of social desirability and faking on personality and integrity assessment for personnel selection. *Human Performance*, **11**, 245–269.

Ones D S & Viswesvaran C (2001) Integrity tests and other criterion-focused occupational personality scales (COPS) used in personnel research. *International Journal of Selection and Assessment*, **9**, 31–39.

Ones D S, Viswesvaran C & Schmidt F L (1993) Comprehensive meta-analysis of integrity test validities – findings and implications for personnel selection and theories of job performance. *Journal of Applied Psychology*, **78**, 679–703.

Oppler S H, Campbell J P, Pulakos E D & Borman W C (1992) Three approaches to the investigation of subgroup bias in performance measurement review: results and conclusions. *Journal of Applied Psychology*, **77**, 201–217.

Organ D W & Ryan K (1995) A meta-analytic review of attitudinal and dispositional predictors of organisational citizenship behavior. *Personnel Psychology*, **48**, 775–802.

Orr J M, Sackett P R & Mercer M (1989) The role of prescribed and nonprescribed behavior in estimating the dollar value of performance. *Journal of Applied Psychology*, **75**, 34–40.

Orwell G (1949/1984) *Nineteen Eighty-Four* Oxford: Oxford University Press.

Outtz J L (1998) Testing medium, validity and test performance. In: M Hakel (ed.) *Beyond Multiple Choice: Evaluating Alternatives to Traditional Testing for Selection*. Erlbaum, Mahwah, NJ.

Owens W A (1976) Background data. In: M D Dunnette (ed.) *Handbook of Industrial and Organisational Psychology*. Rand McNally, Chicago.

Owens W A & Schoenfeldt L F (1979) Toward a classification of persons. *Journal of Applied Psychology*, **65**, 569–607.

Pannone R D (1984) Predicting test performance: a content valid approach to screening applicants. *Personnel Psychology*, **37**, 507–514.

Parkinson C N (1958) *Parkinson's Law*. John Murray, London.

Parry G (1999) A legal examination of two cases involving employment references. *Educational Management and Administration*, **27**, 357–364.

Pearlman K, Schmidt F L & Hunter J E (1980) Validity generalisation results for tests used to predict job proficiency and training success in clerical occupations. *Journal of Applied Psychology*, **65**, 373–406.

Peres S H & Garcia J R (1962) Validity and dimensions of descriptive adjectives used in reference letters for engineering applicants. *Personnel Psychology*, **15**, 279–286.

Peterson N G, Mumford M D, Borman W C *et al.* (2001) Understanding work using the occupational information network (O*NET). *Personnel Psychology*, **54**, 451–492.

Pingitore R, Dugoni B L, Tindale R S & Spring B (1994) Bias against overweight job applicants in a simulated employment interview. *Journal of Applied Psychology*, **79**, 909–917.

Plomin R (2002) Individual difference research in a postgenomic era. *Personality and Individual Differences*, **22**, 909–920.

Ployhart R E & Hakel M D (1998) The substantive nature of performance variability: predicting inter-individual differences in intra-individual performance. *Personnel Psychology*, **51**, 859–901.

Ployhart R E, Lim B-C & Chan K-Y (2001) Exploring relations between typical and maximum performance ratings and the five factor model of personality. *Personnel Psychology*, **54**, 807–843.

Posthuma R A, Morgeson F P & Campion M A (2002) Beyond employment interview validity: a comprehensive narrative review of recent research and trends over time. *Personnel Psychology*, **55**, 1–81.

Prewett-Livingston A J, Feild H S, Veres J G & Lewis P M (1996) Effects of race on interview ratings in a situational panel interview. *Journal of Applied Psychology*, **81**, 178–186.

Pulakos E D, Schmitt N, Whitney D & Smith M (1996) Individual differences in interviewer ratings: the impact of standardisation, consensus discussion and sampling error on the validity of a structured interview. *Personnel Psychology*, **49**, 85–102.

Pynes J & Bernardin H J (1989) Predictive validity of an entry-level police-officer assessment center. *Journal of Applied Psychology*, **74**, 831–833.

Quinsey V L, Harris G T, Rice M E & Cormier C A (1998) *Violent Offenders: Appraising and Managing Risk*. American Psychological Association, Washington, DC.

Raju N S, Burke M J & Normand J (1990) A new approach for utility analysis. *Journal of Applied Psychology*, **75**, 3–12.

Range L M, Meynert A, Walsh M L, Hardin K N, Ellis J B & Craddick R (1991) Letters of recommendation: perspectives, recommendations and ethics. *Professional Psychology: Research and Practice*, **22**, 389–392.

Raymark P H, Schmit M J & Guion R M (1997) Identifying potentially useful personality constructs for employee selection. *Personnel Psychology*, **50**, 723–736.

Rayson M, Holliman D & Belyavin A (2000) Development of physical selection procedures for the British Army. Phase 2. Relationship between physical performance test and criterion tasks. *Ergonomics*, **43**, 73–105.

Ree M J & Earles J A (1991) Predicting training success: not much more than g. *Personnel Psychology*, **44**, 321–332.

Ree M J, Carretta T R & Teachout M S (1995) Role of ability and prior job knowledge in complex training performance. *Journal of Applied Psychology*, **80**, 721–730.

Ree M J, Earles J A & Teachout M S (1994) Predicting job performance: not much more than g. *Journal of Applied Psychology*, **79**, 518–524.

Register C A & Williams D R (1992) Labor market effects of marijuana and cocaine use among young men. *Industrial and Labor Relations Review*, **45**, 435–448.

Reilly R R & Chao G T (1982) Validity and fairness of some alternative employee selection procedures. *Personnel Psychology*, **35**, 1–62.

Reilly R R & Israelski E W (1988) Development and validation of minicourses in the telecommunications industry. *Journal of Applied Psychology*, **73**, 721–726.

Reilly R R, Zedeck S & Tenopyr M L (1979) Validity and fairness of physical ability tests for predicting performance in craft jobs. *Journal of Applied Psychology*, **64**, 262–274.

Reiter-Palmon R & Connelly M S (2000) Item selection counts: a comparison of empirical key and rational scale validities in theory-based and non-theory-based item pools. *Journal of Applied Psychology*, **85**, 143–151.

Richman W L, Kiesler S, Weisband S & Drasgow F (1999) A meta-analytic study of social desirability distortion in computer-administered questionnaires, traditional questionnaires, and interviews. *Journal of Applied Psychology*, **84**, 754–775.

Ritchie R J & Moses J L (1983) Assessment center correlates of women's advancement into middle management: a 7-year longitudinal analysis. *Journal of Applied Psychology*, **68**, 227–231.

Robertson I T & Downs S (1979) Learning and the prediction of performance: development of trainability testing in the United Kingdom. *Journal of Applied Psychology*, **64**, 42–50.

Robertson I T & Downs S (1989) Work-sample tests of trainability: a meta-analysis. *Journal of Applied Psychology*, **74**, 402–410.

Robertson I T & Kandola R S (1982) Work-sample tests: validity, adverse impact and applicant reaction. *Journal of Occupational Psychology*, **55**, 171–183.

Robertson I T & Makin P J (1986) Management selection in Britain: a survey and critique. *Journal of Occupational Psychology*, **59**, 45–57.

Robertson I T, Baron H, Gibbons P, McIver R & Nyfield G (2000) Conscientiousness and managerial performance. *Journal of Occupational and Organizational Psychology*, **73**, 171–180.

Robie C, Schmit M J, Ryan A M & Zickar M J (2000) Effects of item context specificity on the measurement equivalence of a personality inventory. *Organizational Research Methods*, **3**, 348–365.

Robinson D D (1972) Prediction of clerical turnover in banks by means of a weighted application blank. *Journal of Applied Psychology*, **56**, 282.

Robinson S L & Bennett R J (1995) A typology of deviant workplace behaviors: a multidimensional scaling study. *Academy of Management Journal*, **38**, 555–572.

Roche W J (1965) A dollar criterion in fixed-treatment employee selection. In: L J Cronbach and G C Gleser (eds) *Psychological Tests and Personnel Decisions*. University of Illinois Press, Urbana, IL.

Roehling M V (1999) Weight-based discrimination in employment: psychological and legal aspects. *Personnel Psychology*, **52**, 969–1016.

Rosse J G, Stecher M D, Miller J L & Levin R A (1998) The impact of response distortion on pre-employment personality testing and hiring decisions. *Journal of Applied Psychology*, **83**, 634–644.

Roth P L & Bobko P (1997) A research agenda for multi-attribute utility analysis in human resource management. *Human Resource Management Review*, **7**, 341–368.

Roth P L & Bobko P (2000) College grade point average as a personnel selection device: ethnic group differences and potential adverse impact. *Journal of Applied Psychology*, **85**, 399–406.

Roth P L, Bevier C A, Bobko P, Switzer F S & Tyler P (2001) Ethnic group difference in cognitive ability in employment and educational settings: a meta-analysis. *Personnel Psychology*, **54**, 297–330.

Roth P L, Bevier C A, Switzer F S & Schippmann J S (1996) Meta-analyzing the relationship between grades and job performance. *Journal of Applied Psychology*, **81**, 548–556.

Roth P L, Van Iddekinge C H, Huffcutt A I, Eidson C E & Bobko P (2002) Corrections for range restriction in structured interview ethnic group differences: the values may be larger than researchers thought. *Journal of Applied Psychology*, **87**, 369–376.

Rothstein H R (1990) Interrater reliability of job performance ratings: growth to asymptote level with increasing opportunity to observe. *Journal of Applied Psychology*, **75**, 322–327.

Rothstein H R & McDaniel M A (1992) Differential validity by sex in employment settings. *Journal of Business and Psychology*, **7**, 45–62.

Rothstein H R, Schmidt F L, Erwin F W, Owens W A, & Sparks C P (1990) Biographical data in employment selection: can validities be made generalisable? *Journal of Applied Psychology*, **75**, 175–184.

Rotundo M & Sackett P R (1999) Effect of rater race on conclusions regarding differential prediction in cognitive ability tests. *Journal of Applied Psychology*, **84**, 815–822.

Rotundo M & Sackett P R (2002) The relative importance of task, citizenship, and counterproductive performance to global ratings of job performance: a policy-capturing approach. *Journal of Applied Psychology*, **87**, 66–80.

Russell C J & Domm D R (1995) Two field tests of an explanation of assessment validity. *Journal of Occupational and Organizational Psychology*, **68**, 25–47.

Russell C J, Mattson J, Devlin S E & Atwater D (1990) Predictive validity of biodata items generated from retrospective life experience essays. *Journal of Applied Psychology*, **75**, 569–580.

Russell C J, Settoon R P, McGrath R N *et al.* (1994) Investigator characteristics as moderators of personnel selection research: a meta-analysis. *Journal of Applied Psychology*, **79**, 163–170.

Ryan A M & Lasek M (1991) Negligent hiring and defamation: areas of liability related to pre-employment inquiries. *Personnel Psychology*, **44**, 293–319.

Ryan A M & Ployhart R E (2000) Applicants' perceptions of selection procedures and decisions: a critical review and agenda for the future. *Journal of Management*, **26**, 565–606.

Ryan A M & Sackett P R (1992) Relationships between graduate training, professional affiliation and individual psychological assessment practices for personnel decisions. *Journal of Applied Psychology*, **45**, 1–22.

Ryan A M, Ployhart R E & Friedel L A (1998) Using personality testing to reduce adverse impact: a cautionary note. *Journal of Applied Psychology*, **83**, 298–307.

Ryan A M, Daum D, Bauman T *et al.* (1995) Direct, indirect and controlled observation and rating accuracy. *Journal of Applied Psychology*, **80**, 664–670.

Ryan A M, McFarland L, Baron H & Page R (1999) An international look at selection practices: nation and culture as explanation for variability in practice. *Personnel Psychology*, **52**, 359–391.

Rynes S & Gerhart B (1990) Interview assessments of applicant 'fit': an exploratory investigation. *Personnel Psychology*, **43**, 13–35.

Rynes S L, Orlitsky M O & Bretz R D (1997) Experienced hiring practices versus college recruiting: practices and emerging trends. *Personnel Psychology*, **50**, 309–339.

Saad S & Sackett P R (2002) Investigating differential prediction by gender in employment-oriented personality measures. *Journal of Applied Psychology*, **87**, 667–674.

Sacco J M, Scheu C R, Ryan A M, Schmitt N, Schmidt D B & Rogg K L (2000) *Reading Level and Verbal Test Scores as Predictors of Subgroup Differences and Validities of Situational Judgement Tests*. Unpublished paper.

Sackett P R (1998) Performance assessment in education and professional certification: lessons for personnel selection. In: M Hakel (ed.) *Beyond Multiple Choice: Evaluating Alternatives to Traditional Testing for Selection*. Erlbaum, Mahwah, NJ.

Sackett P R & Dreher G F (1982) Constructs and assessment center dimensions: some troubling empirical findings. *Journal of Applied Psychology*, **67**, 401–410.

Sackett P R & Ellingson J E (1997) The effects of forming multi-predictor composites on group differences and adverse impact. *Personnel Psychology*, **50**, 707–722.

Sackett P R & Ostgaard D J (1994) Job-specific applicant pools and national norms for cognitive ability tests: implications for range restriction correction in validation research. *Journal of Applied Psychology*, **79**, 680–684.

Sackett P R & Wanek J E (1996) New developments in the use of measures of honesty, integrity, conscientiousness, dependability, trustworthiness and reliability for personnel selection. *Personnel Psychology*, **49**, 787–829.

Sackett P R & Wilk S L (1994) Within-group norming and other forms of score adjustment in pre-employment testing. *American Psychologist*, **49**, 929–954.

Sackett P R, Gruys M L & Ellingson J E (1998) Ability–personality interactions when predicting job performance. *Journal of Applied Psychology*, **83**, 545–556.

Sackett P R, Harris M M & Orr J M (1986) On seeking moderator variables in the meta-analysis of correlational data: a Monte Carlo investigation of statistical power and resistance to Type 1 error. *Journal of Applied Psychology*, **71**, 302–310.

Sackett P R, Schmitt N, Ellingson J E & Kabin M B (2001) High-stakes testing in employment, credentialing and higher education: prospects in a post-affirmative-action world. *American Psychologist*, **56**, 302–318.

Sadri G & Robertson I T (1993) Self-efficacy and work-related behaviour: a review and meta-analysis. *Applied Psychology: an International Review*, **42**, 139–152.

Saks A M (1994) A psychological process investigation for the effects of recruitment source and organisation information on job survival. *Journal of Organizational Behavior*, **15**, 225–244.

Salgado J F (1994) Validez de los tests de habilidades psicomotoras: meta-análisis de los estudios publicados en Espana (1942–1990). *Revista de Psicologia Social Aplicada*, **4**, 25–42.

Salgado J F (1995) Situational specificity and within-setting validity variability. *Journal of Occupational and Organizational Psychology*, **68**, 123–132.

Salgado J F (1997) The five-factor model of personality and job performance in the European community. *Journal of Applied Psychology*, **82**, 30–43.

Salgado J F (1998a) Sample size in validity studies of personnel selection. *Journal of Occupational and Organizational Psychology*, **71**, 161–164.

Salgado J F (1998b) Big five personality dimensions and job performance in army and civil occupations: a European perspective. *Human Performance*, **11**, 271–289.

Salgado J F & Anderson N (2001) Cognitive and GMA testing in the European Community: issues and evidence. *Human Performance*, **15**, 75–96.

Salgado J F & Moscoso S (2002) Comprehensive meta-analysis of the construct validity on the employment interview. *European Journal of Work and Organizational Psychology*, **11**, 299–324.

Sarchione C D, Cuttler M J, Muchinsky P M & Nelson-Gray R O (1998) Prediction of dysfunctional job behaviors among law enforcement officers. *Journal of Applied Psychology*, **83**, 904–912.

Saville P & Willson E (1991) The reliability and validity of normative and ipsative approaches in the measurement of personality. *Journal of Occupational Psychology*, **64**, 219–238.

Schippmann J S, Prien E P & Katz J A (1990) Reliability and validity of in-basket measures. *Personnel Psychology*, **43**, 837–859.

Schleicher D J, Day D V, Mayes B T & Riggio R E (2002) A new frame for frame-of-reference training: enhancing the construct validity of assessment centers. *Journal of Applied Psychology*, **87**, 735–746.

Schmidt F L (1992) What do data really mean? Research findings, meta-analysis and cumulative knowledge in psychology. *American Psychologist*, **47**, 1173–1181.

Schmidt F L (2002) The role of general cognitive ability and job performance: why there cannot be a debate. *Human Performance*, **15**, 187–210.

Schmidt F L & Hunter J E (1977) Development of a general solution to the problem of validity generalisation. *Journal of Applied Psychology*, **62**, 529–540.

Schmidt F L & Hunter J E (1978) Moderator research and the law of small numbers. *Personnel Psychology*, **31**, 215–232.

Schmidt F L & Hunter J E (1981) Employment testing: old theories and new research findings. *American Psychologist*, **36**, 1128–1137.

Schmidt F L & Hunter J E (1984) A within-setting empirical test of the situational specificity hypothesis in personnel selection. *Personnel Psychology*, **37**, 317–326.

Schmidt F L & Hunter J E (1995) The fatal internal contradiction in banding: its statistical rationale is logically inconsistent with its operational procedures. *Human Performance*, **8**, 203–214.

Schmidt F L & Hunter J E (1998) The validity and utility of selection methods in personnel psychology: practical and theoretical implications of 85 years of research findings. *Psychological Bulletin*, **124**, 262–274.

Schmidt F L & Rader M (1999) Exploring the boundary conditions for interview validity: meta-analytic validity findings for a new interview type. *Personnel Psychology*, **52**, 445–465.

Schmidt F L & Rothstein H R (1994) Application of validity generalisation to biodata scales in employment selection. In: G S Stokes, M D Mumford & W A Owens (eds) *Biodata Handbook: Theory, Research and Use of Biographical Information in Selection and Performance Prediction*. CPP Books, Palo Alto, CA.

Schmidt F L, Berner J G & Hunter J E (1973) Racial differences in validity of employment tests: reality or illusion? *Journal of Applied Psychology*, **53**, 5–9.

Schmidt F L, Gast-Rosenberg I & Hunter J E (1980a) Validity generalisation results for computer programmers. *Journal of Applied Psychology*, **65**, 643–661.

Schmidt F L, Hunter J E & Outerbridge A N (1986) Impact of job experience and ability on job knowledge, work sample performance, and supervisory ratings of job performance. *Journal of Applied Psychology*, **71**, 432–439.

Schmidt F L, Pearlman K & Hunter J E (1980b) The validity and fairness of employment and educational tests for Hispanic Americans: a review and analysis. *Personnel Psychology*, **33**, 705–723.

Schmidt F L, Hunter J E, Croll P R & McKenzie R C (1983) Estimation of employment test validities by expert judgement. *Journal of Applied Psychology*, **68**, 590–601.

Schmidt F L, Hunter J E, McKenzie R C & Muldrow T W (1979) Impact of valid selection procedures on work-force productivity. *Journal of Applied Psychology*, **64**, 609–626.

Schmidt F L, Hunter J E, Pearlman K & Hirsh H R (1985a) Forty questions about validity generalisation and meta-analysis. *Personnel Psychology*, **38**, 697–798.

Schmidt F L, Ocasio B P, Hillery J M & Hunter J E (1985b) Further within-setting empirical tests of the situational specificity hypothesis in personnel selection. *Personnel Psychology*, **38**, 509–524.

Schmidt-Atzert L & Deter B (1993) Intelligenz und Ausbildungserfolg: eine Untersuchung zur prognistischen Validitat des I-S-T 70. *Zeitschrift fur Arbeits- und Organisationspsychologie*, **37**, 52–63.

Schmit M J & Ryan A M (1993) The big five in personnel selection: factor structure in applicant and nonapplicant populations. *Journal of Applied Psychology*, **78**, 966–974.

Schmit M J, Kihm J A & Robie C (2000) Development of a global measure of personality. *Personnel Psychology*, **53**, 153–193.

Schmitt N & Pulakos E D (1998) Biodata and differential prediction: some reservations. In: M Hakel (ed.) *Beyond Multiple Choice: Evaluating Alternatives to Traditional Testing for Selection*. Erlbaum, Mahwah, NJ.

Schmitt N, Clause C S & Pulakos E D (1996) Subgroup differences associated with different measures of some common job-relevant constructs. *International Review of Industrial and Organizational Psychology*, **11**, 115–139.

Schmitt N, Schneider J R & Cohen S A (1990) Factors affecting validity of a regionally administered assessment center. *Personnel Psychology*, **43**, 1–12.

Schmitt N, Gooding R Z, Noe R A & Kirsch M (1984) Meta-analyses of validity studies published between 1964 and 1982 and the investigation of study characteristics. *Personnel Psychology*, **37**, 407–422.

Schneider B, Smith D B, Taylor S & Fleenor J (1998) Personality and organisation: a test of the homogeneity of personality hypothesis. *Journal of Applied Psychology*, **83**, 462–470.

Scholz G & Schuler H (1993) Das nomologische Netzwerk des Assessment Centers: eine Metaanalyse. *Zeitschrift fur Arbeits- und Organisationspsychologie*, **37**, 73–85.

Schrader A D & Osburn H G (1977) Biodata faking: effects of induced subtlety and position specificity. *Personnel Psychology*, **30**, 395–404.

Schuler H & Moser K (1995) Die validitat des multimodalen interviews. *Zeitschrift fur Arbeits- und Organisationspsychologie*, **39**, 2–12.

Schuler H, Diemand A & Moser K (1993) Filmszenen. Entwicklung and Konstruktvalidierung eines neuen eignungsdiagnostischen Verfahrens. *Zeitschrift fur Arbeits- und Organisationspsychologie,* **37**, 3–9.

Scott S J (1997) *Graduate Selection Procedures and Ethnic Minority Applicants.* MSc Thesis, University of East London, London.

Senior B (1997) Team role and team performance: is there 'really' a fit? *Journal of Occupational and Organizational Psychology,* **70**, 241–258.

Seymour R T (1988) Why plaintiffs' counsel challenge tests, and how they can successfully challenge the theory of 'validity generalisation'. *Journal of Vocational Behavior,* **33**, 331–364.

Shapira Z & Shirom A (1980) New issues in the use of behaviorally anchored rating scales: level of analysis, the effects of incident frequency, and external validation. *Journal of Applied Psychology,* **65**, 517–523.

Sharf J C (1988) Litigating personnel measurement policy. *Journal of Vocational Behavior,* **33**, 235–271.

Sharf J C (1994) The impact of legal and equal employment opportunity issues on personal history enquiries. In: G S Stokes, M D Mumford & W A Owens (eds) *Biodata Handbook: Theory, Research, and Use of Biographical Information in Selection and Performance Prediction.* CPP Books, Palo Alto, CA.

Shermis M D, Falkenberg B, Appel V A & Cole R W (1996) Construction of a faking detector scale for a biodata survey instrument. *Military Psychology,* **8**, 83–94.

Shore T H (1992) Subtle gender bias in the assessment of management potential. *Sex Roles,* **27**, 499–515.

Silvester J, Mohammed A R, Anderson-Gough F & Anderson N (2002) Locus of control, attributions and impression management in the selection interview. *Journal of Occupational and Organizational Psychology,* **75**, 59–78.

Simon H A & Noonan A M (1994) No smokers need apply: is refusing to hire smokers legal? *Employee Relations Law Journal,* **20**, 347–367.

Smith J E & Hakel M D (1979) Convergence among data sources, response bias, and reliability and validity of a structured job analysis questionnaire. *Personnel Psychology,* **32**, 677–692.

Smith M (1994) A theory of the validity of predictors in selection. *Journal of Occupational and Organizational Psychology,* **67**, 13–31.

Smither J W, Reilly R R, Millsap R E, Pearlman K & Stoffy R W (1993) Applicant reactions to selection procedures. *Journal of Applied Psychology,* **46**, 49–76.

Sparrow J, Patrick J, Spurgeon P & Barwell F (1982) The use of job component analysis and related aptitudes on personnel selection. *Journal of Occupational Psychology,* **55**, 157–164.

Springbett B M (1958) Factors affecting the final decision in the employment interview. *Canadian Journal of Psychology,* **12**, 13–22.

Spychalski A C, Quinones M A, Gaugler B B, & Pohley K (1997) A survey of assessment center practices in organizations in the United States. *Personnel Psychology,* **50**, 71–90.

Steiner D D & Gilliland S W (1996) Fairness reactions to personnel selection techniques in France and the United States. *Journal of Applied Psychology,* **81**, 134–141.

Stevens C K (1998) Antecedents of interview interactions, interviewers' ratings and applicants' reactions. *Personnel Psychology,* **51**, 55–86.

Stinglhamber F, Vandenberghe C & Brancart S (1999) Les reactions des candidats envers les techniques de selection du personnel: une etude dans un contexte francophone. *Travail Humain,* **62**, 347–361.

Stokes G S & Cooper L A (2001) Content/construct approaches in life history form development for selection. *International Journal of Selection and Assessment,* **9**, 138–151.

Stokes G S, Hogan J B & Snell A F (1993) Comparability of incumbent and applicant samples for the development of biodata keys: the influence of social desirability. *Personnel Psychology,* **46**, 739–762.

Sturman M C, Cheramie R A & Cashen L H (2001) *The Consistency, Stability, and Test–Retest Reliability of Employee Job Performance: a Meta-Analytic Review of Longitudinal Findings.* Cornell University Center for Hospitality Research, Ithaca, NY.

Sullivan L & Arnold D W (2000) Invasive questions lead to legal challenge, settlement and use of different tests. www.siop.org/tip/backissues/TopOct2000/24Sullivan.htm.

Super D E & Crites J O (1962) *Appraising Vocational Fitness by Means of Psychological Tests.* Harper and Row, New York.

Taylor P, Mills A & O'Driscoll M (1993) Personnel selection methods used by New Zealand organisations and personnel consulting firms. *New Zealand Journal of Psychology*, **22**, 19–31.

Taylor P J & Small B (2002) Asking applicants what they would do versus what they did do: a meta-analytic comparison of situational and past behaviour employment interview questions. *Journal of Occupational and Organizational Psychology*, **74**, 277–294.

Teague P (1994) EC social policy and European human resource management. In: C Brewster & A Hegewisch (eds) *Policy and Practice in European Human Resource Management.* Routledge, London.

Terpstra D E & Rozell E J (1993) The relationship of staffing practices to organizational level measures of performance. *Personnel Psychology*, **46**, 27–48.

Terpstra D E & Rozell E J (1997) Why potentially effective staffing practices are seldom used. *Public Personnel Management*, **26**, 483–495.

Terpstra D E, Mohamed A A & Kethley R B (1999) An analysis of Federal court cases involving nine selection devices. *International Journal of Selection and Assessment*, **7**, 26–34.

Tett R P, Jackson D N & Rothstein M (1991) Personality measures as predictors of job performance. *Personnel Psychology*, **44**, 407–421.

Tett R P, Guterman H A, Bleier A & Murphy P J (2000) Development and content validation of a 'hyperdimensional' taxonomy of managerial competence. *Human Performance*, **13**, 205–251.

Thorndike R L (1986) The role of general ability in prediction. *Journal of Vocational Behavior*, **29**, 332–339.

Tiffin J (1943) *Industrial Psychology.* Prentice Hall, New York.

Tziner A & Dolan S (1982) Evaluation of a traditional selection system in predicting success of females in officer training. *Journal of Occupational Psychology*, **55**, 269–275.

Tziner A & Eden D (1985) Effects of crew composition on crew performance: does the whole equal the sum of the parts? *Journal of Applied Psychology*, **70**, 85–93.

Ulrich L & Trumbo D (1965) The selection interview since 1949. *Psychological Bulletin*, **63**, 100–116.

Umeda J K & Frey D H (1974) Life history correlates of ministerial success. *Journal of Vocational Behavior*, **4**, 319–324.

Vance R J & Colella A (1990) The futility of utility analysis. *Human Performance*, **3**, 123–139.

Vance R J, Coovert M D, MacCallum R C & Hedge J W (1989) Construct models of task performance. *Journal of Applied Psychology*, **64**, 447–455.

Varca P E & Pattison P (1993) Evidentiary standards in employment discrimination: a view toward the future. *Personnel Psychology*, **46**, 239–258.

Vernon P E (1950) The validation of Civil Service Selection Board procedures. *Occupational Psychology*, **24**, 75–95.

Vernon P E (1982) *The Abilities and Achievements of Oriental North Americans.* Academic Press, New York.

Vernon P E & Parry J B (1949) *Personnel Selection in the British Forces.* University of London Press, London.

van der Vijver F J R & Harsveld M (1994) The incomplete equivalence of the paper-and-pencil and computerised versions of the General Aptitude Test Battery. *Journal of Applied Psychology*, **79**, 852–859.

Vinchur A J, Schippmann J S, Switzer F S & Roth P L (1998) A meta-analytic review of predictors of job performance for sales people. *Journal of Applied Psychology*, **83**, 586–597.

Vineberg R & Joyner J N (1982) *Prediction of Job Performance: Review of Military Studies*. Human Resources Research Organisation, Alexandria, VA.

Viswesvaran C & Ones D (1999) Meta-analyses of fakability estimates: implications for personality measurement. *Educational and Psychological Measurement*, **59**, 197–210.

Viswesvaran C & Ones D S (2000) Measurement error in 'big five factors' of personality assessment: reliability generalisation across studies and measures. *Educational and Psychological Measurement*, **60**, 224–238.

Viswesvaran C, Ones D S & Schmidt F L (1996) Comparative analysis of the reliability of job performance ratings. *Journal of Applied Psychology*, **81**, 557–574.

Viswesvaran C, Schmidt F L & Ones D S (2002a) *Is There a General Factor in Job Performance? A Meta-Analytic Framework for Disentangling Substantive and Error Influences*. Unpublished paper.

Viswesvaran C, Schmidt F L & Ones D S (2002b) The moderating influence of job performance dimension on convergence of supervisory and peer ratings of job performance: unconfounding construct-level convergence and rating difficulty. *Journal of Applied Psychology*, **87**, 345–354.

Viteles M S (1932) *Industrial Psychology*. Norton, New York.

Wagner R (1949) The employment interview: a critical summary. *Personnel Psychology*, **2**, 17–46.

Waldman D A & Avolio B J (1986) A meta-analysis of age differences in job performance. *Journal of Applied Psychology*, **71**, 33–38.

Waldman D A & Avolio B J (1989) Homogeneity of test validity. *Journal of Applied Psychology*, **74**, 371–374.

Walsh J P, Weinberg R M & Fairfield M L (1987) The effects of gender on assessment centre evaluations. *Journal of Occupational Psychology*, **60**, 305–309.

Weekley J A & Jones C (1999) Further studies of situational tests. *Personnel Psychology*, **52**, 679–700.

White L, Nord R D, Mael F A & Young M C (1993) The assessment of background and life experiences (ABLE). In: T Trent & J H Laurence (eds) *Adaptability Screening for the Armed Forces*. Office of Assistant Secretary of Defense, Washington, DC.

Whitney D J & Schmitt N (1997) Relationship between culture and responses to biodata employment items. *Journal of Applied Psychology*, **82**, 113–129.

Wiesner W H & Cronshaw S F (1988) A meta-analytic investigation of the impact of interview format and degree of structure on the validity of the employment interview. *Journal of Psychology*, **61**, 275–290.

Wilk S L & Sackett P R (1996) Longitudinal analysis of ability, job complexity fit and job change. *Personnel Psychology*, **49**, 937–967.

Wilkinson L J (1997) Generalisable biodata? An application to the vocational interests of managers. *Journal of Occupational and Organizational Psychology*, **70**, 49–60.

Williams C R & Livingstone L P (1994) Another look at the relationship between performance and voluntary turnover. *Academy of Management Journal*, **37**, 269–298.

Williamson L G, Malos S B, Roehling M V & Campion M A (1997) Employment interview on trial: linking interview structure with litigation outcomes. *Journal of Applied Psychology*, **82**, 900–912.

Wilson M A, Harvey R J, & Macy B A (1990) Repeating items to estimate the test–retest reliability of task inventory ratings. *Journal of Applied Psychology*, **75**, 158–163.

Wilson N A B (1948) The work of the Civil Service Selection Board. *Occupational Psychology*, **22**, 204–212.

Witt L A, Burke L A, Barrick M R & Mount M K (2002) The interactive effects of conscientiousness and agreeableness on job performance. *Journal of Applied Psychology*, **87**, 164–169.

Woehr D J & Arthur W (in press) The construct-related validity of assessment center ratings: a review and meta-analysis of methodological factors. *Journal of Management*.

Wood R & Payne T (1998) *Competency-Based Recruitment and Selection.* John Wiley & Sons, Chichester.

Yoo T-Y & Muchinsky P M (1998) Utility estimates of job performance as related to the data, people and things parameters of work. *Journal of Occupational Behavior,* **19,** 353–370.

Zazanis M M, Zaccaro S J & Kilcullen R N (2001) Identifying motivation and interpersonal performance using peer evaluations. *Military Psychology,* **13,** 73–88.

Zeidner M (1988) Cultural fairness in aptitude testing revisited: a cross-cultural parallel. *Professional Psychology: Research and Practice,* **19,** 257–262.

Zickar M J (2001) Using personality inventories to identify thugs and agitators: applied psychology's contribution to the war against labor. *Journal of Vocational Behavior,* **59,** 149–164.

Zwerling C, Ryan J & Orav E J (1990) The efficacy of pre-employment drug screening for marijuana and cocaine in predicting employment outcome. *Journal of the American Medical Association,* **264,** 2639–2643.

Author Index

Subject Index